KING ALFRED'S COLLEGE
READING
ROCK AND ROLL

D1427445

READING ROCK AND ROLL

AUTHENTICITY, APPROPRIATION,

AESTHETICS

EDITED BY

KEVIN J. H. DETTMAR AND **WILLIAM RICHEY**

WITH A FOREWORD BY

ANTHONY DeCURTIS

Columbia University Press New York

COLUMBIA UNIVERSITY PRESS

Publishers Since 1893
New York   Chichester, West Sussex

Library of Congress Cataloging-in-Publication Data
Reading rock & roll : authenticity, appropriation, aesthetics / edited
by Kevin J. H. Dettmar and William Richey ; with a foreword
by Anthony DeCurtis.
p.   cm.
Includes bibliographical references and index.
ISBN 0–231–11398–6 (cloth). — ISBN 0–231–11399–4 (pbk.)
1. Rock music—History and criticism. 2. Music—Philosophy and aesthetics.
I. Dettmar, Kevin J. H., 1958–   . II. Richey, William, 1956–   .
III. Title: Reading rock and roll.
ML3534.R3844 1999
781.66—dc21   99–11659

CONTENTS

DANCING ABOUT ARCHITECTURE

ANTHONY DeCURTIS

Writing about rock & roll is no job for the self-esteem impaired. Despite more than three decades of credible and in many instances groundbreaking work, rock criticism has not yet attained a stature comparable even to that of film criticism, let alone writing about more traditional areas of the arts. And, for a variety of complicated reasons, it most likely never will.

Far more than writers in any other genre, rock critics are subjected to caricature and condescension, much of it generated—and, indeed, validated—by the form's own practitioners. More bewilderingly, while rock critics in the mainstream press are routinely assumed to be cozying up to their subjects, relations between artists and writers on the music scene have typically been . . . well, let's say tense. While that's probably true in most genres—battles between artists and critics are hardly shocking news—things, again, seem peculiarly charged on the rock front. Rockers have been particularly fond of disparaging critics, often in pretty funny ways.

The late Frank Zappa once characterized rock criticism as interviews with people who can't speak by people who can't write for people who can't read. Some years later, David Lee Roth opined during his stint as a young lion with Van Halen that the reason rock critics liked Elvis Costello and didn't like him is that most rock critics looked like Elvis Costello and didn't look like him. Not that Costello himself has been especially generous toward critics. In fact, my favorite putdown of music critics is a statement that is typically attributed to him: "Writing about music is like dancing about architecture."

Fair enough. Much rock writing is snotty, adolescent, and dismissive, so why shouldn't artists respond in kind? As in so much critical writing of late, rock critics have routinely aspired to supplanting their subjects, and they've succeeded at least in their own work and their own minds, if nowhere else. The degree of cultural—and material and sexual—envy in much rock writing is disturbingly palpable. "These people are too rich, too coddled, too fawned over, too stupid (or, at least, certainly not as smart as me) for their own or anyone else's good" runs the subtext of much rock writing. At the same time, critical writing itself has become an impenetrably self-aggrandizing performance that replicates the very tendencies it allegedly is attacking.

What's especially intriguing about those three remarks about rock critics, however, is that two of the people who made them—Zappa and Costello—virtually owe their careers to the music press. (Van Halen's multiplatinum sales came without initial critical support, indeed, in the face of critical denunciation. Rock-critic self-loathing—or do I mean self-interest?—generated a rethinking of the band around the time of its biggest success with the album *1984*, and the group became a hip guilty pleasure. To say then that you disliked Van Halen was the ultimate middle-brow sin.) Horrific though his music may be, an artist like Michael Bolton has every right to disown critics and embrace the audience that buys his albums regardless of how badly they are received. Zappa and Costello don't.

All that said, however, writing about music *is* in many ways like dancing about architecture—or should be. The comment is meant to suggest a pretentious futility, a pathetic inability to accept something simply for what it is. But to me it suggests virtues that rock writing should strive to achieve. Rock criticism should take inspiration from its subject but at the same time be completely distinct from it. It should aspire to a similar level of artistic achievement. It should be sensual, physical, and smart. And ultimately it should be able to stand on its own terms without requiring the stature or notoriety of its subject to justify itself.

At this stage of its development, rock writing spans an absurdly broad range of forums: from national consumer magazines to local weeklies, from e-zines to university press anthologies, from daily newspapers to record-store giveaways. That spectrum is only going to continue to grow, and each context imposes its own constraints and offers its own possibilities. For all this diversity, however, rock criticism remains in a cultural ghetto. That's because, certainly in the popular press, its audience—like that of the music itself—consists primarily of young people, and despite the United States' obsession with youth, that audience still lacks cultural clout. And young people, of course, are the least likely audience to place its faith in critics. In the academy, the subject of rock & roll is still quite disreputable. But even if all of this is true, so what? Does any of it matter? And if it does, can anything be done to change it?

I think it does matter because a significant opportunity is being missed. The most positive development in my view would be the encouragement of a critical language that can run the full spectrum of the contexts in which the writing occurs, a development that *Reading Rock & Roll: Authenticity, Appropriation, Aesthetics* goes a long way toward achieving. That's not to say that no distinction should be recognized between *TV Guide* and *Semiotext(e)*, although that might not be a bad idea. Still, one of the often overlooked advantages of writing about popular music is that it is popular. From average readers to experts, many more people are at least potentially interested in it than are likely to pursue other equally worthy subjects. Conversely, for those writing in more broadly distributed media, the popularity of the subject does not require a superficial treatment. It's very possible, in short, to shoot the gap—between seriousness and fun, between the newsstand and the library, between passion and analysis.

This is hardly a call for serious writing to become as celebrity struck, ego-obsessed, and marketing-oriented as the mainstream press or for popular writing to lose any of its zip, timeliness, and energy. There are many approaches to this work and many ways to reach, engage, build, and inspire an audience of smart, informed listeners and readers.

Talking across various cultural barriers is one way to move things in the right direction, and, again, this volume makes valuable strides towards that goal. Artists and writers, journalists and academics should find new ways to communicate instead of retreating into their separate worlds, content to speak only to themselves. No one ever discusses it in public, but intellectual insecurity often lurks behind journalists' eye-rolling dismissal of academic pop culturists. And jealousy of the glamour and relatively large readership of the popular press often underlies academics' condescension toward journalists. Not that anybody will in fact admit to them, but are these rarely acknowledged motivations really worth acting on?

It is often the sad case that the fewer the spoils to fight over, the more vicious the backbiting that characterizes the field. That charge has frequently been leveled at the academy, but, alas, the fair targets for it are far more plentiful. Criticism of all types is hardly in great shape at the moment—at least as far as the general public is concerned—and writers about rock music are far more united in the difficulties they face than they are divided by their various theoretical approaches. Fine collections like this one aside, dancing about architecture is no easier than it ever was, and everyone is surely dancing as fast as they can. But as long as critics continue dancing only with themselves, it really won't matter much whether they're dancing at all.

Anthony DeCurtis
NEW YORK CITY

READING
ROCK AND ROLL

INTRODUCTION

KEVIN J. H. DETTMAR AND WILLIAM RICHEY

The important thing about theoretical positions is that they lead you to deci-
sions that you wouldn't have taken otherwise, or you wouldn't have permitted:
good taste would have militated against them.

—Brian Eno

Traditionally, the humanities have been structured according to a series of familiar oppositions: high versus popular culture, timeless versus ephemeral value, original versus imitative art, work versus play, art versus entertainment. To our way of thinking, such distinctions have always seemed both highly artificial and counterintuitive, because we were raised straddling both sides of this divide.[1] We came to British literature through the British Invasion: the Beatles and the Stones, the Sex Pistols and Elvis Costello, prepared our minds for Shakespeare & Co., and we pounded out our dissertations on Blake and Joyce to *Remain in Light* and *Louder than Bombs*. And still today—now that we should know better—we feel comfortable teaching Jim Morrison alongside William Blake and suggesting that Richard Thompson's is a more impersonal poetics than any T. S. Eliot was ever able to realize.

In this pleasant confusion of the artistic realms, we are, of course, hardly alone. An entire generation of critics, emerging from Ph.D. programs in the humanities at the same time that cultural studies was gaining currency, have turned their attention to popular culture topics, and recently these trends have resulted in an explosion of so-called scholarly work on rock music. During the first six months of 1997, both Duke and UCLA hosted major conferences on popular music; universities across the nation are now offering courses on rock history; and a number of important critical studies of popular music have recently been published by major academic and trade presses. Still, despite this growing interest, the range of critical approaches available to scholars in this field remains rather limited because, to a large degree, the academic study of rock has been dominated by the sociological bent of the Birmingham School of cultural studies.[2] This influence is clear in Lawrence Grossberg's and Dick Hebdige's pioneering studies of rock subcultures, in the more recent work of Angela McRobbie, Tricia Rose, and Andrew Ross, and even in mass-marketed books such as those of Ray Pratt and Reebee Garofalo.[3]

Without question, this scholarship has greatly advanced the study of popular music by reminding us that this music isn't made in a vacuum and by situating it clearly within its institutional and cultural contexts. They have, however—largely as a result of the Birmingham School's distrust of purely formalist analysis—tended to shy away from detailed examinations of specific artists or texts.[4] In his introduction to *Microphone Fiends*, for instance, Andrew Ross suggests that the volume's contributors have focused on the question "What then is popular music good for?" Thus the collection's structural/functional imperative—an emphasis on "the need to assess the function of popular music, along with its associated youth cultures"[5]—comes at the cost of aesthetic critique, and the volume's writers never go very far toward answering the equally urgent question "What *is* popular music, and what formal features account for its popularity?" Similarly, even though Simon Frith confronts these very sorts of issues in his most recent book, *Performing Rites: On the Value of Popular Music*, he rarely analyzes individual artists or songs. He does discuss the Pet Shop Boys and Portishead, but these passages are the exception to the rule, serving principally as the intro and outro to his more abstract meditations on cultural value and aesthetics. Otherwise, when he alludes to specific artists, Frith almost invariably includes them as parenthetical references, as quick, unanalyzed illustrations of his general points: "What is it about a record that makes us say, 'I just don't believe it!' (my reaction to Paul Simon's *Graceland*, for example)?"[6] In the collection of essays that follows, we have elected to take a much more textually oriented approach. While we, too, recognize the pitfalls of a myopic sort of New Critical reading, and we certainly no longer see texts as wholly self-determined and independent objects, we believe that poststructuralist and postmodern theories of textuality enable readings that pay close attention to the minutest details of individual compositions while still situating these texts within their social, historical, political, and cultural contexts. In short, we feel that to be a responsible close reader, one must—to paraphrase Fredric Jameson—always contextualize.

In order to enact such nuanced and multilayered readings, we have sought throughout the collection to take an *inter*textual approach to rock music. Rock songs, ordinarily constrained to rather brief compass, are at their best as dense and densely allusive as imagist poetry; in order to accomplish any lasting musical or cultural work in three or four minutes, both the musical and lyrical texts must be highly associative, allusive, even quotational. On one level, this suggests that the critic must explore the ways in which rock lyrics, like poetry, allude to other verbal texts, such as the ways in which rock artists have invoked the literary muse in countless pop standards, from Kate Bush's pithy synopsis of *Wuthering Heights* to David Bowie's grandiose dramatization of Orwell's *1984*, *Diamond Dogs*, to U2's sly use of P. B. Shelley's *Alastor* to parody contemporary media culture in their concert performance of "Mysterious Ways." Rock's intertextuality, though, is even more frequently self-referential in nature because throughout its history rock music has revisited the lyrics of previous songs—for example, the Beatles' reprise of "She Loves You" during the fade-out of "All You Need is Love" or, more recently, Veruca Salt's simultaneous allusion in "Volcano Girls" to their riddling first hit, "Seether," and to the Beatles' most self-referential song, "Glass Onion": "Well here's another clue if you please / The seether's Louise."[7]

On another level, adopting an intertextual approach to rock also means considering the music's aural dimension, something largely beyond the scope of standard literary analysis and ordinarily of little interest to sociologically oriented critics. Literary critics do, of course, like to believe themselves sensitive to the "music" of literary texts; but when we talk about the music of a poem, we are generally speaking metaphorically. Thus, while a poet may refer to a Bach toccata or a Beethoven string quartet, he can evoke these other art forms only through the silent medium of writing. By contrast, George Martin could hire an actual quartet to play on "Eleanor Rigby," simultaneously converting Paul McCartney's simple pop tune into something like a European art song and suggesting a seriousness of purpose and depth of meaning that the lyrics alone cannot sustain. In addition to this familiar kind of high cultural appropriation, rock musicians often add texture, complexity, and humor to their recordings by borrowing musical motifs associated in the listener's mind with specific songs.[8] The Smithereens, for instance, wittily adorn their paean to a well-known tax evader, "Gotti," by undergirding it with the bass line from George Harrison's "Taxman"; the Kinks string together a series of tired rock & roll riffs in "Do It Again" to represent soni-cally the sense of boredom and repetition that the lyrics describe. This type of allusive and quotational strategy, of course, reaches its logical extreme with the rap and hip-hop technique of sampling; a couple of bars lifted from Led Zeppelin's "The Ocean" lay the foundation for the Beastie Boys' "She's Crafty," and M. C. Hammer's appropriation of the signature riff from Rick James's "Super Freak" was seen by many—including James—as an untalented upstart's attempt to glom onto an established artist's reputation. Even the type of recording sound associated with a particular producer (e.g., Phil Spec-tor, Brian Eno, Steve Albini) can immediately evoke a series of predictable responses and resonances among musically sophisticated listeners—which is why, presumably, a well-established artist such as David Bowie recruited Brian Eno to help engineer his 1977 comeback album, *Low*, and why the Rolling Stones have sought the services of the Dust Brothers and others to help them shake the dust off the tired Stones formulas on their most recent album, *Bridges to Babylon*.

Finally, rock's status as a multibillion dollar industry designed to saturate us with immediately identifiable sonic and visual images also affords a kind of intertextuality unavailable to most other artistic media. An obvious instance of this type of image trafficking is the way in which bands have generated entire careers for themselves by imitating the sound of previous artists: Badfinger and Oasis have in different eras achieved commercial success by brazenly cannibalizing the music of the Beatles—and would there ever have been a Tom Petty had there not first been the Byrds? More revealing, how-ever, is the intertextual dynamic created when rock musicians cover songs first made famous by other artists. In recording Johnny Cash's trademark "Ring of Fire," the congenitally sarcastic New Wave band, Wall of Voodoo, relied on our familiarity with the original recording and our associations with Cash's voice to set up a series of cognitive dissonances. The song may have remained the same, but our experience of it certainly did not. On the other hand, U2 has skillfully exploited the image of Johnny Cash in an opposite, yet equally provocative way. By having Cash sing "The Wanderer"—the final track on their *Zooropa* album—they seemingly imbue their vision of a postapocalyptic wasteland with a deeper sense of poignance and sincerity because Cash's storied voice is associated in the public mind with a man whose very public struggles with drugs, alcohol, and love prove that he has "walked the line." But, at the same time, the fact that Cash is appearing on this album, in which the band is consciously attempting to distance itself from its own reputation for sincerity, necessarily makes us wonder if the song and Cash's presence aren't also subject to the ironic perspective of the rest of the CD—an impression reinforced by the self-conscious way in which Cash is credited in the liner notes: "THE WANDERER STARRING JOHNNY CASH."

The most challenging rock music has always taken advantage of these multiple dimensions to complicate and enrich what seems to be a univocal message, and, to a large degree, we believe that it is this verbal and aural polyphony that makes it worthy of serious study. It is also this sort of complexity that places such demands on rock critics as they seek to listen to and account for each channel of these multitracked recordings. One seemingly simple song may serve to make this point: "Something in the Way," from Nirvana's best-selling album *Nevermind.* Sonically, the song is the most stripped-down track on the album; frustrated at finding the most appropriate way to lay down the track, producer Butch Vig—not usually known for his refined sensibilities or sensitive touch—finally decided to record Cobain sitting alone on the studio's waiting-room sofa, strumming chords on a nylon-stringed guitar, singing in a barely audible whisper, recorder levels cranked to 11. Such a setting seems poetically appropriate to the song's loneliness and pain; this basic track, then, resembles a frail, listless "All Apologies": just a boy and his guitar. The lyrics are somewhat cryptic, in the way that Cobain's lyrics are often cryptic (though not, in this case, indecipherable to boot): the basic narrative concerns a man living in a tent under a bridge, eating the fish he can catch, and generally having a miserable time ("It's O.K. to eat fish, / 'Cause they don't have any feelings").

But the song is far more knowing than this skeletal outline would suggest. To begin with, the lyrics aren't simply "lyric"; they aren't merely the untutored outpourings of Cobain's tortured soul or the spontaneous overflow of powerful emotion. "Something in the Way" is a song with a Beatles' song hidden inside—George Harrison's "Something"—and once recognized, the Beatles intertext profoundly complicates the verbal and aural texture of the song. Harrison's "Something" is, for all the sophistication of its melodic line and arrangement, at heart what Paul McCartney might call a "silly love song": "Something in the way she moves / Attracts me like no other lover. . . ." Cobain's song, on the other hand, is not about a mysterious, sensual Something but a something *in the way.* And while George Harrison declares, "I don't want to leave her now / You know I believe and how," Cobain's narrator doesn't know who, or what, to believe in—or how. Along these same lines, the melodic structure of the chorus is effectively the same as the opening bars of "Something," only shifted into a minor key; that certain something no longer hovers tantalizingly just out of reach but is completely, cruelly unattainable. Such a sentiment might, of course, have been uttered straight up, with no intentional intertextual echo; for a pop audience raised on the Beatles, however, the ironic invocation here does a lot of musical and discursive work for Nirvana: it implicitly critiques the dominant ideology of pop love songs, points out the hold the Beatles still exert on the contemporary romantic imagination, and suggests some of the ways the musical and emotional landscape has shifted since the Beatles.[9]

Thus "Something in the Way" must be read not as a self-contained lyric utterance—or not as this only—but as a calculated contribution to the ongoing conversation between the tradition and the individual talent. At least one other intertextual dimension of the song carries significant freight, for "Something in the Way" exists not just in the context of Anglo-American pop music but quite explicitly within the context created by the album *Nevermind*. That context itself is a complicated one—too complicated to explore in very much detail here; perhaps the most salient characteristic of the album with which "Something in the Way" must contend is its sometimes withering irony. "Something in the Way" comes last on an album that opens with two of the most ironic—even mocking—songs to have enjoyed pop success in the nineties, "Smells Like Teen Spirit" and "In Bloom." In such a rough neighborhood, a song like "Something in the Way" might have a difficult time establishing the sincerity of its intentions, especially given its ironic and self-conscious musical and lyrical procedures; those intentions are signaled in part by a cello, unaccountably added to the chorus in the final mix—a sort of diacritical marker of the authenticity of the song's communication. "Something in the Way" isn't on the face of it the most complex song in the Nirvana catalog, or on *Nevermind*, yet even this folksy, bluesy ballad requires listeners who can process the sonic materials on a number of levels, almost simultaneously. How often has rock criticism encouraged us to listen in this multifaceted way? Or tried to show us how?

Clearly, then, one way in which this collection differs from other academic studies of rock music is its tighter focus on individual texts. But there is a more expansive dimension to our project as well, for—like other recent studies such as Frith's *Performing Rites* and Theodore Gracyk's excellent *Rhythm and Noise*[10]—*Reading Rock & Roll* shares an interest in the aesthetics of rock music. In this case, though, our approach differs because our focus is considerably wider. Rather than trying to discover a methodology specific to rock itself, we seek to explore the larger question of what rock music reveals about late-twentieth-century aesthetics as a whole. This broader focus is perhaps most visible in those essays that analyze the two-way dialogue between rock and other nonmusical discourses: how rock has appropriated and been appropriated by contemporary fiction, film, and visual art. But we would also argue that the study of rock music has in and of itself much to contribute to our more general understanding of postmodernism. Unlike most other high or popular art forms, rock & roll (according to the canonical stories) came into being at approximately the same time that postmodernism was beginning to exert its influence on American and European culture. On July 5, 1954, Elvis Presley recorded "That's All Right" at Sam Phillips's Memphis Recording Service; just eighteen months earlier that harbinger of postmodern drama, Samuel Beckett's *Waiting for Godot*, had premiered in Paris, and eighteen months later *Godot* would celebrate its U.S. debut. As a result, rock has from the beginning served as an artistic laboratory where many of contemporary art's most significant and exciting tendencies have taken shape. Pop artist Andy Warhol, for instance, famously took the Velvet Underground under his wing in 1965 as manager and patron, but it would, in retrospect, be difficult to say whether Andy ever taught the vu as much as they taught him.

Thus, in our view, postmodern rock is not a recent development but something that has been around since rock's inception. With its rather mongrel pedigree and its intimate association with mass media and high-tech modes of production, rock has been a highly self-conscious and often ironic art form from the get-go and by no means the bastion of sincerity and countercultural opposition that much rock writing has made it out to be. To put it another way, for every Joni Mitchell[11] or Bruce Springsteen, there has always been a Ray Davies or Frank Zappa ready to poke fun at rock's earnestness; at every Woodstock there has been a Sha Na Na waiting to puncture its millennial pretensions. As we write this, the most obvious high-profile sincere, politically committed band in the business would have to be Rage Against the Machine. Yet a quick Internet search turns up a parody web page, "Rage Against the Coffee Machine," featuring downloadable songs such as "Our Copier Broke Down, Motherfucker" and thanking "Evil corporations, without which this very angry album would not have been possible."[12] Perhaps every Beatles spawns its own Rutles.

Given this understanding of rock, our take on the issue of authenticity is necessarily very different from that of a critic such as Lawrence Grossberg. As he argues in his 1992 study, *We Gotta Get Out of This Place: Popular Conservatism and Postmodern Culture*, rock's claim to authenticity once enabled it to assume a "special place" in the lives of postwar youth:

> The ideology of authenticity legitimated the fact that rock mattered by providing the measure of its difference from other cultural forms—rock differed absolutely from mere entertainment—and grounding that difference in rock's claim to have an excess. The ideology of authenticity renders the musical form and lyrical content of rock secondary to, or at least dependent upon, an excess which may be defined stylistically, or by rock's youthfulness and fun, or by the fact that rock matters. This excess distinguishes between musical/cultural practices and between fans, although the two dimensions do not always correspond. It can be marked in a number of ways: inauthentic vs. authentic; center vs. margin; mainstream vs. underground; commercial vs. independent; co-opted vs. resistant; pop vs. rock.[13]

But with the rise of postmodernism and what is for Grossberg its musical avatar, punk, these notions of authenticity have been replaced by a logic of "ironic nihilism" or "authentic inauthenticity" that sees every identity as "equally fake" and all images as "equally artificial" (226). Consequently, rock now "offers neither salvation nor transcendence, neither an anarchy of fun nor a narcotic of bliss. Rock is a site of temporary investment, without the power to restructure everyday life" (237).

Grossberg's thesis has been so influential in rock criticism that many of the essays in this collection respond to it, explicitly or implicitly, calling into question his opposition between the authenticity of the past and the inauthenticity of the present. Furthermore, many of the essays argue that despite—and in many cases because of—its increasingly ironic strategies, rock continues to represent a robust source of opposition to the status quo. To use Grossberg's terms, "postmodern" rock continues "to matter" and affect the "everyday lives" of its listeners; postmodern rock, however—ironic rock, self-conscious rock, intertextual rock, metarock—at the same time requires different listening strategies of its listeners. If critics like Grossberg are prone to throw up their hands and mourn that authenticity and commitment have gone out of rock, its most complex and challenging texts will fall on deaf—or, as Simon Reynolds would call them, "blissed out"—ears.[14]

One final feature, we believe, distinguishes this collection from others of its type: our attempt to harness the kind of energy found in the best rock journalism but rarely seen in so-called academic writing. Perhaps the quintessential example here is the wild-child/martyr of rock writing, Lester Bangs. The jacket copy for his posthumous selected writings, *Psychotic Reactions and Carburetor Dung*, bears the motto "Rock 'n' Roll as Literature and Literature as Rock 'n' Roll." In his magnificent introduction, Greil Marcus gives Bangs's myth momentum by eulogizing him as "rock's essential wild man, a one-man orgy of abandon, excess, wisdom, satire, parody" and suggests that the only way latter-day readers can tap into Bangs's magic is "to accept that the best writer in America could write almost nothing but record reviews."[15] Bangs's frenetic and opinionated writing continues to elicit strong opinions today; what is beyond dispute, however—and what many of rock's more sober critics would do well to bear in mind—is that the passion of a writer who cares deeply about the music can cover a multitude of sins. Who but Lester Bangs could title an article about American punk in *Creem* magazine "James Taylor Marked for Death?" and get away with it?

While few have attempted to co-opt Bangs's neanderthal, "gonzo" style[16]—and those few unsuccessfully—writers at magazines such as *Rolling Stone* and *Spin* continue to turn rock's raw power into powerful prose. Popular writers such as Robert Christgau, Greil Marcus, Robert Palmer, Anthony DeCurtis, and Elysa Gardner never disguise their genuine love for the music and find the risk of writing from the position of music consumer and fan—rather than simply as critic—to be well worth taking. One noteworthy recent example of the contagious energy of this kind of writing is Gina Arnold's *Route 666*. Nothing we've read recently conveys as vividly what it feels like to be crazy in love with a rock band:

> Francesca is staring fixedly at the stage. Slowly, she bends her knees so her mouth is right by my ear. "Dance," she hisses into it. "It intimidates people."
>
> We begin to flail wildly away in time to "Wolves, Lower," our arms swinging in slo-mo, fancying ourselves a lot like Morrissey in the "How Soon Is Now" video. Soon we've cut ourselves a hole a full arm's length in circumference in the crowd around the stage. It's June 1984, and she and I are standing nose to nose with R.E.M. at the Catalyst in Santa Cruz, an hour's drive south of the Bay Area. We'd heard the gig announced on the radio that afternoon and, convinced it'd be sold out, each left her

respective workplace on a trumped-up excuse ("That was my mom. I have to quick take the cat to the vet!") and bought a pair of tickets, one for the other.[17]

Arnold is a fan—a rabid fan—yet surely no Pamela Des Barres (author of the infamous *I'm With the Band: Confessions of a Groupie*).[18] *Route 666* is a wonderful marriage of intelligence and passion in the service of the music, capturing along the way the essence of the music she loves. This is essentially what Mark Crispin Miller said in his famous review of Greil Marcus's *Mystery Train*: "There is more of rock's spirit in this book than there is in rock music."[19] Or as Michael Stipe says in the promotional blurb on the back cover of Anthony DeCurtis's collection *Present Tense*: "This shit rocks!"[20]

The writers collected here share with journalistic writers a desire to create a more lively and passionate style of rock criticism; we refuse to let theoretical discourse squeeze the life out of our prose. Surely there's something perverse about invoking a notion such as Althusser's "ideological state apparatuses" and the music of Abba in the same sentence. Instead, we feel that rock & roll writing can, without sacrificing its intellectual rigor, express both the energy of the music and the personal voice of the writer—can, in the words of Susan McClary and Robert Walser, demonstrate "a greater willingness to try to circumscribe an effect metaphorically, to bring one's experience as a human being to bear in unpacking musical gestures, to try to parallel in words something of how the music *feels*."[21] Such an approach—at once informal and theoretically informed—will yield, we hope, a collection that will appeal to both academic and general readers alike.

Michael Coyle and Jon Dolan's essay opens the collection with an examination of the issue of authenticity, reexamining the traditional dichotomy in rock criticism between authentic artistry and commercial success, the belief that "real" rock is a challenge to the hierarchy, a return to a purer, uncommercialized form. Coyle and Dolan, however, contend that this obsession with authenticity is not indigenous to rock music and analyze how this kind of rhetoric crept into the discourse of rock & roll when performers became songwriters and singers aspired to be accepted as visionaries.

R. J. Warren Zanes's "Too Much Mead? Under the Influence (of Participant-Observation)" sounds a dissenting note by examining a number of the central concepts of this book. At the core of his argument is the belief that appropriation bears within it an implicit critique of the myth of authenticity and its conception of art as the unique product of an originating genius; Zanes also suggests how rock & roll influences the aesthetic practices of other art forms, exploring the curious relationship between underground music in 1980s' New York (a scene in which Zanes was an integral member, as guitarist for the Del Fuegos) and the postmodern art practices of the same period and place (Prince, Barbara Kruger, Cindy Sherman, and others). Somewhat vexingly, however, Zanes concludes by suggesting that an overinvestment in irony hardly answers nagging questions about authenticity, a quality that rock fans and performers, and perhaps even cultural studies scholars, desire as fervently today as ever.

The next four essays explore the ways that artistic appropriation has been used both to critique existing race and gender politics and to envision a new set of social relationships. Marilyn Manners analyzes Madonna's and Courtney Love's periodic reinvention of themselves as a means of escape from the pervasive media tendency to pigeonhole them. Manners draws out buried links among addiction, female sexuality, and writing that evoke other, underlying aspects of the "disorienting" role of powerful women in rock: the interminable quest for Truth that continues to haunt reactions to popular art is informed by—indeed saturated with—gender assumptions. In "Ask Any Girl," Patricia Juliana Smith argues that the conventions of the girl group create an environment rich in homosocial implications. Though the Boy is both subject and object of girl-group fantasies, he exists primarily in the third person for the lead-singer persona; by extension, the backing vocalists represent the commercial audience for girl-group music: a primarily female and adolescent audience that interacts and identifies with other girls by exchanging male-centered fantasies. While Smith interrogates the smiling face of girl-group homosociality, Ashley Dawson explores the troubling appropriation of skinhead iconography within the underground movement known as Queercore. Certain forms of gay style and cultural identity have always been based on a dangerous fascination with the most hegemonic forms of heterosexual masculinity; the irony of such mimicry, Dawson suggests, corrodes the iron façade of straight masculinity by revealing the erotic charge latent within such hardness. Finally, the dizzying array of appropriations out of which George Clinton weaves his heteroglossic vision is the subject of Mark Willhardt and Joel Stein's essay. Drawing on the work of critics such as Henry Louis Gates, Jr., and Houston Baker, they examine Clinton's uses and abuses of the discourses around him and chart the political ramifications of these intertextual strategies.

The next several essays continue to investigate the various interconnections among the aesthetics, politics, and economics of rock. John Alberti applies the Brechtian concept of the faux-naïf to one of the pioneers of alternative rock, Jonathan Richman, to examine how his seemingly juvenile music functions as a site of resistance. Alberti believes that Richman's invocation of the faux-naïf not only operates in the simplest sense of asking his listeners to regress to a childlike condition but in so doing exposes how many of the critical and audience reactions to his performances reveal contradictory attitudes toward the dominant cultural practices to which alternative rock claims to represent an alternative. Sean Portnoy's essay on rave culture exhibits an equally political focus. Contesting both those who condemn contemporary dance music as fascist and those who celebrate it as liberatory, he ultimately suggests that the most effective tools of rave's critique reside in its attempt to challenge traditional notions of aesthetic, intellectual, and physical property. In "The Riot Grrrls and 'Carnival,' " Neil Nehring invokes Mikhail Bakhtin to provide a refreshingly positive spin on the anger of the riot grrrl movement. Reenvisioning this anger as energy, he argues that any criticism that cannot read such anger as anything but negative or nihilistic no longer has much to say to us. Nehring's essay focuses on one very short Bikini Kill song, "Carnival," that he reads as simultaneously a confrontational piece about sexual abuse, a parodic treatment of traditional notions about "sluts," and finally as a kind of musical carnival.

No book-length consideration of rock's uneasy and shifting aesthetics would be complete without a consideration of the recent work of U2, and so we have included two essays that approach U2's postmodern reinvention through rather different theoretical lenses. In her discussion, Robyn Brothers directly addresses some of the political implications of postmodern rock. By arguing that U2's newly ironic stance simultaneously criticizes the commodification of contemporary culture and embraces the potential benefits of the very systems it targets, she makes clear that their brand of postmodern inauthenticity is anything but a "depoliticized nihilism." Atara Stein's essay explores how on two recent albums (*Achtung Baby* and *Zooropa*) U2 has self-consciously deconstructed one of the most traditional forms in rock & roll: the love song. The lover's project of self-creation and self-glorification, Stein demonstrates, is also a metaphor for the band's own violation of its fans' expectations, moving away from its previous incarnation as the intensely sincere "Conscience of Rock 'n' Roll" to a far more unstable and ironic stance.

The last two essays widen the collection's focus once again to consider explicitly the aesthetic implications of other artistic media (fiction and film) using rock as a source for their intertextual work. Pamela Thurschwell's essay explores the prominent role of Elvis Costello in particular and pop music more generally in two recent novels: Bret Easton Ellis's *Less than Zero* and Nick Hornby's *High Fidelity*. Despite the radically different cultural contexts of these two books, Costello provides not only their titles but a frame of reference against which to assess the politics and emotional terrain they cover. Finally, our own cowritten essay discusses the appropriation of rock by yet another media: film. Focusing on the use of largely schlocky seventies' music in several recent movies (*Reality Bites, Wayne's World, Reservoir Dogs,* and *Pulp Fiction*), we argue that these soundtracks do not simply evoke a period mood but create the kind of unstable postmodern irony that Linda Hutcheon and Fredric Jameson describe. Even as these filmmakers acknowledge the cheesiness of this musical effluvia, they suspend judgment on it and actually seem to take delight in it.

As these brief synopses suggest, the essays collected in *Reading Rock & Roll* chime in from all over the theoretical map; the result is an eclecticism we're pleased about. Although some critics have recently begun to launch into jeremiads about the lack of any central, unifying theory in rock writing, this heterogeneity can be read as a sign of the field's vitality: rather than pursuing a unified field theory of rock discourse—what Jean-François Lyotard would call an oppressive "metanarrative"—scholarly work on rock music seems at present to be more interested in responding to Lyotard's call for the multiplication of small narratives. As the epigraph from Brian Eno suggests, the beauty of a theory is that it allows you to read a familiar object differently and thereby reanimate it for yourself and others. Many different theories allow many different kinds of rediscovery and magic to happen.

That's enough from us. On with the show.

NOTES

1. The most thoroughgoing examination and critique of these terms is Andreas Huyssen's *After the Great Divide: Modernism, Mass Culture, Postmodernism* (Bloomington: Indiana University Press, 1986).
2. For a brief history of the Birmingham School by one of its founders, see Stuart Hall, "The Emergence of Cultural Studies and the Crisis of the Humanities," *October* 54: 11–90.

3. See Lawrence Grossberg, *We Gotta Get Out of This Place: Popular Conservatism and Postmodern Culture* (New York: Routledge, 1992); Dick Hebdige, *Subculture: The Meaning of Style* (New York: Routledge, 1993); Angela McRobbie, *Postmodernism and Popular Culture* (New York: Routledge, 1994); Andrew Ross and Tricia Rose, eds., *Microphone Fiends: Youth Music and Youth Culture* (New York: Routledge, 1994); Ray Pratt, *Rhythm and Resistance: Explorations in the Political Uses of Popular Music* (New York: Praeger, 1990; Washington, DC: Smithsonian Institution Press, 1994); Reebee Garofalo, *Rockin' Out: Popular Music in the USA* (Boston: Allyn and Bacon, 1997).

4. In their introduction to the *Cultural Studies* anthology, Cary Nelson, Paula A. Treichler, and Lawrence Grossberg write "Although there is no prohibition against close textual readings in cultural studies, they are also not required. Moreover, textual analysis in literary studies carries a history of convictions that texts are properly understood as wholly self-determined and independent objects as well as a bias about which kinds of texts are worthy of analysis. That burden of associations cannot be ignored" (Lawrence Grossberg, Cary Nelson, and Paula A. Treichler, eds., *Cultural Studies* [New York: Routledge, 1992], p. 2).

5. Ross and Rose, introduction, *Microphone Fiends*, p. 3.

6. Simon Frith, *Performing Rites: On the Value of Popular Music* (Cambridge: Harvard University Press, 1996), p. 71.

7. "Seether," on Veruca Salt's first album, *American Thighs* (Geffen 24732, 1994), builds up a mysterious riot grrrl ethos through a series of "neither/nor" constructions: Seether is neither "loose nor tight," "black nor white," etc. "Louise" is Louise Post, the band's dynamic front woman. The band's very name is itself intertextual, referring to the snotty-nosed brat in Roald Dahl's *Willie Wonka and the Chocolate Factory*.

8. In recent years, rock's forays into the classical realm have become even more common and ambitious. No longer are rock musicians content with merely weaving together series of thematically related pop songs into rock operas; they now are attempting to write full-scale "serious" compositions, such as Paul McCartney's *London Oratorio* and *Standing Stone* or Joe Jackson's *The Seven Deadly Sins*. At the same time, classical musicians have also begun experimenting with rock-inflected projects: consider, e.g., the Brodsky Quartet's collaboration with Elvis Costello, *The Juliet Letters*, or Phillip Glass's *Low* and *Heroes* symphonies.

9. For the members of Nirvana, and especially for Kurt Cobain, the Beatles are the inescapable reference point for all subsequent rock experimentation; in an interview, Dave Grohl complained, "When it comes down to pop, there's only one word—the B word. . . . Beatles. We might as well play fucking Beatles covers for the rest of our careers." According to Chris Novoselic, "They started it, they did it best, they ended it" (Chris Mundy, "Nirvana vs. Fame," reprinted in *Cobain*, by the editors of *Rolling Stone* [Boston: Little, Brown, 1994], p. 30).

10. Theodore Gracyk, *Rhythm and Noise: An Aesthetics of Rock* (Durham, NC: Duke University Press, 1996).

11. Even this convenient opposition between naive and knowing rock artists isn't airtight; Joni Mitchell, after all, lets us hear her singing on cheap airline headphones on "This Flight Tonight," from her fourth album, *Blue* (1971), and, of course, Bruce Springsteen's irony in "Born in the USA" caught Ronald Reagan napping—such that Reagan adopted this almost despairing song as a campaign anthem. Even folk idols such as Joni Mitchell and Bruce Springsteen aren't the two-dimensional cutouts to which a simplistic "authenticity" standard threatens to reduce them.

12. "Rage Against the Coffee Machine," http://weber.u.washington.edu/mamster/ratcm/ (October 1997).

13. Grossberg, *We Gotta Get Out of This Place*, p. 206.

14. Simon Reynolds, *Blissed Out: The Raptures of Rock* (London: Serpent's Tail, 1990). In some of his more recent writings, such as "Cinema, Postmodernism, and Authenticity" (in *Sound and Vision: The Music Video Reader*, ed. Simon Frith, Andrew Goodwin, and Lawrence Grossberg [London: Routledge, 1993]), Grossberg has gone so far as to suggest that "the ideology of authenticity is becoming irrelevant" and has acknowledged that "the way in which rock matters, its place in the fan's everyday life, is changing" (203). Still, for him, the prevalence of irony and self-consciousness in rock is a fairly recent phenomenon and one that represents a sharp break from the ideology of the past.

15. Greil Marcus, introduction to Lester Bangs, *Psychotic Reactions and Carburetor Dung* (New York: Vintage, 1988), pp. xii, x.

16. The reference, of course, is to the "gonzo" journalism of Hunter S. Thompson, pioneer of the generation of U.S. journalists who sought the truth of a story not by achieving an objective distance from the subject but via a full immersion in the story. It's certainly no coincidence that Thompson wrote his greatest book, *Fear and Loathing in Las Vegas*, on assignment for *Rolling Stone*.

17. Gina Arnold, *Route 666: On the Road to Nirvana* (New York: St. Martin's, 1993), p. 57.

18. Pamela Des Barres, *I'm With the Band: Confessions of a Groupie* (New York: Beech Tree, 1987).

19. Quoted in Greil Marcus, *Mystery Train: Images of America in Rock 'n' Roll* (New York: Dutton, 1975), n.p.

20. Anthony DeCurtis, *Present Tense: Rock & Roll and Culture* (Durham, NC: Duke University Press, 1992).

21. Susan McClary and Robert Walser, "Start Making Sense! Musicology Wrestles with Rock," in *On Record: Rock, Pop, and the Written Word*, ed. Simon Frith and Andrew Goodwin (New York: Pantheon, 1990), pp. 288–89.

1

MODELING AUTHENTICITY, AUTHENTICATING COMMERCIAL MODELS

MICHAEL COYLE AND JON DOLAN

Right in the middle of a contradiction, that's the place to be.
—Sam Shepherd

Let's start with three postmodern morality tales: You're watching your MTV, and your MTV is laughing at you. Two tiny Japanese women are jumping up and down on two itty-bitty beds, playing off a canned hip-hop groove, and hollering "I know my chicken! / you got to know your chicken."[1] Their aggressively playful look could be a come-on, and it could be a put-down. If you're quick, you wonder if they're giving you supermarket advice ("you gotta know your chicken"), spoofing a playground dis ("you gotta know you're chicken"), or troping on a pimp's solicitations. But, quick or not, this video moment vanishes as you confront it. An instance of contrived disposability, the Cibo Matto video has a finger on your semiotic trigger.

In an upstate New York college radio station, an old *Rolling Stone* cover slowly yellows on the control room door. On it, Nirvana stand posed and poised as the latest big thing. Kurt Cobain shows that he's a rebel by wearing a white tee shirt on which he has scrawled, in black magic marker, "Corporate Magazines Still Suck." In choosing that photo for its cover, *Rolling Stone* successfully appropriates the gesture and by so doing associates itself with the rebellion: a good strategy, tried and true, that has been selling copy for over a quarter century now.[2] This salacious confusion of traditional ideological distinctions remains irrelevant to the students who DJ at the station, own *Nevermind* (Subpop/Geffen DGCD 24425),[3] and keep the image on display.

Working at his desk in Minneapolis, rock critic Jim Walsh is wearing his heart on his sleeve in more or less the same way that he'd love all his favorite bands to hang their souls on their strings. A talented writer and a pop music critic for the *St. Paul Pioneer Press-Dispatch*, Walsh verily embodies roots-rock integrity. Today he's writing an article for *Spin* about his favorite new band of 1995, a country-rock outfit called Son Volt. The band is fronted by former Uncle Tupelo guitarist Jay Farrar, and Walsh celebrates Farrar as an explicit inheritor of such authenticity-starved sixties' legends as Gram Parsons. He likens Son Volt's songs to "evergreens" and honors Farrar's "love affair with the Mississippi River." Taking a page, perhaps, from Greil Marcus, Walsh embowers the record in the discourse of cultural "tradition." He discovers "roots" in the self-conscious mysticism of Farrar's lyrics that run deep into the American earth. With this idea Walsh hits his stride and produces a line more absurdly profound—or maybe profoundly absurd—than a hundred Farrar lyrics: "Son Volt is less interested in modern rock air-play or MTV rotation than they are in contributing to an on-going tradition."[4] There you have it. You gotta know your chicken.

These episodes become postmodern morality tales not in and of themselves but in the spaces among them, in the context formed by their juxtaposition. Think again about the Cibo Matto video. MTV has remained a favorite topic—if not target—of critical commentary since its first broadcast of 1 August 1981. Presenting videos that are both performances and promotions, the very nature of MTV deconstructs the opposition between art and commerce on which so much trade—corporate and critical—depends. Moreover, as it represents a primarily visual medium designed to sell sound recordings, MTV's semiotic promiscuity has made obvious a condition that the acolytes of rock tradition have only recently begun to acknowledge: that is, unlike jazz (at least until recently), rock is primarily about recordings and not performance.[5] Whereas early jazz musicians made records only to boost the price of their personal appearances, rock musicians tour to promote records.[6] The recording and not the performance is the "real" thing. Excepting recent and important trends in hip hop or DJ performance, where fans go to hear familiar music remixed beyond recognition, late-twentieth-century audiences go to hear musicians give a sense of a record rather than the other way around. MTV, by its very nature more than by its programming, demonstrates rock's spectacular nature. For rock audiences seeing is believing; rock plays live largely as spectacle, which is why acoustically horrific venues such as arenas or stadiums are increasingly appropriate. MTV did not create this condition; it has capitalized on it and on the outrage its irreverence to rock piety still some-times produces.

Cibo Matto's bouncing on little beds signifies—sells records—precisely because it's done in a house still haunted by Kurt Cobain's ghost and har-rowed by the specter of authenticity. Their chicken-core chorus parodies the importance of knowing what's what. And yet it's not at all that Cibo Matto answer the "traditionalism" of Son Volt with something "revolutionary." In fact, Son Volt and Cibo Matto are not really so different. Late in 1995, when both groups made their recording debuts, they occupied the same ephemeral space in the hit story that is rock history. Neither produced a big hit, though Cibo Matto got more critical props. By 1998 Sun Volt was going nowhere fast, while Cibo Matto was working on a second album and made an appearance on Warner Brothers' popular TV show *Buffy the Vampire Slayer*. Even so, both groups attracted the attention of college radio; both bands presented a version of mid-nineties pop success; and both bands were hooky, to say the least. Both *Viva! La Woman* and *Trace* yield approximately the same number of hooks, although these hooks differ in kind: Cibo Matto's are sleekly synthetic, whereas Son Volt's are evocatively evasive, organicist with-out quite being organic. Still, hooks are hooks, and popular recordings depend on them to get airplay and public notice. It isn't so much the differ-ences between the records per se that's of interest as the differences in their marketing and consumption. Granted, marketing routinely works to fabri-cate difference, but why do we need to know that Son Volt is not concerned with MTV rotation, whereas Cibo Matto confronts it? What kind of distinc-tion are roots-minded critics making when they expect Cibo Matto to have the staying power of a cardboard match while Son Volt will endure to carry the torch of tradition? Why is modern rock airplay antithetical to ongoing tradition, and what does ongoing tradition have to do with a commercial record?

The larger question might be, what commercial music has to do with authenticity in any form? The music industry invokes tradition primarily as another marketing strategy. But tradition, and an authentic relation to it, clearly means more than that not only to critics such as Jim Walsh or Greil Marcus but also to fans and musicians. Kurt Cobain, after all, died for it. The merest suspicion of show-biz hype regularly destroys the reputations of aspiring alternative rock groups. Indeed, the sudden success and somewhat less sudden self-destruction of Nirvana is inescapably the crux on which this question now hangs. In the 1990s the ethics of indie integrity systematically catch new bands in what no doubt one day will be remembered as an impossible double bind. If they win big, sell lots of records, and make their music available to the millions, they lose credibility in Coolsville; on the other hand, to maintain their alternative status—to lose commercially—means that ultimately they will never escape the alterna-ghetto. It might seem that it's only through another loss that an alternative musician can win: fame must be posthumous. However tragic Cobain's personal loss, Nirvana continues to move lots of product.

Quoting Neil Young, Cobain's suicide note recited a primary lesson from what Cobain called "Punk Rock 101": "It's better to burn out than to fade away."[7] However, the effect of Cobain quoting that consummate survivor, Neil Young, transforms a simple lesson into a complex series of media melodramas immediately played out in public responses to the death, to the note, and to Cobain himself: Courtney Love's grief and anger over his grave; media neo-cons Rush Limbaugh and Andy Rooney wondering why anyone should be surprised by a drug user's suicide and dismissing Cobain as insignificant; alternative pioneer Michael Stipe speaking publicly of the project he and Cobain had been planning; and thousands of other commentators trying to explain what really happened to the most promising rock star of the nineties. In the 1992 cover shot for *Rolling Stone*, while bandmates Dave Grohl and Chris Noveselic offer the smiles of guys who are damn happy to be there, Cobain himself cops a stone-cold glare through his three-day beard and lounge-lizard shades. He's shooting for James Dean sex appeal, Dylan ambivalence, Clash defiance, and he's missing on every mark. All told, Cobain looks more lame than likely.

The only thing really interesting about Cobain is the DIY tee shirt, reading "Corporate Magazines Still Suck," which plays on an SST Records tee shirt of the time that read "Corporate Rock Still Sucks." Cobain's indie in-joke, no doubt lost on many *Rolling Stone* readers, links Cobain to a punk ethos that his success meant was no longer his to share. Between the early and middle eighties, SST Records had set the pace for U.S. punk labels, releasing records by Hüsker Dü, the Minutemen, and Black Flag, the first band Cobain ever saw in concert. By 1992, however, label owner and former Black Flag guitarist Greg Ginn had exchanged his DIY management philosophy for the guidance of what one insider called business major types, a species as far removed from punk identity as any imaginable. While Cobain was touring for *Nevermind*, SST was releasing little more than overpriced reissues of old Minutemen records and marketing self-reflexive tee shirts like the one Cobain parodies on the *Rolling Stone* cover shot. Punk had gone corporate, and corporate rock sucked. Kurt Cobain knew it sucked, knew he'd been sucked in, and hated himself for being there.

"*Nevermind* embodies a cultural moment," Michael Azerrad wrote in April 1992; it's "an anthem for the 'why ask why?' generation," a refusal of industry-standard music.[8] Azerrad was looking for a sound bite, and so he copped Budweiser's "Why ask why?" slogan in an effort to capitalize on the street credibility of a band that had just grown huge. But, apart from the burlesque of tagging Nirvana fans with a corporate hook, his comment underscores a contradiction fundamental to what we now can't help calling the alternative industry. That contradiction involves the inescapable complicity of music and marketing in late-century America, a complicity that inevitably involves writers who take popular music as their subject. Cobain, not surprisingly, seems to have consented to Azerrad's estimation very uncomfortably and only in part. "I don't want to sound egotistical," he protested, "but I know [*Nevermind*] is better than a majority of the corporate shit that's been crammed down people's throats for a long time."[9] Nevertheless, Cobain continued, "I'm a spokesman for myself. It just so happens that there's a bunch of people that are concerned with what I have to say." Cobain clearly was in a troubling position. The obvious difference between "a bunch" and the millions who have purchased *Nevermind* renders uneasy the difference between speaking for yourself and writing an anthem for a generation. How do you complain about "corporate shit" when you are the shit, and how do remain true to your own voice when the industry makes a killing off your every gesture, even your suicide?

When Courtney Love stood in front of thousands of her dead husband's mourners and called him an "asshole" for not getting out while he still had the chance, she was wrestling with the same thirty-year-old hegemony.[10] The music she made on Hole's *Live Through This* (Geffen 24631, 1994), and the Madonna/Medusa of punk rock image she cultivated, responded directly to the hyperdisconsolate "Leonard Cohen afterworld" in which Cobain had found himself.[11] And yet Love's orgy of grief and rage prompted widespread cynicism from the press and elicited skeptical responses from many of her husband's fans, who felt themselves the real inheritors of his legacy. Her curses seemed scripted, the very spittle running down her chin seemed the exploitation of an energy she could tap into only so long as Kurt Cobain's ghost followed her onstage, on TV, and into the tabloids. She couldn't win either.

The band that did win was Green Day. Originally from the Bay area, they began releasing their first, retro-nuevo Ramones-like singles about the same time Nirvana was gracing the cover of *Rolling Stone*. Those singles did increasingly well and drew enough attention that Green Day was quickly signed by Reprise Records. Almost immediately thereafter they became the targets of punk purists. The subculture monthly *Maximum Rock'n'Roll* was warning its readership against Green Day on the grounds that they would one day be huge. After they signed with Reprise, *Maximum Rock'n'Roll* began treating Green Day as if they had contracted some sort of pop-industry plague and regularly attacked their every success as if sticking by their side might summon the wrath of the punk-rock furies. Once their album *Dookie* (Warner 45529, 1993) became a pop sensation, the purists began hollering "I told you so." But Green Day took it all in stride, and as the screams of "sell-out" grew louder, they grew better, more self-assured, and maybe even more fun to love.

The absurdity of this moment, particularly in view of Azerrad's sense of "the cultural moment" only one year before, is hard to miss. Green Day was selling out of its market niche and in the process bringing punk-rock music and ethics to people that *Maximum Rock'n'Roll* would never reach. Touring large halls with gay punks Pansy Division, Green Day had fourteen-year-olds singing a line the likes of which Cobain might have spoken in his darkest and loneliest moments: "Sometimes I give myself the creeps."[12] Yet Green Day responded to its fifteen minutes of fame with little more than a shrug; "I never really thought that being obnoxious would get me to where I am right now," singer Billie Joe Armstrong mused when his turn came to be on the cover of *Rolling Stone*.[13] Green Day had won. They won on their own terms, in their own way, and probably for themselves only.

The phrase "cultural moment" is imprecise, to say the least. The struggle between recording artists and industry suits has been retold now countless times. Think of three hugely influential—and popular—examples just from the seventies, by which time principled opposition had already become artistic dogma: the Kinks's *Lola Versus the Powerman and the Money-go-round* (Warner 6423, 1970), Pink Floyd's *Wish You Were Here* (Epic 33453, 1975), and the Sex Pistols's *Never Mind the Bollocks* (Warner 3147, 1977), the last of which anticipates not only something of Nirvana's attitude but even the title of *Nevermind*. Similar examples remain abundant as far back as the Byrds's "So You Want to Be a Rock 'n' Roll Star" (1967), but between the Byrds's hippie cynicism and Chuck Berry's populist anthem from a still earlier period, "Johnny

B. Goode" (1958), emerges a world of difference.[14] That difference marks a profound discursive development, a development that pointedly separates us from the tradition about which Jim Walsh writes so nostalgically. But this nostalgia is more than the merely wistful longing for an organic tradition that never quite existed; it unwittingly (at least in Walsh's case) serves to mask an increasingly antisocial contradiction.

Musicians make records so that their music can be heard, but they must make them without appearing to be in the embrace of the corporate beast. Nirvana's example is by no means singular, however much it helped shape the nineties version of the authenticity paradigm or informed some peculiarly nineties examples. Cobain's crosstown rival, Eddie Vedder, has made a career of protesting the burden and pain of international celebrity. He doesn't sing about giving himself the creeps, but he's been widely quoted as saying that, when he sees his face filling some magazine page, he "hates that guy." Younger bands, however, increasingly respond with something of the same slacker indifference played out by Green Day. Indeed, in the context of this dilemma, the whole notion of "slacker" begins to make sense. In a culture that coheres largely on the basis of its identity as a market, where bands are said to have sold out even before having paid for their first records, a slack attitude toward success might mean survival.

Consider the highly touted slacker band Pavement. They made their brilliant record *Slanted and Enchanted* late in 1991 and saw it released by Matador Records the next year. *Slanted* (Matador Records OLE 038–2, 1992) is still regarded by many as the height of indie music and of college radio; it seemed the *Murmur* (I.R.S./A&M 70014, 1983) of its generation, a semipopular hit that suggested massive, R.E.M.-scale success to come.[15] But although *Slanted* brought only success enough that they could quit their day jobs, Pavement quickly became fair game for street-level prosecution. They anticipated sellout accusations, however, ironizing them by playing with the constraints of their hipper-than-thou image. They resisted the slacker rap by telling radio interviewers that they were striving to get tight (and added that getting tight wasn't easy); they wrote self-conscious songs about going "out on tour with the Smashing Pumpkins" ("nature kids and they ain't got no function");[16] and during live performances they introduced their songs with one-liners such as "This is from the soundtrack to *Reality Bites II*." As Pavement has developed since, its increasingly self-conscious meta-rock has become more challenging. "I don't think we're a cultural moment," Songwriter and lead singer Steve Malkmus told an interviewer on the release of

Brighten the Corners (Matador/Capitol 197, 1997),[17] defusing any of his band's lingering Nirvanaesque implications. Malkmus's comment doesn't imply a refusal of success but a refusal of the terms that made it so difficult for Nirvana to take pride in the work that made it successful. Masters of the discourse, Pavement don't defend their authenticity as alternative musicians but instead ridicule the very expectation that authenticity has anything to do with their records.

The contradiction acted out by these celebrated examples obscures the very conditions within which pop music signifies and sells—or sometimes sells and so signifies—but few fans or musicians have seen this apparent double bind as keenly as Green Day and Pavement. Most fans do not wish to see themselves as consumers, even though they pay for recordings or concert tickets. They prefer instead to see the issue in terms of the constant and necessary resistance of rock to the industry on whose support its life depends but whose authority must always be resisted, a condition whose very structure suggests the relation of the young to their parents, at least insofar as that relation has been constructed in the United States since the Second World War. In other words, the situation is conceived of in the same terms used by critical theory to distinguish the genuine from the ersatz.

Few critics have played a more influential role in defining the relevance of authenticity to American music than Dave Marsh. Marsh's tastes have always run to American idioms, black and white, and he has made no secret of the fact that he writes not for college kids but for working people: Marsh has never shown much interest in the youth culture at which rock is primarily targeted. These qualities perhaps explain why, in the seventies and almost alone among the major critics, he rejected punk and favored populist rockers such as Bruce Springsteen. But although betting on a different horse, Marsh, too, was then anticipating a revival, and his writing exemplifies how ideology critique in the name of authenticity reproduces itself. In effect, Marsh saw Springsteen's music as a recapturing of the American dream, a dream that is always greater than the means by which we pursue it:

> Over the past decade, rock has betrayed itself. It gnaws at my marrow to recall a hundred sellouts, from the rock opera movies that were all glamour and no heart, to the photos of rock celebrities with international jet-set fugitives. The inevitable result was records that were made not with feeling but because there was a market demanding product, and concerts

performed with an eye only toward the profit margin. Rock became just another hierarchical system in which consumers took what was offered without question.[18]

This language of betrayal and its inevitable result, of the prostitution of music to market, informs the familiar and proudly repeated narrative of most rock histories. As Marsh retells it, this narrative reveals its foundational nature. New sounds are almost invariably proclaimed as liberations from the devitalizing control of industry, even as such proclamation generally inserts the new into an established pattern. Real rock is always a rebellion, always a disrespect to the hierarchy, a blow to the empire. The authentic article is never the commercial article. And so the musical departure from conformity becomes a return to form. The discourse about rock (contributed to by musicians, fans, critics, and latterly by the industry) finds authenticity in its own self-reinscription.

Discourses, as Michel Foucault has proposed, typically work in such fashion. They reproduce themselves, police themselves, institutionalize themselves. They secure their authority even in speaking their own violation. But it's interesting to consider that the discourse of rock 'n' roll is every bit as heterogeneous a mixture of borrowings as the music itself. Even today rock discourse includes critical writings, fan testimonies, the explanations of musicians, and the puff and grease of record labels, managers, and promoters: a positive carnival of forms from tabloid revelations to professorial ponderings. Overlapping both textually and contextually, these forms all make their appeal by claiming some concern or privileged perspective unavailable to the others: all insist on their distinctiveness. Critical reviews and essays evaluate recordings; academic studies engage in ideology critique; fanzines offer audience-based discussions and make public the lives and personalities of stars, becoming adulatory fact sheets for newer-than-new bands. But however distinct their subject matter or the generic features of their forms, all intone their concern for authentic expression.

Things have not always been so. The kind of narrative offered by Marsh and so many others did not originally figure in accounts of rock 'n' roll. Elvis, for example, in one of his most revealing interviews, disclaimed any title to authenticity: "The colored folks been singing it and playing it just like I'm doin' now, man, for more years than I know. They played it like that in the shanties and jook joints, and nobody paid it no mind 'til I goosed it up. I got it from them."[19] In this simple statement Elvis was not trying to give himself a lineage; he was simply trying to deflect increasingly clamorous charges of immorality. His candor was no doubt further enabled by his personal indifference to where the music came from, so long as his presentation of it was the thing currently attracting the attention of millions. Elvis knew his chicken, and he didn't care whether it came before or after the egg.

The point is that authenticity is usually a story about origins, a genealogical narrative, but here at the origin of rock 'n' roll as culture (to paraphrase Nick Tosch),[20] we find no concern whatsoever with the genuine or authentic. Elvis not only disclaimed originality, he made it clear he expected the whole rock 'n' roll thing to end at any moment; he was fully prepared shortly to be singing ballads like Perry Como or Dean Martin were. His rock 'n' roll career, he might have said, involved no carrying of the torch but the brief flare of a cardboard match. Quite simply, the pervasive concern for authenticity was not initially brought into the discourse of rock 'n' roll as industry and as signifying practice by musicians; neither did it come from a first generation of fans grown troubled over commercial exploitation.

The concern to distinguish authentic rock from industry pablum developed from sources antithetical to all that rock 'n' roll represented to its early audiences. On the one hand, the notion of authenticity derived from fiercely intellectual objections to the very nature of consumer culture. In particular, the attacks of German critical theorists Theodor Adorno and Walter Benjamin provided a rhetoric whereby to imagine a preindustrial, precommercial pastoral: to imagine forms of artistic expression that were the genuine expression of total forms of life. This rhetoric has been and remains broadly compelling, inspiring such disparate studies as LeRoi Jones's powerful indictment of crossover success, Blues People, and the Beat celebration of bebop that informs the writing of Jack Kerouac.[21] Both Jones and Kerouac exemplify a broad pattern in fifties' America, whereby an elitist conception was slowly internalized by audiences or markets that it was initially designed to critique. Through the work of such influential intermediaries, this conception gradually came to exert pressure on broader, mainstream audiences. Of these, none was more important for the shaping of rock discourse than, ironically enough,'the college and coffeehouse scene of the late fifties and early sixties, the scene most commonly referred to both by those who lived it and by subsequent historians (most of whom write nostalgically of their younger days) as the "folk" scene.

Of course, it wasn't folk music at all. That is, the music known as folk was controlled by self-appointed custodians from the intelligentsia: professors, collectors, museum curators, and other intellectuals. This control is not absolutely a terrible thing, but acknowledging its definitive presence can help us understand the impact of folk on the commercial music that was theoretically its antithesis. Folk was itself formalized by commercial and semicommercial interests. Since its first articulations in the thirties, the very idea of folk music has been caught up in romantic ideas about "the folk," in expectations that it somehow voices the soul of that mythical political convenience, the common man. The expectation has been that folk music sounded from the bedrock of U.S. culture, whereas pop is no more stable than the shifting sands of commercial fortune.

This contrast has long been authorized by the granting or withholding of such federal funds as those that sent folklorist and Librarian of Congress Alan Lomax across Depression-era America. His work was funded by New Deal ideals, but contemporary state agencies such as New York's NYSCA (New York State Council on the Arts) continue to regulate the presentation of so-called folk culture to consumer society. This regulation comes not so much in the form of restrictive prohibitions as in the qualities sought under official guidelines for grants to nonprofit venues and organizations. In other words, the state continues to protect the purity of our cultural spring waters. The constitutive power of government guidelines operates then with no nefarious intention, and these guidelines typically respect the discourse of "the folk." As Philip Ennis explains, the definition of folk music has included many related components: "music that is collectively owned, of ancient and anonymous authorship and transmitted across generations by word of mouth; a canon celebrating life in the past and urging change for tomorrow, the performance being on simple instruments in natural settings . . . the joyful performance by specially gifted but not 'professional' artists."[22] All these characteristics point toward a pastoral vision of preindustrial America.

Folklorists such as Lomax toured such of the United States' "living libraries" as "Negro Prisons" (94), Appalachian churches, or the shanties of migrant workers in search of vestiges of lost ways of life. They were interested in the real life of America, as opposed to the sundry ephemera created by self-conscious fashion; they were interested in the life and soul of the nation, but they sought it in the form of "fossils" (93) from earlier stages of U.S. history. They assumed, as have later critics such as LeRoi Jones or Greil Marcus, that forms of music derive from forms of life: an organicist conception fundamental to all notions of authenticity. It is certainly true that not all the earliest collectors of folk music were quite so idealist; beginning in 1920, for example, Ralph Peer began touring the South, for the Okeh label, looking for new material (92). But Peer's drive to find something new for the fledgling recording industry took him south, rather than into the clubs of New York, because he knew that anything commercial was always already more like other things commercial than like anything outside the system. In other words, however profit-oriented his search, it was directed by a valorization of the authentic essentially similar Lomax's.

The so-called folk music scene of the late fifties and early sixties grew directly from such curatorial impulses. The music was performed by professionals—they made their living from it—who disclaimed professional ambitions, and it was performed in intellectual settings—folk festivals, coffeehouses, recording studios—rather than in "natural settings" (if such things really exist), settings whose very presentation declared the presence of cultural activity and banked on that presentation being understood. Performance styles and stagings thus contradicted most of the characteristics prized by the first collectors—and they couldn't have done otherwise. But the entire scene did try to preserve the "aura" of the folk, and it did so on the basis of what might have seemed stark contradictions: experienced performers worked to seem naive and sincere, their primary "experience" being of "the world" or "the road" rather than of the industry, and they strove never to give the impression that they were interested in money or fame.

It's hard to imagine a music more antithetical to all this sincerity than early rock 'n' roll. Rock 'n' roll throughout the second half of the fifties was party music: music to dance to, music to love to, music to dream to. It was not concerned with its legitimacy as culture; it was not troubled by questions of legitimacy at all. Rock 'n' roll not only promoted stars, as pop music did, but made them and disposed of them with unprecedented alacrity. The only obvious similarity to folk music was the fact that rock 'n' roll audiences seemed more interested in the song than in the singer. This situation among folk audiences pertained because the music was by definition a common heritage, passed down the generations anonymously. Rock 'n' roll, by contrast, demanded novelty, and there didn't seem to be enough of it to go around. Most early rock hits were instantly covered by several other artists, so that there would often be two or more different versions of a single song competing in the marketplace, and that was fine with consumers. They thought they were buying songs, not singers, and, though the huge cult that developed around Elvis began to change that sense, it remained in place for nearly ten years more.

As Ennis sums it up, "folk delivered to rocknroll its music, its performance sites, and a set of beliefs about 'the people' " (316). In 1967 Bob Dylan put it more simply, and more elliptically: "Strap yourself to a tree with roots, you ain't goin' nowhere."[23] Denounce it as the roots fallacy, or admire what might be called the inspired authenticity riff, in the last thirty years folk-derived notions of roots have functioned to authorize successive modes of commercial product. These notions inform not only the marketing of music but also the way that the vast majority of rock fans experience their relation to pop music. And yet neither roots fallacy nor authenticity riff can really suffice to explain what has been happening. While the first term suggests a misguided people, the second suggests an industry capable of exciting attention whenever needed. Both suggestions oversimplify the dynamic. The sometimes massive audiences for alternative music are fickle and, by comparison with a professional collector like Lomax, unpredictable in their tastes. And for every Son Volt that the industry or its critics successfully market as authentic there are scores—hundreds—of failures. Moreover, the term "authentic" now has more applications than Microsoft Windows: it arises with regard not only to alternative acts but also to hip-hop, blues, jazz, and world-beat music, and it means something different in every case. Authenticity is a sign and not a quality, and like any sign it functions differentially and deferentially. In the world of commerce, authenticity is simply a matter of trademark.

Although the preoccupation with authenticity is more a phenomenon more American than British, it was in certain ways the British Invasion that prepared its way. The first wave of British pop stars polarized U.S. audiences, so that college-educated youth retreated into their coffeehouses to wait out the excited screaming of the modsters. But for both sides of that opposition, the British Invasion transformed youth music into a site on which to stage identity formation. Subsequent events would make that process more self-conscious.

By the summer of 1967 the impress of the folk scene on the new, post-Beatlemania and post-Newport rock music helped create a space for serious young writers to raise expectations for serious pop achievement from pop recordings. In New York, Robert Christgau began writing for *Esquire* and shortly after for the *Village Voice*. In San Francisco, Greil Marcus began writing for the *San Francisco Guardian* and then for a fledgling magazine known as *Rolling Stone*. Such writers mixed leftist sociology and what they could salvage from still hostile critical theory with techniques previously associated with jazz criticism and even literary criticism. Rock 'n' roll stars became artists, and the writing of consumer guides for record buyers became an act of conscience.

Almost immediately, changes in the music confirmed and resonated with the work of these early countercultural writers. Dylan's turn to electrified music a couple of years earlier had helped create a renewed market for U.S. bands. By 1968 many of these new bands began trying to recover vernacular idioms that had apparently been buried by all the moneymaking associated with the British Invasion. The turn of these new bands to countrified or folkified rock was meant to signify a rejection of consumer culture, and it proved a commercially substantial gesture. In 1968 Roger McGuinn took the Byrds straight into the figurative fields. The record they made, *Sweetheart of the Rodeo*, remains among the most listenable records of that very productive year, and many critics still revere it as one of the best rock records ever made. *Sweetheart* was a country record. Its waltz signatures, its twang, its traditionalist clichés, and the genuinely fake accents in which they were delivered all courted a history that, somewhere along the line, McGuinn and company felt was theirs to appropriate.

They appropriated pretty cleanly. Unlike Dylan's return to the simple, *John Wesley Harding* (Columbia CK-9604, 1968), or the Band's neo–farmer's almanac, *Music from Big Pink* (Capitol C2-46-69, 1968), there were no trap doors hiding beneath *Sweetheart's* relentless pursuit of the genuine country article. It had its straight readings of Dylan songs; it said "I like the Christian life"; it placed itself in the blue Canadian Rockies; it sang about families on relief. In an extraordinary leap of faith, it believed that these were real places and things, and it testified to them with affected drawls and steel guitars. *Sweetheart* was and is the genuine fake. By comparison, *Big Pink* and *John Wesley Harding* were complex records, packed with uneasy metaphors, tricky characters, and performances that were at once rich and thin. The Byrds's album was right up front, as though to exclaim: Hey, we're playing country now! McGuinn and cohorts Chris Hillman and Gram Parsons did not share Dylan's or the Band's desires to reinvent themselves within the context of an agrarian experience. They just wanted to sound like a country band.

Irony folds over irony. McGuinn's turn to country was not only, or not merely, a matter of individual taste and discernment. His turn to country followed fault lines created by the pressure of massive cultural upheavals, but those lines are especially visible in the often mutually disdainful interaction of rock 'n' roll with the so-called folk scene of the late fifties and early sixties. The friction between these subcultural audiences is, as cliché would have it, overdetermined. The friction grew heated for reasons of class and was complicated by questions of race: coffeehouse audiences laid claim to Leadbelly (Huddie Ledbetter), Mississippi John Hurt, and Odetta, while the pop audiences packed into movie theaters claimed Little Anthony, Sam Cooke, and the Supremes. Both groups, in other words, embraced forms of African-American tradition, but the one sought roots, while the other sought, in Barry Gordy's golden phrase, "the sound of young America." Eventually, the difference proved dialectical: the British Invasion overwhelmed both scenes, and when that red-coat tide retreated, very different forms emerged in its wake. What Dave Van Ronk and others somewhat self-righteously referred to as "the great folk scare" subsided;[24] the self-conscious folk music that flourished just before the invasion never recovered as an important market. But then neither did rock 'n' roll. Instead, amplified big-beat pop reinvented itself and in the process sublated its argument with folk. Rock music, as opposed to rock 'n' roll, took form both with the electric muscle of the Animals and the Yardbirds and with the self-conscious hunger for legitimacy that had characterized coffeehouse folk. Folk died and came back as McGuinn's Byrds, as electric Dylan, as R.E.M., as Son Volt, and as just about every other band that has wanted to offer more than the flavor of the month.

This process is especially visible in rock's reverence for the blues. Over the first forty years of its recorded history, the blues changed constantly. Its artists, from Bessie Smith, to Billie Holiday, to Big Joe Turner and Muddy Waters, rarely worried about their cultural legitimacy but sought commercial success whenever and however they could find it. White rockers ever since the British Invasion have, by contrast, struggled to prove their right to play the music: "Got to pay your dues, if you wanna sing the blues," as legendary bluesman Ringo Starr succinctly puts it.[25]

Punk found its first audiences by disclaiming tradition. Twenty years later, punk has become a tradition in its own right, and it reinscribes authenticity with a vengeance, a vengeance that is often, unfortunately, self-directed. Punk rock, or alternative rock, defines itself in opposition to the mainstream and in so doing becomes the perfect expression of capitalist society. It survives, as does the mainstream, by constantly revolutionizing the instruments of its own production and thereby the relations of production to performance and with them the whole of its relations to its audience.[26] Punk reproduces itself by ceaselessly assaulting its own foundations. Pop eats itself.

In this way, Cibo Matto, Nirvana, and Son Volt all respond to and within the same discursive expectations. Son Volt's very name bespeaks an effort to naturalize amplified music. Nirvana rages against the very limits that define its excellence. And Cibo Matto? Let's look again, and look through critical discourse. Writing for the *Village Voice*, Evelyn McDonnell affirms that Cibo Matto "speak for and to a community living outside the usual boundaries, in a worldwide web of cafés and digitized communication, where one pledges allegiance to more than the black or white noise of one's roots."[27] McDonnell's equation of "roots" with so much "white noise" (or "black noise") is rich in possibility. It's not just that the authenticity riff begins to sound by this point like so much white noise but also that the whole business becomes an increasingly unnecessary irritant in the U.S. understanding of race. The notion of "roots" is and always has been freighted with all kinds of political baggage.

Cibo Matto escape much of this by virtue of their national origin, a condition they submit to play at most every opportunity. They are a duo, Miho Hatori ("singing, howling, moaning, sighing, thigh tapping") and Yuka Honda ("pushing buttons, keyboarding, beach guitar"); their name is broken Italian for "food craziness," and their sound is b-boy beats, trip-hop slips, bossa nova asides, ambience, and pop.[28] They scream "a horse's ass is better than yours," command "shutup and eat," and coo "lie down here, baby,"[29] creating a play of sexual significance that affronts and cuddles the pigeonhole of cutesiness to which two Japanese women would otherwise likely be consigned, and all of this despite the fact that, as Chris Norris writes in *New York*, "Cibo Matto is more lower East Side than Japanese."[30] In other words, they are an irascible Disneyland of contradictions. Or the undoing of any postmodern morality tale. They're also one hell of a pop group.

Their appropriations and samples sound slick and smart, but the manner of their appropriations is still smarter. That manner extends even to the packaging of their debut CD. Compare, for example, the photo on the inside of the CD case with the cover photo of Dylan and the Band's *Basement Tapes*. Both photos are shot (or meant to be seen as shot) in a basement. The boys from Woodstock establish their authenticity, their contact with the real USA, by posing among circus performers and sideshow freaks; Cibo Matto's cover suggests Japanese cyberporn, but the inside photo places them in a hip-hop hipster's basement, surrounded by DJ equipment and DJ types. But they also have on hand loads of guitars, a couple of drum kits, and a Marshall stack, as well as, front and center, five very loud-looking skateboards. They stand, in other words, amid the paraphernalia of U.S. pop culture (which has long included Japanese cartoons), and they look wholly at home.

It's not just that the discourse of authenticity deconstructs itself in the presentation and marketing of Cibo Matto but that Cibo Matto would have been inconceivable without the idea of roots to ignore. Their arch cuteness and their gimmickry simply wouldn't signify in a pop world with no expectations of the authentic to satisfy. Yet it's through the manipulation of that gimmickry that Cibo Matto mock themselves, the gimmickry, and the discourse. All the songs on *Viva!* save one are about food: it is an album about consumption and about its own consumption.

The music industry is a difference-generating machine that operates by means of comparatively few discourses. Most of these, like the celebratory marketing of celebrity, are more or less what they seem. But the discourse of authenticity proposes to ground audiences and performers alike in a place outside discourse, a place somehow free of the star-making machinery, a place where audiences and artists yearning for what is genuine can commune with an ageless and priceless heritage. That proposal may have little more immediate substance than the wind in Jim Walsh's evergreens, but like that wind it continues to demonstrate its power to move those who hear it. Our point has been to show how the same yearning informs such diverse pop phenomena as Son Volt, Nirvana, and Cibo Matto. Authenticity is not a quality but a way of affirming quality that now figures in many of the ways in which audiences and performers use recordings in identity formation. "Right in the middle of a contradiction, that's the place to be":[31] the discourse of authenticity encourages us to perceive our condition as being in the middle, caught between plain truth to ourselves and alluring sellout. It would indeed be the place to be, if only we could get through the ceaselessly differing and deferring dynamics of consumer culture to find it.

NOTES

1. Cibo Matto, "Chicken," on *Viva! La Woman* (Warner Brothers 9 45989–2, 1996).
2. *Rolling Stone*, 16 April 1992. The cover story about and interviews with Nirvana are by Michael Azerrad.
3. Nirvana's third album, released in September 1991.
4. Jim Walsh, "The Sun Also Rises," *Spin* 4 (April 1996): 55. Sun Volt's first album is called *Trace* (Warner Brothers 46010, 1995).
5. Theodore Gracyk's *Rhythm and Noise: An Aesthetics of Rock* (Durham, NC: Duke University Press, 1996) is the most thorough exploration of this tension.
6. See Evan Eisenberg, *The Recording Angel: The Experience of Music from Aristotle to Zappa* (New York: Penguin, 1987), especially pp. 142–50; and Roger Johnson,

"Technology, Commodity, Power," *Computer Music Journal* 18, no. 3 (fall 1994): 25–32.

7. Neil Young, "Hey Hey, My My," on *Rust Never Sleeps* (Reprise/ Warner 2995, 1979). Cobain's suicide note was reproduced in newsgroups: e.g., alt.music.nirvana (the National Capital FreeNet), 12 April 1994, 14:00:00. Four years later Courtney Love returned to the line her husband has virtually transformed into a trope for the dilemma of pop authenticity: the song "Reasons to Be Beautiful" from Hole's acclaimed album *Celebrity Skin* (Geffen DGCD 25164, 1998) submits that "when the fire goes out you better learn to fake / It's better to rise than fade away," an obvious off-quotation from "Hey Hey, My My."

8. Michael Azerrad, "Nirvana," *Rolling Stone*, 16 April 1992, p. 39.

9. Kurt Cobain, quoted in ibid., p. 39.

10. Reprinted in Editors of *Rolling Stone*, *Cobain* (Boston: Little, Brown, 1994), p. 94.

11. Kurt Cobain, "Pennyroyal Tea," on *In Utero* (Geffen 24607, 1993).

12. Green Day, "Basket Case," *Dookie*.

13. *Rolling Stone*, 26 January 1995, p. 4.

14. The Byrds, "So You Want to Be a Rock 'n' Roll Star," *Younger Than Yesterday* (1967; reissue, CBS Sony 46705, 1995); Chuck Berry, "Johnny B. Goode," *Chess Masters* (Chess 4016, 1983).

15. It was *Murmur* that largely launched the contemporary alternative scene.

16. Pavement, "Range Life," on *Crooked Rain, Crooked Rain* (Matador/Atlantic 92343, 1994).

17. Personal conversation between Jon Dolan and Steve Malkmus, 4 October 1997.

18. Dave Marsh, *Born to Run: The Bruce Springsteen Story* (Garden City: Doubleday, 1979; rept., London: Omnibus, 1981), p. 6.

19. "Elvis Defends Low-Down Style," interview with Kays Gary for the *Charlotte Observer*, 27 June 1956, quoted in Peter Guralnick, *Last Train to Memphis: The Rise of Elvis Presley* (Boston: Little, Brown, 1994), pp. 288–89.

20. See Nick Tosch, *Unsung Heroes of Rock'n'Roll: Rock in the Wild Years Before Elvis* (New York: Harmony, 1991). Although sometimes inaccurate (particularly about Hardrock Gunter), this is an outrageously funny and pointed book.

21. LeRoi Jones, *Blues People: The Negro Experience in White America and the Music That Developed from It* (New York: Morrow/Quill, 1963). See Jack Kerouac, *The History of Bop* (Montclair, NJ: Caliban, 1993). The essay was written on 20 February 1953 and first printed, as "The Beginning of Bop," in *Escapade* (April 1959), after having been rejected by Gilbert Millstein of the *New York Times* in 1953.

22. Phillip Ennis, *The Seventh Stream: The Emergence of Rocknroll in American Popular Music* (Hanover, CT: Wesleyan/University Press of New England, 1992), p. 88. See generally pp. 88–98 and also pp. 316–20.

23. From "You Ain't Goin' Nowhere," by Bob Dylan, copyright 1967. Dylan's first recording of the song, with the Band, is now available on *The Basement Tapes* (Columbia C2K33682, 1975); according to Greil Marcus's program notes, this

recording was made between June and October 1967, though Barney Hoskyns has recently proposed that the date could in fact fall between May and November of that year; see Honskyns, *Across the Great Divide: The Band and America* (New York: Hyperion, 1993), p. 139. Dylan recorded the song again in October 1971, with Happy Traum on banjo; this recording is available on *Greatest Hits Volume II* (Columbia C2K31120, 1971). The Byrds's recording of the song was made in March 1968 and released on *Sweetheart of the Rodeo* (Columbia CS-9670, 1968).

24. See Dave Van Ronk, "The Urban Folk Scare," in Bruce Pollack, *When the Music Mattered: Rock in the 1960s* (New York: Holt, 1983). The very title of Pollack's collection is a case in point about rock's quest for authentic importance.

25. Ringo Starr, "It Don't Come Easy" (Apple 1831, 1971), later collected on *Blast from Your Past* (1975; reissue, Capitol C2-46663, 1988).

26. We're paraphrasing, of course, from part one of Marx and Engels's *Communist Manifesto*, trans. A. J. P. Taylor (New York: Penguin, 1967), p. 83.

27. Evelyn McDonnell, "Slice and Dice: Cibo Matto's *Viva! La Woman*," *Village Voice*, 23 Jan. 1996, pp. 53, 56.

28. Liner notes to *Viva! La Woman*.

29. "Beef Jerky," *Viva! La Woman*.

30. Chris Norris, *New York*, 5 Feb. 1996, 38–39.

31. A quotation of a quotation: U2's Bono quoting Sam Shepard, as recorded in Bill Flanagan's *U2 at the End of the World* (New York: Delacorte, 1995), p. 83. Thanks to Michael Sheehan for bringing this odd conjunction to our attention.

2

TOO MUCH MEAD?

UNDER THE INFLUENCE (OF PARTICIPANT-OBSERVATION)

R. J. WARREN ZANES

A lot of great bands over the years have been lost to higher education.
—Gerard Cosloy

Rock culture has a somewhat ambivalent relationship with formal education. The road from the club to the academy isn't populated by an unusually high number of bandits or marked by a particularly nasty terrain, but, more often than not, it is the route that goes unrecommended—at least, as the above epigraph suggests, if you're asking for directions from the so-called underground. At the other end of that journey's map, in the academy, feelings are less consistent. In contrast to the disdain for rock music voiced so (in)famously by Allan Bloom, within cultural studies the rock sphere is often privileged as a locus of social expression; the reverse route goes recommended. In fact, just as "the authentic" is that which rock fans and performers are forever struggling to define, many academics working under the wide banner of cultural studies display a similar fortitude as regards seeking out authenticity, without, of course, labeling it as such; in their case, the authentic often comes to be associated with lived experience, a lived experience in which consumption is not a matter of passivity but of negotiation, sometimes bitter and often refusing any social artifact the sanctity of intrinsic meaning. And many scholars find marks of this authenticity in popular music culture. Understood quite generally, their view often suggests that in lived experience meaning comes through struggle, is never final, whereas in traditional academic culture, as characterized by opponents of a figure such as Bloom, the transmission of canonical texts is inseparable from the transmission of canonical meanings. If there was a struggle, one might say that it has been settled, in advance and for you.

Not surprisingly, as certain strands of cultural studies scholarship enact this search for authenticity, discovering it in, for instance, various fan groups, subcultures, and producers of music, in those sites and in those practices where, as the argument commonly goes, appropriation is the governing principle, it often seems that an academic search for authenticity, particularly susceptible to something like projective identification, risks a distortion of the object of study that is perhaps beyond the inevitable distortion resulting from any scholarly framing. That is to say, popular music culture sometimes becomes the surface on which certain academic interests are both projected and, following this, protected; however fluid the borders between the two spheres, going from the academic to the sites of music culture (to settle, one might say, rather than simply to break in a new pith helmet) can only result in an altered relation to the authentic, a contingent category if ever there was one. The stakes involved in defining it necessarily depend on context, on one's social positioning, a fact that seems deserving of more attention. If, as Simon Frith claims, the "rock aesthetic depends, crucially, on an argument about authenticity," one must account for the shifting ground on which authenticity is argued.[1] In many respects, the academic aesthetic, too, depends crucially on an argument about authenticity. And that argument, inevitably, will not converge in its various makeups with those issuing from popular music culture.[2]

If within cultural studies, as I've suggested, authenticity and appropriation have frequently become terms nearly synonymous, I argue that in music culture the skills associated with appropriation are generally much less important to that culture than the academic report sometimes suggests. Not uncommonly, irony is the rhetorical cloak that allows the appropriator to move in and out of different dramas of consumption. Academic interests in appropriation and irony have had an enormous impact on the study of authenticity as the central category of valuation in popular music cultures, not infrequently leading to the suggestion that authenticity is, so to speak, no longer the issue. In popular music cultures, however, I argue that authenticity continues to have meaning in a way that does not easily coexist with a truly ironic distance or what has been constructed as a postmodern canniness. Authenticity remains a matter of intense importance, and, despite the weight often given it within cultural studies, irony figures in as little more than a surface play, effecting relatively insignificant changes.

It strikes me that this ironic distance of the performative, appropriating mode, in a strange way (and in tension with the claims that such performances are constitutive of identity), requires a rather secure, a priori sense of identity; otherwise, what is the centeredness that keeps one from falling under the sway of a costume that reduces the sense of insecurity or fragmentation that is the subject's lot, a costume, that is to say, that pays off socially, gives a sense of belonging that finally diminishes insecurity? It is in popular music culture that what I'm calling the subject's insecurity (one might just as well call it self-alienation) is often managed through identifications with others, frequently ideals, that confer a sense of coherent selfhood, temporarily replacing what is otherwise experienced as a tenuous, threatened selfhood. And when identifications (often the fantasies that stage desire) are felt to diminish a sense of threat, there is little room for irony. The needs that popular music has long been celebrated as answering, particularly in relation to the identity-youth intersection, do not lend themselves to ironic distance, quite the opposite: the investments are for real, even as they are ephemeral in nature. While something like sampling often involves an ironic mode of quotation, and examples of irony as a practice extend well beyond this celebrated instance, ironic distance is decidedly incompatible with the larger promises popular music culture offers the subject, a matter I'll elaborate on in this essay.

Accepting that appropriation offers a model of the consumer's agency that is empowering—and not simply for the consumer—I nonetheless cannot help responding to the fact that when I force myself to see the practices of music culture as involving ironic distance, I force myself to see music culture as I have never seen it. And while, as an academic, I've had some success in doing just this, my own experiences, past and present, leak through, leaving me with a disjunction that must be understood. The participant (in the sites of music culture) and the observer (ultimately speaking of that culture to an academic audience) are forced to negotiate, with the political stakes in a representation of popular music culture, of course, playing a part in such negotiations. I can recognize appropriation as being central to music culture practices, but it is not an appropriation involving a shrewd, distanced business of knowingness, in which the agent gains power by standing at a distance from the objects in which he/she invests. That is a picture that cannot easily be reconciled with what I believe to be the psychic life of the fan, the performer, the listener.

Larry Grossberg suggests that one postmodern authenticity, what he calls "authentic inauthenticity," is the most "purely ironic" form and the "most pervasive strategy in what is often thought of as 'postmodern' culture." His description of this is important to my argument: "If every identity is equally fake, a pose that one takes on, then authentic inauthenticity celebrates the possibilities of poses without denying that this is all they are."[3] While I find myself agreeing with Grossberg in a number of places, his account of irony ultimately leaves too little room for fantasy and identification as central to the life of the fan/subject. As I feel I must argue again, popular music, perhaps particularly in relation to the experiences of youth but certainly not restricted to them, is not engaged with at a distance; instead, it is a thing of intimacy and surprising faith. And the ironic investment simply does not do for the individual what such faith does. While cultural studies in general (and subcultural studies in particular) has offered a way of understanding agency in its micro forms, particularly as appropriation, the enthusiasm for uncovering its many instances has proved both useful and limiting for the study of popular music culture. A celebration of the appropriating mind has finally placed emphasis on a rational agency and threatened to make fantasy, by nature incompatible with ironic distance, something for those who are simply not in the know, postmodernity's dupes.

Running the risk of reproducing the mythic insider's account, in this essay, I take my own experiences in the music business and in the university as my starting point.[4] I set out from the confusion of tongues that marked my academic, textual engagement with the popular music culture I had left behind. In this confusion, the participant and the observer were separated rather than joined by the hyphen between them, a symptom that led me to question the manner in which discourses of authenticity are constructed on shifting grounds and must be understood as such. My earlier experiences, taking place on the ground that was the eighties music business, came to something of a close when, after several years of touring, recording, seemingly selling out, and claiming authenticity, I entered the university. And though my academic interests are more directly aligned with the visual arts, cultural studies scholarship has been important to my work in that area, finally allowing me to stay in touch with a growing body of scholarship that has, in my view, produced the most critically urgent readings of rock culture yet available. There is little point in denying that this work has afforded me a more complicated understanding of my experiences in the music business. Retroactively, I have come to appreciate the social meaningfulness of music and music culture as it structured my own experiences, which, before this, seemed largely without sense, without any kind of mooring in a wider social grid.

At the same time, as I've described, there is often a nagging disjunction among my experience of rock music, my retroactive understanding of the social needs it answers as based on this experience, and the accounts of rock culture offered from within cultural studies, particularly as regards rock culture's empowering potential. Curiously, it's the scholarship I have encountered in exploring the discourses of contemporary art, no less than the art itself, that acts as a kind of translating field here, helping me to understand and hopefully explain the disjunction already mentioned. The work of artists such as Richard Prince and Cindy Sherman encouraged me to think through the intersections at which identity and the discourses of authenticity are bound as projects. Their work, as I see it, doesn't simply signal our release from myths of authenticity; rather, it addresses, often indirectly, certain anxieties that emerge when identity is thought of not as the possibility of an authentic Self but as a construction. Such a moment is shown to be significant because our relationships with images, primarily in the form of identifications with media images, become, almost paradoxically, more intense. Prince and Sherman suggest that subjectivity, despite its constructedness, is never, especially when the stakes are highest, something that is easily approached ironically. Put simply, their work reminds me that theorizing the possibilities of a fluid identity should in no way mask the anxieties that emerge as one faces the prospect of living that fluid identity.

Most importantly, such anxieties are often managed by turning with renewed intensity to the very notions of authenticity (of an authentic, essential Selfhood, for instance) that seem to have been obviated or at least rendered archaic. And popular music culture often provides the various media through which this turn is made possible. Fantasy, not irony, is the issue of greatest import at this crossroads. Herein one can begin to see the powerful nostalgic dimension of popular music culture, particularly as it is bound to a particular historical ground on which subject formation, as a kind of struggle, takes place. Allowing irony too significant a place disallows a clear view of this turn. In writing to Walter Benjamin, Theodor Adorno referred to his study on jazz as "revealing its 'progressive' elements (semblance of montage, collective work, primacy of reproduction over production) as façades of something that is in truth quite reactionary."[5] In a sense, I think that something "in truth quite reactionary" takes place in popular music culture. A film like *Sonic Outlaws*, for instance, demonstrates the ease with which a nostalgic, romantic conception of the artist as outsider can be mobilized to validate supposedly radical underground practices. Despite the film's celebration of appropriation as a practice, the authenticity of the performers is claimed on familiar, modernist terms. One has to ask why this is so rather than deny that it is taking place. Understanding popular music culture's potential conservatisms, however—bound as they are to discourses of authenticity—first requires a discussion of authenticity as a mobile concept, one that has assumed a few particularly notable models even as it has continued to do essentially the same work.

DEFINING AUTHENTICITY: DISTANCE; OR, THE TRAIL OF CRUMBS AND THE SHOT SALESMAN

A friend of mine recently gave me a clipping from the classifieds section of his hometown newspaper:

> *Singer/Songwriter in search of musicians to complete band presentation.* Full length album complete. Web site/fan club. Showcase gigs commencing in the fall. Highly visible major league Producer, Engineer, prominent NY Attorneys. Presently choosing management of some caliber. Publishing deal under way, talking to several major labels at very high levels already. *No access problems. Commercial Radio Pop music,* lyric oriented, loosely reminiscent cross reference of Bryan Adams, Collective Soul, James Taylor to name a few. *Seeking young, good looking, unjaded, nonwriting guitarist, bassist, B-3/piano-player & drummer. Male or female.* Attempting to create band/family environment with long view.

If authenticity is typically defined by negation—an elaboration of the authentic often begins with a denunciation of the inauthentic—the band represented by this clipping could hold the negative position for a disparate number of authenticities as they are defined relationally, definition by negation always requiring an other. In its classical form, authenticity is associated with at least a degree of spontaneity. Spontaneity, in turn, is frequently opposed to artifice. The chain of associations and oppositions simply grows from here; what becomes obvious in any discussion of authenticity, however, is that the terms that proliferate are slippery: "artifice," "spontaneity," "real," "sold out," and so forth. The barren quality of these terms, at least when taken out of a specific context, makes it clear that any argument mobilizing them will require a very pronounced definition through negation: the slippery vocabulary needs to be anchored in an unambiguous relational situation so as to become meaningful. As a lynchpin in the classical model, an opposition between authenticity and commercial artifice is constructed.[6] And such an opposition is typically articulated with recourse to images and tropes of distance.

Paul Westerberg's "World Class Fad" presents the sentiments of underground authenticity in a manner that betrays this recourse to images of distance: "If you want it that bad you're a world class fad / Remember where you started from."[7] The song's point of view, in my reading, is that of a gatekeeper of the underground way of life (which is not to say that such a point of view should automatically be taken as Westerberg's; rock knows forms other than autobiography). One can almost envision the father speaking in advance to the prodigal son about the distance, expressed as physical but ultimately moral, that will be put between them, though here the father's "forgiveness" is shot through with judgment and isn't forgiveness at all.[8] Further, it would be difficult to disentangle the song's sentiments from the discourse of authenticity as it is associated with the always current myth of the sellout, that Faustian pact of the music business that is everywhere talked about, the morality tale that keeps one honest but is finally difficult to discern (if purity is opposed to corporate influence, as it still commonly is, few are untainted). In such a morality tale, the move from authenticity is a move away, a movement through space that can be reversed only by following the trail of crumbs, signifiers of a poverty that, in art world discourses, is associated with truth or authenticity. In arguing "the central place of romanticism (its language of art and genius) in rock ideology," Andrew Goodwin and Simon Frith rightly suggest a ground shared by art discourses of authenticity and those of popular music.[9] The equation between poverty and truth that I've isolated marks only one such intersection. Another comes in the founding paradox of this first model of authenticity.

In "World Class Fad," selling out is a conscious decision one can make, a decision involving a deliberate move away from one's roots. While authenticity is claimed in spatial terms, the implication is that such spatial changes involve a fixed authenticity and a move away from this point that involves inauthentic maneuverings. Thus, just as authenticity is defined relationally, it is also seen as a fixed point, that is to say, as an anchored, intrinsic authenticity, the tarnishing of which is ultimately determined by the choice of the subject rather than by our perspective of that subject within a system of differences. While relying on a spatial, relational model in order to give form to the sellout, to make authenticity meaningful, there is a paradoxical move in which an attempt is made to veil the relational dimension of authenticity; authenticity becomes intrinsic as it is argued to be a matter of the subject's intentions, an inside job, so to speak, rather than a relational mode. This is what I have called the founding paradox of a spatial model of authenticity.

While acknowledging that, as a construct, authenticity serves different needs in different spheres of cultural production and reception—a point that I've already suggested is important to my argument—I want to make explicit the manner in which differently situated discourses of authenticity intersect. As Frith and Goodwin argue in the citation above, what they call "rock ideology" seems to have inherited its language from romantic conceptions of art and genius, which, if they have not been generated in the art sphere, have often been given their most bombastic form in that context. At the same time, I hope to show that channels of inheritance are not marked simply by a one-way flow. In a case in point, as the critical art of the late seventies and early eighties made its move on the galleries, calling into question the assumptions supporting the institutions of art while still being enmeshed in them, it was, for some artists, punk-rock strategies that initially suggested some ways of doing this, offering practical models with which to engage questions of art as a social practice.

Richard Prince, associated with Cindy Sherman, Barbara Kruger, and others who have together been referred to as the "pictures group," has been very open in crediting punk rock as one component establishing the conditions of possibility that sustained his project. He claims that his "rephotography," the practice of photographing other photographs, was "a very punk thing," involving not only appropriation as a strategy but a blissful lack of specialized skills; he knew next to nothing about using a camera, referring to his punk progenitors in terms that betray an interest in an art based not on a skill but on a willingness to abandon the imperatives associated with it: "Sure, they couldn't play like Eric Clapton, but Eric Clapton probably couldn't play like them."[10] From punk, Prince borrowed a gesture—learn three chords and form a band—that challenged the connection between virtuosity and genius, finally forcing a partial destabilization of the category "genius" (not to suggest that the term "genius" could not be grafted onto an art that challenged the central place given skill in systems of valuation, as the cases of Duchamp and Warhol already made clear). As punk's raw energy opposed itself to the slick studio productions of the seventies, rephotography unsettled the terrain on which Ansel Adams's "fine prints" might otherwise go unchallenged as the model of value in art photography.

Beyond the common ground of practical method, however, Prince's work shares with punk a deliberate play with and challenge of the romantic constructions of authenticity as they commonly organize representations of the artist and of art.[11] It is this critical dimension, in both art and music spheres, that has commonly been explained as involving an ironic, self-reflexive positioning within the cogs of the art and music businesses.[12] The spatial conception of authenticity elaborated above thus seems to find itself facing a challenge from within. Prince manages to tease out what I earlier called the founding paradox of a spatially defined authenticity (an authenticity that I suggested is active in Westerberg's "trail of crumbs") as it underpins modernist rhetorics in the visual arts. If in underground rock rhetorics such as those I've associated with the "trail of crumbs" authenticity is imagined to be anchored—an intrinsic authenticity—yet at the same time can only be expressed in relational terms, through negation, Prince allows one to see this very same mode of rhetorical operation as it permeates the high modernist visual arts, something I'll discuss below.

In his *Jokes, Gangs, Hoods* catalog, one of Prince's appropriated "photo-sentences" speaks directly to a spatial conception of authenticity: "I'm so far underground, I get the bends." Undoubtedly stolen from the same marketplace where he pilfered the majority of the work comprising his 1992 Whitney Museum retrospective, it bears a sentiment that is the suit worn threadbare in the closet of rock culture rhetorics: the underground exists at a remove from commercial artifice, and it suffers for its purity/authenticity. Of course, while it can be understood as a critique of authenticity in general, Prince's work has commonly (and rightly) been understood as a critical exploration of the high modernist tenets particularly exemplified in the writing of Clement Greenberg and the work of the abstract expressionists Greenberg championed, a high modernism that, like so much authentic rock culture, is explicitly defined, through images of distance, against a denigrated commercial sphere. In this light, Prince's work is understood as a critique of the autonomous art object, which, in Greenberg's formulation, is said to exist within a frame that defends against the poisons of commercial culture and further the whims of historical contingency.

Greenberg's writing advocated an art that would move closer and closer to autonomy, that would focus on "the characteristic methods of [the] discipline to criticize the discipline itself—not in order to subvert it, but to entrench it more firmly in its area of competence."[13] The distillation of painting, the pursuit of its essence and designation of its area, was presented as a project that required transcending the spectacle of commerce, particularly as it was manifest in the artifacts of popular culture. While not associated with the Greenberg camp, Yves Klein's explanations of the negative, spectacular effect resulting from the juxtaposition of more than one color within a painting offers a good example of how autonomy—the purported goal in the pursuit of essence—was defined as existing both outside of spectacle, something long associated with commerce, and, for Klein, outside of language itself, as beyond relational systems of difference in general: "In my judgment two colors juxtaposed on one canvas compel the observer to see the spectacle of this juxtaposition of two colors . . . but prevent him from entering into the sensitivity, the dominance, the purpose of the picture. This is a situation of the psyche, of the sense, of the emotions, which perpetuates a sort of reign of cruelty, and one can no longer plunge into the sensitivity of pure color, relieved from all outside contamination."[14]

In a painting such as Klein's *Blue Monochrome*, one can see the result of such efforts to distill painting, to "entrench it more firmly in its area of competence." The title, as if demonstrating the supposedly extraneous nature of language to such a modernist investigation of pictorial purity, can tell us nothing we don't already know about the painting: it is indeed a blue monochrome. In the purity of the canvas, Klein represents an attempted flight from social confines and the "cruelty" of spectacle. Purportedly "relieved from all outside contamination"—particularly, we must assume, the contamination of language (manifest in that system of difference that is the juxtaposition of two colors)—the work at once liberates the observer from a "reign of cruelty" and allows "him" to enter into a situation wherein "he" is dominated by the "purpose of the picture."

The freedom of the modernist experience of an autonomous art is clearly related in terms of power. Perhaps inadvertently, Klein exposes this modernist conception of freedom in such a way as to highlight its connection to domination: we are free to be dominated. The maintenance of an authentic art is quickly articulated in terms of struggle. But, importantly, struggle, inherently relational, is again at the heart of an authenticity (in this case figured as purity) that is claimed nonetheless to be intrinsic, autonomous, essential. This is the very paradox I saw at work in Westerberg's lyrics: just as underground authenticity is claimed to be anchored, self-defined, it can only be expressed in relational terms. The struggle of the relational, the situation of dominance that is involved in a definition by negation, is the repressed that exists at the heart of a purported purity or authenticity, a repressed that cannot but emerge as such purity or authenticity is given expression.

Prince's *Shot Salesman* (1988), a large canvas painted, importantly, in an unmistakable Yves Klein blue, plays with the idea of this impossible repression of struggle at the heart of any construction of authenticity. At the middle of the vast, blue canvas, silk-screened in small yellow block letters, is a joke, one of the very forms through which Freud suggests the repressed might emerge: "A traveling salesman's car broke down on a lonely road late at night in the middle of nowhere. He walked to the nearest farmhouse and asked the farmer if he could stay the night. 'No,' said the farmer and then shot the salesman in the head with a shotgun." Prince's disruption of the monochromatic surface brings him into dialogue with Klein on several levels. First, Klein's prescription to "plunge into the sensitivity of pure color, relieved from all outside contamination" is made impossible, as Prince reveals, through the introduction of those small block letters at the heart of the monumental, blue canvas, the struggle, the act of domination that is at the center of any campaign for purity. He makes the return of the repressed the very subject of the work. Further, the spatial description of an autonomous, authentic art's pure status, its existence outside "contamination" and systems of difference in general, is shown to be a rhetorical operation rather than an aspect of the artwork itself.[15]

As regards the joke, Prince selects one that focuses on the opposition that is finally something of an obsession in both high modernist rhetorics of authenticity and in authenticities of rock: that differentiation between commerce and art/authenticity. The so-called naturalness of art, its declared existence outside language and within the frame that secures autonomy, can only be fought for, and never, as Prince's *Shot Salesman* suggests, on fair terms. The ill-fated meeting of the salesman (giving off the stench of commerciality, artifice) and the farmer (metonymic stand-in for the natural, for art and the artist, for authenticity) allegorizes the struggle required to protect the supposed autonomy of the authentic art object, an autonomy that, paradoxically, can only be posited relationally. What critiques of high modernist rhetorics have gone on to suggest is that this insistence on autonomy and, in turn, authenticity takes place only under the banner of ideological investment. One might say that whenever authenticity is defined (and perhaps most clearly when it is defined in opposition to the commercial), specific interests are being served. A hierarchizing of taste such as one finds in the art/commerce divide both reinforces and produces social differentiation along historically specific lines. Some have argued that in the case of high modernist claims to authenticity, the investments made were often, in the last analysis, conservative, protecting a sphere of art that was coded as male, that privileged an individuality altogether similar to that valorized in a capitalist ethos, that, in fact, recalled the dominant power at several levels. Not surprisingly, abstract expressionism, the materialization of Greenberg's autonomy thesis, became both the style most common to corporate boardrooms and what has been called our official art, an art that screams freedom, though a bit too emphatically for comfort. If any defense of authenticity is a defense of social interests, it seems worth asking what interests are being defended when rock music's various authenticities are persistently defined against a commercial artifice, a question I'll approach after first elaborating on two further models of authenticity that reproduce the conception of authenticity as distance but with different effects.

RECONCEIVING DISTANCE: AUTHENTICITIES IN THE MACHINE OF COMMERCE

Before looking at an authenticity founded on ironic distance, I want to mention a model of authenticity—really a strand of what I've called the classical model—in which distance from commerce is figured more as a temporal than a spatial remove. Anthony DeCurtis makes a statement that exemplifies this approach: "By the mid-1980s, rock & roll was well on its way to becoming terminally safe. . . . Artists seemed to be tripping over themselves in their eagerness to sell out."[16] What's worth pointing out in this statement is not that it represents any kind of rarity but that it comes at the beginning of a collection of writings dedicated to theorizing rock & roll in a manner that takes into account the facts "that art is created in a social context; that hard distinctions between elite and popular art are ill-advised; that art created by minorities and working-class people is worthy of serious discussion."[17] That is to say, DeCurtis joins Prince and so many others in challenging long-held beliefs in an autonomous art, an art said to transcend social context. And, as part of this project and in line with much of the recent work on popular culture, DeCurtis insists that the elite (art)/popular (artifact) split be understood as a social construction. The spatial orientation of the high modernist autonomy thesis, the claim, among others, that art remains outside commercial culture, is clearly up for critique on several levels.

What eludes DeCurtis's theoretical agenda, however—what is finally overlooked—is the manner in which high art/low art distinctions can be deemed worthy of critique at the very moment that the rhetorics common to such distinctions can be mapped onto further distinctions between so-called authentic rock music and commercial, sellout rock. If the high art/mass culture opposition has been disrupted, this does not mean that its logics have not returned to support an opposition within mass culture, specifically in the differentiation between the authentic and the commercial, the sellout. This takes place despite the degree to which authenticity is no longer claimed, in spatial terms, as a distance from the commercial but is viewed instead as existing within the commercial yet somehow not partaking of it. As I began to argue above, the absence of a spatial distance model is compensated for by the introduction of temporal distance that underpins this particular picture of authenticity. Bands in the eighties, we are told, seem to be "tripping over themselves in their eagerness to sell out." Implicit in the statement is the notion of a past that was less densely populated with sellouts. A current authenticity can (and does) thus become a matter of levels of intimacy with this past, a model of authenticity that is not necessarily more nostalgic than others but is certainly more explicit in its nostalgia.[18]

Rather than agree with DeCurtis that the eighties marked a particularly conspicuous moment in a fall from grace that found rock musicians aching to make it, one might instead question whether both the rage against commerciality and presence of the sellout became more pronounced simply because commerciality was increasingly difficult to pin onto any one particular faction in the rock music sphere. In the eighties, rock video certainly made it impossible to avoid the fact that promotion and art have a rather happy marriage; it wasn't simply the Pat Boones of the world who could be castigated for their interest in commercial packaging. And given such a scenario, wherein commerciality is more difficult to isolate at the level of modes of production and packaging, authenticity is often fought in temporal terms, terms under which the latest generation always seems to be the sickest and the few who escape such a condition—one might take Nirvana as an example—are presented as having the most in common with a purer past. Following this model, of course, one can't help stumbling across a number of nou-

veau Dylans, those exceptions who, even as they sample, immerse themselves in quotation, and so on, seem to be in direct dialogue with the spirit of
the purer past (again, given the pervasiveness of this model of authenticity,
it's no surprise that popular music has been widely recognized as being
obsessed with its own history, as deeply nostalgic).

In my own band experience, I tended to demarcate authenticity in the
classical manner, as a real thing contrasted to a commercial artifice. The Del
Fuegos' practice space in Boston, two floors beneath a donut shop and pizza
place, a netherworld from which the plague of the next millennium will
surely come, was on the block that faced the Berklee School of Music, an
institution that was easily associated with commerce and artifice. As regards
maintaining authenticity, this was a matter of great convenience: we simply
avoided the other side of the street. While music students populated the side-
walks, their hands a blur as they passed over fretboards, even daring to read
music in public, we stood opposite, outside the reach, importantly, of written
music and in the world of feeling (Yves Klein's modernist rhetorics are echoed
on several levels). Of course, we didn't articulate it with such precision, but,
in essence, this was our spatial conception of authenticity: we just made sure
our guitars were out of tune, and Mass. Ave. did the rest of the work. Even
as we started to get around a bit and forged unambiguous connections to corporate sponsorship, linking ourselves to a major label affiliation and—I can
still feel the curious warmth of Mephistopheles' handshake—shooting a beer
commercial (the visibility of which was finally mortifying), we fought for our
authenticity along the same lines.[19] If the commercial functioned as a major
setback to our authenticity, we argued our position through various practices
that might be associated with the first two models of authenticity I've mentioned: we established an Other wherever we could, that is, we isolated acts
that seemed to have sold out more than we had, acts that seemed closer to
the machine of commerce, so that we could establish a relational situation
wherein we assumed the authentic pole (there's always an Other to be constructed!); we brought ourselves, wherever possible, in contact with figures
associated with an authentic past (this meant getting James Burton to play on
a record, Tom Petty to sing on an album, Merry Clayton to sing back-ups,
thus allowing us to profit from a temporal authenticity); we used equipment
that spoke of the pure era in rock & roll. While we didn't deal with such
issues in any kind of self-reflexive manner and our motives were not one
dimensional, we fought for our authenticity with various temporal and spatial distance models, though without recovery. And given the forms of

authenticity we had mobilized up to that point and the rock cultural moment in which we were acting, our thoughts never turned toward a further model of authentic distance, the ironic model of distance, a model that seemed to change the terms altogether.

IRONIC AUTHENTICITY: WE DON'T HAVE TO GET OUTTA THIS PLACE

While theory and practice often interpenetrate in a manner that disallows any discussion of either simple deterministic relations or discreet registers, one might safely argue that antifoundationalist epistemologies have left a rather clear mark on various sites of cultural production. Among the practices that have reflected this influence and challenged the idea of an intrinsic authenticity or purity, one can locate Prince's rephotography and, say, the elaborate performativity of the New Romantics. In both of these cases, the challenges posed have also led, perhaps inadvertently, to new models of authenticity. Rather than argue that antifoundationalism leads to a frightening relativism (wherein all positions become equal and any discourse of authenticity is rendered hollow rather than hallowed), it seems more important to question whether it merely reconfigures authenticity under new guiding terms consistent with this particular epistemic moment. Indeed, a new authenticity does emerge from the critical play with romantic or classical authenticities that has come to be associated with postmodernism, an admittedly elastic rubric under which New Romanticism and Prince can both find a home. The figures who seem to be engaging in such play, confounding the spatial and temporal conceptions of authenticity in which the authentic in some way stands apart from (commercial) artifice, become the bearers of a new authenticity, an authenticity born not of spatial or temporal distance but of ironic distance.

For many, the authenticity founded on, for instance, a temporal distance involves too nostalgic a view of the past. And, as it is often (and hastily, I believe) understood, nostalgia is a semideluded state, the sleep of sentimentality that is an act more of forgetting than remembrance. What is not infrequently portrayed as a more sophisticated sensibility arrives through the introduction of irony. Sophistication and irony are quickly brought together. If it is accepted that there is little hope of getting outside the commercial and if claiming a kinship with a purer period of music making or a form of music making in which commercial interests are less all determining is viewed simply as a prelapsarian fantasy, positions within the commercial might be differentiated at the level of one's investments in its various dramas and in the costumes those dramas demand one wear. The notion of a self-conscious, knowing performativity thus becomes central, finally allowing one to take on the features of the sellout while maintaining authenticity through the acknowledgment that it is all, finally, play; in the extreme, the earnestness of a classical model of authenticity quickly becomes another sleep of sentimentality, and irony, from some angles, comes to look increasingly like a savvy, politically crucial stance. Yet, while this seems to undermine the very notion of authenticity, such is the case only if authenticity is narrowly equated with what I've called a classical model.

Even if one could believe in the complete collapse of the classical model, I find it difficult to believe that the needs managed within the sphere of popular music culture and through its products, particularly through the discourse of authenticity, are themselves rendered irrelevant in this collapse. If estimating authenticity is ultimately an act of judgment, it is a judgment affecting as much the judge as the object in question. The need to suppose authenticity in an Other—put simply, the need to declare that an act's authenticity is inseparable from the fantasy that such authenticity might be conferred on oneself as a subject—is ultimately a deep-seated subjective need that has found a particularly powerful home in popular music culture, and this need does not simply drop out when a particular model of authenticity, such as the classical, is challenged. The general need answered by the discourse of authenticity cannot be confused with any one particular model of authenticity.

If the Sex Pistols entered the machine of the music business with a sneer that set them apart—even as they entered its most suspect, commercial corners—so, too, Richard Prince first enacted his critical project from within the very walls (of the museum) that his project would seem to be destabilizing. If authenticity seems always to be distinguished as an apartness, this third form of authenticity, commonly attributed to both Prince and the Sex Pistols, is marked by an apartness of attitude. As Andrew Goodwin argues, rock authenticity might be "located in an act's perceived ability to manipulate and construct media imagery."[20] With the media being a main component of the commercial network against which classical authenticity is defined, irony allows one to enter into the dark heart of commerce in order to manipulate it from within. Clearly, it's quite easy to map a heroic model of authenticity onto this Robin Hood–esque conception of manipulation. Even while allowing the subversive potentials of this model, one has to acknowledge that such a hero is constructed in a manner that quite plainly reproduces certain elements of the classical purity; the ironic hero is not infected, is not overcome by the machinery of commerce as s/he moves through it, and thus acts as a kind of double agent whose true self can be appreciated by those in the know. If, as I suggested above, one of the primary needs answered by a belief in, say, a performer's authenticity is that somehow the fan arguing such authenticity will share in the profits, will have some of this authenticity conferred on him or herself, in the ironic model this shared knowingness puts more stress on that act of conferral: understanding the performer's double agency makes for an enhanced intimacy between the performer and the fan. Thus authenticity's work at an intersubjective level, particularly in relation to its role in the construction of something like an ideal ego toward which the subject directs itself, is not diminished as the postmodern kicks in but instead is given a new depth. Popular music culture does take up irony, but it does so in a manner that can easily be misconstrued.

I want first to look at such a moment as interesting because academic discourses and popular discourses seem to be converging as never before. Larry Grossberg, whose account of the irony-authenticity intersection is perhaps the most suggestive theoretical account available, sounds an important warning that speaks to this moment: "Confusing the two contexts [that of the fan and that of the critic] can often lead to serious misunderstandings in which critical and everyday categories slide into each other."[21] Such a confusion is especially pronounced when the increasingly specialized language of the critic is taken up by the performer and in the popular context more generally. It doesn't take much looking to uncover examples wherein what I'm calling "academic" discourses emerge in a more popular context so as to defend an ironic authenticity; in a recent *Spin* review of the Jon Spencer Blues Explosion one finds evidence of this: "Though [Spencer's] been playing dumb since a scathing review by a black critic called his act a 'coon show,' Spencer, a former semiotics major, is a master of tweaking cultural symbols for maximum provocation." The reviewer goes on to praise the band for the fact that they "raise questions about cultural ownership and racial dialectic, but never try to answer them" and, further, for their capacity to "conflate parody and true appreciation, verging on saying something sincere."[22] Skirting closure, escaping the myth of artistic "sincerity," they seem an instance of what might be called "theory in action." Or, to name a more notorious case, U2's Bono has alluded to Baudrillard in explaining his band's shift from a painfully earnest self-presentation to an ironic, we're-just-manipulating-the-media-here self-presentation. In that same issue of *Spin*, U2 is applauded for something along these lines: "It's pretty standard rock star behavior, hanging out with models, but U2 very publicly approached it as high camp, as if they were doing it for intellectual, not libidinal, reasons. It was all part of the band's switch from over-the-top sincerity to ultravivid irony."[23]

That irony allows a new model of authenticity seems obvious. That academic discourses and popular discourses share a language as never before also seems obvious enough. However, I maintain that irony has been embraced as little more than surface play in popular music culture, and below it the business of authenticity is carried on with great consistency. The importance in arguing this has much to do with the manner in which a celebration of irony has brought on something like a regression in popular culture studies, a regression that I believe has been particularly pronounced in popular music studies. For instance, the U2 and Jon Spencer examples demonstrate the manner in which irony allows an act to be set apart not only from the commercial machine within which it operates but also from its own practices, which, under the cloak of irony, can be understood as separable from their operator, a separation that, if we don't see it, leaves us in the position of the dupe. Grossberg describes this situation in its extreme form: "If one fails to see the irony, one is left only with the despair of illusions and lies, a depoliticised nihilism."[24] Of course, it would be wrong to explain an individual's capacity to see and appreciate irony would as a natural gift; this mode of seeing, like any other, is learned, at least to a significant degree. If, as I've already suggested, appropriation has long been a privileged practice within cultural studies and it is a practice that can be appreciated only if one sees that an object's meaning resides not in the object itself but in the uses made of it in local situations, cultural studies does, in a sense, groom one for the appreciation of irony as an operating mode (not to equate any and all appropriation with irony, of course, but to suggest that all irony does involve a kind of appropriation).

As a way of seeing, this capacity to look for and find the ironies that sometimes underpin appropriating practices is a way of seeing that, in many ways, is connected to an academic moment in which discourses of antifoundationalism are pervasive, in which various models of reading against the grain are practiced and taught. The examples of Jon Spencer and U2 betray the manner in which ironic distance and appropriative strategies are often explained and validated with recourse to academic parlance. But further, as practices, appropriation and irony are better learned through some contact with the academic—where such practices are most conspicuously discussed and valorized—than with no contact at all. Finding exceptions, noble savages of irony, does little more than veil what demands attention. Too often, the dupe who fails to see the irony is often the one who has not learned its language, and privileging those who have learned its language is merely to buttress a privilege that is already secure. The stakes involved in privileging irony must be acknowledged. Despite the fact that the exchange between the club and the academy is a two-way affair in some cases, that academic interests and those of fans and performers often seem to allow a dialogue that needs no translating apparatus, I think the common interests are too often imagined to be more extensive than they in fact are, a situation that finally leads to a great deal of projective identification on the academic side of things. While there is the threat of perpetuating an old elitism in a new form, equally problematic is the manner in which this celebration of irony has obscured the subjective needs (which, if expressed through fantasy, for instance, are finally coded as a weakness, a failure) that have often been managed through authenticity as popular music culture's governing discourse.

In a sense, Richard Prince and Cindy Sherman are both objects of a projection similar to that which popular music culture endures. Particularly in the case of Sherman, I believe there is a tendency to reduce her work to a powerful argument for the micropolitical possibilities embedded in the ironic, performative practice. As one argument related to this general tendency goes, Sherman demonstrates that one can adopt a pose or put on a costume that carries with it a subversive potential or social power, however limited that power may be, and, once a profit is turned from putting on that costume and using its power or potential, put on another costume that will pay off in the same fashion. Agency is thus discovered in this cunning adaptability; a kind of postmodern chameleonism becomes a potentially transgressive operation. And while it would be ridiculous to say that this reading of Sherman's project is incompatible with the work itself, I believe too singular an emphasis on this particular dimension obscures the anxieties to which I believe her work gives form.

When the empowering aspect of performativity is stressed, the cunning of the individual enacting this performance emerges, necessarily, as a power that is ultimately the power of reason. Opposed to the individual who fails to see the irony and is "left only with the despair of illusions and lies," this cunning performer becomes a new, albeit somewhat modified, version of the sovereign, autonomous agent. As I've suggested, such an opposition risks reproducing not only the self in possession of itself but, as a kind of counterpart, the very dupe (the mass consumer who is all passivity, who buys into the "illusions" of popular culture and misses the irony, failing to read against the grain) that cultural studies has so long and so often argued to be something of a false construction. While this version of things sees the ironic hero emerge from behind the various performances, from behind the ironic practices, one could just as well argue that in Sherman's work the individual is effaced. While there is a clear suggestion in her work that a postmodern subjectivity is not founded on an essential identity but quilted together from the various possibilities that preexist the individual, this evacuation of the subject leaves us with more of an absence, a vacuum, than a position filled by a new, albeit more slippery, hero. Again, this projected heroism is the effect of the enthusiasm shown for the transgressive possibilities embedded in appropriation as it relates to identity, an enthusiasm that strikes me as emerging less from Sherman's work than from dominant agendas of cultural studies. If this enthusiasm obscures the anxieties around postmodern identity as they are expressed in Sherman's work, a similar enthusiasm transforms the landscapes of popular music into something that becomes unrecognizable. As I've argued, fantasy drops out. Despite what the good book tells us, one's generosity is not always the finest gift one can give, a lesson that might be remembered for cultural criticism.

In Valerie Steele's essay "The F Word," Steele and Jane Gallop, cited in the essay, remark on strategies of an ironic performativity. Steele elaborates on Gallop's claim that Gallop learned something about the possibilities of costume from "gay men friends," further describing the manner in which Gallop discovered that "women can project the same kind of irony when they adopt ultra-femme wear." Gallop goes on to qualify the possibilities of this ironic approach: "I don't think you can pull it off at a cocktail party, or as a secretary or receptionist, when you're supposed to be advertising your sexuality. But in the academic world, because femininity is so deeply excluded—from the lectern, from the position of knowledge—that sort of dress operates in some kind of interesting tension with other expectations." While this is perhaps unsettling in the sense that the receptionist and the secretary are denied the privilege of ironizing through an "ultra-femme" costume, I believe that Gallop sheds light on the very important fact that irony doesn't work equally well from everywhere. Rather than question what might be seen as Gallop's reproduction of academic privilege, I think one might recognize that she rightly narrows the field of possibilities as regards the ironic performance. Gallop readily admits the degree to which her performances became a kind of cause célèbre, remarking that one of her skirts "became famous before I did," a comment that draws attention to an ironic performance quite different in nature from Sherman's. Sherman's project, in my reading, sees the autonomous individual lost behind the wall of poses; in Gallop's, the unique individual emerges through ironic practices; in some respect, these practices do indeed make a name for Gallop.[25]

This brings me to an important point at which I have again to turn to the specifics of popular music culture. In some sense, I believe that Gallop allows one to see that different economies of identity exist in different cultural spheres. She is right to point out that the ironic performativity from which she profits will not everywhere function the same. The disruptive nature of her conference practices is contingent on the conditions of possibility that make such practices meaningful. Importantly, it was in an academic context that the disruptive force was felt, in a context where irony is a strategy both practiced and valorized. This antiessentialism of the object is both in line with antifoundationalist thinking in general and with the privilege given ironic performativity as it relates to identity. Equally so, Sherman's and Prince's capacities to suggest the possibilities and anxieties of a postmodern identity have everything to do with the context of production. In popular music culture, investigations and practices of irony face obstacles unique to that culture, something to which I will turn now.

THE WAGER OF DEMOCRACY

If ironic performativity means different things under different conditions, I want to argue that in popular music culture it finds some of its least fertile soil. When such practices are in operation—it would be ridiculous to argue their total absence—they are processed in much the way Gallop's have been, as evidence of a unique personality at work beneath the surface, as a model of postmodern heroism. The U2 and Jon Spencer examples demonstrate the manner in which irony, as a popular music practice, becomes little more than a new appearance of an old model of authenticity, buttressing the intrinsic worth of these particular acts. When authenticity based on spatial and/or temporal distance is exchanged for an apartness of attitude, this does not mean that authenticity does not remain the matter of most importance in rock music culture. If one agrees that we have entered a postmodern era that has given rise to what Peter Sloterdijk, in a less celebratory instance, has called "enlightened false consciousness," wherein we are no longer willing to drink down the elixir of master narratives, rock culture plays a somewhat atavistic role.[26]

Particularly if the master-narrative rubric can be extended to include the narrative of the American Dream that is the eroded keystone in a stateside democratic mythos, I argue that our emancipation from master narratives is hardly complete across the social landscape. Importantly, a postmodern mindset does not emerge everywhere with the same force, and one might understand the levels of force as being in reverse proportion to the presence of so-called healthy master narratives that hold some kind of teleological promise, some emancipatory kernel. If it is clear that not everyone can become president (race, class, gender, leisure interests, and so forth determining our chances at securing that unfortunate post), in certain realms of society, a rise to cultural power remains a decided possibility. This is not to say that its appearance as a possibility, egalitarian in nature, is a simple social fact rather than a fantasy promoted in advance by a dominant ideology, but rock culture's curious existence as one of the American Dream's most conspicuous lasting outposts is not without its testimonials. Bands actually do emerge from nowhere, from bedrooms and garages, and make a splash. Again, I don't mean to say that this is commonplace, but the fantasy of a cultural rise to power is not without its anchors in reality. One might again make a comparison with the art world: while the myth of the natural artist persists, the SoHo galleries not infrequently house the work of artists with a cultural capital that can't be easily separated from its transmission through institutions of learning. The art world is recognized, with good reason, more as a stronghold of elite tastes than as a place that might be culturally penetrated by one without the institutional passport. While exceptions are not uncommon, the emergence from nowhere is more unlikely there than within popular music culture.

My point is not to mythologize popular music culture as a last frontier. Rather, I want merely to suggest that autodidacticism without institutional credentials more commonly leads to pop music careers than it does to high-profile artistic careers. Given this, the sovereign, authentic individual of the American Dream, the self-made man, that figure supposedly known only to a faded ideological moment, enters rock culture with a persistence that has been largely ignored as the end of ideology and the age of irony have supposedly rendered such silly stories insignificant—except, that is, to the few who embrace their illusions (not the ones, the advocates of irony tell us, who will lead the next cultural revolution).

If, as Susan Stewart suggests, nostalgia is a pervasive "social disease" that finds the sick longing for an authentic state of being, it is a longing that finds temporary resolution in fantasy, which, in turn, has several points of insertion in rock culture.[27] In my own experience, growing up with rock music meant long hours with the music and with an image bank that always promised an elsewhere. When Hal Foster refers to " 'perfect' images that make us 'whole' at the price of delusion, of submission," he draws attention to a scenario that I would argue leaves little room for ironic or performative relations to those images.[28] The need to believe that social elevation is not out of the question is a need that rock culture is commonly imagined as capable of answering, and it is an elevation that involves a rise to wholeness, to an authenticity in which the self is a self-presence. A modernist purity is at the center of this vision. Thus it is of little surprise that practices involving ironic distanciation are hardly a threat to the greater promises of rock culture; they are merely incorporated into these promises of authenticity. Importantly, this is not to say that rock culture is simply a culture of delusion. I quote Foster merely to draw attention to an aspect of rock culture (the fantasy of wholeness) that is often ignored in cultural studies and, in turn, to suggest a dimension in the experience of subjectivity that has itself been ignored. I think one reason for this is that the fantasy of wholeness has come to be coded as a delusion and, as such, seems to risk appropriation by a conservative right argument against rock music and its offshoots. This risk of appropriation by the right cannot, however, be given more power than it is due; it cannot be allowed to determine readings of rock cultural practices. As Stuart Hall argues, "We do tend to think that the right is not only always with us, but is always exactly the same: the same people, with the same interests, thinking the same thoughts."[29] While it seems important to strategize, when the right is too much with us there is a certain narrowing of the possibilities of a cultural criticism that is perhaps itself the greater threat. To understand the workings of rock culture, particularly in relation to the subjectivity of the fan, one must temporarily abandon the aspirations of a model of empowerment that steadfastly refuses fantasy, that risks constructing fantasy as a form of supplication and appropriation as canniness.

A postmodern moment producing a longing for the authentic must be recognized more consistently for its nostalgia. Baudrillard suggests that "when the real is no longer what it used to be, nostalgia assumes its full meaning. There is a proliferation of myths of origin and signs of reality; of secondhand truth, objectivity and authenticity."[30] Thus the postmodern sensibility can be thought of as marked by a perceived loss and, in turn, a longing for the authentic (though I wouldn't necessarily claim that this longing is particularly postmodern). It is important to see how the authenticity that is fought for in rock culture answers a social need, how rock culture takes on a particularly important role under the postmodern, as something like an outpost of a modernist sensibility that with some degree of clarity reflects subjectivity as a process founded on a relation to ideal images toward which striving takes place (one might again think back to Klein's rhetorics).

I have suggested that different cultural products and spheres of production play different roles in what might be called postmodernity's management of longing. If at one site the postmodern seems to challenge what I will crudely call modernist beliefs (in, say, the art world), to the point of displacing them, at another the losses faced by this displacement are managed through nostalgia. If in the academy one sees, even amid the various waves of backlash, an embrace of the antifoundationalism that is at the core of postmodernism, in rock culture a longing for the very authenticity this view challenges is both particularly virulent and carefully managed, the two tendencies necessarily being difficult to marry within one sensibility. Thus the projection onto rock culture of something related to an antifoundationalist ethos is notably obfuscating, primarily because the discourse of authenticity is not waning; rather, it is on the rise, moving about, sometimes under the veil of irony.

While in the academy myths of authenticity are daily deconstructed, I believe it is often in popular culture that the resultant longing is managed. And this longing is made ideologically specific as it is bound to what I call the wager of democracy, through which ideology and the demands of the subject are brought together. To take one example of a popular cultural form, the sitcom could be said to manage longing in a way that is finally quite different from the management I have attributed to rock culture. At the episodic level, the sitcom—*Gilligan's Island* is a suitable example, although something like *Friends* works within the same frame of logic—promises release from a containment. What drives the narrative within the single episode of *Gilligan's Island* is the possibility that this containment might be overcome: the castaways might get back to civilization. Of course, in the end, viewing revolves around seeing how every effort to escape will inevitably fail. It is, after all, promised. Episodic dynamism is always overcome by formal stasis. As Steve Neale and Frank Krutnik claim, "the situation is not allowed to change but is rather subjected to a recurring process of destabilization-restabilization in each episode."[31] The comedic dimension, of course, makes the harsh reality of containment, of the near impossibility of rising, a possible subject matter. And, importantly, in the sitcom the containment typically results in a reformation of community, whether of family or friends, reminding us that that is all we really need anyway. In this respect, the sitcom might finally be understood as more adept at managing containment than at managing a longing for some authentic existence outside that containment. The nostalgic impulse to return, argued by Baudrillard, is insistently foreclosed on. But the sitcom enacts this foreclosure by merrily reminding us that our longing for an elsewhere is only something like a failure of our own gratitude. The message, as community is restored despite our ill-founded dreams of an elsewhere, is that there's no place like home (in the Dorothy sense, that is). The sitcom thus restores the original meaning, this latter meaning, to a phrase that might otherwise be the very slogan of what Anthony Giddens calls the "post traditional order": "There's no (longer any) place like home."[32]

Rock culture, however, manages longing by maintaining a connection to what might be called, alluding to Pascal, the wager of democracy. Put simply, one could say the confines of democracy are tolerated because implicit in its ethos is the notion that we might rise, as individuals, and be recognized, in turn recognizing ourselves as authentic: we might as well believe in democracy just in case its biggest promises come true. And, importantly, the wager of democracy, focused on rising, is about the possibility of establishing distance. In relation to this, and compared to the sitcom, rock culture houses big promises. It maintains a link with an otherwise faded myth of recognition, and this by persistently envisioning an authenticity that can be reached by overcoming the foreign body of commercialism, whether by physical distance, temporal distance, or ironic distance. One can begin to see why ironic distance is so easily absorbed into a more modernist dream of authenticity: it fulfills the most immediate demand on any authenticity—distance. As Ernesto Laclau claims, "fantasy becomes an imaginary scenario concealing the fundamental split or 'antagonism' around which the social field is structured."[33] The fantasy, implicitly nostalgic, of arriving at authenticity requires the prerequisite fantasy of an intrinsic commerciality, a fantasy that finally conceals the fact that what Stewart refers to as "the necessarily insatiable demands of nostalgia" can never be met.[34] Rock culture, however, holds out the promise that such a longing might be satisfied.[35]

In a sense, authenticity is guarded as an ideal, continues to be argued as intrinsic because desire needs this primary point of destination. As I've already suggested, that which we confer with authenticity is integral to our own hopes of one day being recognized as authentic; this conferral is at the heart of any defense of an act's authenticity and thus remains of paramount importance to the subject. In Kaja Silverman's words, "desire is directed toward ideal representations which remain forever beyond the subject's reach."[36] But the futility of such strivings toward an ideal is obscured beneath the field of possibility that makes rock culture the locus of great cultural import that it is. It rarely serves to remind us of our containment. If a postmodern sensibility were everywhere in effect, allowing one to see the situation as it is, a knowingness resulting in what Larry Grossberg has described as the "collapse . . . between the authentic and the inauthentic," the promise of rock culture, bound as it is to the wager of democracy, would hardly continue to matter in quite the same way.[37] That it matters is intimately bound with its promise of individual recognition (which, again, is inseparable from the revelation of authenticity in an Other). The intersubjective dimension of the judgment of authenticity is thus the dimension that finds an ideal established, often an act, that both confers some sense of authenticity on the judging subject and sets up a goal for that same subject. Just as Lacan's mirror stage introduces an ideal ego that functions as a promise of potential wholeness (among other things, of course), so too establishing the authentic is forever about demarcating the possibilities of a subject's future.[38] Such needs are those not of the dupe but of the subject.

An individual's desire for a sense of completion is thus enacted through engagement with an Other who is idealized in the manner Silverman refers to when describing a desiring relationship with "ideal representations." This relation, allowing less room for irony, is at the base of relations between fans and performers, even fans and fans. The completeness envisioned in the star, for instance, is hardly diminished if that star inhabits multiple selves or plays with images. Privileging this play as somehow effecting or simultaneously emerging with a new ironic sensibility at the level of reception fails to acknowledge that desire can run its course, incorporating irony, and most often does. "The collapse, or at least the irrelevance, of the difference between the authentic and the inauthentic," which Grossberg locates as a possibility in rock culture, seems to be incompatible with the intersubjective relations of popular music culture as they lend themselves to the process of subject formation.[39]

CONCLUSION

The manner in which the Sex Pistols have generally been recuperated as authentic rather than as problematizing the very notion of authenticity allows a useful comparison with Richard Prince. If Prince was quickly validated along rather traditional lines of artistic merit (the museum's power here cannot be underestimated), that validation nonetheless allowed a frequent elaboration of his work as involving an extended critique of the rhetorics underpinning modernist authenticities. The Sex Pistols are more commonly celebrated as challenging the artifice of commercial music, as reinjecting an otherwise fading authenticity into rock and roll. We see them set up alongside Little Richard, the Who, even Springsteen. The absorptive power of rock's discourse of authenticity has long suggested that authenticity has particularly powerful meanings and that its relational work, its construction of difference, is deeply rooted in this. The introduction of irony has not changed that. If anything, it has changed only our view of popular music culture. Before suggesting some important reasons why an interest in irony has assumed the centrality it has, I want to outline some of the general opposition that the idea of irony as a liberating force has faced.

"Authentic inauthenticity," which Grossberg explains as a knowing, ironic stance, is not unrelated to Sloterdijk's notion of "enlightened false consciousness": hardly populated by dupes, the social landscape is perceived as producing inhabitants grown too savvy for a "false consciousness" to do the work it once did, inhabitants who have changed the terms of alienation by grasping its mechanics. Sloterdijk, however, less eager to invest in the possibilities of such a moment, sees as problematic this "radical, ironic treatment of ethics and of social conventions, as if universal laws existed only for the stupid while that fatally clever smile plays on the lips of those in the know."[40] In another attempt to counter the overvaluation of the ironic, Slavoj Žižek castigates "the underlying belief in the liberating, anti-totalitarian force of laughter, of ironic distance . . . [because] in contemporary societies, democratic or totalitarian, that cynical distance, laughter, irony, are, so to speak, part of the game."[41] Ironic knowingness, in this understanding, is not just another pose but perhaps one with particularly powerful veiling capacities. In the worst case, it denies its own relation to the construction of difference. In fact, Žižek draws attention to the dangers of privileging it without consideration of its potential as a mode of critical disengagement: "Cynical distance is just one way—one of many ways—to blind ourselves to the structuring power of ideological fantasy" (33). Because ironic distance is constructed as a being-in-the-know, in privileging it, the power of fantasy is often bracketed off as an object of critical study. Imposed on popular music culture, this simply obscures too much. As long as this ironic sensibility is privileged, I believe that it will discourage investigations of rock culture that might foreground the role of fantasy. Regardless of ironic play, as Simon Frith and Howard Horne contend, "It's as if artists, conscious of their own artifice, still crave for some unambiguous mark of authenticity and are thus haunted by the idea of real street credibility."[42] And I would hardly exempt rock musicians, fans, and cultural studies scholars from this scenario.

What Susan Stewart views as a longing for the authentic is easily related to Frith and Horne's craving for "real street credibility." And this notion that one can get at a "real street credibility" requires that something stand as an obstruction to such an accomplishment, thus finally explaining the impossibility of its fulfillment. Herein lies the importance of cultivating the category of commercial artifice. And even Grossberg can be found enriching such a category: "We may point to the increasing ease and rapidity with which various styles of rock and roll have been incorporated into, and exploited by, commercial interest . . . and reduced to harmless stereotypes."[43] "Harmless stereotypes" become the backdrop for a rather traditional authenticity. Žižek offers an example of how a fantasy of the Other allows—is in fact required for—a fantasy of such fulfillment of authenticity. Taking a Nazi fantasy of the Jew figure as his example, Žižek suggests that, "by transposing onto the Jew the role of the foreign body which introduces in the social organism disintegration and antagonism, the fantasy-image of society qua consistent, harmonious whole is rendered possible."[44] Within rock culture, a fantasy of an intrinsic authenticity requires that the commercial be kept alive as rock culture's "foreign body," the prerequisite fantasy that keeps the engine in motion. And, as structuring oppositions such as this never stand alone but always allow ideological investments to be woven into the chain of associations that lead from the primary opposition, one must study this primary opposition to see just how interests regarding gender, class, race, and sexuality are joined with it. Declaring the end of authenticity merely encourages a turning away from an ideologically loaded structuring opposition.

Judith Butler's notion of an antiessentialist performativity argues that, "if subversion is possible, it will be a subversion within the terms of the law, through the possibilities that emerge when the law turns against itself and spawns unexpected permutations of itself. The culturally constructed body will then be liberated, neither to its 'natural' past, nor to its original pleasures, but to an open future of cultural possibilities."[45] To a degree, I believe this notion of subversion characterizes the work done by the "pictures group." Within rock culture, however, a widespread desire for the authentic produces a different ground on which subversive practices are possible: the pervasive longing for something close to what Butler sees as the fiction of a " 'natural' past" makes rock culture an unlikely site for both the performativity she theorizes and the "authentic inauthenticity" presented by Grossberg.

Importantly, portrayals of rock culture as a suitable home for ironic play have been less responses to conditions in rock cultural settings than to both the dim view of popular culture and the valorization of traditional curricula associated with certain factions within the conservative right. Allan Bloom remains my convenient example. And while I agree that the cultural politics being played out in the context of this debate are important, attempts to elaborate on the complexities of the popular in reaction to the conservative trend have often done just the opposite: veiled the complexities.

Robert Walser's *Running with the Devil*, a much-lauded account of heavy metal music, does a great deal to complicate widespread understandings of heavy metal culture as a society of knuckle draggers with more than a passing interest in the forces of evil. And for the most part its efforts are persuasive. But, at points, Walser's defense of heavy metal is so insistent that one might wonder whether countering the dim view of heavy metal is the only thing at stake for Walser. In arguing against an uncritical understanding of metal as simply misogynistic—"blatant abuse of women is uncommon in metal videos"—Walser makes one of many moves that overcompensate.[46] His agenda—to challenge the common view of heavy metal as a social phenomenon—is surely possible without such countersimplifications. I find myself questioning whether Walser, in taking such an approach, is finally offering a more sophisticated picture of heavy metal or simply making its contradictions more palatable.

Regarding the proper response to a conservative disdain for popular culture, the question might be, "If they tell us to 'Just say no,' should we bark back, 'Just say yes!'?" To this I would just say no. The tactic of inversion can be debilitating for cultural studies. If the conservative right is reified as the opposition, issues such as drugs—in the case of the "just say yes!" allusion— are responded to with only the right's moral crusade in mind. David Lenson's *On Drugs* offers one example of where this might work on the subject: he claims that drug experiences (not simply using but buying and so forth) "may involve knowing people of other ethnicities, classes, races, and sexual orien- tations than those of parents and their social circle . . . so drugs becomes a code word for the child first associating with and then turning into the Other, and triggers parental fears of their once-dependent infant becoming inde- pendent. What runs through the skein of public imagery is not regression, then, but the opposite: the prospect of premature adulthood."[47] This kind of empowerment study is obviously a rant against a constructed "straight" soci- ety, not a critique of drug culture that might demonstrate how, for instance, that culture contributes to keeping a cultural Other in a position of margin- ality or how it is generally depicted through racial stereotypes.

Stuart Hall's admonition is worth repeating: "We do tend to think that the right is not only always with us, but is always exactly the same: the same people, with the same interests, thinking the same thoughts." Part of the ten- dency of cultural studies toward what has been called the affirmative model, which tends to bracket the negative critique and focus on empowerment, results from this simplification of the conservative right as a political oppo- nent, which further privileges the transgressive potentials of popular culture in such a way as to suggest that critical negativity, the turn away from empowerment studies, always risks flirting with the right's conservatism. But, paradoxically, this forestalls any critical activities that might see how social ground that is commonly associated with left-leaning principles (e.g., underground rock and roll) is healthy in its relations with a cultural conser- vatism. Simplifying the right as a body certainly allows a further simplifica- tion of what have commonly been thought of as left spaces.[48]

This is not to say that either the affirmative or the negative approaches offer the truth of what is out there but that they are choices to be made by the critic. One can find good reason to take either approach, though the deci- sion is not always already made for cultural studies work. In fact, an imbal- ance in favor of the affirmative continues to dog cultural studies. It is my belief that a rigorous critique of rock culture authenticity is incompatible, so far, with a "theory of cultural empowerment."[49] Uncovering the potential empowerment in rock culture first requires that what I've called the negative critique establish the ground on which transgression is possible. To put it in a more extreme light, even what Susan Stewart refers to as the "social disease" of nostalgia might be looked at as potentially empowering, though rock music's place in the social management of longing renders it particularly susceptible to the invasion of conservative values. But I think it more productive to take this route—to assess the conservatism before setting out to challenge it—than to imagine that within rock culture there is no longer a distinction made between authenticity and inauthenticity and to locate in this an empowering sensibility. I think there is a very real connection between a rock cultural desire for authenticity and rock culture's fertility as a soil for traditional values, including romantic notions of artistic genius, gender norms, a nostalgic longing that is often aimed at a mythic past (a past not unrelated to the traditional family values espoused in mainstream political rhetorics), and so forth. Very often empowerment studies strive too insistently to counterbalance the view that popular culture effects, in Adorno's words, "the control of the individual consciousness."[50] This is not to say that such a project is without value. But when accounts of popular culture begin to populate the social landscape with creatures surprisingly well-fed on empowerment, on irony, on a decidedly rational agency, that landscape becomes unrecognizable. If the threat being reacted to is a new conservative right that would prefer to instill a traditional canon in the academy and devalue popular culture as an object of study, I would argue that such a threat cannot dictate a cultural studies agenda. And, if this happens, who might we say cultural studies is for?

NOTES

1. Simon Frith, "Towards an Aesthetics of Popular Music," in *Music and Society*, ed. Susan McClary and R. Leppert (Cambridge: Cambridge University Press, 1987).

2. While my primary interest here is rock music culture, I will discuss tendencies within popular music culture more generally. This essay deals with issues that cannot easily be deemed irrelevant to one strand or another of popular music culture's fabric; such a reflex, separating off something like an avant-garde that is exempt from (and often seemingly above) common logics, is a pervasive and problematic move in popular music studies. In a sense, this essay addresses some of the problems that have resulted from the desire to make exemptions of this sort.

3. Lawrence Grossberg, with T. Fry, A. Curthoys, and P. Patton, *It's a Sin: Postmodernism, Politics, and Culture* (Sydney: Power, 1988), p. 43.

4. Of course, that I took the path from the club to the academy doesn't mean that I

understand this itinerary to be singular in providing a truer vision of rock culture, that I would feel comfortable contributing to a discourse that promotes the idea of an authentic, insider account as somehow set apart and hence capable of providing cultural studies with a missing truth; I certainly don't remember leaving the party with any such thing. This, however, does not change the fact that the gulf between certain academic accounts of rock cultural practices and my own experiences might mark a point at which some productive questions can be asked, despite the estimable poverty of personal testimony as source for theoretical generalizations. In Joan Scott's "The Evidence of Experience" she suggests that the uncritical appeal to experience is hardly innocent in its obfuscating powers: "When experience is taken as the origin of knowledge, the vision of the individual subject . . . becomes the bedrock of evidence on which explanation is built. Questions about the constructed nature of experience, about how subjects are constituted as different in the first place, about how one's vision is structured— about language (or discourse) and history—are left aside" ("The Evidence of Experience," *Critical Inquiry* 17 [1991]: 777). I take this as an admonition in advance, without, of course, imagining that I can live up to each and every one of its implicit suggestions.

5. Theodor W. Adorno, "Letters to Walter Benjamin," in *Aesthetics and Politics*, ed. Perry Anderson, Rodney Livingston, Perry Anderson, and Francis Mulhearn (London: New Left, 1977), p. 125.

6. In a recent phone interview with author Stanley Booth, I asked about Otis Redding as a kind of embodiment of soul (soul, of course, being inexorably bound with authenticity in its classical forms). Our discussion became most exacting, most concrete only when Michael Bolton was introduced as a comparison figure, at which point Otis Redding's authenticity could be described more effectively. Such is the nature of what I've called an "unambiguous relational situation."

7. *14 Songs* (Warner 45335, 1993).

8. Of course, it is worth remembering that throughout Westerberg's career he has, in what I would argue is an implicitly critical fashion, played with the defining features of commerciality (read "*inauthenticity*"). If at various points a denigrated commerciality was dependent on, for instance, the use of synthesizers, or the willingness to drift into bubblegum chord changes, or an affiliation with a major label, or a tendency toward what Elvis Costello has referred to as the "Fuck me, I'm sensitive" school of lyric writing, Westerberg, in embracing various negative terms and making them work for him, often helped demonstrate that such terms were fallible, that the underground/commercial binary was always susceptible to a decentering.

9. Simon Frith and Andrew Goodwin, eds., *On Record: Rock, Pop, and the Written Word* (New York: Pantheon, 1990), p. 181.

10. Richard Prince, personal interview, April 1995.

11. The idea of a romantic construction of authenticity is borrowed from Frith and

Goodwin but also appears in Larry Grossberg's work. I've called it the "classical model of authenticity." In rock-music culture in particular, the romantic is the classical. I'll use both terms to suggest the same model.

12. See Dick Hebdige, "Style as Homology and Signifying Practice," in Frith and Goodwin, *On Record*, p. 62.

13. Clement Greenberg, "Modernist Painting," reprinted in *Art in Theory: 1900–1990*, ed. Charles Harrison and Paul Woods (Cambridge: Blackwell, 1992), p. 755.

14. Yves Klein, "Sorbonne Lecture 1959," reprinted in *Art Into Theory 1900–1990: An Anthology of Changing Ideas*, eds. Charles Harrison and Paul Woods (Oxford: Blackwell, 1997), pp. 804–5.

15. Derrida, of course, has explored the connection between authenticity and writing, exploring in Rousseau and Levi-Strauss a tendency to establish writing as a condition of inauthenticity. Klein's desire to escape language so as to attain purity is consistent with this theme that Derrida sees as recurring in Western thought. See particularly "The Violence of the Letter," in Jacques Derrida, *Of Grammatology*, trans. Gayatri Spivak (Baltimore: Johns Hopkins University Press, 1974).

16. Anthony DeCurtis, "The Eighties," in *Present Tense*, ed. Anthony DeCurtis (Durham, NC: Duke University Press, 1992), pp. 5–6.

17. Anthony DeCurtis, preface to idem, *Present Tense*, p. x.

18. My suggestion here is not that nostalgia is a tendency of the weak. As I think Derrida makes quite clear, there is a nostalgic dimension to any argument for authenticity. And, as I suggest in this essay, we have not yet come upon a moment in popular music culture where the discourse of authenticity is not central, even as its forms shift; that is to say, popular music culture in general is deeply nostalgic, not simply certain strands within that culture. Contrary to what I see in Derrida, however, I believe that denigrating nostalgic tendencies without assessing the character of those nostalgias is a mistake, primarily because nostalgia might be the most powerful political tool of our time, one worth considering as potentially oppositional rather than simply conservative.

19. Although, in the case of this last blasphemy, some came to our defense as the ship went down—among them, Elvis Costello, who suggested that there is a difference between a young band doing a commercial to keep itself in motion and Phil Collins doing one in order to keep a country estate in gardens—it caused declines in our authenticity stock from which we never really recovered. Some fourteen years later we remain protagonists in a kind of morality tale that has outlasted the presence of our albums in any but our parents' collections. In a recent *Rolling Stone*, a member of Everclear holds the Del Fuegos up as an example of what can go wrong when a band does a high-profile beer commercial as we did. It's a story we can perhaps tell better than anyone, but the moralistic dimension that is generally a part of the telling—think of the character in *It's a Wonderful Life* who asks for his money back when George Bailey needs the community to rally behind him in order to rescue the Savings and Loan—in the mid-eighties the under-

ground took a similar view of any band embracing the wrong element of the world, and this moralistic dimension was often lacking in our telling. Ultimately, were we to have had the chance to rethink the choice of such sponsorship, we would have rejected it without question. But significantly, the grounds for making such a decision would have been career grounds, that is to say, business grounds. Authenticity, without a doubt, is as much the language of the market as it is of art. In our experience, we came to see the manner in which they were one in the same.

20. Andrew Goodwin, *Dancing in the Distraction Factory* (Minneapolis: University of Minnesota Press, 1992), p. 35.

21. Lawrence Grossberg, "Is There Rock After Punk?" in Frith and Goodwin, *On Record*, p. 112.

22. *Spin* 13 (March 1997).

23. Ibid.

24. Grossberg et al., *It's a Sin*, p. 45.

25. Valerie Steele, "The F Word," *Lingua Franca* (April 1991): 17–20.

26. Peter Sloterdijk, *Critique of Cynical Reason* (Minneapolis: University of Minnesota Press, 1987), p. 5.

27. Susan Stewart, *On Longing: Narratives of the Miniature, the Gigantic, the Souvenir, and the Collection* (Durham, NC: Duke University Press, 1993), p. ix.

28. Hal Foster, *Recodings* (Seattle: Bay, 1985), p. 83.

29. Stuart Hall, *The Hard Road to Renewal* (New York: Verso, 1988), p. 162.

30. Jean Baudrillard, *Simulations* (New York: Semiotext(e), 1983), p. 12.

31. Steve Neals and Frank Krutnik, *Popular Film and Television Comedy* (New York: Routledge, 1990), p. 235.

32. Anthony Giddens, *Modernity and Self-Identity: Self and Society in the Late Modern Age* (Stanford: Stanford University Press, 1991), p. 2.

33. Ernesto Laclau, preface to Slavoj Žižek, *The Sublime Object of Ideology* (New York: Routledge, 1989), p. xi.

34. Stewart, *On Longing*, p. 23.

35. As I've already argued, if the American Dream is demystified as regards political egalitarianism, from the perspective of a cultural rise to social power, such a dream remains decidedly achievable. There, in fact, the rise from nothing itself becomes a mark of the authentic. This doesn't simply mean that fame—being recognized as a performer—is the only possible avenue to authenticity. There is an equally powerful desire to be recognized (as authentic) by another performer or even by a fan group.

36. Kaja Silverman, *The Subject of Semiotics* (New York: Oxford University Press, 1983), p. 176.

37. Lawrence Grossberg, *We Gotta Get Out of This Place: Popular Conservatism and Postmodern Culture* (New York: Routledge, 1992), p. 227.

38. Of course, this also suggests that it would be worth extending this comparison

point, elaborating on the ways in which aggressivity toward the ideal expresses itself in popular music cultures.

39. Grossberg, *We Gotta Get Out of This Place*, p. 227.

40. Sloterdijk, *Critique of Cynical Reason*, p. 4.

41. Slavoj Žižek, *The Sublime Object of Ideology* (New York: Routledge, 1989), p. 27–28.

42. Simon Frith and Howard Horne, *Art Into Pop* (London: Methuen, 1987), p. 21.

43. Lawrence Grossberg, "Is There Rock After Punk?" in Frith and Goodwin, *On Record*, p. 112.

44. Slavoj Žižek, *Enjoy Your Symptom* (New York: Routledge, 1992), p. 90.

45. Judith Butler, *Gender Trouble* (New York: Routledge, 1990), p. 93.

46. Robert Walser, *Running with the Devil* (Hanover, CT: Wesleyan University Press, 1993), p. 117.

47. David Lenson, *On Drugs* (Minneapolis: University of Minnesota Press, 1995), p. 91.

48. See Kobena Mercer, "Skin Head Sex Thing: Racial Difference and the Homo-erotic Imaginary," in *How Do I Look? Queer Film and Video*, ed. Bad Object–Choices (Seattle: Bay, 1991), p. 192. Mercer's essay offers an excellent example of how cultural studies might confront the conservative right as an opposition. In it, Mercer responds to an earlier essay he wrote on Robert Mapplethorpe's photographs, in which the possibility of the argument's potential appropriation by rhetorics such as those of Jesse Helms is not taken into account. As he says, "For my part, I want to emphasize that I've reversed my reading of racial signification in Mapplethorpe not for the fun of it, but because I do not want a black gay critique to be appropriated to the purposes of the Right's antidemocratic cultural offensive" (192). He draws attention to the importance of a "politics of enunciation" (197). But what I find of value is not simply that he, in a sense, turned his argument around in the name of countering a conservative right argument but that this was done with a very specific right attack on culture in mind. His fight is against a concrete instance in right's war on culture. Too often the right is seen not in such specificities but as something closer to a monolith.

49. Simon Frith and Andrew Goodwin, introduction, "From Subcultural to Cultural Studies," in *On Record*, p. 42.

50. Theodor Adorno, *The Dialectic of Enlightenment* (New York: Continuum, 1993), p. 351.

3

FIXING MADONNA AND COURTNEY

SEX DRUGS ROCK 'N' ROLL REFLUX

MARILYN MANNERS

"Madonna is a great inspiration to a lot of people and she definitely deserves respect on a certain level, but her music has always sucked."
—Courtney Love

"I do think she knows not what she says."
—Madonna (on Courtney Love)

For much of their careers, fluidity and metamorphoses have described Madonna's and Courtney Love's experiences as women in rock. Yet each has faced pervasive and stubborn tendencies to fix her flux, from each other as well as from people in general. For many, Madonna has represented sex, Courtney drugs. If Madonna is pop idol, Courtney is postpunk train wreck. Madonna has been considered too much in control; Courtney too out of control. Even relations between them become frozen in stereotypical contours, often of the catfight: "Madonna's interest in me was kind of like Dracula's interest in his latest victim"; "I am fascinated by Courtney Love, but the same way I am by someone who's got Tourette's syndrome walking in Central Park."[1] Notably, each draws attention to something very wrong with the (other's) body. Both suggest unnatural symptoms of orality and roaming abroad that uncannily echo more general perceptions of their disturbing relations to female sexuality and physicality, including the maternal body. One was a madonna too long without child; the other a junkie mother. Both needed fixing.

To a certain extent, and in irony-laden contexts, a legitimizing fix recently came for both in the form of cinematic presentation of some of their own supposed faults. In Madonna's portrayal of Evita's calculated gold digging, her dramatic rise to fame and power, and her masterful manipulation of public image can be traced the narrative thread of many unauthorized Madonna biographies. Yet, coupled with her pregnancy during the final stages of filming, Madonna's hyperbolic self-representation garnered considerable respect, if not unanimous praise. Similarly, Courtney Love emerged in the same Academy Award year (1997) as a clean, sober, and serious presence large because of her generally lauded portrayal of Althea Flynt, a character not entirely unlike Courtney Love in her association with pornography (Love was once a stripper, for example) and especially drugs.

But far before Love's startlingly straight *Harper's Bazaar* cover—captioned "Courtney Love and America's Most Stylish Women" (September 1997), which, as it happens, was also a performance ("I dressed up as Donatella [Versace]")[2]—much interest in her seemed to derive exactly from a desire to fix her somehow. That might involve catching her out as heroin user, halting her fluidity as a self-defined feminist ("It's not like feminism was just invented. It's just that it's taken on a new face—my face, for one"),[3] or just fixing her good (the defining moment of the latter is the widely reported incident in which she "started a fight with Axl Rose himself at 1993's MTV Awards [Axl to Cobain: 'Shut your bitch up, or I'm going to knock you to the pavement']").[4] Madonna, of course, has had a longer and more complex popular history, and as I will detail later, reactions to her have shifted dramatically over the years. Yet fairly consistently she has functioned as a pop diva contrast to the seriousness of so-called real rock. Comparisons of Madonna to female bands reproduce this tendency: when Babes in Toyland, an "angry" female band, uses Cindy Sherman photographs for cover art, for example, both band and art are treated seriously; when Madonna refers seriously to working in the mode of Sherman on her book *Sex*, she is by and large ignored or ridiculed. Indeed, Madonna's use of irony or parody frequently encounters doggedly literal interpretation, especially when sexuality—on any level of representation—is concerned. These reactions range from reading "Material Girl" as allegory rather than parody to utterly serious repetitions of her ironic remarks about advertising for a sperm donor. That is, Madonna's binds tend to be double: she is flighty yet the ground against which real art can be measured; not serious enough to produce real art yet transparently serious in revealing her purportedly real desires.

Spin magazine covers promise "The Real Madonna" (January 1996) and that "Courtney Love Comes Clean" (May 1994). Beyond the latter's rather typical allusion to addiction and recovery, these iconic inscriptions are not entirely unrelated. Avital Ronell has drawn comparisons between the addict and the artist: " Like the addict . . . a writer is incapable of producing real value or stabilizing the truth of a real world. . . . The drug addict offers her body to the production of hallucination, vision or trance, a production assembled in the violence of non-address. . . . Going nowhere fast, as we say." What Ronell calls the "constitutive adestination of the addict's address" applies to more than addiction, certainly. "Adestination" suggests links among addiction, female sexuality ("going nowhere"), and writing ("non-address") that evoke other, underlying, aspects of the "dis-orienting" role of powerful women in rock. The fan's (critic's, reporter's) interminable quest for Truth ("the real," "com[ing] clean"), which continues to haunt reactions to popular art, is, of course, informed by—indeed saturated in—gender assumptions.[5] To have no fixed address, to roam (sexually, to tour, to rock hard, to produce ambiguity rather than be defined as enigma itself), remain, for many, unthinkable prerogatives for women in rock. "And yet," as Luce Irigaray has argued, "that woman-thing speaks. . . . It speaks 'fluid,' even in the paralytic undersides of that [phallocratic] economy."[6] It/she also writes, sings, screams, and says "fuck." A lot.

SEX LINE

Madonna and Courtney Love, although accorded more attention than most, are but two of many figures in the contemporary artistic discourse regarding female sexuality. Some women grab their crotches in public (Madonna and Roseanne) or display them parodically in various genres of glossy magazines (e.g., Courtney Love in *Vanity Fair* or Sandra Bernhard in *Playboy*). Some, such as riot grrrls—or more recently, Skin in the group Skunk Anansie—make concrete the notion of sex symbol by baring their flesh and scrawling on it "slut," "rape," "fuck you," or "clit rock." These women are displaying neither a passive offering of sex (as commodity, as fetish that arrests the gaze or the narrative) nor a renewed claim of female essence (however positively intended as a celebration of the body). Instead, their gestures trace a contested relationship between body and signification that is not adequately described by simply inverting Laura Mulvey's dictum into woman "as *maker*, not *bearer*, of meaning."[7] A closer rendering would be Hélène Cixous's threat: "We're going to show them our sexts."[8]

Women's contemporary cultural production often has to do with a self-conscious sense of agency or identity as process, and indeed with a sense that concepts of agency and identity may be problematic. It also has to do with intended and actual audience: the presumed spectator is no longer—necessarily—male or heterosexual. As Susie Bright reminds us, "When Madonna grabs her crotch and pulls, gay, straight and bi hearts beat a little faster."[9] Yet taking such things into her own hands or showing all there is to show—showing too much, some would say—is no guarantee of power, and such gestures can still be recuperated into the realm of the not-enough. When Courtney Love displayed her diaphanously covered crotch in *Vanity Fair* (September 1992), her gesture was at one and the same time ignored and the topic of anxious speculation: her particular crotch shot was both literally and figuratively overshadowed: by her pregnancy, by rumors of her continued drug use, and by moralizing concern (in the article and elsewhere) over whether her baby (or, perhaps more to the point, Nirvana's Kurt Cobain's) would come out well. In an almost too neat illustration of Luce Irigaray's observation that, in Western culture, concerning woman there is "nothing to see,"[10] Courtney Love's cigarette (but not her pubic hair) was airbrushed out of the *Vanity Fair* photo.

If Madonna's oft-repeated crotch grabbing is probably not exactly what Gayatri Spivak had in mind when she wrote, over a decade ago, about "reclaim[ing] the excess of the clitoris" (Irigaray argues in *This Sex Which Is Not One* that the female sex is not one but multiple, thus similarly nonrecuperable), neither is it defined simply by a "uterine" economy of reproduction: "Even as we reclaim the excess of the clitoris, we cannot fully escape the symmetry of the reproductive definition. One cannot write off what may be called a uterine social organization . . . *in favor of* a clitoral. The uterine social organization should, rather, be 'situated' through the understanding that it has so far been established by excluding a clitoral social organization."[11]

For all the obsessive attention paid to Madonna's or Courtney Love's actual reproduction, neither figure can be entirely contained within a uterine order (in relation to their public images, their female bodies, or their cultural production); there is far too much slippage, too much movement back and forth between pleasure and responsibility, excess and order, transgression and organization. Whatever their personal experiences, their "sexual" acts contribute to undoing the reproductive imperative, and varieties of these acts are as disparate as publicly admitting to abortions in an increasingly repressive climate (Madonna), or lyrics that scramble the daddy-mommy-baby triad: "Your milk turns to mine / Your milk turns to cream" (Hole, "Softer, Softest," *Live Through This* [DGC 24631, 1994]).

POP TRAP

Madonna has been taken extremely seriously for her business acumen and ability to manipulate images, but her claim to understand Cindy Sherman, an artist deemed serious, and moreover to employ similarly ironic strategies in *Sex* apparently convinced almost no one. Referring to work done by Modleski and Huyssen on the way in which high and popular culture are often masculinized and feminized, respectively, Schulze, White, and Brown have shown the same effect at play in Madonna's reception: rock is masculine/serious; Madonna is feminine/fluff.[12] In the same collection of essays, *The Madonna Connection*, in which their article appears, David Tetzlaff reproduces quite precisely the same old divisions between high and popular: "The semiotic process through which Sherman's images acquire their status as feminist critique is dependent on their location within the world of high art. . . . In high culture, [postmodernist style's] fragmentations and pastiches of popular symbols signify a challenge to the modernist canon of the establishment, and in popular culture, they don't really signify anything at all." In short, for Tetzlaff, "A Cindy Sherman image says, 'Interrogate me.' A Madonna image says, 'Buy Me!' "[13] But Sherman herself has not always been so confident about such distinctions; discussing her series of history portraits, she has admitted, "I felt a little uncomfortable about how successful they were. . . . I thought people would think they were trite and that I was sort of selling out and that they looked very commercial and kind of cute."[14] On the other hand, although Madonna underwrote Sherman's 1997 Museum of Modern Art show, Sherman maintains a characteristic distinction between them: "What she does with her identity is about *her identity*, while what I do is about other characters."[15]

No one, to my knowledge, has remarked that Cindy Sherman's general departure from a "cool" (detached, ironic, postmodern) aesthetic in earlier work lands her recent work in a territory that approximates (I do not say appropriates) riot grrrl/angry women imagery. Yet it seems unlikely that information—or images—only flows in one direction (down, of course).

Two of the band Babes in Toyland's album covers (for *Fontanelle* and *Painkillers*) not only look like riot grrrl images and/or recent Cindy Sherman photographs but *are* in fact Cindy Sherman photographs. Some would doubtless argue that the alternative/critical music of Babes in Toyland cannot be usefully compared with Madonna's more mass-based pop appeal, yet arguing thusly leads us back into the trap Schulze, White, and Brown warn against: " 'Rock,' therefore . . . is adult, innovative, authentic, serious, and committed actively and unselfishly to social issues. 'Rock' is art. Madonna, in contrast, is 'pop'—juvenile, formulaic, artificial, shallow, self-centered, escapist fantasy, committed to making a profit. . . . Clearly, pushing Madonna to the bottom rungs of the pop cultural ladder makes a space at the top for pop music 'art.' "[16] And the irony should not be lost on us that Madonna has claimed to be doing serious work that will change people's lives and sexuality (regarding "Justify My Love" and *Sex*, notably), whereas Kat Bjelland of Babes in Toyland has complained: "Everyone wants us to shoulder this like—I don't know what it is—feminist girls slut cause—I don't know what it is—bad girl cause. And the main reason I wanted to get in a band was to do music, and I didn't realize that it entailed all this political sh— stuff."[17] Perhaps it should be noted as well that both Madonna and Bjelland have published dating tips.[18]

Since *Evita* and motherhood and the generally respectful response to *Ray of Light* (Warner 46847, 1998), attention seems increasingly to be focused on Madonna's authentic inner self, the real Madonna exposed at last; as one of the more playful versions has it, "in its digitalized, navel-gazing way, *Ray of Light* is Madonna's most radical, mask-free work."[19] Yet if Madonna is moving, however tentatively, up the rock hierarchy, she seems less eager than most to reproduce and support that order, as her comments on those who have come to fill her "Low-Other" position suggest: "I like [the Spice Girls]. I know I'm not supposed to. Every time someone says something bad about them, I say, 'Hey, wait a minute, I was a Spice Girl once.' "[20]

alt.fan.addiction

Courtney Love's position in the contemporary discourse of women in rock has sometimes been that of central emblem of addiction in a postmodern allegory: she has served as a nexus of addiction, absorbing, enacting, embodying, or deflecting its multiple aspects. Violence and the Maternal, death and recovery, consumption and desire, gender and sexuality: all traverse the figure of Courtney Love, defining it, negating it, forming and deforming a reflection of what may be a pervasive cultural addiction to addiction itself. The figure of Courtney Love brings to mind time and again Ronell's question: "What if 'drugs' named a special mode of addiction . . . or the structure that is philosophically and metaphysically at the basis of our culture?"[21]

Love shouts in "Drown Soda" (*Ask For It* [Caroline 1470, 1995])—louder and louder each time—"Just you wait till everyone is hooked." Following her career and reactions to it might easily make one feel that day has already arrived. Courtney Love has, at any rate, achieved a sufficient degree of public recognition across age groups that she and a Hole concert (no mention of Cobain or Nirvana and no jokes at Courtney's expense) were referred to in the highly unlikely venue of a *Rockford Files* special. That the reference was neutral—and passing—is anomalous, however. In a more typical vein, Mia Ferraro, of the band Bobsled, recently claimed laughingly that she "got kicked out of Hole for doing drugs."[22] Any spin, straight or ironic, on Courtney Love in such a context would have to go very far indeed to outdo Barbara Walters: her fixation on Love's drug use (during an interview on "The Ten Most Fascinating People of 1995") was so concentrated as to seem almost parodic. She asked Love whether she does drugs in front of her daughter and whether she was on drugs at the moment, insisting that those were the questions "everyone" wanted to ask. Love's response included insisting, equally forcefully and repetitively, that the reason she was being interviewed in the first place was that her band Hole doesn't "suck," implying that perhaps there were other questions that "everyone" might like asked of her.[23] Tripping up or returning her critics' own criticism is one of the many modes of Courtney Love's ironic performative strategies. She might make certain that she is the first to bring up and comment on drug use (e.g., telling an interviewer that she bought a tee shirt with "My Drug Shame" written on it and laughing that she can't wear it because "It wouldn't even be ironic on me");[24] she writes song lyrics mocking her "bad motherhood" ("I don't do the dishes, I throw them in the crib");[25] she has posted numerous and notorious *America Online* messages that occasionally erupt into spontaneous pedagogical sessions, for instance, on feminist icons: "Re; Plath, Dumbass, sit down with 'Ariel' tell me.? If your not FUCKED when your done you have rotten taste"(11 April 1995; characteristic orthography preserved).

Irony, however, especially ironical contrast, seems to be a mode that the media tries to appropriate for its own use regarding the figure of Courtney Love. The 1995 *Vanity Fair* cover story, which was meant to remedy its earlier treatment of Love as a junkie mother (in Hirschberg's 1992 "Strange Love" article), displays Love both as a baroque, gold-tinged, feather-winged angel (on the cover and in the lead photo) and (in two facing full-page black-and-white photos) as a thumb-sucking, artfully deranged KinderWhore and as an exposed torso (only), with Love's hands covering (part of) her bare breasts.[26] A *Newsweek Special Issue* section on "Hitmakers," even less subtly, ran a two-page "Good Courteney [Cox], Bad Courtney [Love]" photo spread.[27] Such phrasing not only accurately plays off (other, presumably) media portrayals of Love but also alludes to Hole's song "Good Sister/Bad Sister" on their first album, *Pretty on the Inside* (Caroline 1710-2, 1991). In *Newsweek*, the good Courteney (color photo) is swathed in demure pink, while the bad Courtney's black-and-white shot abounds in irony, even without the contrast to the good Courteney: ominous shadows fill the middle and background; Courtney is foregrounded with face raised, eyes closed, hands uplifted in prayer, dressed in a torn babydoll dress, with heart-shaped earrings and what appears to be a bent spoon hanging from a black ribbon around her neck. Angel/Devil, Virgin/Whore, Dirty/Clean: defining terms for Love yet terms that can be deployed ironically, as they are here for grabbing audience attention. The catch, of course, is that Love set the irony in motion in the first instance.

Numerous thumbnail descriptions of Love's contrasts seem intended to convey her many complexities yet often display annoyance that they cannot penetrate and expose the real Courtney Love. The following appears in a *Spin* cover article that is actually entitled "Endless Love" but is marketed on the cover as "COURTNEY LOVE: Confessions of a Diva—The Untold Story":

> Heroine, villain, feminist, slut, poet, punk, fashion plate, gossip, punching bag, bitch, survivor, wife, mom: Love slips into each of these roles as if born for the part. Her deeply confessional songs—"I may lie a lot, but never in my lyrics," Love says—are sometimes revised during her shows for extra voyeurism and bloodletting. . . . Love's life bleeds heavily into her art, and vice versa. Don't bother trying to untangle what is real from what is artifice; at this point the knot is so gnarled that the strands are barely traceable.[28]

When it is no longer merely a question of interchangeable roles or true confessions but rather of ambiguity's shifting grounds, the tone and rhetoric here becomes increasingly anxious and almost hostile. Don't bother, indeed.

ON LINE

Madonna and Courtney Love have often been figured as conventional female doubles, whether as evil twins (hyperblond ambition) or as good/bad sister (clean/addicted, mother/whore). Indeed, an MTV advertisement features a parody of Madonna and Love as the twisted sisters of *What Ever Happened to Baby Jane?*[29] A very large "Courtney Love" in a big-bowed babydoll dress feeds a rat to a muscular, wheelchair-bound, nipple-tassel-wearing "Madonna." A common pattern is crystallized here: Madonna's and Love's work has always included exaggerating and tweaking gendered images; their audience picks up on these excesses, often (unlike in this case) recommending that they be reined in yet at the same time reproducing them (and, as here, sometimes exaggerating them further).

Comparisons of Courtney Love with Madonna, which are pervasive, have sometimes made Madonna seem like America's sweetheart, however. Or perhaps it is more accurate to say that in terms of female genealogy in popular music, Love has often filled the role in the popular imaginary that Madonna filled during and after the period when her book *Sex*, her album *Erotica*, and the film *Body of Evidence* were released, a period (late 1992 to early 1994) that culminated in her much-maligned 31 March 1994, appearance on *Late Show with David Letterman*. During this time, vituperative reactions of the sort Love often receives emerged in a range of print, as the following titles and tags indicate: "The Booby Trap," "Despotica," and "S & M Lite" (*LA Weekly*); "The New Voyeurism: Madonna and the Selling of Sex" (*Newsweek*); "Publicity Whore," "Exposing Her Body of Evidence," and "Madonna: The Crack of Yawn?" (*Film Threat*); "Like Aversion" and "Desperately Seeking a Future" (*Entertainment Weekly*). Matt Groening even ran a parodic Akbar and Jeff's *Sex* ad ("Calling All Carnal Consumers! You've Seen Her Breasts—Now See the Best!"), which announced the(ir) book as "Grim and Joyless Pseudo-Sadomasochism—The Kind America Likes!"[30] Groening, typically, hits a number of targets—and levels—with his parody. Both *Sex* and its U.S. audience could be—indeed were—charged and countercharged (by author Madonna and by readers ranging from reporters and critics to the man on the street) with "grim and joyless pseudo" one-thing-or-another, misreading irony and/or the public sexual climate, going too far or not going far enough—misrepresentation in general.

It is as banal as it is necessary to repeat that male musicians are not subjected to the same scrutiny, criticism, name-calling, vitriol, or condescension as are female artists and that reactions explode even more dramatically when it is an issue of women who work in the discourse of female sexuality. Rock critic Lorraine Ali has well documented in a short article for the *Los Angeles Times* the very different standards (moral, personal, behavioral, parental, etc.) to which male and female rock artists are held.[31] Both Courtney Love and Madonna have drawn attention to this fact themselves, as have a number of their fans and critics; indeed, this uneven situation is far from restricted to the music world. Kathy Acker has made statements on this subject that could have been voiced by Madonna or Love: "Sexuality is something that we [women] were defined by, and now we want to define it. Every time there is a wave of censorship this is what I think it is about. It's not against sexuality—it's against women wanting to reclaim sexuality."[32] One of Madonna's versions runs: "I'm being punished for being a single female, for having power and being rich and saying the things I say, being a sexual creature. . . . If I were a man, I wouldn't have had any of these problems."[33]

But knowing all this and knowing it well does not necessarily prepare one for the degree of hostility that has regularly been unleashed in the general direction of Courtney Love in the newsgroup alt.fan.courtney-love. A mild example is a thread that ran with "Cuntney" in the subject heading on March 14, 1996. In contrast, Madonna's newsgroup postings prior to the announcement of her pregnancy were generally characterized by an almost clinical commitment to (sometimes obsession with) her ratings and her awards (or lack thereof) and news of her professional activities, sprinkled lightly with more personal gossip. December 1995 saw comparative threads on Madonna and Love appear on both newsgroups—called (on alt.fan.madonna) "Courtney Rules!!!" and (on alt.fan.courtney-love) "Courtney Love: Big on talent, low on class." Discussion of relative talent and who copies the other's look was interspersed with material that, not surprisingly, continually harked back to sex and drugs. On the anti-Madonna side, postings included: "Courtney's a lot of fun! She's not some sex crazed deep dark sex lady with the fuck all the time look in her eyes like Madonna!"; "Well, at least drug addict Courtney has a baby, which Madonna wishes to have. And Courtney was married when she had it! :-) Even drug addicts got it more down than 'The Sex Goddess Madonna.' Tell me something about sex Madonna!" The anti-Courtney postings typically and rapidly escalated to more extreme statements: "Courtney wouldn't be able to have a fuck-look since she's high all the time, and no guy would ever want her"; "Your vain attempts at any kind of common threads between Madonna and that ludi-cris scuz are ridiculous. Are you aware of the suicide pact between courtney and her now dead husband that involved killing their baby as well?"; "court-ney love is a wretched bitch of a hag with NO musical talent whatsoever and her only claim to fame is that she was married to Kurt Cobain. She should take the same route that her husband did!!!!!!!!!! Stupid cunt. . . . . . Madonna rules the world and could kick the shit outta courtney any day" (all postings from "Courtney Rules" thread on alt.fan.madonna). The violence evinced in any number of online postings regarding Courtney Love make that space sometimes appear like an eerie equivalent of the punk concert mosh pit filled with "sporto" boys (Love's term), a physical and sexual hazard that Love has encountered regularly both in concert and on the Net. One mosh rape fantasy (?) on alt.fan.courtney-love had as subject heading "I fingered her."

Mark Mardon writes in an e-zine (*Come: The Journal of Eclectic Journeys*) that Courtney Love has been elevated to mythological status, taking on aspects of harpie, Medusa, vampire, Cleopatra. Along the way, he refers to a number of online reactions to Love, both positive and negative. Yet in the three that he cites as among those from Love's passionate defenders are to be found the following phrases: "Okay, so she's loud, obnoxious, and potentially violent"; "She looked like a very sexy zombie"; "Sure, she talks the talk—sometimes (maybe even often) in a shrill, irritating voice."[34]

The World Wide Web may have had a parodic homepage called "Madonna's Biological Clock Countdown" ("Desperately Seeking Semen," www.comcentral.com/madonna.htm [no longer active]) with a hot link to "Courtney Love's Birthing Tips," but it is also homebase for Tom Grant's elaborate conspiracy theory about Kurt Cobain's death, featuring Courtney as its murderous engineer.[35] There are, however, numerous similarities among responses to Madonna and Love to be found as well. On the news-groups of both, there are frequent requests for nude pictures, particularly of breasts, a situation that might well indicate an audience segment unlikely to browse newsstands (where such photos have not been entirely rare) and/or one that may be male adolescent enough to unabashedly express desire for such maternal attributes. On both groups, Madonna and Love are the butt of jokes; these too revert with unerring precision to the female body: "What is the difference between Wayne Gretzky and Courtney Love? Wayne Gretzky showers after three periods" (alt.fan.courtney-love). In a long posting (Subject: "Girlfriend, you should've remained 'Like a Virgin' ") criticizing Madonna's disastrous development ("perversion" is the term used) of a "slut persona," a series of jokes has a telling finale: "Q: Why is Madonna like a railway track? A: She gets laid all over the country! Q: What's the first thing Madonna does in the morning? A: She gets up and goes home! Q: Why is Madonna like a door knob? A: Everyone gets a turn! Q: What's the difference between Madonna and men? A: Madonna has a higher sperm count!" (alt.fan.madonna).

Over and again, everywhere, the types of Virgin, Whore, Mother appear, along with typical, related dichotomies: clean/dirty, aggressive/passive, attraction/fear. What I want to begin to suggest here is that the utterly banal stereotyping that one consistently encounters in reactions to Madonna and Courtney Love is itself caught in a bind: it often seeks to limit, contain, fix these women, yet it is also (unintentionally) part of a discursive process that the artists themselves have set in operation. This is decidedly not to say that Madonna or Love is in any way asking for it (the title of a Hole song, by the way) or responsible for the violent, hostile, or just plain stupid misogyny sometimes exhibited by their audiences, both professional and amateur. It is to argue, however, that while the power Madonna and Courtney wield is in part undeniably sexual, it is also certainly discursive as well. That body and language are intricately linked is part of both Madonna's and Love's artistic message, which may help explain not only their power but also their threat.

Madonna's pregnancy and motherhood have certainly catapulted her image into a realm that is sometimes associated with the female body's problematic or nonexistent relations with language. In that sense, it is tempting to read some degree of irony in the fact that she both deferred the announcement of her pregnancy and then made no statement herself, instead having her publicist do so. Online, the outpouring of good feeling over Madonna's pregnancy on alt.fan.madonna was somewhat eerie, as though the full weight of her name had finally hit home and fans were stunned with joy and apprehension over an imminent Second Coming. While the media relentlessly repeated variations of sorry puns (Material Girl Becomes Maternal Girl!), alt.fan.madonna generated scores of nearly identical postings expressing personal amazement and best wishes. Early on, the most interesting aspects of the thread concerned sporadic complaints that the media had not demonstrated more creative play with Madonna's song titles, or even name, when conveying news of the pregnancy. Only later in the torrent of postings did hints of more stereotypical reactions emerge: whereas original postings mentioned what a good year 1996 had turned out to be so far for Madonna, these later postings began to suggest, explicitly, what good timing the pregnancy was in terms of her slipping career and/or how it fit in with her propensity to control everything in her life: "This is great news!!! It can only help her both musically and artistically. Due in Aug/Sep? I'm betting her sales and airplay will increase due to this everyone watch!!!"; "Shrewd shrewd career move—she's reclaimed her throne as the world's premier PR artiste. . . Go MO!!"; "I don't mean to sound overly cynical . . . but Madonna's pregnancy almost assures good grosses [for *Evita*] here in the U.S.A.!" At least one posting analyzed the development of Madonna's image reinvention that led so inexorably to pregnancy at that time:

> Granted, Madonna does clearly want a baby for all the "loving" reasons, but the timing is shrewd, savvy, and intelligent. She's been toning her image down for the last two years, and what a better way to prepare the public for a kinder, gentler Madonna than a baby which will be born before Evita premieres. Imagine the marketing stunt: Madonna has baby in September/October, thus the magazines are filled full of photos with Madonna and Baby, therefore burying the image of Madonna as sex-obsessed pop star from the Erotica era. We all know how much Maddy has riding on this film—the timing seems too perfect. Maddy wanted a child, but she seems to have chosen the perfect time—as usual. YOU GO.

Once again, Madonna is seen as too much in control—unnaturally in control—even if that control is figured positively, as here.

Courtney Love, on the contrary, has typically been considered far too out of control. Yet a recent *Playboy* article, to name but one example, thinks differently. Arguing that Love craves "crossover stardom," it posits that "she has the requisite cunning, smarts, drive, cunning, talent—did we mention cunning?—to go the distance."[36] Certainly, it is unreasonable to expect that a media, or a culture, based on oppositional thought, hierarchies, and quick fixes will suddenly develop complex critical strategies regarding any cultural icon, but it can nonetheless be fascinating to watch as a huge swath of the cultural discourse begins to leap over the bar that demarcates dirty from clean, whore from mother, madwoman from magnate. Yet even the newly sanitized image of Courtney Love has recently been sullied by the release of Nick Broomfield's film *Kurt and Courtney*, which has been busily reviving the evil Courtney figure, both within the film (with its accusations that she tried to hire a hit man to kill Kurt) and without (her threats to sue blocked the film's screening at Sundance and bolstered attendance when it was shown at the alternative Slamdunk festival; in the words of the *L.A. Times*, "Courtney Love Got Slamdunked").[37] And *The Tonight Show* continues to bank on laughs at the "dirty" Courtney: in a February 5, 1998, skit on Clinton's many women, a punch line ran, "This afternoon I'm going to nail Courtney Love in the Rose Garden. Be there!"

The banal double binds that everywhere restrict women in rock can sometimes appear in the most unexpected places as well. One book on gender and rock, *The Sex Revolts: Gender, Rebellion, and Rock 'n' Roll*, while forwarding a critical stance toward gender fixing in rock, itself continually reproduces such assumptions in (the third and final) section of the book, titled "Lift Up Your Skirt and Speak," which covers women in rock. The authors, Simon Reynolds and Joy Press, conclude that "even the most striking and powerful of the new female artists are musical traditionalists, bringing new kinds of subject matter and subjectivity to masculine formats."[38] Such an argument leads at times to almost comical impasses regarding the relation of the female body to musical performance: "A sort of politically-correct version of the Runaways, L7 show that trying to be as hard as the boys is just a dead end. Surely women have more to offer rock than the same old hardened, repressed armature of cool? Are L7's notorious antics—like the incident at the 1992 Reading Festival when singer/guitarist Donita Sparks pulled her tampon out of her vagina and hurled it into the crowd—really that much of an improvement on heavy metal's ritual feats of misbehaviour?" (248).

From its (critical?) repetition of phallorhetoric ("as hard as the boys," "the same old hardened, repressed armature") to its startling comparison of bloody tampon tossing with hypermasculine "ritual feats of misbehaviour," this passage indicates both a willful blindness to difference and a tendency toward fixing its female subjects that will round out the book's argument. *The Sex Revolts* is perhaps most useful as a document that reminds us how easily academically sanctioned gender criticism on women in rock can mirror the conflicting constrictions expressed in much more popular venues, such as newsgroups. For Reynolds and Press, women just can't seem to do anything right. If "female artists who appear to put their sanity in jeopardy . . . run the risk of being dismissed as 'merely' mad" (269), women who exercise control over themselves or their product are castigated soundly: "For some, Latifah's aura of self-discipline and sagacity doesn't have the magnetic, mesmerising allure of more 'unsound,' male rappers. Latifah's version of sovereignty is closer to benign despotism than gangsta rappers' tyranny and terrorism (although she did entitle an early song 'Wrath of My Madness'). She's too dignified, too much of a positive role model to be baaad" (299).

But if Queen Latifah is criticized for a relatively boring "benign despotism," Madonna is dubbed an "image fascist":

> We find little in the way of liberation in Madonna's work precisely because it seems so much like work. In Bataille's terms, Madonna's self-serving makes her servile rather than sovereign. There's a grim, aerobic, almost Protestant strenuousness to the Madonna spectacle, and while her reward is obviously the narcissistic enjoyment of her own image, it's hard to see what the payback is for the audience. . . . In most of her music, for all its burnished state-of-art production, there's a lack of real grain and swing. (321–22)

Their pushing of Madonna to the bottom of the rock ladder—a common tactic that I discussed earlier in this essay—allows Reynolds and Press to mention but then completely to disregard Susan McClary's exhaustive and convincing analysis of the radical form of some of Madonna's music.[39] That they do not bother to argue with McClary's analysis but merely dismiss it in passing makes their closing complaints that female musicians are still just replicating masculine forms exasperating not merely on the level of gender criticism but on the level of old-fashioned logic as well.

Remarkably, *The Sex Revolts* treats Courtney Love almost reverently in comparison, recognizing that "her body has become the battlefield for a struggle of ownership": "Love's performance is a striptease that removes too many layers to be titillating, exposing a subcutaneous realm of female horror that makes men flinch and recoil. . . . Speculum becomes spectacle, the invisible interior is displayed. . . . It's as though one of Charcot's female patients has taken charge of her own theatre of hysteria and transformed the humiliation of being an exhibit into an empowering exhibitionism" (349, 262). If loaded with flashy and dualistic (interior/exterior, e.g.) rhetoric, this description at least has the merit of pointing toward the gynogymnastic quality of the gender-"twitching" (Kathy Acker's term) often employed by Courtney Love. And Madonna.

"FEMMENISTE" THEORY?

"I know the aspect of my personality, being the vixen, the heart-breaker and the incredibly provocative girl is a very marketable image. . . . But it's not insincere. You just can't take it seriously."
—Madonna[40]

"When I say 'I am doll heart' I want to grab my pussy. Not in a Madonna way; it's very ironic. It's not aggressive, hey, I'm a man. I'm not a man. I couldn't stand it. I'm just the opposite. I am, I guess, a 'femmeniste.' "
—Courtney Love[41]

Although reading about Madonna and Courtney Love sometimes produces the slightly sickening feeling of always everywhere finding the same old thing, following their own cultural production (music, videos, interviews, etc.) can resemble tracing the contours of an emergent cultural and gender theory. This would be a theory that certainly challenges, for example, more traditional feminist theories of victimized female body, women's language as liberating self-expression, or female image as consumable object, at the same time that it refers to and plays off (yet does not negate) those theories. Similarly, their work on race, particularly as an extended interrogation of hyperwhiteness (bell hooks has thoroughly critiqued Madonna's appropriation of African-American culture),[42] and on bisexuality (which both have played at but declared the game untrue) demonstrates how they may exceed, and yet remain entangled in, more conventional feminism's assumptions and limits.

I now return for a moment to Kathy Acker, not only because she is generally considered to operate on an entirely different cultural register from Madonna or Courtney Love or because she herself has spoken enthusiastically about Madonna and riot grrrl bands (or because she released an album with the Mekons) but because she has also been part of this emergent theory:

The body is always connected to the imaginary, and whatever that is for women's bodies, that imaginary does not exist in our society. That is *major* to me, especially as I grow older, to try to find out what that imaginary is—try to locate the body, get in there, listen to it and find out how it could possibly exist in the world. A lot of women now are working around the question of "what's our sexuality," "what's our imaginary," "what's our body?" It's coming from theorists, people like Susie Bright, it's coming from all over the place. So why is the body central? Because our bodies have been denied, because maybe Gloria Steinem is allowed to say that we should be equal to men, but when it comes to menstruation it's "hide that dirty pad!"[43]

Sexuality/imaginary/body: the difficulty of these realms, theoretically, concerns where and how (or if) language comes into play. Before her untimely death, Acker was working on a new theory of myth and of a female imaginary, by means of languages of the body: dreams, masturbation, bodybuilding, tattooing, and piercing. Madonna and Courtney Love are also working at the very friable borders of language and body, albeit somewhat differently (although Love claims writing tactics that are usually associated with Acker: plagiarism and automatic writing).[44] Both certainly employ genre- and gender-blending strategies, mixing male and female gestures or mixing musical performance with performance art, with the latter's strong association with and history of work on feminist sexualities. Both also play along the borders of truth and falsehood (excessive artifice, revealing too much, "truth or dare," "live through this"), problematic borders for mainstream Anglo-American feminist theory, which has long privileged and little questioned the (truth) value of the confessional mode.

Madonna and Courtney Love are furthermore constantly preoccupied with issues of interpretation and presentation, reading, misreading, and various forms of duplicity, including irony: "They didn't get the joke. The whole point is that I'm *not* anybody's toy. People take everything so literally," Madonna has complained.[45] Courtney Love says, "When I wrote *Live Through This*, I didn't write one word that had anything to do with my inner life. That's my gift, my gimmick," and, "One of the most famous things that happens to everyone is mis-hearing a lyric. That's where some of the best stuff comes from."[46] Both take negative criticism and incorporate it into their own artistic production: "Oops, I didn't know I couldn't talk about sex—(I musta been crazy)" (Madonna, "Human Nature," *Bedtime Stories* [Sire/Maverick

9362 457670, 1995]). "Since my persona is so demonized and so huge and so not what I am about, I can practically do anything I want behind that persona, artistically. That's kind of a gift and a positive thing" (Love).[47]

Madonna and Courtney Love have, finally, generated a language body, a fluid entity that operates both on the most simple and on the most complex terms. Love, Hole, Madonna: their having set these and other terms and phrases—"Like a Virgin," "Material Girl," *Sex*, "Live Through This," "Good Sister, Bad Sister," "Pretty on the Inside"—into play sometimes gives one the impression that nothing said about them, however laudatory or derogatory or even simply descriptive, can ever exceed or escape their own language body. Article titles, online subject headings, pull-quotes, and citations quoted throughout this essay have constantly referred, first and foremost, back to Madonna's and Love's own cultural production, including their own self-naming. Merely dropping a last name (Ciccone) or switching a first name to a last name (Courtney Love, née Love Michelle Harrison) has spawned a vast maternity. Article titles punningly vie for attention, using terms that come preloaded: "Hole: Angry Love Songs," "Love Hurts," "Strange Love," "Love Story," "In Love with Courtney," "The Hole Truth," "The Trials of Love," "Love Conquers All," "Endless Love." For all the outcry over the excessive and scandalous circulation of their bodies, there has been precious little attention paid to the scandalous circulation of their language.

In the often-scorned realm of image, where language and body meet and intermingle, Madonna and Courtney Love have staked claims to producing provocation, fun, outrage, art—and feminist theory. Cixous's twenty-year-old injunction to "write the body" takes on additional nuance when the body writes as much as writing bodies. Images produced by Madonna and Love unravel easy assumptions about surface and depth, truth and falsehood, the banal and the serious, language and body, sex and drugs and rock 'n' roll. Madonna and Courtney Love—in language-body-image—are excessive indeed in a realm of feminist theorizing that is still being imagined.

NOTES

1. Cited in Lynn Hirschberg, "Strange Love," *Vanity Fair* 55 (September 1992): 232; cited in Bob Guccione, Jr., "Live to Tell," *Spin* 12 (January 1996): 45.
2. Ann Powers, interview with Courtney Love, *US* 238 (November 1997): 128.
3. Cited in Ann Powers, "The F Word," *Spin* 9 (July 1993): 39.
4. *BAM*, 23 April 1993, p. 42.

5. Avital Ronell, *Crack Wars: Literature Addiction Mania* (Lincoln: University of Nebraska Press, 1992), p. 106.

6. Luce Irigaray, *This Sex Which Is Not One*, trans. Catherine Porter (Ithaca, NY: Cornell University Press, 1985), p. 111.

7. Laura Mulvey, "Visual Pleasure and Narrative Cinema," in *Visual and Other Pleasures* (Bloomington: Indiana University Press, 1989), p. 15.

8. Hélène Cixous, "The Laugh of the Medusa," in *New French Feminisms*, ed. Elaine Marks and Isabelle de Courtivron (New York: Schocken, 1981), p. 255.

9. Susie Bright, *Susie Bright's Sexual Reality: A Virtual Sex World Reader* (Pittsburgh: Cleis, 1992), p. 56.

10. Irigaray, *This Sex Which Is Not One*, p. 26.

11. Gayatri Chakravorty Spivak, "French Feminism in an International Frame," in *In Other Worlds: Essays in Cultural Politics* (New York: Routledge, 1988), p. 152. Emphasis in original.

12. Laurie Schulze, Anne Barton White, and Jane D. Brown, " 'A Sacred Monster in Her Prime': Audience Construction of Madonna as Low-Other," in *The Madonna Connection: Representational Politics, Subcultural Identities, and Cultural Theory*, ed. Cathy Schwichtenberg (Boulder, CO: Westview, 1993), p. 18.

13. David Tetzlaff, "Metatextual Girl: → patriarchy → postmodernism → power → money → Madonna," in *The Madonna Connection*, p. 256. Greg Seigworth, on the other hand, straightforwardly applies a comment about Cindy Sherman to Madonna in "The Distance Between Me and You: Madonna and Celestial Navigation (or, You Can Be My *Lucky Star*)," also in *The Madonna Connection*, p. 304.

14. Cited in Amei Wallach, "Tough Images to Face," *Los Angeles Times*, June 7, 1992, "Calendar," p. 77.

15. Cited in Julie L. Belcove, "The Sherman Act," *W* 26 (June 1997): 188.

16. Schulze, White, and Brown, " 'A Sacred Monster in Her Prime,' " p. 18.

17. Interview on *In Concert*, ABC, June 23, 1993.

18. Madonna in *Sex* (New York: Warner, 1992); and Bjelland, "Charm School," *Details*, July 1993, p. 68.

19. Barry Walters, "Madonna Chooses Dare," *Spin* 14 (April 1998): 72.

20. Cited in Walters, "Madonna Chooses Dare," p. 76. "Low-Other" is the term used by Schulze, White, and Brown, " 'A Sacred Monster in Her Prime.' "

21. Ronell, *Crack Wars*, p. 13.

22. Pleasant Gehman, "Girl Trouble! Will LA's Bobsled Go Over in Tai Pei?" *BAM*, 19 April 1996, p. 9.

23. "The Ten Most Fascinating People of 1995," ABC, 1995.

24. Raphael, *Grrrls* (New York: St. Martin's, 1996), p. 4.

25. "Plump," *Live Through This*.

26. K. Sessums, "Love Child," *Vanity Fair* 58 (June 1995): 106–15.

27. "Good Courteney, Bad Courtney," *Newsweek*, 1995, pp. 48–49.

28. Craig Marks, "Endless Love," *Spin* 11 (February 1995): 45.

29. Such readings may also come from supposed friends, apparently: after a dinner party both attended, one of the guests whispered to a journalist that "Madonna and Courtney together are like Joan Crawford and Bette Davis, and it's hard to tell who's who" (Ingrid Sischy, "Madonna and Child," *Vanity Fair* 61 [March 1998]: 206).

30. Matt Groening, "Life in Hell," *LA Weekly* , *6–12 November 1992, p. 6.*

31. *Lorraine Ali, "Courtney Love and the Flip Side of Criticism," Los Angeles Times,* 27 May 1995, F1 and F6.

32. Lisa Palac, "Kathy Acker: The *On Our Backs* Interview," *On Our Backs* (May/June 1991): 38.

33. Sheryl Garratt, "An Interview with Madonna," *Medio Magazine* 2, no. 1, http//www.clark.net/pub/wmcbrine/html/Medio-view.html (13 February 1996).

34. *Come: The Journal of Eclectic Journeys,* www.sirius.com/~memardon/Come/Love_Myths.html (1997).

35. Available at www.nirvanaclub.com/grant01.htm.

36. Neal Karlen, "Love Hurts," *Playboy* 43 (February 1996): 104.

37. Amy Wallace, " 'Kurt' Finally Finds a Home," *Los Angeles Times,* 20 January 1998, F1.

38. Simon Reynolds and Joy Press, *The Sex Revolts: Gender, Rebellion, and Rock 'n' Roll* (Cambridge: Harvard University Press, 1995), p. 387.

39. Susan McClary, "Living to Tell: Madonna's Resurrection of the Fleshly," *Feminine Endings: Music, Gender, and Sexuality* (Minnesota: University of Minnesota Press, 1991), pp. 148–66.

40. Cited in Gillian G. Gaar, *She's a Rebel: The History of Women in Rock and Roll* (Seattle: Seal, 1992), p. 335.

41. Cited in Raphael, *Grrrls,* p. 31.

42. bell hooks, "Madonna: Plantation Mistress or Soul Sister?" in *Desperately Seeking Madonna,* ed. Adam Sexton (New York: Delta, 1992), pp. 218–26.

43. Cited in Benjamin Bratton, "A Conversation with Kathy Acker," *Speed* 1, no. 1, http//www.arts.ucsb.edu80/~speed/speedPast/1.1/acker.html (12 December 1995).

44. See Raphael, *Grrrls,* pp. 9–10.

45. Cited in Gaar, *She's a Rebel,* p. 333.

46. Cited in Raphael, *Grrrls,* pp. 6–7, 8–9.

47. Ibid., p. 10.

4

"ASK ANY GIRL"

COMPULSORY HETEROSEXUALITY AND GIRL GROUP CULTURE

PATRICIA JULIANA SMITH

for Terry Castle

From the end of the 1950s to the end of the 1960s, hundreds of musical expressions of female adolescent romantic (if not clearly sexual) desire and its concomitant angst found their way onto the popular music charts in the United States, Great Britain, and numerous other nations. Beyond a doubt, the basic epistemology of the average girl group song is unapologetically and uncritically male-centered. Some feminist critics have dismissed these boy-fixated confections as frivolous or debasing.[1] To do so, however, is to miss or misunderstand their essential homosociality, the homosociality of a female adolescent subculture existing within a larger social ethos of compulsory heterosexuality.[2]

While The Boy is both subject and object of girl-group fantasies, he is only rarely a physical presence in these minimelodramas. Absent, in love with someone else, dead, merely fantasized, or otherwise disembodied, The Boy exists primarily in the third person for the lead singer/persona, while the second-person preceptors are other girls.[3] In the most immediate sense, the other girls are the background singers, who in call-and-response fashion abet and advise their enamored and afflicted sister through the interpolation of such interjections as "Go ahead, girl . . . Ain't nothing but love, girl" (Martha and the Vandellas' "[Love Is Like a] Heat Wave" [1963]) or such nonsense vocables as "Da Doo Ron Ron" (the Crystals [1963]), "Shoop Shoop" (Betty Everett's "The Shoop Shoop Song" [1964]), "Hey La" and "Bah-Ooh" (the Angels' "My Boyfriend's Back" [1963]), or the quintessential "Doo Lang Doo

Lang" (the Chiffons' "He's So Fine" [1963]) that serve semiotically to convey an inarticulable if not unspeakable empathy.[4] By extension, the backing vocalists represent the commercial audience of girl-group music: primarily female adolescents who interact and identify with other girls by exchanging male-centered fantasies.

In this manner, girl-group music functioned, throughout a decade of sea changes in attitudes toward female sexuality, as a demotic adolescent female form of what has come to be known in critical discourse as "homosociality." Anthropologist Gayle Rubin and French feminist theorist Luce Irigaray have defined the structures of patriarchal society as being based on a structure of "traffic in women," whereby men consolidate the basis of their cultural and economic powers through an exchange of dependent and objectified women.[5] Similarly, René Girard has demonstrated how "triangular desire" is a vital aspect of such exchange, one that operates as a modes of enacting repressed and forbidden homosexual desires.[6] More recently, Eve Kosofsky Sedgwick, who coined the term "homosociality," has posited that homosociality and its objectification of women exchanged among men (as well as the related notion of separate spheres for men and women) is a means of enforcing compulsory heterosexuality, while the violations of this code are tantamount to social treason.[7] Girl-group music, which represents the conditions of adolescent girls, perhaps the most dependent, disempowered, and disenfranchised sentient beings in society, takes the concept of homosociality, albeit unwittingly, one step further. Created within the context of a historical period during which the nuclear family stood as a social paradigm of normalcy, these recorded performances provide a cultural document of the predominant sexual mores of the 1960s, particularly the earlier years of the decade when heterosexuality was the only visible option, early marriage and motherhood were the rule rather than the exception, unwed pregnancy incurred social stigma, and birth control was ineffectual if not completely inaccessible. Under these conditions, teenage girls, desexualized by the same social forces that would compel them eventually to become wives and mothers, possessed little more on which to base their system of "traffic in boys" than fantasy and emotionality, two of the few entities that were theirs and theirs alone. It has been easy—perhaps useful, for some—to dismiss girl groups and the music that expressed the anxieties of these conditions as mouthpieces for the self-subjugation of women and girls; rather, I would suggest, they merit critical attention as they provide us with a documentation of and insight into changes in female consciousness and social conditions throughout a watershed period of change and dissent.

If one were to seek a foundational moment of girl-group music and its ethos, one might well look to the Chantels' recording "Maybe." In October 1957 five African-American schoolgirls entered a recording studio that had, in an earlier time, been a Roman Catholic church. The oddity of this setting is apt, for the musical, social, and cultural backgrounds of the young women in this group were a similarly curious mixture. Students at St. Anthony of Padua School in the Bronx and well trained in the vocal demands of Gregorian Chant by the nuns, Arlene Smith and her companions crossed, perhaps unwittingly, numerous demarcation lines of race, culture, and gender in committing their adolescent plaints to disc. Typically, black female vocalists of the mid-1950s were, like Ruth Brown and LaVerne Baker, solo acts, lone women in the predominantly male world of rhythm and blues; their roots were solidly in the gospel traditions of southern evangelical and Pentecostal churches. As the articulators of sensuality and forbidden pleasures, they had limited access to mainstream airwaves, and their best recordings were routinely sanitized and covered by "nice" white girls like Georgia Gibbs and Gogi Grant, who accordingly reaped a far greater share of royalties and recognition. All-female vocal groups, like the Chordettes and the McGuire Sisters, were, on the other hand, generally white and relentlessly ladylike. The Chantels, whose very name derives from that of French nun St. Jeanne Françoise de Chantal, were, by contrast, simultaneously passionate and chaste in both their material and their demeanor, as befits their Catholic (and therefore Eurocentric) circumstances and apparently middle-class aspirations.

These conditions, including the homosociality that is particularly pronounced in Roman Catholic education, clearly inform the Chantels' greatest hit. Charlotte Grieg aptly notes that for "the first time in a pop setting," a "devotional" tone blended with "simple rhythm 'n' blues backing" and "youthful yet heartfelt wailing from the girl lead singer":

> In "Maybe," a girl seemed to be talking to her friends; their voices followed her story, emphasizing their agreement, their interest, their shared emotions in a private female world. . . . In the adult world of gospel, women often sang in a call-and-response pattern, the powerful lead singer telling her story and baring her soul, seeking affirmation from

the choir and congregation; but the Chantels' high, ethereal harmonies and purity of tone, which derived from an altogether different strain of church music, added a totally fresh element, one that seemed to chime perfectly with an emerging pop sensibility amongst teenage girls.[8]

Grieg's interpretation may be inaccurate in a strictly literal sense: "Maybe" is a direct address apostrophizing a loved one whom the protagonist hopes will "come back to stay," if only she performs the right actions and prays enough, "every night" and "every day."[9] Yet Grieg nonetheless discloses the atmosphere the lyrics convey. The loved one is neither present nor, for that matter, embodied. Indeed, no characteristic of the object of desire—not even gender, actually—is revealed, save absence. This absence is so profound that while the vocalist posits that physical contact ("if I hold your hand . . . if I kiss your lips") might reestablish (or simply establish) a mutual affection and that "the Lord" might be willing to "send you back," she pessimistically concludes that her love will "come to me only in my dreams," just before repeating her initial list of "maybes." Accordingly, the singer's plaint becomes more of a soliloquy or prayer that the loved one will never hear. Her audience, then, is the fundamental female adolescent one: other girls. Behind Smith's lead vocal, the other Chantels provide a wordless cry of sympathy, interrupted only by the occasional chant of "maybe, maybe, baby," in agreement with the protagonist's desperate hopes. Maybe our heroine will be with her true love someday; but, given the overall tone of despondency, probably not. Rather, the recording suggests the likelihood that she will always remain in the company of girls, that realm of homosociality where the fantasized possibility—if not probability—of eventual heterosexuality becomes the primary topic of discourse.

"Maybe," with what Grieg aptly describes as its "homemade feel," found success not merely as a rhythm-and-blues (i.e., "black") record but became a Top 20 pop hit as well.[10] The Chantels' early girl-group sound subversively defied racial categorization; indeed, because many girl groups were comprised of faceless session singers with little in terms of public identity, it would eventually become difficult, in many cases, to determine whether the girls singing on a given record were black or white. But perhaps even more subversive in its demure way was the Chantels' reversal of gender roles. For Arlene Smith, the "older guys" in "doo-wop" ensembles "represented the pinnacle of glamour," a glamour out of her reach until she discovered Frankie Lymon and the Teenagers (13). In the popular success of "Why Do Fools Fall in Love," Smith discerned not only the possibilities of adolescents empowered to access the private domain of the "older guys" but also a certain feminine quality in Lymon's "lovely high voice" that allowed her to believe that girls could be recording stars as well: "I thought if he could do it. . . . It seemed so far removed, but I made a conscious decision to do the same" (15).

That Smith and the other Chantels were conscious, at least on some level, of their trespass into a gender-restricted territory is obliquely suggested by early publicity photos. Armed, as it were, with the emblems of musical masculinity, the girls strike various poses wielding guitars, maracas, and drumsticks, at times doing so while another member pounds away at a piano. Their parodic machismo would insinuate that girls could readily appropriate a guy thing, but also—albeit inaccurately—that the Chantels were truly independent young women who did not need to rely on a male backing band. Simultaneously, however, whatever threat of gender transgression they presented was undercut by their ultrafeminine attire—semiformal prom gowns replete with billowing crinolines—and the fact that their awkward handling of the instruments indicated a complete unfamiliarity with them. Semiotic ambiguities notwithstanding, with "Maybe" and a handful of lesser hits—virtually all of which manifest self-blame for a shattered romance and a peculiarly Catholic and oxymoronic bleakly prayerful hope for reconciliation—the Chantels established a new medium of what, in the context of the early sixties, might best be called "girl culture."

That this highly occulted and relatively undefined substratum of the rock-and-roll universe has long existed is rarely considered by even the most thorough historical or sociological overviews of popular music. Cultural critic Iain Chambers, drawing on the studies of Angela McRobbie and other social critics, has nevertheless noted the significance of adolescent female homosociality as an integral part of both the ambience of youth culture and the formation of British rock music in the late 1950s and early 1960s. The dance hall, a venue traditionally devoted to heterosexual adventure, was, according to Chambers, more often than not a site of strict and ritualistic homosociality where gender differences were sharply defined: "Dancing involved rigid ground rules that had been persuasively laid down elsewhere, outside the walls of the dance hall or youth club. Consequently, girls tended to arrive in groups and couples and danced amongst themselves, while the majority of boys lounged around the walls, talked and smoked, stared down alien males, and conserved their masculinity."[11] Similarly, these dualistic modes of homosociality were echoed in the sexes' approach to pop music:

> The sexuality that was stamped on the public sentiments and postures of rock 'n' roll was predominantly masculine in shape. There were few girls who could embrace the rough "street" iconography and unpolished directness associated with the music and hope to escape the crippling censure of their family, friends, neighborhood and school. . . . Yet girls were deeply involved in pop music. . . . With other options discouraged or barred, the girl fan was encouraged to organise her commitment around a romantic attachment to the star. The result: for the majority of girls, the sounds of pop were deeply associated with a largely hidden female "bedroom culture" of pin-ups and a Dansette record player. . . . It was this domestic space that was permitted rather than the public areas of streets, clubs, coffee bars and amusement arcades.   (42–44)

This phenomenon, however, was hardly limited during the period to the working-class British girls that Chambers and his sources note. In the United States and conceivably most other first-world nations, postwar social mores prepared young women for the conventions of compulsory heterosexuality at the end of adolescence yet simultaneously restricted any outward expression of desire or sexuality on their part. Accordingly, these least powerful members of society were effectively shoved into a secret and fantasy-filled dream world, the locus of which was the aforementioned bedroom—or, in more affluent circles, a rec room—where teenage girls, solitarily or collectively, engaged the angst of their precarious position in life.[12]

The gender dichotomies of late 1950s and 1960s rock culture are moreover hardly confined to behavior in response to the music. Rather, several very different gender-related strains developed in the 1950s: the macho tough guy, whose songs focus on sexual conquest (e.g., Jerry Lee Lewis); the pretty boy, whose songs are informed by a sentimental attachment to an often unappreciative female love object (e.g., Paul Anka); and, of course, that perennial standard, the yearning girl. As the 1960s dawned, certain aspects of this dichotomy grew more pronounced.[13] While the girl-group paeans to The Guy proliferated, guys such as the Beach Boys and Jan and Dean, while unquestionably heterosexual, concerned themselves in song with such apparently nonsexual yet utterly homosocial endeavors and obsessions as surfing, cars, and motorcycles. While occasional acknowledgment is given to the presumably daring girls on the periphery of these activities in the songs of these groups and others of their ilk, the Beach Boys explain (in "I Get Around") that "none of the guys go steady 'cause it wouldn't be right / to leave your best girl home on a Saturday night."[14] Rather, one presumes, the potential "best girl," who is nonetheless left alone by the "best guy" getting around with the other guys, retreats to fantasy of her own "bedroom culture," provided, of course, that she is considered by The Guy at all.[15] And it is this enclosed culture of girls pondering their limited options and sharing their hopes and fears with their female peers that is articulated in "Maybe" and the greater number of the girl-group recordings created during the ensuing decade.

The Chantels' success was, like nearly every aspect of girl culture, ephemeral; less than two years after "Maybe," Smith had departed, and the reorganized Chantels were history by 1961. In their wake, however, many more girl groups came to the fore—if, in many cases, for only the duration of a hit record or two—so many that during the earliest years of the 1960s more female-performed recordings placed on the pop charts than at any time before or after, and the creation and production of the girl-group sound became a veritable industry. The most prominent center of this industry was the Brill Building in New York City, a latter-day Tin Pan Alley where young songwriters individually and collectively turned out pop hits in massive quantities. Al Kooper, later and better known for his work with Bob Dylan, recalled the psychic drag act facing those who supplied the girl groups with their material: "Every day from ten to six we'd go in there and pretend that we were thirteen-year-old girls and write these songs. That was the gig."[16]

Arguably, in light of Kooper's comment, the songs given voice by the various girl groups were merely interiorizations of male-inscribed discourse and dictates on what constituted proper and acceptable (i.e., male-centered) conduct and thought on the part of the female sex. It is equally arguable that virtually no aspect of girl culture, given the social and economic dependence and powerlessness that characterized female adolescence in this prefeminist period, was completely female—or adolescent—in origin. Yet such arguments, interminable as they are, overlook the fact that the most significant Brill Building girl-group hits of the early 1960s were not, strictly speaking, male-authored; rather, they were the creations of three Jewish-American married couples barely out of their teens: Carole King and Gerry Goffin; Ellie Greenwich and Jeff Barry; and Cynthia Weil and Barry Mann. The crosscultural implications of the collaboration between Jewish songwriters and singers who were usually African-American are significant, particularly in the context of the then-nascent civil rights movement: "Suddenly, there was an interpollination of black voices with white melodies. . . . There were . . . black girls singing Jewish melodies that didn't quite work out; here was a new form of music. . . . Suddenly you had this dichotomy of cultures; and it worked, it worked perfectly."[17] Equally significant, however, was the further inculcation of white middle-class mores—already evident in the Chantels' recordings—in a traditionally black musical mode.[18] Mediated through the authorship (if not the authority) of the aforementioned young marrieds, wedlock became the common goal and greatest possible good in girl-group lyrics while the anxieties and contradictions of the quest for this exalted and presumably felicitous state informed their most frequently articulated plaints.

As was true of almost all aspects of life in the early 1960s, the manner in which young women were to achieve the goal of marriage was fraught with rules. That marriage was the expected end—often in every sense of the word—for the female adolescent was a given. In order to arrive at that state, she would have to make herself sexually attractive to her male peers (and sexually competitive with her female peers), yet she could not be sexual (or, for that matter, have sexuality) unless and until she reached the honeymoon suite. Conversely, given the double standard of the day, adolescent males were not subject to any such pressure to remain pure, nor was such emphasis on marriage as an ultimate goal part of their socialization; indeed, the reverse was true, as one can discern from most male-authored/male-performed rock recordings of this or any other period. Further, The Guy could easily dump a girl who wouldn't for a girl who would (although he wouldn't marry a girl who would, at least not willingly). Accordingly, teenage girls found themselves in a double bind, caught between the dictates of parents and society and the importunings of The Guy, even a triple bind, if one considers the girls' own, often barely defined or articulated desires. Yet the consequences of sexual transgression were dire. The lack of effective—much less accessible—means of birth control and the social ostracism that would result from unwanted pregnancy made the stakes particularly high for any young woman, as motherhood would virtually obviate her chances in the marriage market. (Except, of course, those cases in which a rushed and parentally enforced wedding designed to rescue respectability sent many a teen bride to the "Chapel of Love" well before her time. But this sort of short cut to the main goal, while utilized frequently enough, was never matter for song lyrics.) Therefore, for the girl seeking the grand prize in the nuptial sweepstakes—or, for that matter, mere social acceptability—reputation was of the utmost importance as an indicator of valuation in the marriage market or, as Gayle Rubin would have it, the "traffic in women."

The singular importance of reputation is obvious in the lyrics of numerous girl-group recordings. A case in point is the Angels' "My Boyfriend's Back," a song that provides a peculiar twist on the theme of fidelity to the absent boy so common at the time.[19] Here, the singer/persona chastens the miscreant who "hung around and bothered me every night" while the Boyfriend was gone and "said things that weren't very nice" (presumably about her lack of virtue) when she rejected him. For this major affront to a girl's means of social survival, the creep will pay the price upon the return of the Boyfriend, who's "gonna save my reputation" by administering a severe beating to the one who would have cuckolded him. Although the members of this particular white girl group presented themselves as semitough and somewhat tawdry, their song indicates the extreme importance of avoiding at all costs any speculation or gossip about promiscuity: marriage market values being what they were, even girls who came across as cheap could not afford to be seen as free.

No group, however, explored the multifaceted angst of female adolescent existence as thoroughly as the Shirelles, who, having stayed on the charts for nearly five years, had the greatest longevity of any girl group associated with the Brill Building song factory. Reputation, sexual deception, and potential disappointment ("Will You Love Me Tomorrow" and "Tonight's the Night"), absent guys ("Dedicated to the One I Love" and "Soldier Boy"), faithless guys ("Baby It's You"), guys who have lost interest ("A Thing of the Past" and "Don't Say Goodnight and Mean Goodbye"), jilting fiancés ("Big John"), and competition with other girls ("Stop the Music") were all within their scope. The Shirelles were unusually frank—for a girl group, at least—in their subject matter, most of which is conveyed by means of direct address to the party concerned, if not as an interior monologue. In this manner, they articulated the confused aspirations and apprehensions that many girls felt and would like to have been able to express but were too inhibited and repressed to do so. In this sense, the Shirelles functioned within the realm of girl culture—and this may well explain their ongoing popularity—as sympathetic surrogates for the average anxiety-ridden teenage girl.

But even the seemingly bold Shirelles never forgot that girls would still need to turn to other females at times for advice, reassurance, and even social correction. Their "Foolish Little Girl" is a dialogic mini-(soap) opera in which, after a spoken and smugly accusatory exposition, the eponymous persona/singer is scolded by the lead singer and the rest of the group because "you didn't want him when he wanted you," and, as he is about to marry someone else, she is warned not to disrupt the ceremony: "You'll keep quiet if you're smart."[20] But, of course, as the song's title affirms, she is far from smart; indeed, her apologia, which she asserts repeatedly to the other girls, is lamely banal: "But I love him." Yet what is a girl to do? Given the social and sexual pressures on the average female adolescent in the early sixties (which might in part account for the high incidence of Valium addiction among adult women in the following decade), one means of solace—if not exactly escape—was a retreat to the homosocial world of girl culture, where one could share one's distress and apprehensions with others who were experiencing or had experienced the same, a group that at times could include the originary source of female homosociality: Mom. And in "Mama Said," the Shirelles, who would seem to have left no stone of fretfulness unturned, defy the unappreciative boyfriend armed with a mother's words of wisdom: "She said, 'Someone will look at me like I'm looking at you, someday,'" and, when that occurs, the heroine will discover that "I don't want you any old way."[21] Thus, even on days when it seems that "chapel bells are calling for everybody but me," one may take comfort in Mama's advice: "Don't worry . . . there'll be days like this."

The Shirelles were hardly the only girl group to deal in such giving and getting of advice; indeed, a whole subgenre of songs devoted to admonition and counsel between girls (or between mother and daughter and subsequently passed on to other girls) flourished in the girl groups' heyday. If the fictive singer/persona's equally fictive mother warned her to hold out for true love and avoid the mere simulacrum (as in Jan Bradley's "Mama Didn't Lie"), so did she warn several hundred thousand (or, in the case of the Supremes' "You Can't Hurry Love," far more than a million) young female consumer/listeners of the same. Indeed, through its inherent homosociality, girl-group music had as one of its functions the expression of the altruistic impulse of any decent girl to protect all other members of macrocosmic and microcosmic girl culture from the dangers continually presented by the male sex and the desires thereof. Consequently, numerous girl-group songs warned against involvement with unfaithful and deceitful males (e.g., the Marvelettes' "Playboy" and "Too Many Fish in the Sea," the Chiffons' "Sweet Talkin' Guy"), commiserated that a good man is hard to find (e.g., the Velvelettes' "Needle in a Haystack"), offered redoubtable if unorthodox modes of truth detection (e.g., Betty Everett's "The Shoop Shoop Song [It's in His Kiss]," the Crystals' "Girls Can Tell"), propelled the reluctant headlong into "true romance" (e.g., the Exciters' "Tell Him," the Essex's "Easier Said Than Done"), advocated the termination of wrongheaded romance (e.g.,

Martha and the Vandellas' "You've Been in Love Too Long"), and consoled the losers in the ongoing game of love (e.g., the Jaynettes' "Sally Go 'Round the Roses").

Such songs would seem to present the drawing of us-against-them battle lines in the war of the sexes. Indeed, the stressful decorums of female adolescence and the pursuit of love might readily be said to involve more struggle than bliss, for, as the Supremes asserted in the title of one of their early recordings, one need only "Ask Any Girl" to discover what *every* girl, presumably, suffered every day. Accordingly, a retreat to the sympathetic, all-female world of girl culture would, in many cases, seem the safest and sanest route. Yet this too was fraught with taboos, ones so unspeakable that they had no place in girl-group music. Homosociality, as its critics have pointed out, is designed to privilege heterosexuality and thus must absolutely proscribe anything that even appears to be its opposite. In girl culture, where contact with other females is the quotidian, girls are effectively devalued among themselves; to 'like' another girl too much would devalue The Guy, who is valuable because he is inaccessible. Because sexual contact—that is, *hetero*sexual contact—is surrounded by so many restrictions and properly belongs only in the legally and religiously approved state of matrimony, it is therefore privileged and special. To like another girl too much—or to prefer the company of other girls over the stressful social conventions and interactions of heterosexual romance—is to deny the very specialness of heterosexuality and its ultimate stage, marriage. And to deny this is to upset the entire design of the family-based social order, if not that of Nature itself.

Regardless of her true feelings about her preordained biological destiny, the disempowered and dependent adolescent girl was in no position to pursue any such inclinations. Therefore, while girl culture and girl-group music provided no outlet for the exploration of this particular anxiety, it did allow for its disavowal. The boyfriend, no matter how diffident or distant, became the emblem of heterosexuality, a credential a girl could display for other girls' approval. It is small wonder, then, that so many Guy-oriented love songs are in the third, rather than second, person. They are not directed to the male love object himself but rather to the community of girls, represented by the backing singers, who must, through their affirmation, testify to the rightness, as it were, of the lead singer/persona's heterosexuality, albeit a rigidly virginal heterosexuality. Consequently, the early 1960s' pop charts were lavish with various female boasts about The Guy and the singer/persona's claim to him.

Remarkably, there is no one set of characteristics that makes an individual male desirable. He could be rich (the Ad Libs' "The Boy from New York City"), poor (the Crystals' "He's Sure the Boy I Love"), a nonconformist (the Crystals' "He's a Rebel"), lovably eccentric (the Murmaids' "Popsicles and Icicles"), almost superhuman (the Essex's "A Walkin' Miracle"), simply irresistible (the Raindrops' "Kind of Boy You Can't Forget"), utterly plain (Mary Wells's "My Guy"), sweet and kind (Darlene Love's "A Fine, Fine Boy"), or boorishly insensitive (Lesley Gore's "Maybe I Know"). All that was really required was that he was male and that the girl claimed her possession of him, as is evinced in what is perhaps the most abject of all girl-group recordings, the Chiffons' "I Have A Boyfriend."[22] Indeed, as long as one could display this evidence of sociosexual normalcy in the presence of other girls, little else seemed to matter.

Lest there be any doubt that these outpourings were for the benefit of other females, a certain dialogism developed in much girl-group music. While the Shirelles' previously discussed "Foolish Little Girl" dispensed admonition to a peer who had failed in her duty to cherish appropriately the boy she was so fortunate to have (an aberrant behavior in and of itself), a number of songs warned off other girls who might encroach too closely on the singer/persona's property. The Cookies' "Don't Say Nothin' Bad (About My Baby)" is constructed around the supporting vocalists' repetition of the title phrase and listing of accusations against the ne'er-do-well boyfriend, to which lead singer Earl-Jean McCree, the possessor of one of the lowest contralto voices in the pop music of the period, assertively responds, "He's good . . . to me, so you better shut your mouth."[23] Likewise, in the unambiguously titled "Keep Your Hands Off of My Baby," Little Eva informs the putative best friend that she is entitled to share her makeup, clothes, and other worldly goods freely, but female friendship has definite limits: "This boy is *mine*."[24]

That no mere girl could have priority over The Guy attained the condition of a law of nature, a truth universally acknowledged.[25] And just as the adolescent female could spend an incredible amount of her time interacting with and confiding in other girls but could not allow herself to like them too much, so might she purchase girl-group records in massive quantities and listen to them interminably yet never define herself as a fan of these female performers. Great adulation might be devoted to such vapid teen idols as Ricky Nelson, Frankie Avalon, Fabian, or others of their ilk, who could serve as surrogate love objects until a girl could find an appropriate boy to claim; members of girl groups, however, tended to be nameless and faceless. Critic Jim

Curtis speculates that this was the result of both the racism and the internalized sexism that then predominated:

> If the Teen Idols were all personality (i.e., television exposure) and no performance, the black girl groups . . . were all performance and no personality. They didn't become celebrities because they rarely appeared on *Bandstand*, and the teen magazines which reported what Fabian had for breakfast didn't feature the girl groups, both because they were girls and because they were black. Their records did well, nevertheless, in part because their lyrics dealt with the generalized situation of being a teenager in love.[26]

There can be no doubt that racism was a significant factor in the relative anonymity of girl-group vocalists in the years immediately preceding wide-reaching civil rights legislation. At the same time, while they might appear more often on teen-oriented television programs, even white girl-group members—as well as most of the white female solo performers of the day, with the possible exception of Lesley Gore—were given scant fan magazine coverage. Regardless of her race or her relative musical talent, the social inequality of the sexes was such that the female singer was insignificant in comparison with male stars, just as the average teenage girl was generally less valued by society, school, and family than were her brothers.

Perhaps no one understood—or exploited—this disparity between the sexes and the races more than the "Tycoon of Teen" Phil Spector, who presided over the last and possibly most decadent flourishing of girl-group music before the so-called British Invasion changed the face of pop music during the mid-1960s. Comprising equal parts musical ingenuity and megalomania, Spector was a self-created (if self-contradictory) Jewish-American rock-and-roll Wagner who concocted "little symphonies for the kids" performed by a recording studio repertory company of African-American Valkyries, Norns, and Rhinemaidens.[27] And, as far as Spector was concerned, these women—with the possible exception of his bride-to-be, Veronica Bennett, the lead singer of the Ronettes and later known as Ronnie Spector—were devoid of individual identity and thus interchangeable.[28] Thus, when Spector gained access to Gene Pitney's "He's a Rebel" and intuited a potential hit, he chose Darlene Love, surely the finest singer at his disposal, and her group, the Blossoms, to record it. But Love and company, while very much in demand as session singers, were virtually unknown to the public. Spector, in his capacities as both producer and label owner, therefore issued the record under the name of the Crystals, another group under his control who had already had two Top 20 hits, "There's No Other Like My Baby" and "Uptown," in the previous year. Spector's intuitions were correct, and "He's a Rebel" became his label's first recording to reach the number one position in the pop charts. But no member of the Crystals sang on what was to be "their" greatest hit—nor on its follow-up, "He's Sure the Boy I Love," which was also recorded by Love. Granted, the Crystals' lead singer, Barbara Alston (who would soon be replaced by Love soundalike La La Brooks on such hits as "Da Doo Ron Ron" and "Then He Kissed Me"), was no match for Love's vocal talents. Still, all the women involved were compromised artistically and economically by this name game, for which Spector offered the apologia that he owned the names of the groups under contract to him and could utilize them as he so chose. The echoes of institutional slavery inherent in this situation are nonetheless appallingly evident.

Given his extraordinary capacity for egocentricity and monomania, it perhaps stands to reason that Spector would have the capability to drive girl-group music to its penultimate extremes as a mode of expressing female teen distress and fantasy. Under his aegis, the Crystals, Darlene Love, and the Ronettes turned out, in the short span of two years, a prodigious number of odes (mostly written by Spector in collaboration with the recently married Jeff Barry and Ellie Greenwich) to that final goal of compulsory heterosexuality: marriage. "Why Don't They Let Us Fall in Love" and "So Young" (both by the Ronettes) and "Not Too Young to Get Married" (by Bob B. Soxx and the Blue Jeans, a studio group fronted by Love) remonstrated against parental restrictions against teen marriages. In the last recording, the singer/persona protests "What kinda difference can a few years make? I gotta have you now or my heart will break."[29] This would imply that having—whether it be having and holding (i.e., possessing) the other or, more prosaically and perhaps more precisely, having sex—could be achieved only through the social benedictions of marriage. In this sense, these songs fairly accurately represent the mores still in effect in the early 1960s. But as neither this song nor any other of its ilk bespeak the praises of marital responsibility, marriage can only be interpreted as an endless consummation of "true love" to which one's elders could pose no obstacles. Hence the young girl's frustrated sexual desires, which no respectable girl felt free to define as such, were reconfigured as merely a wish for that most proper and respectable condition for any female: that of the wife.

If this unprecedented musical obsession with marriage leaves the actual conditions of the matrimonial state a bit hazy, there is no lack of detail about the main *public* event involved. The Spector-Barry-Greenwich opus "Chapel of Love," originally recorded by Love and subsequently a hit for the Dixie Cups, tells little about the bridegroom, other than "Gee, I really love him."[30] But the grandiosity of the event is nonetheless apparent, so much so that even the pathetic fallacy can be brought to bear on the proceedings: "Spring is here, the sky is blue / the birds all sing as if they knew." The dream of the perfect end to girlhood is achieved, and it is so right, so *natural* in this construct, that even Nature itself conspires to make it perfect, the unknown groom notwithstanding. Nor is this anonymity peculiar to "Chapel of Love." Hearing Darlene Love's "(Today I Met) the Boy I'm Gonna Marry," the listener is struck by the singularity of the notion that a young woman could not only fall in love with but also automatically recognize her future husband at first sight. But even more singular are the quasi-religious manifestations that indicate that "This is it": "He smiled at me and the music started playing 'Here Comes the Bride' "; and, subsequently, "On my hand a band of gold appeared before me."[31] Lest we doubt the veracity of these aural and apparitional portents, she assures us that this "sweet sensation . . . wasn't just my imagination." As the song offers nothing by means of an actual description of The Boy himself, one might be hard pressed to understand exactly what it is about him in particular, preternatural revelations notwithstanding, that makes him *The Boy;* the clue, however, lies within the singer/persona's assertion that "He's all I've wanted all my life and even more." Like the groom in "Chapel of Love," he is only barely real, if real at all. He is the Apparitional Boy, a simulacrum, a composite photo that comprises all of the adolescent girl's fantasies about what the fairy tale bridegroom should be. And as he exists primarily in third person, he is the object of the female fantasy gaze, the token of exchange among girls.[32]

The supreme Spectorian expression of the apparitional boy between girls was saved, however, for his minion Ronnie and her group. From the beginning, the Ronettes had been different from the Crystals and the Blossoms; different, indeed, from virtually any other girl group. All members of the same family, seemingly identical, and racially indeterminate (a mixture of black, white, and native American), they were the products of a street-smart form of girl culture peculiar to the New York rock-and-roll scene, one in which a tough, aggressive homosocial inaccessibility allowed for the creation of their femmes fatales image. Charlotte Grieg notes that the Ronettes were "part of a female underground that still exists today: teenage girl clones who turn up to clubs in groups to devote their whole evening to serious dancing, who know that when all kitted out in exactly the same gear—however seductive or outrageous—they are totally unapproachable."[33] This inaccessibility, Grieg observes, made them "the first true girl pop stars to induce hysteria on a par with Elvis" (57), in this case with male fans, not the usual female ones. In their media enticement of the male fan/consumer, the Ronettes employed a rhetoric that deviated from that of their contemporaries: "Traditionally, the lead singer in the girl group told her friends about her latest boyfriend, in classic teenage girl-talk style; but Ronnie sang directly to the boy himself. . . . Here, for the first time, were unequivocal expressions of adoration addressed by girls to boys; this was seductive, but unnerving stuff. Since when had it been the girl's prerogative to implore 'Be My Baby' to the boy who took her fancy?" (59). But the Ronettes rage was short-lived; their last Top 40 hit, "Walking in the Rain," was recorded little more than a year after "Be My Baby" entered the Top 10. In this final magnum opus, the group reverts to the traditional girl-group formula. But with a vengeance: not only is the boy no longer the interlocutor of Ronnie's direct address but his only presence is in his very absence; Mr. Right, an extraordinary paragon with whom the singer/persona is already in love, has yet to be seen. This is apparent from the beginning: "I want him, and I need him / And someday, some way (whoa-oh-whoa-oh-oh) I'll meet him."[34] But if the bridegrooms and prospective bridegrooms in earlier Spector melodramas are ciphers, the fantasy lover is described in psychological and physical detail ("kinda shy, and real good-looking, too"); more specifically, he will be known to his lover by his penchant for "walking in the rain, / and wishing on the stars up above, / and being so in love." After a description of their projected life together, the song enters into an almost prototypical scenario of girl-group dialogism: the other Ronettes call out the names of supposedly real-life boys ("Johnny," "Bobby"), only to have each refuted ("No, no, he'll never do. . . . No, it isn't him, too"). All conclude, in harmony, that these young men are all unacceptable because "they would never . . . go walking in the rain" or participate in any of the other special, even fetishized activities. Thus, in the end, even the Ronettes indulge in the shared fantasy of The Boy who is not.

As if Spector realized that this was, in fact, the end of the Ronettes—and, for that matter, his own—hit-making career, he furnished "Walking in the Rain" with sound effects of thunderclaps and rain showers worthy of any demotic *Twilight of the Gods*. For it was, by then, 1964. John F. Kennedy, the president who embodied the ideals of the American Camelot, was recently dead, his assassination a media spectacle; an increasingly unpopular war was escalating in Vietnam; and the Beatles and their British colleagues had begun to reshape U.S. perceptions of popular music. Life was no longer so simple, and young women began to have inklings—and so popular music told them—that there were other possibilities besides going to the chapel and getting married. As the ending roar of thunder resolves itself in "Walking in the Rain" and the recording begins to fade out, Ronnie moans for her yet-to-materialize love, "I've been wishing and hoping. . . ." This concluding phrase, whether intentionally or not, is a curious allusion to a record breaking onto the U.S. charts in September 1964, just as "Walking in the Rain" was being recorded, a recording by the Beatles' leading female contemporary, one that took all the conventions of girl-group music and subverted them thoroughly and permanently.

"Wishin' and Hopin', " Dusty Springfield's cover version of a minor hit by Dionne Warwick, herself a former second-string Shirelle, would seem to be, on the surface at least, just another girl-group advice song. Indeed, Springfield modeled her vocal style primarily after that of black American girl-group singers.[35] But the advice goes against the grain of fantasy heretofore the norm: "You won't get him thinkin' and a-prayin', wishin' and a-hopin.' "[36] Moreover, in this pre-Pill era, it is incredibly *bad* advice: "Just do it, and after you do you will be his." This was startling stuff, indeed; three decades before it became a commercial buzz phrase, every schoolgirl knew full well what unspeakable activity "just do it" signified. Even more incongruously, Springfield, though a true devotee of American soul music, was white, British, and queer: the complete antithesis of everything associated with the girl-group ethos. Issued by such a spokeswoman, then, the advice put forth in "Wishin' and Hopin' " might be subversive, but it was probably better not taken seriously; indeed, it can be seen as an early example of the sort of queer camp that would become more commonplace—and subsume girl-group music—in the techno-pop eighties.[37]

Although the Beatles themselves covered girl-group songs such as "Chains," "Boys," and "Baby It's You" on their first album, they are often cited as a causal factor in bringing about the end of the girl-group era. This, however, is an oversimplification. As performer/songwriters, the Beatles were among the first to obviate the need for song factories such as the Brill Building. Moreover, as the sixties progressed, the Barry-Greenwich and Goffin-King songwriting partnerships that created the messages of true love and eternal bliss through marriage were terminated—ironically—by divorce, just as the marriage of Phil Spector and Ronnie Bennett effectively ended the Ronettes' career.

Still, in the transitional year 1964, a unique if ephemeral quartet of schoolgirls from Queens rose meteorically to the top of the charts, and in their proverbial fifteen minutes of fame, the Shangri-Las pushed girl-group sensibility to its outer limits. Protégées of Spector wannabe George "Shadow" Morton (who, like Spector, collaborated with Barry and Greenwich in supplying his group with songs), they specialized in the performance of girl-talk dialogistics—spoken bits of conversation between group members interpolated into the song itself—against a backdrop of gothic terror displaced onto a contemporary urban, working-class setting with an ample dose of soap opera sensationalism mixed in for good measure. The elements of advice and the shared male fantasy object were all there, but the advice was either poorly heeded or of no avail in a world in which unsympathetic parents and, by extension, society at large conspired to keep the teen heroine from redeeming through her love the street-tough boy of her desires. ("He's good bad, but he's not evil," we are assured in "Give Him a Great Big Kiss," their only decidedly cheerful hit.)[38] But these stylistic innovations and the girls' "tough chick" posturings were not enough to give the Shangri-Las their permanent place in rock history; rather, their most memorable accomplishment was the incorporation of necrophilia into the already stale convention of fantasy boys shared among girls.

Death played a substantial role in much of the Shangri-Las' output, usually in some combination with parents, guilt, manipulation, and blame. In "Give Us Your Blessing," for example, an eloping couple is are killed in a car crash because of their emotional distress over parental disapprobation, while in "I Can Never Go Home Any More," the singer/persona melodramatically narrates her history, in which she fights with her mother and runs away with The Guy (who is the focus of the mother-daughter discord) but soon falls out with the boyfriend, only to find that her mother has died in her absence, presumably of a broken heart. But while these morbid offerings are all variations on the typically adolescent "Imagine how you'd feel if I died" fantasy, the Shangri-Las' biggest hit, "The Leader of the Pack," is structured around The Dead Guy as fantasy object of exchange among girls. The recording begins with almost stereotypical—and spoken—adolescent female gossip and speculation about "Betty," the lead singer/persona, and her relationship with the eponymous biker "Jimmy" ("Is she really going out with him?"), until the interlocutors see "Betty" and turn the questions on her. In this present-tense discourse, it is obvious that they are unaware of Jimmy's current condition, as they ask "Is he picking you up after school today?"[39] It would seem unlikely that they could be so completely unaware of an event as spectacular as that which is about to be related (or that "Betty" would be in school immediately thereafter, even though she sings in the end that "in school they all stop and stare / I can't hide the tears, but I don't care"), but this dialogue is merely intended to function as an incentive to narrative. Even the anachronistic sequence of events is part of the shared necrophiliac fantasy; what matters is not that "the Leader of the Pack" is "gone gone gone," but rather that the singer/persona is able to re-create (if not actually create), with an immediacy augmented by overpowering sound effects, a tale of parental interference and bigotry ("They said he came from the wrong side of town," "They told me he was bad / but I knew he was sad") and the literally fatal consequences thereof. After Jimmy's crash reverberates through the track—punctuated by the singer's shouts "Look out! Look out!"—all the girls join together in a hymnlike apotheosis to his memory. Yet, peculiarly, here and at various other points in the recording, the enjoyment of distress is more obvious than the distress itself. Indeed, enjoyment of distress plays a significant role in the exchanged fantasy, for his dying young and handsome only enhances the romantic hero's value, not only for the singer/persona but for her backing vocalist peers (and, by extension, her commercial audience) as well: "The leader of the pack's demise . . . had the added advantage of sustaining true romance indefinitely. For the teenage girl, the resolution of love was still marriage; and yet this was unlikely to work out if you fell in love with the bad boy. How much better to have him dead and maintain everlasting adoration for him that way."[40] In effect, the Shangri-Las presented what is most likely the furthest extent to which such exchanged adolescent romantic-sexual fantasies could be taken. The consummation so dreaded by the parents can never occur, thus what might have happened can always remain in the realm of the purely imaginary. Moreover, so extravagant is the singer/persona's scenario that any other girl will be hard pressed to top it; therefore the other girls can only participate in the vicarious pleasure afforded by empathetic (if not sympathetic) participation, a demotic twist on the Burkean sublime that encompasses homosocial envy and desire.

While "The Leader of the Pack" was, in the short run, a huge success, its extraordinary intensity and level of fantasy and distress were far too overwhelming for anyone—whether songwriter, performer, or consumer—to endure, much less sustain, for very long. The Shangri-Las' subsequent attempts to take pathos and morbidity to the top of the charts were increasingly futile, and the group itself became just one more casualty in the massive extinction that had struck Brill Building pop by 1965. Yet if the Spector-Barry-Greenwich / Goffin-King girl-group ethos came to a sudden end at mid-decade, it is nonetheless overly simplistic to attribute its demise solely to the British Invasion, for shifts in culture at large had already begun to obviate many of its most cherished assumptions. Nor is the oft-stated claim that girl-group music ended when the British arrived even accurate, for, after the Beatles, the second most popular group during the mid- to late sixties was, in fact, a U.S. girl group. The Supremes, however, along with other Motown girl groups and singers such as Martha and the Vandellas, Mary Wells, the Marvelettes, the Velvelettes, Kim Weston, and later Gladys Knight and the Pips, marked nothing less than a paradigm shift in girl-group music, both in terms of racial autonomy and thematics.

Under the auspices of Berry Gordy, the Motown studios and artists reconfigured girl groups as part of soul music, a specifically African-American mode of cultural expression. Whereas previously Jewish-American songwriters, often young married couples, provided material performed by young women who were usually (but not always) African-American, Gordy and his cohorts produced recordings by black groups of songs written by in-house teams of black (and almost always male) songwriters. This shift in song authorship and record production, indicative as it is of mid-sixties African-American self-determination, pride, and entrepreneurship, is significant in and of itself. But this was not merely a matter of transforming girl-group music into a specifically "black thing." Rather, as Smokey Robinson, Mickey Stevenson, Marvin Gaye, and the teams of Brian Holland, Lamont Dozier, and Edward Holland and Nikolas Ashford and Valerie Simpson displaced Phil Spector, Shadow Morton, Ellie Greenwich and Jeff Barry, Carole King and Gerry Goffin, and Cynthia Weil and Barry Mann as the girl-group songwriters du jour, so did the rhetoric and the most elemental concerns of the songs themselves change. To wit, girl-group music began to show its age, to move away from adolescence and out of the virginal bedroom site of girl culture into an active realm of heterosexuality.

The earliest Motown girl-group recordings were contemporary with the Brill Building hits and in many cases demonstrate parallel concerns; even so, their initially minor differences anticipate later changes. The Marvelettes were, in all likelihood, the queens of the advice song, yet such songs as "Too

Many Fish in the Sea," which begins "Look here, girls, take my advice" and asserts "Ain't gonna love nobody who don't love me," puts forth a sense of control, self-awareness, and pride that is sorely missing from the many self-sacrificial, self-abjecting, or self-deluding offerings of the Brill Building chanteuses.[41] The Supremes, on the other hand, began their recording career in 1961 with the lugubrious "I Want a Guy," an almost stereotypical fantasy of The-Guy-shared-among-girls, but by 1965, the group had recorded a song that not only stands as a refutation of the conventions of the advice song but also marks a rejection of the girl-culture homosociality that configures The Guy primarily as an object of discourse.

"Back in My Arms Again" details a reunion between lovers—and here, unlike most previous examples, certain ambiguous phrases allow for the interpretation of this being a nonplatonic situation—separated by "friend's advice" that "heartaches he'll bring someday." The other girls' best intentions notwithstanding, the singer/persona complains that "all advice ever got me / was many long and sleepless nights." After affirming the superiority of the lover who leaves her "so satisfied," there is a remarkable shift into song as metafiction, as Diana Ross, in the lead-singer/persona role, begins to "dish" her fellow Supremes—by name—as the implicitly jealous disrupters of the "rightful" connection between male and female, girls whose own misery loves company: Mary, we are told, has no authority in love matters as "she lost her love so true," while Flo, on the other hand, "don't know, 'cause the boy she loves is a Romeo." Some might, of course, see in this oddly self-reflexive passage a reflection of the interpersonal strife that would, before long, fragment the most popular girl group of the era, leaving Florence Ballard out in the cold to die, eventually, as a welfare mother while Diana Ross set out in search of solo stardom and Mary Wilson struggled valiantly to keep the group name viable through numerous personnel changes well into the 1970s. But on a larger cultural level, "Back in My Arms Again" signaled the twilight of the girl group as a primarily homosocial signifier, for here an absolute put-down is administered to other girls and their culture of discourse about The Boy. To have him "back in my arms again," as opposed to a fantasy somewhere out in the ozone, is, we are told, what matters now.[42]

When we consider the demographics of the record-buying public, the rhetorical and thematic shifts seen here are hardly surprising. By the mid- to late sixties, many of the Baby Boom generation that formed the biggest part of the girl groups' audience, were in their late teens or early twenties, then an age at which many married and many more embarked on the sexual experimentation for which the decade is, to a great extent, remembered. Moreover, these particular years witnessed the disputation and disruption of previously unchallenged social mores, not the least of which were those concerning sex and sexuality. Recordings by Motown girl groups over the decade show an acute awareness of the manner in which the times were a-changin.' Of the music of Martha and the Vandellas in particular, Charlotte Grieg notes that "there was a contained sexuality . . . that could not be ignored": "The Vandellas songs were much more adult than those of the average girl group and they had an intense, obsessive quality that sometimes made them a little too close to lowdown R&B for comfort. . . . This was not the excitement of teenage romance, nor even the knowing narrative of the sophisticated, independent young woman; it was more the primitive cry of a human being lost and hurt and in the grip of a sexual obsession."[43] As in the lives of listeners, so in popular art: the focus of obsession had shifted from fantasized desexualized romance to sex itself. As early as 1963, Martha and the Vandellas were subverting—as opposed to the Supremes' refuting—the girl-group ethos. In "(Love Is Like a) Heat Wave," clearly a song about sexual awakening, the discourse of advice and interaction among girls is still very much in place. The singer/persona states her problem to the other girls: "Whenever I'm with him, something inside / starts to burning and I'm filled with desire."[44] While the first verse alludes to her concern with sin and immorality ("Could it be the devil in me?"), the explicitly physical symptoms she details force an almost uncomfortable analogy between sexual longing and disease ("Has high blood pressure got a hold on me?"); still, she considers the alternative that perhaps it is only "the way love's supposed to be." After her climactic cry of "yeah, yeah, yeah, yeah!" the other girls intervene with words of encouragement that are sung with an exuberant passion that insinuates their vicarious thrill in their friend's sexual frenzy: "Don't pass up this chance, / it sounds like a true romance." "True romance," however, is hardly the exact term for what this "sounds like." Indeed, while it never quite gets to that dangerous point of demarcation, this shared sexual frenzy among girls comes close to the thin line between the homosocial and homoerotic voyeurism.

Even so, by 1966 Martha and the Vandellas could sing "I'm Ready for Love," another song of sexual awakening but one that evinces no need to consult or share with other girls, a song that makes it quite clear through its direct address that the other girls have nothing to do with what the singer/persona has in mind. And if we need any further indication of how far girl-group music could move away from its original point of view, by 1968, in

"Love Child," the Supremes (now Diana Ross and the Supremes, as if to refute the egalitarian structures and lack of individual identity peculiar to the earlier girl groups) could give a pragmatic social reason for just saying no, one that had little to do with reputation, marriage marketability, or morals; rather, a black child born out of wedlock in this country would be doomed, almost inevitably, to a life of poverty. The song's perspective is a bit conservative compared to that of many of its contemporary recordings and might even seem a bit disingenuous, given the seeming pervasiveness of the Pill by that time; still, even after thirty years, its observations remain sadly true for many such children. All the same, this was a long, long way from "Will You Love Me Tomorrow?"

Whatever happened to the girl groups? One suggestion is that they faded away ingloriously, beginning with the decline and fall of the Brill Building in the sixties and into a final, decadent twilight in the Saturday night fever of the seventies. Surely, the post–Diana Ross Supremes, after a brief flourishing at the beginning of the seventies, went that way, while transient ensembles such as the Three Degrees, Sister Sledge, the outrageous LaBelle, and the cartoonish Weather Girls provided dance music for a predominantly gay male audience during the disco decade. The white girl groups, by contrast, evolved into girl *bands*, beginning with female singers fronting male bands, first in late-sixties West Coast psychedelic groups (Grace Slick with Jefferson Airplane, Janis Joplin with Big Brother and the Holding Company) and subsequently quirky Euro-pop ensembles (Mariska Veres with the Dutch group, Shocking Blue; Agnetha Faltskog and Anni-Frid Lyngstad fronting Sweden's Abba). By the 1980s girl bands such as the GoGo's and the Bangles were doing it for themselves, thus obviating the heretofore requisite male backing band. For African-American female ensembles, rap and hip-hop offered new and very different possibilities by the 1990s. At century's end, groups such as Britain's multiracial Spice Girls might appear to be little more than the latest repackaging of the original paradigm, yet their cheerfully aggressive stance—as opposed to the tortured toughness of, for instance, the Shangri-Las—their extensive and devout following composed mainly of prepubescent girls, and their putative endorsement of "Girl Power" would suggest that any resemblance is purely superficial. In effect, all the newer formations and the music they have created are a far cry from the girl groups of the early 1960s and the sentiments of "Chapel of Love."

I would suggest that the last girl group, in the old original sense, is Bananarama. By their own description three girls who "could sing in tune and everything but that was about it," Bananarama were the protégées of the British pop production team Stock/Aitken/Waterman, the 1980s successors to the music factory tradition of Phil Spector and Berry Gordy.[45] The SAW philosophy of music is, to say the least, simple: as Pete Waterman has stated, "Pop isn't about being intellectual, about slashing your wrists and telling everybody how awful it is. It's not about politics either. . . . No, it's about teenage romance, about boys and girls, about going out and having fun and falling in love" (193). This perspective—anachronistic, perhaps, by the mid-1980s—is very much in line with Brill Building and Motown girl group music; it is hardly surprising, then, that Bananarama's hits include cover versions of the Velvelettes' "He Was Really Saying Somethin' " and the Supremes' "Nathan Jones," as well as remakes of the Beatles' "Help!" and, as their biggest hit, Shocking Blue's "Venus."

Yet, this anachronism in production and material aside, Bananarama, as even the group's name indicates, are a product of 1980s' postmodern techno-pop in whose hands the sensibilities of 1960s are reduced to the condition of pastiche. The outrageous metaphorical conceits of their "Love in the First Degree," for example, can hardly be construed as sincere (if abject) sentiment but are instead a manifestation of a camp imagination. And if Bananarama seemed in their public image little more than "three jolly bimbos" (189). The appearance belies the self-analytical and even dark side of their retro-sixties performativity. "Cruel Summer" might be seen as a revision of Carole King's "It Might As Well Rain Until September," inasmuch as they both present the scenario of a girl left behind for the summer. But while King's opus falls back on bathos and the pathetic fallacy to describe a season made obsessively desolate by the absence of The Guy, the cruelty of "Cruel Summer" is far more diffuse in its origins. The sinister minor chords underscore that "it's a cruel summer now you're gone," although who is gone (possibly "my friends," who are mentioned) is never quite made clear, and the cruelty of the heat, dryness, and city life seems to be simply that: cruel in and of themselves, rather than emblematic pathetic fallacies indicative of separation from the love object.[46] As such, "Cruel Summer" is as much about the stresses of postmodern urban life as it about romantic angst. Moreover, if "Walking in the Rain" and various other Spector-Greenwich-Barry creations were about longing for the actualization of fantasy, Bananarama's "Robert DeNiro's Waiting" cynically posits, amid some very forthright representations of the terrors of the adolescent female condition, that the simulacrum is far better than the real thing.

But if Bananarama were, in fact, a camp pastiche of sixties girl-group style and sensibility, they are, I believe, an accurate indicator of where the last vestiges of girl-group culture has gone. As part of the second British Invasion of the 1980s, Bananarama were partakers in the greater project of gender bending that characterized this particular trend. Among their covers of sixties' U.S. pop was Steam's "Na Na Hey Hey (Kiss Him Goodbye)." As the gendered pronouns remain unchanged from the original male-performed version, a question inevitably arises: is this a girl asking a guy to leave a guy for her, or is she asking a girl to leave a guy for her? Considering that all three members of Bananarama were (along with Boy George's erstwhile "friend," the female impersonator, Marilyn) among the various "girlfriends" in the Eurythmics' video "Who's That Girl?" (in which Annie Lennox, attired as a sixties' chanteuse, eventually proves that "sisters are doing it for themselves" by becoming her own boyfriend), we must come to the conclusion that there can be no definite answer to the question, except that this is girl-group music in a world in which girls are not necessarily girls, or biologically female, or, for that matter, straight.

It is hardly a coincidence, then, that the sixties' girl groups who have managed to stay together for thirty years and still make the circuit of oldies-but-goodies shows derive much of their revenue from playing gay clubs. Moreover, if anyone, post Bananarama, still relies on the ethos of the girl groups, particularly in terms of anxiety-ridden lyrics of unrequited, fantasized, or forbidden love, it is the various and predominantly British gay male pop bands and singers of the eighties and nineties, such as Culture Club, Erasure, Jimmy Somerville, Morrissey, and Marc Almond, among others. Camp hyperbole notwithstanding, such a translation of these modes across lines of gender and sexuality is really quite understandable, for who, besides the present-day queer audience, understands the need for fantasy projection and the desire for the inaccessible, for The Person (if not exactly The Guy) who has yet to appear? For who can allow themselves to engage in what would seem adolescent sentiments more than those to whom society would deny the full rights and privileges of adulthood, those whom society would leave stranded in a permanent adolescence? For who wants to go to the chapel and get married more than those to whom such privilege is legally denied? Perhaps at the fin de millennium, these are no longer the anxieties of teenage girls, who must find girl-group music archaic and uncool by comparison with that of female alternative rock bands. But as long as social mores situate anyone in a subject position analogous to the unseemly, disempowered, and, indeed, feminized one endured by adolescent females in early 1960s, we can be sure that girl-group music will continue to exist, if only to express the everyday distress of that condition.

NOTES

1. I would like to thank Robert Arambel, Joe Bristow, Pat Cramer, Gary Dyer, Andrew Furer, and Colleen Jaurretche for their input while this essay was in progress. My particular gratitude, of many years' standing, goes to my sister Kate Lanehart, who, in those distant days, introduced me to girl group music, and to Sheila Rhodes, who, on many a bad day in graduate school, sat and sang these songs with me, demonstrating that "girl culture" and the better aspects of its concomitant homosociality can extend far beyond adolescence.

2. I use the term "girl group" throughout this essay in the same manner as do most popular music critics and historians; that is, I use it to denote a particular genre of early 1960s pop / rock that was usually—but not always—performed by ensembles composed of adolescent female vocalists who neither played instruments nor, in most cases, composed the material they performed. Accordingly, their function was interpretive and performative rather than creative. The use of the term, however, is extended by many music historians (including Charlotte Grieg, Gillian G. Gaar, and Lucy O'Brien) and anthologizers of reissued girl-group compilation recordings to include female solo vocalists (e.g., Little Eva, Lesley Gore, Mary Wells) whose style approximated that of the girl groups, as well as vocal combos with female lead singers supported by male (or male and female) backing vocalists (e.g., Gladys Knight and the Pips, the Orlons, the Essex, the Jellybeans). The term "compulsory heterosexuality" is taken from Adrienne Rich's influential essay "Compulsory Heterosexuality and Lesbian Existence," in *Powers of Desire: The Politics of Sexuality*, ed. Ann Snitow, Christine Stansell, and Sharon Thompson (New York: Monthly Review Press, 1983), pp. 177–205. It is used here in a self-explanatory manner.

3. For a provocative linguistic and grammatical analysis of girl-group song lyrics, particularly the use of pronouns therein, see Barbara Bradby, "Do-Talk and Don't-Talk: The Division of the Subject in Girl-Group Music," in *On Record: Rock, Pop, and the Written Word*, ed. Simon Frith and Andrew Goodwin (New York: Pantheon, 1990), pp. 341–68.

4. "(Love Is Like a) Heat Wave" has been reissued on *Martha Reeves and the Vandellas: The Ultimate Collection* (Motown 314 530 405 2, 1998); the Crystals' "Da Doo Ron Ron" on *The Best of the Crystals* (ABKCO, 1992); Betty Everett's "The Shoop Shoop Song" and the Chiffons' "He's So Fine" on *The Best of the Girl Groups, Volume 1* (Rhino 70988, 1990); and the Angels' "My Boyfriend's Back" on *The Best of the Girl Groups, Volume 2* (Rhino 70989, 1990).

5. What appears here is a very brief summation of the development of the concept of homosociality, primarily within literary and cultural criticism. As such, it cannot possibly do justice either to the critics who have informed our present understanding of this concept or to the complexities of their work. For a more comprehensive view of the discourse of homosociality, see Gayle Rubin, "The Traffic in Women: Notes Toward a Political Economy of Sex," in *Toward an Anthropology of Women*, ed. Rayna Reiter (New York: Monthly Review Press, 1975), pp. 157–210; and Luce Irigary, *This Sex Which Is Not One*, trans. Catherine Porter with Carolyn Burke (Ithaca, NY: Cornell University Press, 1985), pp. 170–97.

6. See René Girard, *Deceit, Desire, and the Novel: Self and Other in Literary Structure*, trans. Yvonne Freccero (Baltimore: Johns Hopkins University Press, 1965), pp. 1–52.

7. See Eve Kosofsky Sedgwick, *Between Men: English Literature and Male Homosocial Desire* (New York: Columbia University Press, 1985), pp. 1–5, 21–27; and idem, *Epistemology of the Closet* (Berkeley: University of California Press, 1990), pp. 182–212. Terry Castle has subsequently provided a paradigm for a peculiarly female form of a homosocial (and latently homosexual) exchange of men. See Castle, *The Apparitional Lesbian: Female Homosexuality and Modern Culture* (New York: Columbia University Press, 1993), pp. 67–91. More recently, in my own work, I enlarge on the work of these critics in constructing a model of female homosociality. As I have observed, however, as women have been traditionally displaced from positions of economic or social power, their ability to "exchange men" is limited to the purely personal: to their immediate environment rather than society at large. See Patricia Juliana Smith, *Lesbian Panic: Homoeroticism in Modern British Women's Fictions* (New York: Columbia University Press, 1997), pp. 1–16.

8. Charlotte Grieg, *Will You Still Love Me Tomorrow? Girl Groups from the 50s On* (London: Virago, 1989), p. 12.

9. The Chantels, "Maybe," words and music by Richard Barrett, reissued on *The Best of the Chantels* (Rhino 70954, 1990).

10. Grieg, *Will You Still Love Me Tomorrow?* p. 12.

11. Iain Chambers, *Urban Rhythms: Pop Music and Pop Culture* (New York: St. Martin's, 1985), p. 41.

12. But even if the primary locus of girl culture was the girl's bedroom or some other domestic space set aside for adolescent female socialization, the privileged locus was nonetheless the party or the dance where, at least in theory, the sexes intermingled, even if only in the homosocial manner described above. The significance of the party as a site at which teenage girls' psychodramas could be enacted is evident in such recordings as the Shirelles' "Stop the Music" (reissued on *Anthology [1959 1964]* [Rhino R2-75897, 1994]), discussed below; Lesley Gore's "It's My Party (And I'll Cry If I Want To)" and its sequel "Judy's Turn to Cry" (reis-

sued on *It's My Party: The Mercury Anthology* [Mercury 532517, 1996], which, respectively, provide narratives of boyfriend lost and boyfriend regained, both within the context of a party; Claudine Clark's "Party Lights" (reissued on *The Best of the Girl Groups, Volume 1*), which bewails maternal prohibitions that prevent the protagonist from attending a party within visual and aural range; and the Sensations' "Let Me In," *Cruisin' 1962* (Increase, 1962), which protests exclusion from this site of romantic adventure. Moreover, girl-group music included a number of songs that created or supplemented the newest dance, generally relying on the rhyming words "dance" and "romance" to make their point (e.g., the Orlons' "Wah Watusi" [out of print]; Little Eva's "The Locomotion" [reissued on *The Best of the Girl Groups, Volume 2*]; and dance queen Dee Dee Sharp's "Mashed Potato" [reissued on *Dee Dee Sharp Gamble, Cameo Parkway Sessions* (London LP 8514, 1979)]; "Gravy [on My Mashed Potato]" [reissued on *Dee Dee Sharp Gamble, Cameo Parkway Sessions*]; and "[Get on My Pony and] Ride" [out of print]).

13. It is worth noting that during this period a sort of middle ground of gender ambiguity centered on male hysteria/sensibility existed. In particular, singers endowed with quasi-operatic vocal ranges and techniques, such as Roy Orbison, Gene Pitney, and Jay Black (of Jay and the Americans), gave expression to melodramatic outbursts of overwrought male emotionality that had few analogues in female-performed pop music, other than Connie Francis and, somewhat later, British pop star Dusty Springfield (see note 35 below).

14. The Beach Boys, "I Get Around," words and music by Brian Wilson, on *Endless Summer* (Capitol C2-46467, 1974).

15. Ironically, the Beach Boys' Brian Wilson suggests, in his song "In My Room" (on *Endless Summer*) that even macho dudes need "a world where I can go and tell my secrets to." There are moreover some connections between some of Wilson's songs of male hypersensitivity and Phil Spector's anthems of romantic decadence. The Beach Boys' "Don't Worry, Baby," which details the anxieties of a strung-out young man who can only be quieted by a calming young woman (who repeats the title phrase to him), underwent a significant gender transition in its history. The song was originally written for the Ronettes (presumably Ronnie Spector—then Veronica Bennett—would perform the part of the reassuring girlfriend) but was rejected by the group's handler, Phil Spector. Later, Wilson and his group would have a hit with "I Can Hear Music," a song written by Spector, Ellie Greenwich, and Jeff Barry, which had previously been a minor hit for the Ronettes.

16. Quoted in Robert Palmer, *Rock & Roll: An Unruly History* (New York: Harmony, 1995), p. 35.

17. Grieg, *Will You Still Love Me Tomorrow?* p. 37.

18. A by-product of this blurring of cultural and ethnic boundaries is the great difference in the semiotic modes of presentation employed by white girl groups as opposed to their black counterparts. Black groups took great pains to appear ladylike in their manner of dress (i.e., matching semiformal attire) and photo-

graphic poses; indeed, Motown Records founder Berry Gordy, who envisioned his company as "a conduit for upward mobility," established a charm school for his label's girl groups and female soloists so as "to smooth out the 'street' from [the] girls" (Lucy O'Brien, *She Bop: The Definitive History of Women in Rock, Pop, and Soul* [Harmondsworth: Penguin, 1995], p. 77). Charlotte Grieg posits moreover that "the emphasis on desexualized romance and marriage" not only "made the music respectable and acceptable to the white market" but also "was especially important to black teenage girls . . . because it showed that they were no longer outside the mores of white society. Marriage for them . . . represented a step up" (*Will You Still Love Me Tomorrow?* p. 61). But while the contact with white middle-class culture and mores signified upward mobility and social acceptability for many black performers, many white girl groups who appropriated elements of black girl-group musical styles for their acts (e.g., the Shangri-Las, the Angels) presented themselves in a manner that might best be described as either latently or blatantly sluttish. Casually and/or suggestively attired, they suggested that such contact with African-American culture, albeit a very distant one, signified downward social mobility (and respectability) for white girls. It is worth noting, too, that while white female singers certainly had a significant portion of what might be generically termed as girl-group hits, such performers were more often solo acts (e.g., Lesley Gore, Marcie Blane, Peggy March) rather than members of groups. Thus the more socially privileged white girls, while themselves greatly restricted by the circumscriptions of the male-dominated rock world, were not only allowed more latitude and given greater visibility (i.e., on television and in fan magazines) than their black sisters but also enjoyed, to an extent, individual identities not granted the quasi-anonymous group members, who, ironically, routinely backed them on records. On white girl groups and female solo performers of the early 1960s, see Grieg, *Will You Still Love Me Tomorrow?* pp. 69–84.

19. The Angels, "My Boyfriend's Back," words and music by Robert Feldman, Gerald Goldstein, and Richard Gotteher (reissued on *The Best of the Girl Groups, Volume 2*). The absence of the male object of desire, a major trope in girl-group music as far back as the Chantels' "Maybe" is one more aspect of the female homosocial exchange of the fantasized male presence. Its popularity in the early 1960s can be attributed in part to the concept then still generally in force that college education was more important for young men, who would have to support families, than it was for girls, who only wanted their MRS. degree. Equally significant was the then-mandatory military service, which took most young men away from their female admirers for considerable lengths of time. Given the social mores of compulsory heterosexuality I have just outlined, devotion to a love object in uniform was an incredibly useful means of social conformity; not only would one have a love object to use as currency in the verbal/fantasy exchange with other females, but one would also appear to be doing her patriotic duty by reminding the boy of American values, while, simultaneously, the dan-

gers inherent in sexual surrender were at as great a remove as the boy himself. The Shirelles' "Soldier Boy" (reissued on *The Very Best of the Shirelles*) and Diane Renay's "Navy Blue" (reissued on *Growin' Up Too Fast: The Girl Group Anthology* [Polygram 528171, 1996]) are notable examples of fidelity-to-the-absent-boyfriend songs with specifically military themes; others, such as Darlene Love and the Blossoms' "Wait Til My Bobby Gets Home" (*The Best of Darlene Love* [ABKCO 7213-2, 1992]) the Shirelles' "Dedicated to the One I Love" (reissued on *The Very Best of the Shirelles*), Martha and the Vandellas' "I Promise to Wait My Love" (reissued on *The Very Best of the Shirelles*); the Marvelettes' "Please Mr. Postman" (reissued on *The Marvelettes: Greatest Hits* [Motown 34763-5180-2, 1966]), and (conceivably) the Shangri-Las' "Remember (Walking in the Sand)" (reissed on *Best of the Shangri-Las* [Polygram 532371, 1996]) specify no reason for the absence and thus can be applied to any and every female fan/consumer's missing boy fantasy/angst.

20. The Shirelles, "Foolish Little Girl," words and music by Gerry Goffin and Carole King, reissued on *Anthology [1959 1964]*.

21. The Shirelles, "Mama Said," words and music by Luther Dixon, reissued on *Anthology [1959 1964]*.

22. Another competitor for this dubious distinction is "I Sold My Heart to the Junkman" by Patti LaBelle and the Bluebells, a previous incarnation of the 1970s' disco-diva girl group LaBelle.

23. The Cookies, "Don't Say Nothin' Bad (About My Baby)," words and music by Gerry Goffin and Carole King, on *The Best of the Girl Groups, Volume 2*.

24. Little Eva, "Keep Your Hands Off of My Baby," words and music by Gerry Goffin and Carole King, reissued on *The Colpix-Dimension Story* (Rhino 71650, 1996).

25. A curious attempt to circumvent this law may be found in the long-suppressed 1965 recording "You Don't Know" (reissued on *The Best of the Girl Groups, Volume 2*), written and sung by Ellie Greenwich, the supplier of hit songs to virtually every pre-Motown girl group. In this piece, the singer/persona atypically addresses the male love object, who is already claimed by the singer/persona's best (female) friend. Although madly in love with him, she refutes him and elects to suffer in secret for the sake of the friend "so in love with you" who is "like a sister to me." As such, it corresponds to the paradigms of homoerotic desire mediated through a third party of the opposite sex that Sedgwick and Castle delineate. Yet, as I have suggested, it violates an essential rule by placing the concerns and feelings of another girl ahead of the desired boy and the protagonist's own feelings. It is small wonder, then, that "the record failed to pick up crucial radio play and was quickly and unceremoniously mothballed by the label" (Irving Chusid, liner notes to *The Best of the Girl Groups, Volume 2*).

26. Jim Curtis, *Rock Eras: Interpretations of Music and Society, 1954–1984* (Bowling Green, OH: Bowling Green State University Popular Press, 1987), p. 87.

27. Robert Palmer, *Rock & Roll: An Unruly History* (New York: Harmony, 1995), p. 34. The extent of Spector's Wagnerian fixation is evinced in his arrangement of "When I Saw You" for the Ronettes (*The Best of the Ronettes* [ABKCO 7212-2, 1992]).

As the song ends and Veronica Bennett utters her final wail of abjection that "I'd lose my mind over you," the orchestral accompaniment makes allusion to the final leitmotiv of Brünnhilde's immolation scene in the last act of *Götterdämmerung*. While Ronnie Spector would have been an unlikely Brünnhilde under any circumstances, the notion of romantic self-immolation in her involvement with Spector is chillingly ironic. On the history and neo-operatic ethos of Spector's musical regime and the disastrous Spector-Bennett marriage, see Ronnie Spector with Vince Waldron, *Be My Baby* (New York: Harmony, 1990). See also Gillian G. Gaar, *She's a Rebel* (Seattle: Seal, 1992), pp. 47–49; O'Brien, *She Bop*, pp. 72–73; Grieg, *Will You Still Love Me Tomorrow?* pp. 55–59.

28. In the end, however, even Ronnie could be replaced. By 1966, when the Ronettes were slated to be the opening act on what would be the Beatles' final tour, Spector had become so possessive of Ronnie that he forbade her to tour and substituted a Bennett cousin as lead singer. The Ronettes, then, appeared without the singer from whom they derived their name and on whom their identity was based.

29. Bob B. Soxx and the Blue Jeans, "Not Too Young to Get Married," words and music by Phil Spector, Jeff Barry, and Ellie Greenwich, reissued on *The Best of Darlene Love* (ABKCO 7213-2, 1992).

30. Darlene Love, "Chapel of Love," words and music by Phil Spector, Jeff Barry, and Ellie Greenwich, reissued on *The Best of Darlene Love*. A slight shift of pronouns occurs between Darlene Love's 1963 recording of "Chapel of Love" and the Dixie Cups' more familiar 1964 hit version (reissued on *The Best of the Girl Groups, Volume 1*). In the original, the refrain states, "Gee, I really love *him*," which conforms to the common third-person representation of the male object that I discuss, although in this song, as it is about getting married, the groom is also subsumed into the first-person plural "we." The Dixie Cups, however, change this line to "Gee, I really love *you*," which serves on some cognitive level to indicate, if nothing else, the possible actual presence of a groom (as opposed to a pure fantasy thereof). The original, though, can be interpreted as song about a fantasy of a wedding as easily as it can be assumed to be about the real thing.

31. Darlene Love, "(Today I Met) the Boy I'm Gonna Marry," words by Phil Spector, Tony Powers, and Ellie Greenwich, reissued on *The Best of Darlene Love*.

32. That I am alluding—in an only partially tongue-in-cheek manner—in these two sentences to the theoretical paradigms of, respectively, Terry Castle and Eve Sedgwick should, I think, be obvious.

33. Grieg, *Will You Still Love Me Tomorrow?* p. 55.

34. The Ronettes, "Walking in the Rain," words and music by Phil Spector, Barry Mann, and Cynthia Weil, reissued on *The Best of the Ronettes*.

35. Springfield's first album as a solo artist, *A Girl Called Dusty*, is comprised in great part of note-for-note cover versions (transposed down, in some cases, to accommodate Springfield's female tenor voice) of U.S. girl-group hits, including the Shirelles' "Mama Said" and "Will You Love Me Tomorrow?" the Supremes'

"When the Love Light Starts Shining Thru His Eyes," Lesley Gore's "You Don't Own Me," Dionne Warwick's "Wishin' and Hopin' " and "Anyone Who Had a Heart," and Charlie and Inez Foxx's "Mockingbird" (in which Springfield sings both parts), as well as Gene Pitney's "Twenty-Four Hours from Tulsa." On Springfield's queerness, her deployment of camp, and her racial and gender masquerades, see Patricia Juliana Smith, "You Don't Have To Say You Love Me: The Camp Masquerades of Dusty Springfield," in *Camp Grounds: Style and Homosexuality*, ed. David Bergman (Amherst: University of Massachusetts Press, 1993), pp. 185–205.

36. Dusty Springfield, "Wishin' and Hopin,' " words and music by Burt Bachrach and Hal David, on *A Girl Called Dusty* (Mercury, reissued in 1997).

37. Or, for that matter, the nineties, as evinced by the cover version of "Wishin' and Hopin' " by present-day lesbian icon Ani DiFranco on the soundtrack of the 1997 film *My Best Friend's Wedding*. Accompanied by steel drums, organ, gospel-choir backing vocals, and a shrill whistle, DiFranco's over-the-top performance makes abundantly clear what Springfield merely insinuated: that only the truly clueless would want to achieve the goals the song enumerates, much less take its advice to heart.

38. The Shangri-Las, "Give Him a Great Big Kiss," words and music by George Morton, reissued on *The Best of the Girl Groups, Volume 1*.

39. The Shangri-Las, "The Leader of the Pack," words and music by George Morton, Jeff Barry, and Ellie Greenwich, reissued on *The Best of the Girl Groups, Volume 1*. This use of names on the recording has led to some confusion about the actual group personnel. The lead singer was, in fact, Mary Weiss, whose sister Liz (also known as Betty) was a group member as well. The Weiss sisters were joined by a another pair of sisters, twins Mary Ann and Marge Ganser. Frequent squabbles among the members, however, led to constant reconfigurations of the group, with all four rarely performing together at any given time.

40. Grieg, *Will You Still Love Me Tomorrow?* p. 81.

41. The Marvelettes, "Too Many Fish in the Sea," words and music by Edward Holland, Jr., and Norman Whitfield, on *The Best of the Marvelettes* (Motown LP-11258, 1975).

42. The Supremes, "Back in My Arms Again," words and music by Brian Holland, Lamont Dozier, and Edward Holland, Jr., reissued on *Diana Ross and the Supremes: The Ultimate Collection* (Motown 314 530 827 2, 1996).

43. Grieg, *Will You Still Love Me Tomorrow?* pp. 113–14.

44. Martha [Reeves] and the Vandellas, "(Love Is Like a) Heat Wave," words and music by Brian Holland, Lamont Dozier, and Edward Holland, Jr.

45. Grieg, *Will You Still Love Me Tomorrow?* p. 188.

46. Bananarama, "Cruel Summer," words and music by Tony Swain and Steve Jolley, reissued on *Bananarama: The Greatest Hits Collection* (London 828158-2, 1988).

5

"DO DOC MARTENS HAVE A SPECIAL SMELL?"

HOMOCORE, SKINHEAD EROTICISM, AND QUEER AGENCY

ASHLEY DAWSON

Punk . . . a boy whose anus and rectum is a "vagina" for a pederast.
J.D.s, no. 1: n.p.

During a performance while on a tour of the United States to promote a recent album, Morrissey, the enigmatic former lead singer of the UK band the Smiths, projected a series of huge images of young skinheads onto screens behind his band. While Morrissey has always been fascinated by British culture during the postwar period, his recent flirtation with right-wing chic places such nostalgic nationalism in a far more problematic context. Morrissey's paeans to the "suedehead" go to the heart of contemporary debates concerning the destabilizing effects of performance and mimicry. The appropriation of the hypermasculine, racist iconography of skinhead culture by high-profile artists such as Morrissey as well as by sections of the queer underground radically revises the strategies of ironic citation and parody such as camp and drag that have characterized gay and lesbian subcultures.

In *Male Impersonators*, Mark Simpson, discussing the transgressive role of rock music, writes:

> The leading edge of rock 'n' roll must always be searching for the fault line of sexuality, the cusp of gender, where the connection between the two are most fraught. In order to channel desire into consumerism, rock 'n' roll has first to locate the richest sources of desire. Rock 'n' roll has to appropriate images and acts that are unstable and expose the "arbitrary"

nature of gender performance, revel in the "phantasmatic" nature of identity and thus cause some disturbing feedback.[1]

If rock music functions as Simpson suggests, then the current upsurge in the number of bands who actively foreground questions of sexual orientation has much to tell us about popular attitudes toward gender and sexuality. For not only does rock music pick up on shifts in the etiquette through which normality is defined in gendered terms, but it also discloses the fact that this etiquette is itself a social construction. Definitions of gender characteristic of a particular period are consequently revealed as a product of a hegemonic ideology specific to that period. Of course, such hegemony is itself unstable, having constantly to negotiate the vicissitudes of shifting perceptions of identity as well as the very artificiality of gender discussed by Simpson.

Morrissey's opaque suedehead love songs highlight rock music's function as a site for challenges to normative definitions of gender. His interest in the macho drag of the skinhead underlines the performative dynamic of gender identity that I intend to explore in this essay. In addition, the work of homocore groups and performers such as Pansy Division, Tribe 8, the Mukilteo Fairies, God Is My Copilot, and Vaginal Davis—all of whom appropriate and parody hardcore musical style and attitude—links and contrasts the new queer musical production with various queer aesthetic traditions of the past, as well as with contemporary queer politics. Most importantly, these bands use the traditionally ambivalent position of the male rock star as both an identificatory and an erotic object to engage in particularly powerful forms of genderfuck: the erosion of stable, binary gender norms through parodic performance.

Like heavy metal cockrock, hardcore developed alongside and in reaction to many of the transgressive gender practices of the glam rock movement. Despite the relatively traditional, Reagan-era brand of masculinity evident among the majority of hardcore performers, the independent scene has preserved a tradition of genderfuck since the punk explosion in the late seventies. From the glamour boys of the New Romantic movement who kicked off New Wave in the early eighties to the queer roots and sites of house music, forms of transgressive gender performance have been a consistent—if often violently repressed—influence on more commercial genres of popular music.[2] In this essay, I will examine the characteristics of punk and hardcore that have made these movements particularly important sites for the dismantling of masculinist, heterosexist subject positions by queers. The lyrics, musical style, and performative aesthetics of homocore bands aggressively assert a queer politics that militates against dominant norms of gender identity within both the heterosexual and the gay and lesbian mainstream. In addition, the homocore fanzines that comment on the scene and consolidate lines of alternative communication within the queer community generate a fertile noise that disrupts and reconfigures mainstream musical production.

The counterhegemonic musical form through which homocore circulates is an essential element of its anti-identity stance. Indeed, as Philip Brett argues in *Queering the Pitch*, music has historically represented a part of Western culture whose emotive power and ambiguity of meaning has been constructed as feminine and therefore dangerous.[3] Furthermore, rock music itself was built on the expressive forms of marginalized social groups— African Americans, in particular—in order to satisfy and exploit the voracious popular appetite for acts of symbolic subversion. This tendency of rock to appropriate subversive or marginal social identities has led to the elaboration of various underground forms that resist the logic of the market. While such forms of resistance are laudable in theory, they can lead to a debilitating form of avant-gardist elitism that reinstates music as a so-called high art form. This essay will examine documents of the queer underground, including fanzines and lyrics by homocore bands, that participate in the appropriative strategies of rock music while resisting such avant-gardism. I argue that the proliferation of these parodic forms destabilizes hierarchical, binary forms of social organization such as high/popular culture, straight/gay, and masculine/feminine. In particular, I will pursue the following questions: What are the implications of the homocore appropriation of straight male drag? How are such signs recirculated within an underground subculture and how does this recirculation inflect their political significance? What relation does the homocore movement have to previous forms of sexual dissidence? What are the pragmatic political ramifications of homocore's resistance against the ethnic identity model of gay identity? I will thus move from an examination of the erotics of skinhead camp to a more general discussion of the role of subculture within queer politics.

The last few years have seen an eruption of the independent music scene into the mainstream, principally through the signing of a number of alternative bands to major record labels in the wake of Nirvana's pathbreaking commercial success. Indie bands have brought with them an antihierarchical aesthetic inherited from the punk movement of the late seventies. This aesthetic is predicated on an attack on the exclusionary function of musical virtuosity and show biz entrepreneurs. The punk scene drew much of its vibrancy from the assumption that absolutely anyone was qualified to get on stage. The ferment created by this aspect of the scene is perhaps best demonstrated by the now-classic fanzine diagram depicting three chords and captioned, "Here's three chords. Now form a band."

The DIY. (do-it-yourself) philosophy of the independent rock scene also extends to the mechanics of production and distribution: bands tend to record on labels that are independent of the major commercial producers, giving them license to experiment artistically by curtailing some of the constraints of the profit motive. In addition, the indie scene also supports various underground forms of communication, such as the fanzine, which employ cheap technology in order to foster circuits of communication as alternatives to the established press. Indie bands are, then, inheritors of the emancipatory political projects of the sixties such as the underground press and, in particular, of the various offshoots of the Situationist International.[4] Decentralization of authority in all its forms, independence from the iron law of the marketplace, and the utopian horizon revealed by the spontaneous gesture are the underpinnings of their pastiche style. The irony involved in the commercial success of certain segments of the indie movement at a time when, as Donna Gaines has argued, the civil rights of youths have been eroded to the point where a fetishized consumerism is the principle simulacrum of freedom available, explains the enduring urgency of attacks on those who are perceived as selling out.[5]

In addition, however, this commercial success has also brought a radical sexual politics to more widespread popular attention. Mainstream definitions of gender have perhaps been most impacted through the work of the all-women bands associated with the riot grrrl movement.[6] Groups such as Bikini Kill, Bratmobile, and L7 have brought the ferocious rage felt by women toward forms of patriarchal authority onto the stage with them. The fanzines that circulate in the riot grrrl scene further deconstruct patriarchy using the ironic humor and techniques of manipulation learned from media activists such as ACT-UP and Queer Nation. Despite their obvious debt to feminism, many of these artists refuse to be boxed in with the label "angry girl bands," bridling at the assumption implicit in this kind of labeling that anger is actually the province of male bands.[7] In an interview in a riot grrrl fanzine, for instance, members of 7 Year Bitch feel the need to reject explicitly the patronizing accolades delivered by male audience members and rock critics who are surprised that women can play instruments.[8] Riot grrrl groups cope with this sort of reaction by parodying the arbitrary nature of gender categories. The aggressive inversion of pejorative labels for the female body adopted by bands such as Hole—whose name articulates the ambivalently insulting and fearful synecdoche that often inheres within such misogynist labels—is an apt example of such parody.

Faced with this frontal assault on the gender privilege that once accrued to the rock star, male indie rockers have themselves increasingly moved to acknowledge the lability of gender identity. Britpop groups such as Suede have consequently revived the ambiguous sexual identity of the glam rocker of the early seventies. In addition, even performers within the hardcore subculture have grown more self-conscious about gender. An interviewer's question concerning how he became open-minded enough to invite the homocore band Pansy Division to open for his band on a recent national tour prompted the following exchange between Billie Joe Armstrong, lead singer of the neopunk group Green Day, and Chris Freeman, bassist and singer for Pansy Division: " 'Well,' Billie Joe says, 'I mean, I'm not, for the most part, I'm not fully straight—I mean, I'm bi.' But, I ask him, aren't you married and isn't your wife going to give birth to your child soon? 'Yeah,' says Billie Joe. 'See,' says Chris, who's standing nearby, 'sometimes the right people do have children.' "[9] The gentle humor of this exchange, of course, raises the question of the extent to which nontraditional sexuality is becoming a faddish pose. Severed from any social movement, professions of bisexuality may become nothing more than an attempt to cash in on the latest vogue within rock culture of destroying sexual taboos. Rather than simply seeing Billie Joe's comment as a crass appropriation of a sexual subculture, I would like to think about how it reflects a wider social problematic. If subcultural styles represent, as the cultural studies tradition has argued, "magical" solutions to the problems collectively experienced by youth, then Billie Joe's reaction must be taken as part of a more general social reaction against the remasculinization of male identity characteristic of the Reagan-Bush era.[10] As a result of this reaction, the work of artists who are part of the homocore underground is assuming an increasingly visible role within the independent culture and gaining wider acknowledgement from the commercial mainstream.

At a show in a small club in New York City's Lower East Side during the twenty-fifth anniversary celebrations of the Stonewall Riots, a flyer was handed out addressing itself to all "queer punks and other non-mainstream individuals." Clearly intended to skewer the commercial hoopla of the commemoration, the flyer calls for the establishment of a network of nonconformists who find little appeal in the mainstream gay and lesbian communities that dominated the Stonewall festivities. Unlike the mainstream images that circulated during the commemoration, the Morlocks' flyer rejects the constraints of the "gay lifestyle" as well as the straight world. The group's name, borrowed from the subterranean cannibals in H. G. Wells's *The Time Machine*, heightens the projection of underground identity articulated in the flyer. True to the anarchist roots that the flyer proclaims, the homocore groups that answer to this call for a communication collective cannot be said to have a particular set of doctrines. Nevertheless, the opposition of members of homocore groups to the gay community's mimicry of heteronorms was a prominent unifying concern for such alternative queer collectives during the Stonewall commemoration. Given that many of the performers associated with homocore appropriate some of the most aggressive musical forms in the extremely heterosexist genre of rock 'n' roll, how is this rejection of heteroconformism tenable? How do homocore groups conceive of their identities and the feedback their subculture is generating within dominant gay and straight communities? How, finally, does this relate to broader changes in gender norms during the last decade and a half?

Discussing his fascination with skinheads in *J.D.s*, the seminal homocore 'zine he edited along with G. B. Jones, Bruce La Bruce explains the allure of the skinhead subculture on two levels: the ideological and the sexual. On the one hand, La Bruce mentions a former socialist boyfriend who became a white-power skin in disapproving tones; on the other, he describes his recent film dealing with the homofetishization of skinheads. Opposite this explanation is a line drawing of a skinhead in a style copped from gay porn: Complete with Doc Martens, braces, and Union Jack tattoo, the skin fingers the head of his gigantic, erect cock. In a seemingly incongruous juxtaposition, a bar down the center of the illustration announces in script decorated with trippy seventies' sunflowers that this is a "skin pansy." Why this anomalous collage of pansy typography and skinhead masculinity? Why this fetishization of the skinhead?

Certain forms of gay style and cultural identity have always been based on a dangerous fascination with the most hegemonic forms of heterosexual masculinity, from the neoclassical, eugenically tinged German *wandervogel* movement at the turn of the century to gay erotic artist Tom of Finland's charged images of superbutch farm boys and cops fucking on fences. Commenting on the shifts experienced by masculinity during the last decade, Mark Simpson goes as far as attacking gay pornography for its denial of the variability and fluidity of queer sex roles. According to Simpson, the post-Stonewall masculinization of gay representation runs the risk of denying the subversive interchangeability of gay sexual roles: "What gay porn does is to represent a world in which men have sex with men *where there is no such thing as 'gay.'* Tom of Finland's drawings depict a guilt-free (and gay free) world of spontaneous public sex between willing, youthful square-jawed cops and grinning, tattooed sailors. . . . In Tom Land, homosex is discovered to be the most natural, most *masculine* thing in the world. This is an unpleasant conjunction of gay and straight porn."[11] If Simpson's comments hold true, this tendency also reinforces the coding of sexuality by gender preference through the marginalization of nonconventional sexualities. Dominant versions of gay sexual fantasy thus appear to partake of an ambivalent desire to assume the very rigid, hypermasculine identity that it brings into question.

Simpson's attack is, however, predicated on an interpretation of Tom's work that ignores the very performative complexity that is entailed in this fantasy of superpotent masculinity. Queerness is not a quantity that can be represented by a particular physical type or style politics. Instead, queer identity is constituted in and by same-sex desire in *all* its forms. Moreover, the kick in Tom's porn consists precisely in the revelation that the most apparently straight forms of heterosexual masculinity carry a powerful homoerotic charge. Tom's work is thus hardly a denial of homosexuality; rather, it is an affirmation of the homoeroticism that is habitually repressed in the homosocial order and of the seductiveness involved in breaking the taboo associated with this repression.

Bruce La Bruce's interest in the skinhead pansy exemplifies such an erotic collision. The macho category of "skin" and the stigmatized homophobic label of "pansy" are collapsed together in *J.D.s* in a way that underlines the instability of gender identity as well as the performative element of even the most exaggerated forms of masculinity. In order to understand the attraction of the skinhead for La Bruce and, by extension, that of the hardcore genre for queer activists and artists, it is important to gain a sense of why the skinhead constitutes such a compelling example of rough trade.

The skinhead subculture developed in Britain during the late sixties, a time when the social democratic elements of the consensus society established by the postwar Labour government were increasingly fraying. Indeed, as Dick Hebdige has argued, the very existence of youth subcultures is an index of the dissolution of that consensus, though it might also be taken as a sign of the commodification and consequent visibility of "teenage lifestyles."[12] Skinhead style was, according to Hebdige, a simulacrum of working-class identity that was far more unstable than any real version of that identity because of its retrospective, embattled construction in the midst of the ruins of the traditional working-class way of life (57). Skins, however, did not draw only on this mythical image of the dour machismo of the working-class male; they also gained a component of their symbolic repertoire from the "rude boys," the rebellious West Indian youths of the big city:

> Ironically, those values conventionally associated with white working-class culture which had been eroded by time, by relative affluence and by the disruption of the physical environment in which they had been rooted, were rediscovered in black West Indian culture. Here was a culture armoured against contaminating influences, protected against the more frontal assaults of the dominant ideology, denied access to the "good life" by the color of its skin. . . . The skinheads, then, resolved or at least reduced the tension between an experienced present (the mixed ghetto) and an imaginary past (the classic white slum) by initiating a dialogue which reconstituted each in terms of the other. (57)

Skinhead style is, then, characterized by an appeal to an iconic and embattled form of masculinity that is itself inspired by the marks of absolute difference conferred by racializing discourse. Indeed, one aspect of skinhead appropriation that Hebdige neglects is the skins' fascination with rude boy sexuality. Certainly, stereotypical fears/fascinations concerning black sexuality must have figured prominently in skins' acts of appropriation. Such tensions can only heighten the instability of the skinhead project of remasculinization, which involved a masquerade of male identity founded on a pastiche of marginalized forms of masculinity.

Skinhead identity is therefore based on a history that, like most forms of nationalism and ethnic absolutism, represses the hybridity of its origins. Indeed, as Hebdige goes on to argue, the polarizing racial discourses of the period ultimately proved too strong for the skins. Retreating from their early stage of sympathy with the rudies of the inner-city ghettos, skins embraced a virulent white-power ideology that nostalgically fastened on the imaginary rituals of national identity and communal class solidarity. It is this uncompromisingly compromised element, however, that makes skinhead style alluring. If the dour macho pose of the skin is constituted, as Hebdige argues, by a repudiation of the regime of the normal that draws on the resistant core of blackness within and yet outside British culture, Bruce La Bruce's eroticization of the skin brings out the latent homoerotic elements that this strongly homosocial subculture represses and projects onto others in the process of consolidating its identity.

La Bruce, and homocore in general, are in other words involved in a form of mimicry of macho drag that has always been a prominent part of gay culture and that is predicated on gay men's affective and sexual ties with other socially marginalized groups such as working-class and black men. This mimicry brings out the dialectical power relations integral to sexuality. Furthermore, *J.D.s* anatomizes the absolute distinction that must be maintained between hetero- and homosexuality in order to prevent the queering of the former. Thus, in the narrative that begins with the question, "Do Doc Martens have a special smell?" the speaker moves quickly from a fetishistic description of the smell of Doc Martens and the sweaty socks they contain to an account of domination by a skinhead. The skinhead whose slave the speaker becomes shores up his straight identity through domination of his slave; ironically, this domination always returns to the sexual, to the skin's need to be serviced by his slave:

> "You fucking bastard, you like teenage boys?"
> "Yes sir."
> "You're a fucking dirty queer—what are you?"
> "A fucking dirty queer sir."
> "Queers like you are only good for two things—what are they?"
> "Licking boots and sucking cock sir."[13]

The cartoon that accompanies this narrative foregrounds these issues of sexuality and domination. Not only is the object that has elicited the skin's arousal—the sex slave? the reader?—absent from the frame, but the skin himself is in an ambiguous state, with anger flashing across his face while his cock gyrates in the form of a swastika. Is his cock erecting itself into a swastika or losing that form? Does sexual arousal jibe with or augment white supremacist ideology? Whatever the case, the narrative suggests that skinheads both need the sexual attention lavished on them by their slaves while also seeking to disavow the implications of that relation. The skins in this narrative struggle to retain their identity by adopting an aggressive hetero-fucker stance while at the same time being placed in a position of passivity as the object of the queer gaze. The more frantically the skinhead asserts this hetero-fucker status, however, the more he is reduced to the level of the purely physical, to an irresistible pot of honey, a fairy who enacts his macho drag at the behest of queer desire. The more absolute the posited distinction between hetero and homo, the more the one flips over into the other.

On a recent single, the homocore band Mukilteo Fairies enacts a similar parodic deconstruction of straight culture. The front of the single's cover contains an image typical of the world of heavy metal: a giant, smoking cauldron with Satan's head above the title "Special Rites." Having invoked this discourse of satanic rites, one through which the heavy metal fan proclaims his outsider status, the Fairies then present us with an image on the back side of the single that locates such rites on the level of the somatic: inside a corona of song titles, a dark hole looms, a set of claws protruding just beyond its edge. This image foregrounds the straight male paranoia that renders the anus the true site of forbidden rituals. As Mark Simpson writes:

> The performance of masculinity in all its various rites has more to do with the anxiety a man has about his anus than his phallus. Homosexual representation is not just a desublimation of homoeroticism, making scandalously visible the invisible bond that binds men together, but also a desublimation of anality, a publication of that which must be kept private about the male body, and thus a dissolution of the whole masculine sense of self—predicated as it is upon secrecy and paranoia.[14]

Seizing on the fantasy narratives that have been a part of metal culture at least since Led Zeppelin's embrace of J. R. R. Tolkien's work, the Mukilteo Fairies make explicit the homoeroticism implicit in the narcissistic feudal reveries of so many teenage boys.

The Mukilteo Fairies engage in a similarly sly unsettling of straight culture in their musical style. Their cut "Queer Enough For You?" begins the Outpunk label's *Outpunk Dance Party*. After a brief snatch of disco music is ripped with a rending scratch off a turntable, the fury of the Fairies' wall of grunge guitar erupts, the singer screaming out ironic lines concerning queer identity: "I suck my cheeks in when I dance / Dig Erasure and Man 2 Man."[15] Yet such clichés concerning dominant queer identity merge with a writhing sense of anger and threat that reverses the corresponding stereotype of passivity that often attaches to them: "Get 49 enemas every day / so you'd better get the fuck out of my way." In addition, the Mukilteo Fairies tear apart the binary opposition of homo- and heterosexuality by invoking their worn clichés of queer identity amid a welter of furious noise. The lead singer delivers the lyrics in a throttled scream that unsettlingly juxtaposes an ironic invocation of homophobic discourses with the frothing anger of the traditionally male hardcore singer. The Mukilteo Fairies and other bands such as Swine King, which covers a Motorhead song on the same compilation, thus remorselessly out the hardcore rock star by focusing attention on his performance position.

The exaggerated masculinity of a performer such as Henry Rollins, whose pumped-up and tattoo-swathed body dominates the stage, is intended to deflect the homoerotic dynamics implicit in performances in which the male rocker is an object of both identification and erotic desire.[16] The pit of sweaty, moshing, slamming bodies at the average hardcore show engenders a powerful homosocial bonding process whose homoeroticism must be defused by the performer's expressions of righteous masculine anger. Nevertheless, the discomfort generated by this position as object of a tenuously repressed homoerotic gaze is inevitably exacerbated by the macho strutting of the rocker. Such posturing merely underlines the male subject as spectacle that precipitates this homoerotic dynamic in the first place. Homocore groups are not, then, simply appropriating the male rocker's performance position. Rather, in adopting the performance mode of the hardcore band, such groups rearticulate the performance position of the male hardcore star.[17] Mimicking the macho drag involved in this subject position, homocore performers lay bare the instabilities associated with the homoerotic dynamic of such a position. In addition, this process of outing transforms the hardcore performer's physical expressions of anger into an articulation of queer outrage with homophobic discourses.

The Mukilteo Fairies are, however, hardly the first band to denounce homophobia. As early as 1981, the hardcore band MDC (Millions of Dead Cops) recorded "Dead Cops/What Makes America So Straight?" a track that denounces police harassment of queers, African-Americans, and the poor in general: "Call this the land of the free, say its the home of the brave / You know they call me a queen, just another human being."[18] Like MDC, contemporary performance artist and hardcore diva Vaginal Davis remorselessly attacks the racism evident not only within dominant heterosoc but also within the principal style cultures of the queer nation. Vag, a six-feet, six-inch self-described "Amazonian Black Love Goddessa," is a multimedia artist whose forays into music have consistently transgressed and parodied genres of both dominant straight and gay performance. In appearances in support of her hardcore/speed metal band Pedro, Muriel and Esther's *The White To Be Angry* album, Vag struts onstage wearing militiaman chic. Growling down the microphone with prototypical hardcore ire, Vag engages in what José Esteban Muñoz has recently called a parodic disidentification with the modes of macho masculinity that unite militiaman and hardcore performer.[19] As she strips the layers of militiaman garb to reveal the black/Latina queen underneath, Vag peels apart the racial and sexual boundaries that secure dominant identities.

The higher visibility of homocore music today is attributable not only to the inroads made by independent music into the mainstream but also to a crisis in the discourses of masculine identity. During the Reagan era, the political establishment and important sectors of popular culture such as Hollywood engaged in a racially coded project of remasculinization.[20] Faced with the legacy of the bloody, humiliating defeat in Vietnam and the increasing visibility of previously marginalized social groups as a result of the rise of new social movements since the sixties, politicians and sectors of the U.S. cultural apparatus attempted to revive the ideology of American indominability by interpellating the identity of the individual with a national identity based on strength, toughness, and a determination to use force whenever and wherever necessary. The resolution to this crisis in masculine identity took, then, the form of the hysterical male fantasy of Rambo, returning on the silver screen to retake an imaginary Vietnam for us and thereby reclaim our lost honor.

At the same time as this project of remasculinization was being enacted, however, images of the male body were being increasingly commodified. Over the last decade and a half, the male body has been ever more openly depicted as the site of erotic spectacle and stagy desirability. In advertising, for instance, the commodification of men's cocks has advanced inexorably, most prominently in the form of Calvin Klein's giant billboards and scandalous soft-porn ads.[21] Indeed, in the retrospect provided by this process of objectification, the homoerotic nature of many of the Vietnam revisionist films, not to mention beefcake flicks such as *Top Gun*, is screamingly evident: Rambo's pumped-up body minces around the screen in battle fatigues, straining to assert a masculine identity through the carefully applied mousse and makeup. The fact that the sexual charge accompanying this display of physical prowess is available for the consumption of an undifferentiated gaze only led to more exaggerated exertions. Within such a context, the irony involved in queer mimicry of straight male drag corrodes the iron façade of hetero masculinity to reveal the erotic charge latent within such postures of hardness.

There is no guarantee that this exposure of homoeroticism will diffuse the mechanism of disavowal and scapegoating that maintains the homosocial continuum. Even so, popular culture has been quick to respond to this increasing awareness of the unsustainability of gender binarisms. The members of a group like God Is My Co-Pilot now explicitly conceive of themselves as engaged in undermining such binarisms: "We're co-opting Rock, the language of Sexism, to address gender identity on its own terms of complexity."[22] Indeed, their recent album *How to Be* begins with "Carte Celeste," a song that charts their sense of the reductiveness of a polarized model of gender and sexual orientation: "We're off the map—we're in the dark blue dot screen that stands for in between the stars—everything between the big things."[23] Employing the map of the heavens as a metaphor for gender, the group reminds us that this map is a social construct that cannot or will not adequately represent the indefinable spaces between the bright points of light on which we hang our sense of gendered order. In taking up the poststructuralist analysis of the categories of social thought, the band attempts to offer up examples of the greater freedom with regard to gender and sexuality precipitated by an awareness of the arbitrary nature of the categories governing these aspects of life.

Concomitant with this shift has been a growing sense of frustration with the assumptions underlying existing models of gay and lesbian identity. Homocore's ironic appropriation of straight male drag constitutes a challenge not only to heterosexual masculine identity but to the homogenizing tendencies of the ethnic model that underlies existing paradigms of gay identity. This ethnic model of gay and lesbian identity is founded on the assumption that choice of sexual object is *the* determining aspect of subjectivity. As Stephen Seidman explains, the essentializing tenets of this ethnic model have come under fire not only from academic critics concerned with the social construction of identity but from social groups marginalized by the normative tendencies implicit in the model.[24] The facility with which this discourse of identity lends itself to hegemonization by particular segments of the community is built on the normalizing tendency implicit in the lexicon of family, language, and community on which the ethnic identity model is based. The model tends, in other words, to delegitimize the experience and desires of individuals who do not conform to the sexual, emotional, and cultural identities authenticated by the hetero-/homosexual binary.

Despite the attempts of individuals such as Andrew Sullivan and the members of the Log Cabin Society to censure queers who do not conform to mainstream identities, lesbians and gays are evidently neither a homogeneous community nor an inherently progressive group.[25] Ironically, these neoconservatives have redeployed the modernist discourse of normalization that produced the category of "the homosexual" in the first place, seeking in so doing to cast those who have resisted their version of the homogenizing underpinnings of identity politics as beyond the pale of the so-called normal gay community. Predicated on challenging the ethnic framing of same-sex desire as well as on appropriating the erotics of straight male spectacle, a prominent element of homocore is its reaction to the growing profile of such neoconservative groups. Homocore's resistance to this model is a reminder that minoritarian identity, of whatever stripe, is no longer enough to guarantee political progressivism.

Seeking to challenge this assimilationist trajectory, homocore groups reject one of the more prominent aspects of mainstream gay identity: the consumerist lifestyle that, as Michael Warner puts it, gives off the smell of capital in rut.[26] This critique was particularly evident during the Stonewall commemoration, when the divisions within the gay community were blatantly apparent in the heated disagreements over the meaning of Stonewall. Indeed, the grand march that culminated the twenty-fifth anniversary celebration was split in two, one group marching along New York Mayor Giuliani's approved route while another marched up Fifth Avenue in defiance of civic order. This divide further underlines the inability of the ethnicity model underpinning gay and lesbian identity politics to theorize adequately either the forms of hegemony that develop within the community or the role of resistance in relation to issues unrelated to sexual object choice.

Indeed, the Morlocks' flyer with which I began this analysis loudly proclaims its alienation from the official version of the gay lifestyle just as much as it does its alienation from homophobic segments of the independent music scene. For the Morlocks, this lifestyle involves the unnecessary internalization of stereotypes produced by the gay mainstream's closeness to straight society. Likewise, the Mukilteo Fairies' "Queer Enough For You" catalogs clichéd aspects of gay identity not only in order to refute straight assumptions but also as part of a refusal to engage with and participate in the consumption of icons of collective gay identity from a past that no longer seems relevant to many young queers. Homocore refuses the constraints of nominally straight culture as well as those of what it conceives of as a gay subcultural ghetto, whether that ghetto is decorated by photos of Judy Garland or by pink lambdas. Performances by other homocore artists such as Vaginal Davis, who radically inverts the traditional performance position of the drag queen, similarly critique the racial and gender codes of mainstream queer identity.

This attack on the heteronormativity of certain segments of the gay and lesbian community is carried out most intensely in *S.C.A.B.*, a fanzine circulated by the so-called Society for the Complete Annihilation of Breeders. As this association's title makes evident, *S.C.A.B.* originally assaulted the more and less immediate byproducts of the heterosexual lifestyle. For *S.C.A.B.*, however, heterosexism transcends sexual orientation, including not only the desire to breed but the many forms of exploitation that the group argues are destroying the earth, from capitalism to Christianity. In response, *S.C.A.B.* has turned the discourse of hatred of straights, formerly used by Queer Nation to clear a public space for nonconformist gays and lesbians, back against the dominant groups within those communities.[27] The result is a savage parody of mainstream gay and lesbian culture. All concessions to forms of heteronormativity such as gender segregation and new age mysticism are blasted by this parody. The nugatory intent behind the critique is so powerful, the refusal of the traditional parameters of gay and lesbian identity so total, that *S.C.A.B.* is led to embrace the most virulent forms of homophobia. The second issue, for example, engages in its own discourse of classification and objectification, ranking the different bars of Toronto using a "bash code" based on the degree of lesbian and gay identification of their patrons.

The dark satire of this "Guide to Gay Bashing" is characteristic of an antiidentity polemic that aims to shatter the assumptions of intelligibility concerning gender, sexual object choice, and national identity that underlie mainstream gay and lesbian culture. Reacting against the deployment of a parodic nationalist discourse by groups such as Queer Nation, *S.C.A.B.* engages in a counterparody by representing itself as a shadowy terrorist cell intent on undermining queer nationalism. Lauren Berlant and Elizabeth Freeman's discussion of the role of fanzines in articulating a space for a politics beyond Queer Nation's satire of the current hegemonic public sphere is particularly illuminating in relation to *S.C.A.B.*'s parodic methods.[28] Berlant and Freeman stress the importance of counterproduction within the 'zine network. Such counterproduction embodies a form of parody and camp that rejects the authenticity discourse that grounds the ethnic identity model of queer culture. Adapting the disruptive style of the alternative music culture, homocore similarly adumbrates a postidentity, postnational politics founded on the construction of a public sphere independent of the social institutions and cultural hegemony that currently ground definitions of identity.

Homocore thus represents a significant refusal to adopt the heteronormative identity that is supposedly prerequisite to gaining civil rights within the narrowing horizons of a rightwardly lurching political establishment. The context for such a challenge is perhaps best exemplified by the ultimately unresolved battle for gay and lesbian inclusion within the military that followed Bill Clinton's election. Homocore's aggressive assertion of radical difference is an element in a utopian strategy of linking antagonistic minority groups in a politics that refuses to accept the legitimacy of the nation-state as a form of identity. Rejecting the ethnic identity model as well as the lexicon of the nation, homocore reclaims the radical theoretical and political legacy of the Gay Liberation Front. While the GLF's embrace of the polymorphous perverse ultimately led it toward an ethos of sexual individualism, its awareness of the interwoven nature of forms of oppression remains exemplary. This awareness found pragmatic political content through the forging of bonds of solidarity with marginalized blacks, colonized peoples, and oppressed women that appears increasingly enviable given today's fragmented political landscape.[29] Homocore's appropriation of straight male drag and its parody of queer nationalism rearticulate the signifiers of sexual orientation and gender identity, intervening in a cultural formation in which the politics of identity are coming to seem increasingly facile and limiting. The postidentitarian and postnationalist parody carried out by various homocore groups is a particularly important reminder of the political possibilities inherent within a coalitional politics predicated on a refusal of regimes of the normal in all their forms.

This postidentity politics does not, however, constitute a repudiation of identity per se.[30] Rather, the parodic vitriol of various homocore artists generates a radical dissonance that interrupts and refunctions the signifiers of identity in both gay and straight communities. It is this act of bricolage that explains the constant concern with selling out that one finds among these performers: subcultures must constantly attempt to discriminate themselves from the dominant culture in order to reaffirm their difference, their distance from the hegemonic meanings that they appropriate and invert. Homocore is, in the end, a musical subculture and hence is both empowered and circumscribed by the revolution of style typically carried out within such a context. As Dick Hebdige writes in *Subculture*: "By repositioning and recontextualizing commodities, by subverting their conventional uses and inventing new ones, the subcultural stylist gives the lie to what Althusser has called the 'false obviousness of everyday practice,' and opens up the world of objects to new and covertly oppositional readings. The communication of a significant *difference*, then (and the parallel communication of a group *identity*), is the 'point' behind the style of all spectacular subcultures."[31]

Where Hebdige writes commodities, homocore writes gender. Homocore's subcultural stylists denaturalize the hegemonic discourse of gender by appropriating the elements of this discourse and rearticulating them, thereby offering up an alternative reality. Inherent in this process, however, is a tense, interwoven relation between the dominant reading and the subaltern version articulated by the subculture. As a result, homocore must constantly define its boundaries. As Gottlieb and Wald note, this process means that subcultural groups often run the risk of reifying the distinction between the mainstream and their own oppositional culture.[32] I would suggest, however, that this opposition is also the source of much of the energy produced by such subcultures. For it is by occupying the shifting interface between dominant and subaltern knowledges that subcultures are able to engage in their processes of rearticulation. Stripped of this fertile tension, such subcultures are left without the material for their acts of bricolage. As the parody carried out by homocore artists on both the performance position of the straight male hardcore performer and on the dominant gay lifestyle demonstrates, rearticulatory practices offer powerful vehicles for the assertion of difference. Perhaps more importantly, they also offer significant resources for the constitution of vibrant forms of countercommunity.

NOTES

1. Mark Simpson, *Male Impersonators* (New York: Castell, 1994), p. 206.
2. For an overview of queer musics during this period, see John Gill's *Queer Noises: Male and Female Homosexuality in Twentieth-Century Music* (Minneapolis: University of Minnesota Press, 1995).
3. Philip Brett, "Musicality, Essentialism, and the Closet," in *Queering the Pitch*, ed. Philip Brett, Elizabeth Wood, and Gary C. Thomas (New York: Routledge, 1994), p. 12.
4. For an inventive history of the connections between the Situationist Interna-

tional and the punk movement in the UK, see Greil Marcus's *Lipstick Traces: A Secret History of the Twentieth Century* (Cambridge: Harvard University Press, 1990).

5. Donna Gaines, *Teenage Wasteland* (New York: Pantheon, 1990), p. 12.

6. An excellent discussion of the issues raised by this movement may be found in Joanne Gottlieb and Gayle Wald's " 'Smells Like Teen Spirit': Riot Grrrls, Revolution, and Women in Independent Rock," in *Microphone Fiends*, ed. Andrew Ross and Tricia Rose (New York: Verso, 1994).

7. This point is made forcefully in the discussion of the relationship between riot grrrl music and the rock press in Gottlieb and Wald, " 'Smells Like Teen Spirit,' " p. 254.

8. Gottlieb and Wald, " 'Smells Like Teen Spirit,' " p. 254.

9. James Patrick Herman, "Orgasm Addicts," *Village Voice*, 10 January 1995, 57.

10. Andrew Ross introduction to Rose and Ross, *Microphone Fiends*, p. 8.

11. Simpson, *Male Impersonators*, p. 133. Emphasis in original.

12. Dick Hebdige, *Subculture: The Meaning of Style* (London: Methuen, 1979), p. 17.

13. *J.D.s*, no. 7: n.p.

14. Simpson, *Male Impersonators*, p. 81.

15. The Mukilteo Fairies, "Queer Enough For You?" *Outpunk Dance Party* (Outpunk 12, 1994).

16. Gottlieb and Wald, " 'Smells Like Teen Spirit,' " p. 259.

17. The term "rearticulation" derives from Gramsci's theory of hegemony. In defining the term, Cary Nelson describes the way in which rearticulation allows cultural workers "to describe how political discourses either become dominant or organize for resistance by rearticulating existing terms, concepts, arguments, beliefs, and metaphors into new configurations that are persuasive to people in a particular historical context" (*Repression and Recovery* [Madison: University of Wisconsin Press, 1989], pp. 251–52).

18. MDC, "Dead Cops/What Makes America So Straight?" *Millions of Dead Cops* (R Radical Records 1, 1982).

19. José Esteban Muñoz, " 'The White to Be Angry': Vaginal Davis's Terroristic Drag," *Social Text* 52/53 (fall/winter 1997).

20. For an extensive discussion of the parallels between national politics and Hollywood cinema during the Reagan-Bush era, consult Susan Jefford's *Hard Bodies: Hollywood Masculinity in the Reagan Era* (New Brunswick, NJ: Rutgers University Press, 1994). For complementary analyses of the remasculinization of U.S. males during the post-Vietnam period, see also James William Gibson's *Warrior Dreams* (New York: Hill and Wang, 1994) and Cynthia Enloe's *The Morning After* (Berkeley: University of California Press, 1994).

21. For a discussion of this shift in representations of gender during the postwar period, see Andrew Wernick's *Promotional Culture* (New York: Sage, 1991).

22. From the song "We Signify" on God Is My Co-Pilot's album *Straight Not* (Outpunk 8, 1995).

23. God Is My Co-Pilot, "Carte Celeste," *How to Be* (Making of Americans 11, 1996).

24. Steven Seidman, "Identity and Politics in a 'Postmodern' Gay Culture," in *Fear of a Queer Planet*, ed. Michael Warner (Minneapolis: Minnesota University Press, 1993), p. 127.

25. In an excellent article in *The Nation* (July 4, 1994), Tony Kushner deals with the homosexual individualism being curried by Andrew Sullivan and other conservative, white, gay assimilationists. Kushner's article registers the danger of the divide gay conservativism represents as existing between a purported gay majority who share the behavior and aspirations of the so-called straight world and a minority of deviants and malcontents.

26. Michael Warner, in Warner, *Fear of a Queer Planet*.

27. Lauren Berlant and Elizabeth Freeman's "Queer Nationality," in Warner's *Fear of a Queer Planet*, discusses Queer Nation's attempts to clear a space in the public sphere for queer identities using this "I Hate Straights" discourse.

28. Berlant and Freeman, "Queer Nationality," p. 224.

29. See Seidman, "Identity and Politics," for an analysis of Gay Liberation theory.

30. This is one of Stephen Seidman's main concerns in his discussion of the post-structuralist intervention in gay politics.

31. Hebdige, *Subculture*, p. 102. Emphasis in original.

32. Gottlieb and Wald, " 'Smells Like Teen Spirit,' " p. 271.

6

DR. FUNKENSTEIN'S SUPERGROOVALISTICPROSIFUNKSTICATION

GEORGE CLINTON SIGNIFIES

MARK WILLHARDT AND **JOEL STEIN**

PRELUDE: FUNK UPON A TIME . . .

. . . in the Uptown Tonsorial Parlor in Plainfield, New Jersey, there was a young hairdresser named George. By day he processed conks with a touch renowned statewide; by night he sang with the group he had formed when he was thirteen and named after a brand of cigarettes, the Parliaments. In the early 1960s George would leave his coiffuring days behind in order to develop his ever-growing musical influence into a legacy that has lasted thirty years. By gathering a shifting mélange of musicians around himself, George produced—in all senses of that word—the legend that has become Parliament, Funkadelic, the Parliafunkadelicment Thang, P-Funk, The Bomb. And although he may not have invented it, George Clinton became synonymous with The Funk.[1]

IT AIN'T NOTHIN' BUT A PARTY

To a broad discussion of the theoretical implications of popular musics, however, Clinton might seem more a footnote than a central figure. Given his bands' outrageous attire, a cross between David Bowie, Gary Glitter, and *The Wiz*;[2] their unruly sets, where they attempted "to do chaos and order at the same time";[3] the rising and falling popularity of funk; and, not least, Clinton's uncapped imagination and unwillingness to be pinned down to any single style or be co-opted by any single label, he may seem less important to discussions of this sort than many other black musicians, such as various jazz or blues greats, so-called serious musicians. Clinton's attempts to make his mid-seventies output a popular, commercially successful music have been seen as selling out; even Gary Shider, one of Clinton's lead singers and guitarists, felt this way as the change was happening.[4] Why, then, study a music so intent on being sensational? After all, one of Clinton's catchphrases has always been "It ain't nothin' but a party," so why make more out of it than it is?[5]

Like many critical projects, ours stems from the belief that the popular perception that this is all it is misses some of the subtlety and much of the importance of George Clinton's songwriting, self-creation, imaginative packaging, and the political undercurrent—what we call the political funkonscious—present in his oeuvre. For us, Clinton has survived the past thirty years because he has understood not only the musical possibilities of his age(s) but because he understands that critical and popular viability depend on a musical complexity that most acts' formulaic sound cannot achieve. His lyrics allegorize and metaphorize his world; his music retropes blues and spirituals and even nursery rhymes into something all his own, The Funk, where R&B horns, acid guitars, and spacey synthesizers are nailed together by bass and drums hitting then quitting the first beat of the measure, The One. A saying like "It ain't nothin' but a party, y'all" captures only half of what John Wideman calls the "get-happy and stay-strong power" of black music and, in the process, minimizes the cultural and musical accomplishments of George Clinton that we would amplify.[6]

FREE YOUR MIND AND YOUR ASS WILL FOLLOW

One of the constitutive contradictions to Clinton's funk is that it is a party music that is also, before the fact, an intellectual music.[7] This is not to say that chanting "da da da dee da da da da da da da" for five or ten minutes (as happens at P-Funk concerts during "Flash Light") is a particularly enlightening experience. What it does point toward is that Parliament and Funkadelic, Clinton's 1970s incarnations, were bands whose music was conscious of its social dimensions from the very beginning. Early Funkadelic albums dealt directly with the Vietnam War ("March to the Witch's Castle," from *Cosmic Slop*, 1973) as well as with ghetto life ("Cosmic Slop," *Cosmic Slop*). From the start, then, the idea was to "free your mind and your ass will follow."[8]

No doubt, such thinking partially grew from the drug culture that Funkadelic/Clinton drew on and embraced in the early years of the Parliafunkadelicment Thang. Indeed, by the mid-seventies, acid had claimed at least one P-Funk member as a casualty,[9] had caused most others to dry out any number of times, and had exacerbated conflicts over music and money that were sore spots anyway.[10] The notion of freeing the mind, however, was not simply a drug-addled hippie dream. Instead, it was—and continues to be, as it is chanted from the stage and in the audience—a paean to self-awareness and intellectual growth as well as a call to examine the world and attempt to make it better, make it funky. With an overt message such as "free your mind and your ass will follow"—or the equally direct "Think! It ain't illegal yet!"[11]—laced throughout Clinton's work, it seems a bit premature to acknowledge only the fun and not the pedagogical, if not sometimes pedantic, nature of the music itself. Therefore we want to explore certain of George Clinton's seventies output to chart his "political funkonscious," the "absent cause" of contemporary history that is "inaccessible to us except in textual form," here an undercurrent of intellectualization, political representation, and agency that demands elaboration.[12]

GETTING HIP TO THE MOTHERSHIP

Between 1974 and 1980 Parliament recorded eight studio albums on the Casablanca label. The last six of these constitute what we might characterize as an outer-space opera centered on the conflict between the Protectors of the Pleasure Principle and the Perpetrators of the Placebo Syndrome. Dr. Funkenstein, his clones, and his emissary, Star Child, are the primary agents of the former, all "dedicated," as Dr. Funkenstein puts it, "to the preservation of the motion of hips."[13] The Placebo Syndrome is embodied in Sir Nose D'Voidoffunk, the "sucker" who "will not dance, will never dance" because he is too cool to move, groove, or sweat.[14] Dancing, being at one with The Funk, thus becomes a fundamental metaphor for a well-lived life. The space opera, however, offers not only the party where we can "slip a dip in our hips"; it also offers the opportunity to "get hip to the Mothership," to understand and choose between the contestatory alternatives Clinton gives us.[15]

One of the inspirations for Clinton's concept albums appears purely sensational at first: "I was trying to put blacks in places you wouldn't expect to see

'em. I just knew that a nigger on a spaceship would look pretty strange, especially if he looks like he's on a Cadillac."[16] At the same time that Clinton envisioned this literal alienation effect, he also was interested in creating something unified and lasting in terms of rock history: "*Tommy* and *Sgt. Pepper's*, to
me, was the classiest two pieces of music that I had ever seen where everything related to each other. So I wanted to do one of those kind of things."[17]
In essence, then, Clinton wanted to make a black science-fiction cosmos
"where everything related to each other." Being encouraged to "get hip to the
Mothership" was thus an invitation to enter this cosmos—a cosmos, like all
others, comprehensible only through its signs—with Clinton as our guide.

GETTIN' TO KNOW YOU

We may well ask, however, *which* Clin-
ton would be our guide. Despite their distinctions, Dr. Funkenstein, Star
Child, and Sir Nose all share Clinton's voice and even share his body in their
various album-cover representations and concert incarnations. In this case, no
one of Clinton's personae suffices for an interpreter of the whole sign system;
it is only when taken together, as subjectivities of George Clinton that we find
our mediator. Clinton is the man credited with producing and conceiving
every Parliament album, and so the sign system—in concept, in actuation—is
his. He is both inside and outside of it, before it and present within it (and has
survived after it). The Clinton we have to arrive at as our interpreter is thus a
trickster figure, disguising himself in various and fluid ways to make elements
of the interpretation clear, to a degree that even the guise of the producer and
conceiver is simply another subjectivity, the (albeit multiple) One that connects our reality to the science fiction we hear laid out before us.

Of course, trickster figures are a long-standing tradition in African-American literature.[18] One of the most engaging studies of the trickster as interpreter is Henry Louis Gates, Jr.'s *The Signifying Monkey*, in which Gates generates interpretive strategies by reading and rereading modern and postmodern African-American novels. For our purposes, however, Gates's root figure
for these U.S. tricksters, the Yoruba god Esu-Elegbara, is even more important than his literary descendants. In effect, Clinton echoes Esu in his self-rep-
resentations during the space opera. We don't want to claim that Clinton consciously engages Yoruba mythology in making his concept albums, but by
using Esu as a window into the opera, we can understand Clinton's achieve-
ments in valuable new ways.

Esu himself occupies precisely the mediator/interpreter role: "Esu is the sole messenger of the gods (in Yoruba, *iranse*), he who interprets the will of the gods to man; he who carries the desires of man to the gods." As someone shuttling between meanings divine and mortal, conveying both, Esu is also a figure aligned with many qualities: "individuality, satire, parody, irony, magic, indeterminacy, open-endedness, ambiguity, sexuality, chance, uncertainty, disruption and reconciliation, betrayal and loyalty, closure and disclosure, encasement and rupture." All these at once, Esu embodies ambiguity and contradiction. His actual interpretive process is to take the god Ifa's "text of divine will," as encrypted in the divination tool of sixteen palm nuts, and interpret it. Esu essentially becomes the seventeenth palm nut, the supplement that gives meaning to the otherwise unreadable text. Although meaning may be inherent in the divine text, it is unintelligible without the presence of the sole mediator. Essentially, then, Esu *makes* the meaning, his interpretation more a creation than a translation.[19]

As we have suggested, Clinton's "trick" in his rendering of this tradition is to multiply his own subjectivity. Clinton, as the Yoruba say of Esu, "is One, infinitely multiplied" (36). Incorporating various of Esu's qualities into his tripartite space personae and combining them within that much-cited subjectivity "George Clinton," Clinton plays the mediator, the supplement necessary to interpret and interrogate the sign system he also produces. Such an external interpretation of a closed sign system (the science-fiction cosmos) is really an indication that we're not dealing solely with science fiction, which would demand only its own internal voices. What we're really confronting is political allegory, as Clinton's work makes the most sense in the signification of the sign system of history on the science fiction one and vice versa. It's one thing to put blacks on a spaceship; it is entirely another to have that spaceship be equated with "a Cadillac." From the start, then, we're engaged in the political funkonscious that Clinton narrates.

DR. FUNKENSTEIN'S PILL, STAR CHILD'S BOP GUN, AND SIR NOSE'S PLACEBO

Approaching Clinton this way is to see him as both interpreter and model(s) for a political agency. On the one hand, he is Star Child, mediator between Dr. Funkenstein and the "Endangered Species" on Earth who need The Funk to escape the Placebo Syndrome of mindless commercialism.[20] On the other hand, he is a positive agency, Dr.

Funkenstein, and a negative agency, Sir Nose. And on the *other* hand, he is George Clinton, who creates the cryptogram—including his three personae—and helps us begin to see its importance. Clinton succeeds in this trickster pose because he does what all previous tricksters have done: when others want to read him only one way, he keeps his subjectivity fluid and escapes pigeonholing. In order best to understand how this process works, we want to explicate each of Clinton's personae as they occur, particularly in the best and most coherent albums of the space opera, *Mothership Connection* (1975), *The Clones of Dr. Funkenstein* (1976), and *Funkentelechy Vs. the Placebo Syndrome* (1977).

Star Child is the first persona to appear, in the eponymous second song of *Mothership Connection*. Although an intergalactic "Recording Angel," Star Child is not introduced this way. Late in "P-Funk (Wants to Get Funked Up)," the first song of *Mothership Connection*, the "DJ" who introduces the album returns to encourage us to "stay tuned for Star Child." Initially, then, the character's role—and name—is to remind us of so many of those pseudonymed, smooth-talking overnight disk jockeys: Star Child is first brought to us in the familiar guise of a voice on the radio.[21]

However, Star Child almost immediately loses this FM familiarity: addressing the "Citizens of the Universe," he names himself as one of the "Recording Angels . . . come to reclaim the pyramids." Star Child is thus literally what his name says: a child of the stars, an alien. At the same time, the name is full of intriguing overtones. Taking a clue from the address to "Man Child" on *The Clones of Dr. Funkenstein*, we can erase the whole notion of "child" to recognize Star Child as simply a star: rock star, pop star, music star, superstar. Indeed, the connections between the most prominent use of "superstar" in the 1970s, in *Jesus Christ Superstar*, plays into Clinton's persona as well. Star Child is a sort of Christ figure; he is, after all, the one to tell us "You have overcome for I am here."[22] Yet the Christ connection is never complete as Star Child wins his battles without having to sacrifice himself. Moreover, Star Child is proactive in his fight against the Placebo Syndrome, carrying the technology of the Bop Gun with him. Although like Christ in his role as a special one of "God's children" and in his power to save, Star Child is unlike him in his offensive weaponry.

While he certainly comes for a purpose, Star Child is not only interested in "reclaiming the pyramids": his purpose is as much ontological as performative. That is, he *is* the Mothership Connection. What he is is what he does. As the Mothership Connection, Star Child first of all acts as the one to encourage conversion to The Funk: "Put a glide in your stride and a dip in your hip / And come on over to the Mothership." As the funk opera wears on, it is also obvious that he is the primary warrior for The Funk; more than even Dr. Funkenstein, it is Star Child who fights Sir Nose D'Voidoffunk directly.[23] Finally, *Mothership Connection*'s Star Child also brings Dr. Funkenstein's "Supergroovalisticprosifunkstication": it is first a direction to "give the people what they want, / . . . / and they wants it all the time," which becomes the order to "give the people what they need / . . . / and the need is yours and mine." The ambiguity of these lines is key. Star Child, a force for good, seems to be delivering what is essentially a pusher's credo: "give them what they want" and they'll be addicted, experiencing a "need" that will eventually envelop us all. Left with no interpretive gloss, this seems an odd statement, indeed. Yet on the rest of the album it is clear that Star Child "returns" to Earth to help people escape the world dictated by the Placebo Syndrome. Although alien, Star Child is ultimately able to reconnect with earthlings, as can be heard in the softly looped chorus of "Night of the Thumpasorus Peoples": "I am love We are love. . . ." Here the "I" of Star Child has joined the human community in a bond of common "love."

Clinton's initial intergalactic representation is Star Child, the Mothership Connection. As a "connection," Star Child mediates between the Chosen One—Dr. Funkenstein—and the "Endangered Species" of humanity.[24] In this capacity he is much like Esu mediating between Ifa and the Yoruba. Like Esu, Star Child is the messenger, bringing the ambiguous text; unlike Esu, however, Star Child does not pause to interpret that text. His job is that of disruption. It takes the introduction of the Chosen One himself, Dr. Funkenstein, to begin the process of explication and reconciliation. Clinton thus invents not only the messenger and the message but the origin of them both: Dr. Funkenstein.

Even more than "Star Child," the very name "Dr. Funkenstein" is overdetermined. Like Victor Frankenstein, Funkenstein is the creator intent on using science to overcome death (represented by the Placebo Syndrome) and cure the ills of humanity. In this sense, Funkenstein is a "doctor" in terms of both his learning and healing. He acknowledges the latter in his own prescription of himself: "They say the bigger the headache, the bigger the pill. / Call me the Big Pill."[25] However, he is also "the Fiend with the Monster Sound," allowing "creator" to be conflated with "monster/creation" so that the overhanging Shelleyan myth is reinvigorated. Neither creator nor creation can be seen as corrupt; instead, both work together to aid the "Endangered Species."

The Frankenstein myth is further revised in Dr. Funkenstein's desire to create life not only in the form of man but in his *own* form: they are the *clones* of Dr. Funkenstein, after all. Here, then, Clinton eliminates his own mediating persona, Star Child, in favor of direct replication. As the Creator, Dr. Funkenstein is set up as a god, and, like God's, his creations are made in his image. Thus it may only be half-ironic when, describing the "specially designed Afronauts" returning to "release the secrets of the pyramids" and "multiply in the image of the Chosen One, Dr. Funkenstein," Clinton asks "May I frighten you?"[26] Even if you were hip to the Mothership, the idea of multiple befeathered, leathered, and platformed, "freaky and habit-forming" Dr. Funkensteins running around—particularly as harbingers of a new age—was likely to give a moment's pause.[27] Yet, as Clinton points out, "the whole disassociation with the establishment is more scary to the government than if you rob banks or if you're a communist."[28] Therefore even the outrageousness of these "clones" may stand as a fictive model for action outside the established patterns, something to scare the powers-that-be.

This is only half of the clone image, however. Dr. Funkenstein's clones are a larger product of his (musical) technology, that is, they are any of the people "produced" by careful listening to Dr. Funkenstein's message: his audience itself. To be a clone of Dr. Funkenstein is not to *be* Dr. Funkenstein; it is to take his Funk and incorporate it into your own life, "to strut *and* to partake, not just to strut."[29]

Furthermore, the idea that Dr. Funkenstein is the "Big Pill" also helps clarify some of the ambiguity of the Supergroovalisticprosifunkstication. That is, if it reads like an anthem to addiction, it is legitimized somewhat when we understand that the addiction is to the Big Pill, the force for the Pleasure Principle, The Funk, the good. Thus Dr. Funkenstein acts to reconcile the ambiguity that Star Child gave in his deliverance of the speech. Dr. Funkenstein's description of his own identity becomes the interpretation of an otherwise indefinite text.

Funkenstein's clones (representing both themselves and the listeners as "children of production") each possess a "Funky" core element of God that makes them genuine and instrumental—agents—in any change that will take place. However, Funkenstein's own purpose in Clinton's mythos is best perceived not through his own speeches but rather through his clones' refrain: "Take my body give it the mind to funk with the rest. / Hit me with The One and then, if you like, hit me again."[30] Here we return to two currents underlying Clinton's work: "free your mind and your ass will follow" and "The

One." Of the first, the order is reversed here, as the Clones already have the bodies that move to the beat but are not useful until Dr. Funkenstein gives them "the mind to funk with the rest." Here "funk" funktions in two of its most basic ways. First, it indicates the ability to interact (as in "dance") with others, a step absolutely necessary to effect change. At the same time, it is used as an agnominationic shift on "fuck with them," in the sense of "mess with their minds," in the process also changing them. Through his clones's consciousness-raising, Dr. Funkenstein proves himself a model of positive agency, spreading The Funk throughout the world.

Dr. Funkenstein does this by providing the "One" that accomplishes all these ends (a "One" we will address in more detail below). He gives the music for The Funk; his "One" also provides the intellectual power to overcome the prison of the body. This "One" is the magic, again a quality he shares with Esu, which passes along knowledge to the clones and thus the people as well. The One here is essentially the interpretive factor that Dr. Funkenstein controls and uses.

Unlike Star Child and Dr. Funkenstein, Sir Nose D'Voidoffunk seems a more innocuous character, a stock villain. However, given his visual representation and his voice's modulation at the end of "Sir Nose D'Voidoffunk," there is more to this characterization than meets the eye and ear. In a series of strobed photos on the cover of *Funkentelechy Vs. the Placebo Syndrome* we see Star Child shooting the Bop Gun at a stunned Sir Nose. In the frame where Sir Nose is most firmly in the Flash Light of the Bop Gun, he is depicted in a fedora, a two-piece suit, wearing a great deal of gold and holding a cigarette in his left hand. More damning than these superficialities, the self-satisfied pucker and, even more, the knock-kneed, half-bent posture leave little doubt that Sir Nose is a takeoff on Sammy Davis, Jr. And when we hear an imitation of Davis's voice repeating the chorus late in "Sir Nose," whatever reservations we might have had are driven away. Such a depiction is striking. Davis represented a certain type of Vegas sellout, an outmoded, outdated type of funkiness that was out of place in the current urban black scene.[31] His sort of side-mouthed "goo-ga-choo" was part of the syndrome of co-opted black cool—too cool to sweat—that Clinton reacted to. As one critic put it, Sir Nose "represented hypocrisy, constriction, repression of emotion and actions, and death."[32] Sir Nose represents an insincerity antithetical to The Funk, and Sammy Davis, Jr., gave a face to the plastic hypocrisy that Clinton abhorred and literally warred against in his personae of Dr. Funkenstein and Star Child. On a more general level, as Clinton tells it, "we put [Sir Nose] in there to cause conflict between everybody, 'cause that's his gig."[33] Thus the persona of Sir Nose D'Voidoffunk comes to function as a sort of antiagent in the political struggle for The Funk. It is his capacity for disruption and division that Clinton also battles against.

In the end, Scott Hacker's appraisal of Clinton's best-known personae rings true: "Sir Nose, Star Child and Dr. Funkenstein are not just leftovers from *The Wiz* but a troupe of cosmic thespians who play out very definite roles in a more-or-less coherent vision of what things are, in the face of what they could be."[34] Rather than "thespians," we would read the personae as "agents," enacting their roles within an allegorized vision of history that always reaches the realm of reference outside their science-fictive world. Their cosmic agency is meant to help effect what things could be within our own world.

Of course their mouth within that world is George Clinton. In this capacity, Clinton once again reminds us of Esu-Elegbara who is often depicted with two mouths, one speaking for people and one speaking to them, one speaking clearly and one speaking ambiguously. As someone who embodies both the force to cause conflict and the force to resolve it, The One who literally mouths both parts, Clinton takes on the shifting trickster role that allows him critical room and political agency all at once. Like Esu, Clinton is Janus-mouthed in his storytelling and interpreting of his history, talking trash and truth out of both sides of his mouth.

There is one final aspect of Clinton's trickster that we want to touch on here. Just as representations of Esu often depict him with two mouths, so they often depict him as having a large penis, making him "the ultimate copula," a symbol of his connective status.[35] Clinton's own access to this aspect of the copula is twofold. At the height of the Mothership shows, Clinton arrived on stage in a huge fur-covered codpiece, his sexual bravado, ghetto machismo, and urban styling all displayed before him. Ironically, the codpiece physically hides the penis even as it acts to emphasize the size of the copula, the symbol of connection. At the opposite extreme is one of Clinton's early penchants (occasionally reiterated until the early 1980s): stripping naked onstage. Both instances here can be seen as attempts to "connect" with his audience. In the first case, the exaggeration of style and size act to parody style and size, dislodging their significance by showing that "really, style is just a bunch of bullshit, it's just how you carry it."[36] In the second case, disrobed of all his finery, the mediator/interpreter is like any other man in the audience, nothing special. The sense of humility—and humor—of these physical manifestations is key to Clinton's self-image and even to his status as interpreter: "But I know good and well that I ain't said [something deep]. Even if it came out of my mouth, I know that it was the rhythm of the moment and that it really came from somewhere else. . . . I'm the first one to say, 'I ain't shit.' "[37] Like Esu the trickster, Clinton acts as a translator—of that "rhythm of the moment" that is history—by speaking in words both his own and not his own, a moment of Bakhtinian ventriloquation where the discourse of black urban history and the discourse of science fiction collide.

FUNKENTELECHY VS. THE PLACEBO SYNDROME

It is one thing to explicate Clinton as a multiply subjected interpreter in the tradition of Esu-Elegbara. Without some further exploration of the sign system being signified (on), however, such distinctions are only half-complete. Thus we want to turn now to Clinton's mythology within the space opera, paying particular attention to the ways in which he charges his fiction with a political funkonscious.

Although this sign system seems to arrive full-blown on *Mothership Connection*, it actually grows and develops over time.[38] That is, Star Child and the Mothership appear initially, but Dr. Funkenstein doesn't appear until *The Clones of Dr. Funkenstein*, and Sir Nose D'Voidoffunk until *Funkentelechy Vs. the Placebo Syndrome*. (Indeed, we get introduced to other heroes, such as Mr. Wiggles the Worm and Wellington Wigout, and other villains, such as Bumpnoxious Rumpofsteelskin and Sir Nose, Jr., as the story wears on.) The funk opera not only progresses, however; it also flashes back to its own prehistory, in *Clones'* "Prelude," which gives the origins of the sign system and the reason for the return of Star Child and Dr. Funkenstein: "Funk Upon a Time," "specially designed Afronauts capable of funkatizing galaxies" were given to us but "placed among the secrets of the pyramids" until we could fathom their power and "this most sacred phenomenon, Cloned Funk." They would "wait . . . like sleeping beauties" in these "terrestrial projects" until they were released to "multiply in the image of the Chosen One, Dr. Funkenstein." Echoing Star Child's mission (from the previous year) to "reclaim the pyramids," this opening narrative sets up several techniques necessary to write and read the cosmos Clinton produces, a writing and reading that, recalling Esu's meaning making through interpretation, are synonymous.

Perhaps the most evident of these techniques is Clinton's appropriation of literary and colloquial languages. Beginning with the rhetoric of a fairy tale but with the antanaclasis of "Funk" for "Once," Clinton launches into his narrative; it maintains its fairy-tale façade as the funk "would wait . . . like sleeping beauties." (This is also linked to the start of the whole opus, "P-Funk," which sets up the allegorical nature of the opera by including "Once upon a time called *now*.") Linguistic tropes are not the only appropriations made, though, as we find ourselves in both the pyramids, a historical and pop cultural reference, and the "terrestrial projects," with its appropriation of ghetto life. Clinton simultaneously employs parody in his "Afronauts." Closely linked with the appropriations he makes, it is the parodic nature of these appropriations that gives them their force. Gates talks about parody as "motivated Signifyin(g)," and this is precisely what we can see Clinton engaging in throughout the space opera: his appropriations and parody all are motivated signifying on the urban black reality he sees around him.[39] Finally, Clinton invented a new language centered on The Funk itself: the ability to "funkatize" galaxies, Cloned Funk, Dr. Funkenstein. These, too, signify on a deeper funkonscious into which Clinton taps.

EVERYTHING IS ON THE ONE

As elements feeding Clinton's political funkonscious, invention, appropriation, and parody each deserve a longer look. Because Clinton's imaginative additions to the universe, as we just mentioned, are all generated from a foundation of The Funk—as dance, as lifestyle, as noun, verb, adjective, and adverb—it only makes sense to begin there.

The origins and definitions of "funk" are legion. From Charlie Gillet: " 'Funk' had been used as one of those euphemistic black expressions for years: it suggested the smells of sex, a simple lifestyle, and a particular kind of raunchy rhythm which mimicked the sound of love-makers." From Martha Bayles: "In Britain the word means a bad mood; but in the United States it means a strong odor, especially tobacco and bodily smells; and among black Americans it has long been used, along with 'dirty,' 'nasty,' 'low-down,' and 'gut-bucket,' to refer to the rough, bluesy, and above all, polyrhythmic end of the musical spectrum." From Barry Walters: "Trying to put that *thang* called funk into words is like trying to write down your orgasm. Both thrive in that gap in time when words fall away, leaving nothing but sensation." And, not least, several from Clinton himself: "Funk music is basically R&B or black jazz, gospel and all that put together. It is like whatever it needs to be conceptually, lifestyle, whatever it needs to be to make everything all right. . . . It's the positive version of ['fuck it']"; "Funk is a jazz term. It's like, do the best you can and when in doubt, vamp"; "I get off on the funk, to tell the truth . . . 'cause I know how joyful it is."[40] Thus "Funk is its own reward" partially because it can be anything good, wholesome, pleasurable, freeing, "joyful," and life affirming (even the weapons invented for the opera, the Bop Gun and the Flash Light, are funk-centered, the first on the "bop" beat and the second on the "neon light, spot light" of the dance floor).[41] Yet Clinton's funky inventions—like the definition of "funk"—remain open-ended symbols and, as such, remind us of Esu's definitive yet ambiguous interpretations. The Funk is invested with all good possibility and no ultimate meaning: "The funk is never goin' anywhere, it's always comin.' "[42]

The concept of "The One" is similarly ambiguous but no less central to Clinton's imagination. In many ways, all that this essay says about the political funkonscious is really an extrapolation of The One, Clinton's most expansive and malleable concept.[43] Literal, metaphorical, multifaceted, and unique, The One is the linguistic and ideological foundation on which this House of Funk is built. Clinton weaves The One throughout his projects, as he does The Funk, partially because The One *is* The Funk: funk's syncopation is based on the musicians playing around and then meeting on the first beat of a measure. Riffs may be repeated, improvised on, or modulated, but the characteristic relentlessness of funk comes from the fact that it always returns to and emphasizes The One.

Musically, then, The One literally underlies (nearly) every track Clinton has recorded. However, it is the metaphoric multiplicity of The One that really distinguishes it. In the first instance, this is because The One has come to represent not only The Funk but Dr. Funkenstein himself, George Clinton. Clinton remains the individual most associated with the 1970s' funk phenomenon, despite any number of funk bands and well over fifty musicians having worked in his Parliafunkadelicment Thang alone. He has become the highly visible "Father Funk" whose very identity is inextricably aligned with The Funk, The One master of the music of The One.[44] In this role he has become The One spokesman and self-proclaimed "focal point" for the political agency—self-awareness, responsibility, "freeing the mind"—that his music encourages, if not models.[45] Yet within the space opera, as we have seen, Clinton's "One" is revealed as several funkified personae, all unique, yet all united through the "George Clinton" who creates and inhabits them, The "One, infinitely multiplied." Thus Clinton's representational force relies on our understanding of his "One" as a metaphorical composite of various agentive subjectivities.

Another of the instances of The One is as much metaphysical as metaphorical: The One as the one God. Again, this is an aspect best explained within the context of the funk opera, but some sense of it is communicated when, for instance, the 1995 P-Funk All-Stars album *Dope Dogs* (Hot Hands 087426) gives "SPECIALTHANKSTO: 'THEONE' (ASINEVERYTHINGISON . . .)." The divine connection is interesting because it helps us understand the nature and funktioning of The One. Like God, it is the All-in-All, the Alpha and Omega that subsumes differences, opposites, and disparities: Funk's form (repetitions and variations returning to The One), Funk's personae (Clinton's various public selves that are always his "one" self), Funk's message (we are many, we are "one") often contain contradictory and recursive notions where beginning and ends are smudged. Rather than precluding change within an ever-closed tautological doo-loop, however, connecting The One to a divine and expansive Creator within the opera actually gives a stable backdrop against—and from—which change can occur.

Finally, in Clinton's late-seventies productions with Funkadelic, a more directly political aspect to The One can be seen, a politics we will address more completely in a moment. In *One Nation Under a Groove*, The One becomes the unifying principle on which the imagined community, "the nation," is founded. The One is the body politic that we choose either to join or to ignore. That is, we either embrace the narrated political funkonscious and have The Funk, or we don't. And helping us make this choice was precisely the point of Clinton's Parliament project as well: gotta make that body politic *move* already, both physically and metaphorically. "The One," then, is a concept not only shared by Clinton's two 1970s bands—another form of Janus-faced representation—it is also the concept that unifies the political project implicit in Parliament's science fiction and explicit in Funkadelic's nation formation.

OF SPIRITUALS AND BLUES, MOTHERSHIPS AND OL' SMELLOVISION

It is apparent that Clinton's "Funk"-centered inventions generally leave us in a realm of the indeterminate, with merely a number of metonymic and metaphoric possibilities to work from.

The lasting strength of his cosmology comes not from his open-ended inventions but instead from the power of his appropriations and parodies. By absorbing science, popular culture (in both its scientific and commercial guises), and African-American culture into his space opera, Clinton delineates his dual-signifying political allegory. That is, his narrative signifies best when we see its circular connections to a reality outside the opera: properly read, the appropriations and parodies of that reality reveal the signs of the opera as comments on the reality itself.

Although generally more sporadic in its appearance than some of the other appropriations, Clinton's use of science is perhaps most striking because of the very alien quality of its discourse. Sometimes it is punned on and parodied, as in Dr. Funkenstein's mention of the "Chocolate Milky Way"; other times it supports longer points, as in the use of "funkatizing *galaxies*" above.[46] As medicine, it even plays into Dr. Funkenstein's fundamental role as the Big Pill who fights against empty Placebos. At its most complex, though, "science" conveys the root power and message that Clinton projects, something obvious when he reminds us that, "microbiologically speaking," his groove will expand "your molecules, / causing a friction fire." Indeed, this chain reaction only ends in a verbal release as it hits "you on your neutron, / causing you to scream 'Hit me on the proton!' "[47] Funk's "fire" thus creates a "microbiological" shift that causes an uncontrollable need to be "hit"—as the Clones beg to be "hit" with "The One"—"on the proton." Funk moves.

Yet Funk does not *only* move. As we have discussed throughout, the narration of the political funkonscious acts to free bodies but, even more importantly, it also *removes* intellectual constrictions and frees minds. Thus when Clinton cops the term "entelechy," or "the condition in which a potentiality has become actuality," and makes it the "Funkentelechy" that fights the Placebo Syndrome, he is talking about the "scientific" and existential realization of The Funk.[48] As he does this, his chorus chimes out, "How's your funkentelechy?" asking how *our* funk is coming along. They follow this up, however, with "How's your funk-entelech-y?" an aural pun yielding "How's your funk-intellec(t)-y?" The language of science thus works to highlight the bodily and intellectually liberatory elements of The Funk.

But true science is much less in evidence in the space opera than popular science (fiction). At the time these albums appeared, the United States was in the midst of a number of concurrent (pseudo)science trends that captivated the popular consciousness and presses. Erich von Daniken's *Chariots of the Gods?* brought aliens to earth in order to help build . . . the pyramids, themselves a motif we have already seen (and something connected to the seventies fetish for "pyramid power"). Likewise, the mysteries of Easter Island and the Bermuda Triangle filled the grocery store newsstands, the *In Search Of . . .* television specials and movies, and mall bookstores. Steven Spielberg filled our minds with his own impressive mothership in *Close Encounters of the Third Kind*; George Lucas gave us space westerns in his *Star Wars* trilogy.[49] The idea of clones had cropped up in similarly public places, such as the stalwart and popular *Six Million Dollar Man*. Finally, "scientific" advertising theory picked up a fifties idea and reproposed subliminal images as a key to sky-rocketing sales. All these tropes appear in the space opera: Star Child asks whether we are "hip to Easter Island, the Bermuda Triangle"; Sir Nose calls himself the "Subliminal Seducer"; the mothership, clones, and pyramids speak for themselves.[50] By working them into his cosmos, Clinton immediately ironizes these seventies' trends and replaces in them the often-absent element: race.

In many ways, what Clinton does is to return the repressed—raise the political funkonscious—as he addresses the mothership and the pyramids. When, for instance, von Daniken discusses aliens aiding in the construction of the pyramids, nowhere does he address the particularly black history he is updating (or interfering in). Clinton doesn't make the same mistake. The pyramids are the site of the long-hidden secret of the "specially designed Afronauts" precisely because they were built during (arguably) the most powerful black age in history.[51] Likewise, the image of the mothership carries overtones of a return to an absent motherland, itself a theme as old as field spirituals, gospel hymns, and the blues.

As Clinton narrates it, however, the Mothership does not remove anybody. Its salvation comes through what it brings—Dr. Funkenstein, Star Child, The Funk, The One—not what it takes elsewhere. As Hacker emphasizes, "the Mothership symbolized the possibility of a spiritual, not a physical, return to blood and to roots."[52] In many ways, this message connects it to the project of the blues (if we can attach a single project to the blues): the narration of, and triumph over, an often grim reality. Thus when Lightnin' Hopkins sings "Gabriel" or Willie Dixon "Pie in the Sky" or even Muddy Waters doing "Deep Down in Florida," there is a sense of longing for place and release and some hope for fulfillment. (Obviously, this is even more true in the gospel tradition.) Beyond the spiritual connections it makes, this vision of funk and blues also bridges generations. Parliament singer Fuzzy Haskins, who became a gospel-singing preacher after leaving the band, summarizes this link: "We were always connecting the funk to our parents, but with a heavier beat. The blues thing, we grew up with that. That was in our heart."[53] In this way, The Funk and the extraordinarily spectacular and unruly funk opera that seemed such a break from much of what occurred in seventies' black music actually finds some connections with its historical antecedents through its lyrical content if not its musical techniques.[54]

The trope of the mothership, indeed of space travel at all, may well be seen as a reworking of what Houston Baker, Jr., calls the fundamental factors behind the blues of the early twentieth century, the mobile black population and the train track juncture: "The blues musician at the crossing . . . became an expert at reproducing or translating these locomotive energies."[55] Clinton has talked about the origin of his funk as a modified blues: "We realized that the blues was key to [our] music. We just speeded blues up and called it 'funk.' "[56] His funk was thus "the funky blues, the one with the little light groove to it."[57] Indeed, we might say that the "locomotive energies" of blues got translated into the "mothership energies," the "little [Flash] light groove" of Clinton's funk. Just as blues musicians drew on the train whistle and the "instrumental invitation of the *train-wheel-over-track-junctures,*" so the busy-ness of Clinton's funk—especially Bernie Worrell's synthesizer noodlings in songs such as "Flash Light" (*Funkentelechy Vs. the Placebo Syndrome*) and "Everything Is on the One" (*The Clones of Dr. Funkenstein*)—may be indicative of a new black vernacular music.[58] It drives on The One, "travels" in between and returns "home" again on the first beat, a return tied to the idea of "return" embodied in the Mothership itself.

At the same time, the blues notion of the crossroads returns us for a moment to the connections between Clinton and Esu-Elegbara. As a human performer embodying an alien interpreter, as a musician exploring the new juncture of technology (vast amplification and synthesizers) and fictive worlds, as a mediator between science fiction and political allegory, Clinton is posed directly in the center of the crossroads, the mythological home of Esu. Like Esu, "he is, moreover, as master of the roads and crossroads, the master of 'all steps taken,' be these steps taken as one walks or as steps in a process."[59] We have seen the "steps" Clinton takes to create himself time and again; we are in the midst of seeing how his appropriations take steps to narrate and interpret the history that is his political funkonscious. Although his mode of transport in the opera is a mothership, even his literal "steps taken" are noteworthy: "Right now [1985] I say fuck a limousine. . . . I *walked* to see Thomas Dolby. And that gives you strength. Because people ask, man, ain't you tired, and I say I don't feel like I've done shit. I rehearsed for this for 17 years of my life. When I was younger I used to walk down side streets in Newark on Sunday when the stores were closed, screaming 'Parliament, Parliament!'—just so I could hear what it was going to be like when I made it to where I wanted to be."[60] Clinton's vision, his "steps taken," begins in his walking youth, moves through his seventies' position as a trickster at the crossroads inventing a new vernacular, and arrives at a return to walking, that controlled "stepping" that "gives you strength." By playing at the "crossroads," we can see again how Clinton's music and subjectivity are both combined and historically, culturally contingent.

A wider address to popular culture also finds a central place in Clinton's appropriations. The fairy tale overtones we have already noted are matched by revisions of nursery rhymes such as "Three Blind Mice" and "Baa Baa, Black Sheep" ("Baa baa, black sheep, have you any wool? / Yes sir, yes sir, a nickel bag full").[61] Radio is parodied with all the "DJs" used, a move Clinton says was blatantly commercial: using a mock DJ "on a record that got onto radio, made the record sound like it was getting more action than any other, because it sounds like a DJ is talking about it."[62]

This is particularly ironic because commercialism, especially hard-selling items on television, is harshly criticized in Clinton's pop-cultural appropriations; indeed, the Placebo Syndrome is intimately linked to such a "pimping of the Pleasure Principle."[63] Sir Nose is mockingly called "Ol' Smellovision" by Star Child, an instance of jonesing that signifies on his "nose," his relationship to evil (since the devil was known as Old Reekie because of his sulfur smell), and his connection to the insincerity of television ("fake the Funk and your nose will grow").[64] Nowhere are television's and commercialism's empty natures more highly censured than on *Funkentelechy Vs. the Placebo Syndrome.* In "Funkentelechy," "Mood Control" is "brought to you by the makers of Mr. Prolong, / Better known as Urge Overkill, the Pimping of the Pleasure Principle." This sponsorship and program are suddenly interrupted by Dr. Funkenstein, who establishes "Mood *Decontrol*" (emphasis mine) by appropriating prevalent advertising slogans: "You deserve a break today— have it your way"; "How do you spell relief?"; and "I ain't gonna hold the pickles, lettuce or the mayo." In the hands of his "Mood Decontrol," these slogans become acts of rebellion against commercialism, as the last defiant "ain't" shows. Removing them from their initial context and placing them in his own, Clinton gives us a new choice for "relief," for "how to have it your way": The Funk. As something we can participate in and use, The Funk becomes (again) the force that can help liberate us, "decontrol" our lives. Parodying "Let's Make a Deal," Clinton asks perhaps his most important question: "Would you trade your funk for what's behind the third door?" The choice here is between the self-affirming power of The Funk and the unknown and unreliable power of Smellovision's Placebo, commercialism, a trade that only feeds the need to risk and trade even more. If we have trouble deciding, the chorus forces our answer: "When you've taken every kind of pill, / Nothing seems to ever cure your ill." That is, consuming placebos—or consuming and placebos—does not "cure your ill." But the Big Pill, Dr. Funkenstein, The One, The Funk, will. Through his appropriations of television's language, then, Clinton is able to tap into the TV generation's common lore and turn commercialism on its ear, alienating and "decontrolling" the "syndrome" of mindless consumerism.

Finally, Clinton appropriates black life within his opera. One way this happens is through his use of black music. We have already indicated how he retropes the blues; Clinton also takes the heritage of spirituals and appropriates it so that "Swing Low, Sweet Chariot" now becomes the "Swing Down, Sweet Chariot, stop, and let me ride" that accompanies the descent of the Mothership.[65] Rather than being the harbinger of death, the "chariot" is like the "Cadillac" Clinton described, out for a "ride," a ghetto cruise.

The very language and environment of black urban life permeate the opera. Drugs, for instance, are central throughout. After all, the story's fundamental struggle is between the Big Pill and the Placebo Syndrome, perpetuated by Sir "Nose," itself a not-so-oblique reference to cocaine. Street drugs appear in odd places, as in the revision of "Baa Baa, Black Sheep" with its "nickel bag full." Even more indicative of street drugs is The Funk itself. From the start of *Mothership Connection* the chorus, echoing our own needs ("the need is yours and mine"), pleads to "Make my funk the P-Funk; / I wants my funk uncut" because "I wants to get funked up."[66] Here the "uncut" funk is like a pure drug. Being "funked up," then, is to be high on the best life offers. Certainly in this "just say no" age, the connotations of addiction and enervation tend to overwhelm any positive reading we might give. Yet within the context of this allegory, funk's drug is a force for both the "party" and "freeing the mind," in all senses of those words.

Finally, in the Mothership stage shows, Clinton signified on urban style. Taking every element to the extreme, he was able to parody his audience and his world even as he embraced them as the very foundation of his stylings. For instance, the audience's P-Funk–taught forefinger- and pinky-extended hand gesture brought honor to the Afronauts and their mission (and talents) even as it signified on the Black Power fist in its solidarity and defiance. Similarly, Clinton's fur-covered cod/copula, Star Child's oversized sunglasses (now synonymous with legendary bassman Bootsy Collins), and the whole fur-and-denim-and-leather-and-nine-inch-tall-platform-knee-high boots spectacle was taking the ghetto to the edge of the stage, "standing on the verge of getting it on."[67] As Clinton says, "If it's gonna be about glitter, then it's got to be glitter of the highest order."[68] As with all his appropriations within the space opera, the stylistic ones here act as a key part of the narrative of history, the political funkonscious of the 1970s, that Clinton puts on display and articulates.

CODA: ONE NATION UNDER A GROOVE

Even as Clinton's political funkonscious continued to be metaphorized through three more Parliament albums, it emerged conscious and pointed in the Funkadelic album immediately following *Funkentelechy*, *One Nation Under a Groove* (1978). In many ways the greatest P-Funk album, *One Nation* is remarkable in that it leaves behind the highly allegorized story of the space opera in favor of Funkadelic's choice of the urban dance floor as its theater, in every sense of that word. If the Mothership tour was all "glitter," what followed was an antitour of military fatigues, guerilla rock, hard funk—and a change of political tack.[69] Unlike the spacey insights he provided as Star Child and Dr. Funkenstein, Clinton now became the leader of the "One Nation," Uncle Jam, a punning subjectivity shift that signified on his new-found American prominence. In a brief coda to our reading of the political funkonscious, then, we want to glance at Clinton's conscious "Nation" formation.

The ostensible project of *One Nation* is to "free dance music from the blahs,"[70] a slogan indicating a break from both disco and the seventies' malaise or, to steal Amiri Baraka's phrase for the pre-bebop world, "the sinister vapidity of mainline American culture," that "dance music" had come to represent.[71] Unlike the easily discounted pretenses of disco, Clinton's "One Nation" is an unavoidable concept: "So wide you can't get around it / . . . / So high you can't get over it."[72] In a nice play on words, Clinton reminds us that the Nation is both inevitable and, once caught, incurable as well. Here the echoes of Dr. Funkenstein addicting and curing us with The Funk are (similarly) inescapable; now, however, it is the Nation that inextricably holds us. Although this sounds ominous, in reality, the Nation is a freeing concept in that "this is the chance to dance your way / Out of your constrictions" ("One Nation Under a Groove," *One Nation Under a Groove*)? It is interesting to note that as this line gets repeated (as in most P-Funk songs, many, many times), the pronouns shift: though it begins as a lesson to others, "you," it moves quickly to "our" and finally to "my." Unlike the nonparticipatory Dr. Funkenstein, Uncle Jam appears as much a part of the world as the people he talks to, the Nation he leads.

In reality, of course, there is no "nation" here. Instead, Clinton's lyrics conjure what Benedict Anderson calls the "imagined community" of the nation. Rather than the print culture Anderson contends permits this "deep, horizontal comradeship," Clinton uses the music industry—albums, distribution networks (labels and promotion), and concert appearances—to disseminate his ideas. Aural/oral reproduction, not writing, is thus the "large cultural system that preceded [his nation], out of which—as well as against—it came into being."[73]

As a "cultural system," the black music industry already had a history of nationalist overtones, if not directly nationalist music. As Frank Kofsky reminds us, black "nationalist ideas first gained currency within the jazz milieu," a milieu that came to its intellectual head and musical cutting edge during the same decades when Malcolm X, the Nation of Islam, and the Black Panthers enacted their visions of black nationalism.[74] (Indeed, the album cover to *Uncle Jam Wants You* also nods to the nationalism of the Black Panthers by troping the famous photo of leader Huey Newton sitting in his rattan chair, holding spear and gun; Clinton alters it by putting himself in the chair, left hand resting on the Bop Gun, right hand holding up one finger, with the "One Nation" flag flying behind him.) Clinton's funky nationalism thus echoes both a previous generation of funk—as "by 1962 or thereabouts the spontaneity and vitality of funk-soul had been pretty thoroughly depleted through overexposure"—and a previous generation of expressly nationalist musicians, such as Bill Dixon, Archie Shepp, and John Coltrane (50). Yet despite jazz and funk's common roots in black experience, Clinton's nationalism was different because it played out on the grand scale, in stadiums with props and costumes (even if minimal this time around), and played to a relatively widely distributed (FM) radio audience. Clinton's "nation"-making certainly had ties with its jazz forebears, but it was a different creature altogether.[75]

For instance, Clinton's "Nation" used other "cultural systems," such as education, to help define and refine its "nation-ness."[76] In *One Nation*'s song "Groovallegiance," for instance, that most common grade school oath, the

Pledge of Allegiance, is punned into "pledging groovallegiance to the funk" and "pledging allegiance to the flag of funky-funky-Funkadelica." Here, the educational basis for many Americans' social indoctrination to the idea of "the nation" is refigured to create not only a new pledge but a new nation, the United States of Funkadelica, as well.

As in the Parliament opera, it is Clinton's capacity for inventive and appropriative language that creates that "(Not Just) Knee Deep" (*Uncle Jam Wants You*, Priority CD 53875, 1993) identification with "One Nation." Anderson reminds us that "the most important thing about language is its capacity for generating imagined communities, building in effect *particular solidarities*" (133). As P-Funk has aged, the heterogeneous appeal of this language play—and The Funk—has moved Clinton's Nation beyond its primarily black identification in the seventies: "We got off in Minnesota and there was nothing but white people at the gig. See, that's what's weird now—a lot of white people coming to the shows."[77] In one such recent Minnesota show, playing now to a racially diverse crowd, "One Nation" grooving behind him, Clinton proclaimed, "They say we can't do this—well, we're doing this, black and whites together."[78] Essentially, the Nation is becoming more and more "One" within the particular solidarity, the political unity and alternative to what "they say," that Clinton's music provides.

Ted Fox devotes the last pages of his book on Harlem's Apollo Theater to a 1980 P-Funk performance of "One Nation."[79] In particular, he emphasizes the powerful—"One nation under a groove, / Getting down just for the funk of it"—and prophetic—"One nation, we're on the move / Nothing can stop us now"—character of the chorus, something we would also like to underscore as we end our coda. The Nation imagined here is mobile, active, and powerful. It has become that unstoppable agentive force that both represents and brings change. Yet this Nation is not an undifferentiated "it" at all. In a lovely turn that highlights the political force of each funkateer, the Nation is an "us." The Nation may be getting down just for the fun(k) of it, but the chorus also carries an overtone of unified action and political consciousness, a "deep, horizontal comradeship" that cannot be denied.

REPRISE: EVERYTHING IS ON THE ONE

One Nation, One leader, One beat, One struggle united against hypocrisy, One agency with many agents, George Clinton's Funk articulates the political funkonscious of a decade rife with

"Ego-munchies, images doggie bags, and me burger with I sauce on it."[80] Rather than succumbing to this self-centered Placebo Syndrome, Clinton gives us a prescription and model for action, both on and off the dance floor. With Parliament, he retroped the figure of the trickster-interpreter in order to allegorize his present and battle the Noses. With Funkadelic, his rhetoric engaged a national consciousness tapping both history and the "horizontal" connections his music made. A party on the outside, Clinton's Funk is deeply humanistic at its interior. As Greg Tate so aptly encapsulates it: "Besides giving Funk mass appeal and liquid assets, Uncle Jam also gave it a metaphysic, proposing that the bottom of the human soul, its bass elements one might say, are what makes life a song worth singing."[81] So, too, are Clinton's songs always worth singing, over and over and over again.[82]

NOTES

1. Clinton himself addresses this elision of George Clinton with Funk in his introduction to Rickey Vincent's seminal volume *Funk: The Music, the People, and the Rhythm of the One* (New York: St. Martin's/Griffin Press, 1996).

2. Clinton employed *The Wiz*'s costume designer to accouter the Mothership tour. As he put it, "This business is run by association and money. When you can say you've spent $350,000 on something, and Jules Fisher did the spaceships, and Larry Gatsby did the costumes, you've just associated yourself with the Rolling Stones, the Who, Patti LaBelle, *The Wiz*" (G. Tate, *Flyboy in the Buttermilk: Essays on Contemporary America* [New York: Simon and Schuster, 1992], p. 33).

3. V. Reid, "Brother from Another Planet," *Vibe* (November 1993): 45.

4. R. Bowman, liner notes to *Funkadelic? Music for Your Mother: Funkadelic 45's* (Westbound CD 55, LP IIII, 1992), p. 18.

5. Parliament, "Mothership Connection (Star Child)," on *The Clones of Dr. Funkenstein* (Casablanca CD 842620-2, LP NBLP-7034, 1976).

6. John Edgar Wideman, *Fatheralong: A Meditation on Fathers and Sons, Race, and Society* (New York: Vintage, 1994), p. 72.

7. Although never published, Ted Friedman's "Making It Funky: The Signifyin(g) Politics of George Clinton's Parliafunkadelicment Thang" (http://english-www.hss.cmu.edu/music/Friedman-Making.It.Funky.html) began to address the intellectual content of Clinton's music as well. Friedman's abbreviated study might be best understood as a suggestive introduction to all of Clinton's work, however, rather than the more concentrated and detailed analysis of the 1975–79 period that we offer here.

8. Funkadelic, "Free Your Mind and Your Ass Will Follow," on *Free Your Mind and Your Ass Will Follow* (Westbound 2001, 1971).

9. Original Funkadelic guitarist Tawl Ross was left behind in Toronto on the 1973 tour as a result of a severely bad acid trip. After a twenty-year absence, however,

Ross resurfaced recently to cut a well-received album (*Giant Shirley*, 1995) with P-Funk drummer Jerome Brailey.

10. As Vincent puts it: "While his creative input was invaluable, Clinton often brought complete legalistic and financial chaos to his projects" (*Funk*, p. 249). Often, instead of fuller financial recompense, Clinton would give composition credits to his musicians. This had the effect of minimizing his actual importance in the public eye while maintaining his control of whatever monies the bands produced.

11. Funkadelic, "Lunchmeatophobia (Think! . . . It Ain't Illegal Yet)," on *One Nation Under a Groove* (Warner LP 3209, 1978).

12. Fredric Jameson, *The Political Unconscious: Narrative as a Socially Symbolic Act* (Ithaca, NY: Cornell University Press, 1981), p. 35.

13. Parliament, "Dr. Funkenstein," on *The Clones of Dr. Funkenstein.*

14. Parliament, "Sir Nose D'Voidoffunk (Pay Attention—B3M)," *Funkentelechy Vs. the Placebo Syndrome* (Casablanca CD 824501-2, LP NBLP-7804, 1977).

15. Parliament, "Mothership Connection (Star Child)."

16. C. Harris, "President George Clinton: On the State of the Funk Nation," *Pulse!* (December 1993): 57. Scott Hacker points out that this Cadillac was also more literally represented in later stage shows as a "soft-'n'-floppy lamé roadster" ("P-Funk," in P. Kennedy, *Platforms: A Microwaved Cultural Chronicle of the 1970's* [New York: St. Martin's, 1994], p. 148).

17. John Corbett, *Extended Play: Sounding Off from John Cage to Dr. Funkenstein* (Durham, NC: Duke University Press, 1994), p. 150.

18. Good studies of the African-American trickster figure include Eric Sundquist, *To Wake the Nations* (Cambridge: Harvard University Press, 1991); John Willie Roberts, *From Trickster to Badman* (Philadelphia: University of Pennsylvania Press, 1989); Elizabeth Ammons and Annette White-Parks, *Tricksterism in Turn-of-the-Century American Literature* (Hanover, NH: University Press of New England, 1994); and, Lawrence Levine, *Black Culture and Black Consciousness* (New York: Oxford University Press, 1977). For African tales showing tricksters in action, see Paul Radin, *African Folktales*, Bulletin Series (Princeton: Princeton University Press, 1952); for a cogent analysis of such tales, see Robert Pelton, *The Trickster in West Africa* (Berkeley: University of California Press, 1980).

19. Henry Louis Gates, *The Signifying Monkey: A Theory of Afro-American Literary Criticism* (New York: Oxford University Press, 1988), pp. 6, 9.

20. Parliament, "Bop Gun (Endangered Species)," *Funkentelechy Vs. the Placebo Syndrome*. The Funkadelic embodiment of this Placebo Syndrome, "spanking," is detailed most impressively in the liner notes to 1973's *Cosmic Slop* (Westbound 2022) and, even more acerbically, in the "Zeepic Chronicles" elaborated in 1981's *Electric Spanking of War Babies* (Warner LP 3482; reissue, Priority 53874, 1993).

21. Parliament, *The Mothership Connection* (Casablanca CD 824502-2, LP 7022, 1975). In "Making It Funky," Friedman has a brief but astute reading of Clinton's position

with radio listeners in the seventies. Moreover, this use of the radio helps strengthen the connections between seventies glam rock and the Parliament. Clinton's radio pose echoes, for instance, David Bowie's "Starman," whose protagonist's radio fades down only to come "back like a slow voice on the wave of phase / That weren't no DJ, that was hazy cosmic jive" (David Bowie, "Starman," *The Rise and Fall of Ziggy Stardust and the Spiders from Mars* (RCA AFL1-4702, 1972).

22. Parliament, "Mothership Connection (Star Child)."

23. Sir Nose and Star Child battle face to face in "Sir Nose D'Voidoffunk (Pay Attention—B3M)" and "Funkentelechy" on *Funkentelechy Vs. the Placebo Syndrome*, in "Aqua Boogie" on *The Motor Booty Affair*, and in "Theme from 'The Black Hole'" on *Gloryhallastoopid*.

24. Parliament, "Bop Gun (Endangered Species)."

25. Parliament, "Dr. Funkenstein," *The Clones of Dr. Funkenstein*.

26. Parliament, "Prelude," *The Clones of Dr. Funkenstein*.

27. Parliament, "P-Funk (Wants to Get Funked Up)," *The Mothership Connection*.

28. Corbett, *Extended Play*, p. 281.

29. Hacker, "P-Funk," p. 149.

30. Parliament, "Dr. Funkenstein."

31. Davis's 1970s' career included, for instance, such mainstream and whitewashed manifestations as appearances on *Charlie's Angels* and in the *Cannonball Run* movies. By the 1980s, however, Davis had retapped some of his earlier glory, playing highly respectable and respected characters, such as the aging, patriarchal hoofer in *Tap*.

32. R. Clough, *The Motherpage Website*, http://www.duke.edu/tmc/pfunk.html. The issue of Davis's Judaism is not addressed in either Clinton's characterization or our analysis. However, given the idea of "Sir *Nose*" and the anti-Semitism some of the Clinton's "children" in the rap generation have been accused of, a further analysis of these overtones is worth undertaking.

33. Corbett, *Extended Play*, p. 281.

34. Hacker, "P-Funk," p. 154.

35. Gates, *The Signifying Monkey*, p. 6.

36. Corbett, *Extended Play*, p. 147.

37. P. Jebsen, "The Doctor Is On: The George Clinton Interview," *Goldmine* 17, no. 2 (1991): 10, 13.

38. Funkadelic's early album liner notes, primarily written by cover-artist Pedro Bell (in consultation with Clinton), actually prefigure the growth of the Parliament narrative. The ever-expanding Funkadelic notes delineate the Splankadelic Chronicles, told by Sir Lleb of Splankedelia. Like Parliament's music, these notes are allegorical readings of the world of the 1970s and early 1980s, though even less masked than the narrative of the space opera.

39. Gates, *The Signifying Monkey*, p. xxvi.

40. Charlie Gillet, *The Sound of the City: The Rise of Rock and Roll* (New York: Pantheon, 1983), p. 245; Martha Bayles, *Hole In Our Soul: The Loss of Beauty and Meaning in American Popular Music* (New York: Free, 1994), p. 334; B. Walters, "Learning to Funk the Bomb," *Village Voice*, 16 August 1985, p. 63; Jebsen, "The Doctor Is On," p. 10; Corbett, *Extended Play*, p. 189; Reid, "Brother from Another Planet," p. 48. Scott Hacker has an eloquent explication of the "smell" of Funk in his appendix, "P-Funk," in Pagan Kennedy's book *Platforms*. Although important to an overall understanding of The Funk, this olfactory sense is less important within our reading of the political funkonscious.

41. Parliament, "Prelude." The prominence of the Flash Light in relation to both Clinton and The Funk was emphasized in Clinton's first onscreen appearance during PBS's *History of Rock* episode on funk: he entered through a room full of mist, cut only by the beam of a flashlight.

42. Jebsen, "The Doctor Is On," p. 11.

43. Our emphasis on Clinton's use of The One is to credit him neither with its invention nor the musical innovation it engages. As Vincent points out, that distinction goes to James Brown: "By turning rhythmic structure on its head, emphasizing the downbeat—the 'one' in a four-beat bar—the Godfather kick started a new pop trend and made a rhythmic connection with Africa at the same time. James Brown songs hit their accents in 'On the One,' yet drove the furious bluesy fatback drumbeats all around the twos and fours to fill up the rhythms, never leaving any blank space" (Vincent, *Funk*, p. 8).

44. W. Jancik, "Bernie Worrell: The Man Behind Father Funk," *Goldmine* 17, no. 2 (1991): 40.

45. Jebsen, "The Doctor Is On," p. 10.

46. Parliament, "P. Funk (Wants To Get Funked Up)"; "Prelude."

47. Parliament, "Dr. Funkenstein."

48. *The Compact Edition of the Oxford English Dictionary* (Oxford: Oxford University Press, 1971), p. 874.

49. *Star Wars* was parodied often in P-Funk writing. See, for instance, the retreating text in the comic book accompanying *Funkentelechy Vs. the Placebo Syndrome* and the use of the character "Barft Vada" in the liner notes to *One Nation Under a Groove*.

50. Parliament, "Mothership Connection (Star Child)"; Parliament, "Sir Nose D'Voidoffunk (Pay Attention—B3M)."

51. Parliament, "Prelude." Clinton's use of "Egypt" and later "Nubia" is covered in Greg Tate's 1985 interview, reprinted in *Flyboy in the Buttermilk*. "Egypt" as a visual motif is highlighted on Parliament's *Trombipulation* as well. Still, Parliament was not the only funk band using the motif; Earth, Wind and Fire were also well known for their neo-Egyptian outfits and stage shows.

52. Hacker, "P-Funk," p. 148.

53. Bowman, liner notes, p. 11.

54. A useful, broad survey of the forms, styles, and players of twentieth-century blues (and jazz/blues) is Albert Murray's *Stomping the Blues* (New York: McGraw-Hill, 1976). He is particularly good on the connections between church music and blues as well as when breaking down the various formal elements of a blues song. In particular, his chapter "Playing the Blues" (93–128) would be informative for listeners of extended P-Funk pieces.

55. Houston A. Baker, *Blues, Ideology, and Afro-American Literature: A Vernacular Theory* (Chicago: University of Chicago Press, 1984), p. 11.

56. Reid, "Brother from Another Planet," pp. 45–46.

57. Harris, "President George Clinton," p. 60.

58. Baker, *Blues*, p. 8.

59. Gates, *The Signifying Monkey*, p. 31.

60. Tate, *Flyboy in the Buttermilk*, p. 40.

61. Parliament, "Sir Nose D'Voidoffunk (Pay Attention—B3M)."

62. Harris, "President George Clinton," p. 63.

63. Parliament, "Funkentelechy."

64. This is, of course, the Pinocchio theory first espoused by Bootsy's Rubber Band on their 1977 album *Ahh . . . The Name Is Bootsy, Baby!* (Warner Brothers 2972).

65. Parliament, "Mothership Connection (Star Child)."

66. Parliament, "P-Funk (Wants to Get Funked Up)."

67. Funkadelic, "Standing on the Verge of Getting It On," *Standing on the Verge of Getting It On* (Westbound CD 1001, LP 208, 1974).

68. Corbett, *Extended Play*, p. 297.

69. Tate, *Flyboy in the Buttermilk*, p. 40.

70. This slogan is actually used as the subtitle to the Funkadelic album that followed *One Nation Under a Groove, Uncle Jam Wants You.*

71. Amiri Baraka, *Blues People: Negro Music in White America* (Westport: Greenwood, 1963), p. 182.

72. Funkadelic, "One Nation Under a Groove."

73. Benedict Anderson, *Imagined Communities: Reflections on the Origin and Spread of Nationalism* (London: Verso, 1991), pp. 7, 12.

74. Frank Kofsky, *Black Nationalism and the Revolution in Music* (New York: Pathfinder, 1970), p. 27.

75. There are also ties between the jazz world and Clinton's science fiction. See, in particular, John Corbett's excellent examination of Clinton, Sun Ra, and Lee "Scratch" Perry in his essay "Brothers from Another Planet," anthologized in *Extended Play.*

76. Anderson, *Imagined Communities*, p. 4.

77. Tate, *Flyboy in the Buttermilk*, p. 35. Vincent reminds us that Clinton's original audience was primarily black youths on city streets (Vincent, *Funk*, p. 259).

78. This show was at The Cabooze, in Minneapolis, on 8 October 1992.

79. Ted Fox, *Showtime at the Apollo* (New York: Da Capo, 1993), pp. 304–8. It is inter-

esting to note that, though Fox gives prominence to "One Nation," he repeatedly misquotes the lyrics as "One Nation, United, Under a Groove." Though it is possible that Clinton changed the song for this performance, it is more likely that the misprision occurs to help prove Fox's point that the Apollo's closing was achieved with a continued sense of community.

80. Funkadelic, "Promentalshitbackwashpsychosis Enema Squad," *One Nation Under a Groove.*

81. Tate, *Flyboy in the Buttermilk,* p. 17.

82. Although we have dealt with a cross-section of music now twenty years old, Clinton is still quite active, recently domestically releasing the Parliament/ Funkadelic/P-Funk All-Stars CD DOPE DOGS on his One Nation label and *The Awesome Power of a Fully Operational Mothership* (Sony 550, 1996) under his own name. In 1996 he also released *Greatest Funkin' Hits* on Capitol, which included several new versions of older songs, and a two-CD live set, *Live . . . And Kickin'* (Intersound 9284), came out from George Clinton and the P-Funk All-Stars in 1997. During this decade he has also toured extensively with the P-Funk All-Stars, and the Mothership has even made an occasional appearance.

7

"I HAVE COME OUT TO PLAY"

JONATHAN RICHMAN AND THE POLITICS OF

THE FAUX NAÏF

JOHN ALBERTI

There's a surprise opening to the episode of the recent PBS *History of Rock 'n' Roll* devoted to the rise of punk. While the narration gives us the by now conventionalized story of how rock music had lost its power of cultural subversion in the early nineteen seventies and had simply become another segment of the mainstream leisure industry, we see a figure walking toward the camera over a brightly lit green lawn. This figure has been positioned by the structure of the program to represent a decisive rupture in the co-optation of rock music by the corporate music industry, a harbinger of the punk and by extension so-called alternative music scene that would stand along with rap as the last major political irruption to date in the world of popular music. And who is this revolutionary chosen by PBS to stand as punk herald? Lou Reed? Iggy Pop? Maybe even Joey Ramone? No, although all would be dutifully recognized and interviewed by the program for their roles in punk history. Instead, as we begin to recognize the music playing under the narration as early Modern Lovers, the avatar of punk turns out to be Jonathan Richman, self-proclaimed Nature's Mosquito and cult artist par excellence, who proceeds to regale the PBS audience with a tale drawn from (and, in a gesture characteristic of his performing style, virtually a recitation of the lyrics of) his early song "Girlfriend." Clearly, it is the early Modern Lovers songs that Robert Palmer (the main consultant for the series) and PBS had in mind in choosing Richman for this seminal position, but the lyrics from this particular Lovers song ("I'm walking through the Fenway in Boston I got my heart in my hand / I just need, a girlfriend) seem not quite in synch with the anger and anarchy typically associated with punk.[1] Richman leaves his listeners, particularly those who are newcomers to his music, with the question: is he serious or not?

This anecdote and the choice of Richman by the PBS documentary illustrate in several ways the complex function of irony in rock 'n' roll, specifically in those forms of rock practice known as punk and alternative. Irony is also related to central questions concerning whether and to what extent rock 'n' roll can operate as a music of cultural and political resistance, a site for anti-hegemonic practice, in Raymond Williams's terms. The appearance of the PBS documentary itself, along with the creation of Cleveland's Rock 'n' Roll Hall of Fame, mark both a decisive acceptance and an entombment of rock music within bourgeois culture. Rock now has a canon (and thus a potential source of vita-building academic debate) and an official history (along with the requisite "secret histories").

The attempt to canonize a cult figure such as Richman, however, suggests a potential instability within this historicizing process, in that if he represents a part of the official development of rock 'n' roll, he also can be seen as an aberration from it, a strange figure who rhapsodized about the ice cream man and "Rockin' rockin' leprechauns" and performed affectionate covers of "The Wheels on the Bus" and "Angels Watching Over Me" while the punks he supposedly inspired (an inspiration he has consistently disavowed) sang about Antichrists and lobotomies. It would be difficult to dismiss Richman's performances as simply ironic, but they are at the same time far too calculated in their primitivism to accept at face value. While he occupies a central position in the PBS documentary, none of his songs earned a spot on the Hall of Fame's list of the one hundred greatest rock records of all time. He has remained both widely influential yet still little known (although both Neil Young and the Farrelly brothers are working hard to raise his profile, the first by signing him to his record label and boosting his production budget and the second by featuring Jonathan in their films, most prominently as the musical "narrator" of *There's Something About Mary*).

If there is a performative strategy common to both Richman and the early punks, it would be the deliberate invocation of amateurism as a counterpoint to the growing professionalization of mainstream rock. In Peter Wicke's description: "What counted for music in this sub-culture seemed to be defined through the uncompromising negation of those aesthetic criteria which had in the meantime made rock music an accepted part of contemporary cultural activity. The polished sound structures of a rock 'art' concerned with 'content' were now opposed by a challenging dilettantism which only had to sound loud, aggressive and chaotic to be accepted as rock music."[2] But in place of aggression and chaos, Richman turned—or perhaps *returned* is the word—to childhood, both in terms of lyric content and performance style, yet still within the commercial dynamics of the youth music industry. Such a strategy, with its invocation of the soft over the loud, the ingenuous over the cynical, the playful over the defiant, challenges both conventional rock criticism and consumption in ways that help raise crucial questions about the role of irony as alternatively a form of cultural resistance and co-optation within alternative rock. Specifically, Richman's strategic invocation of childhood can be read as a gesture toward the concept of preideological space as a point of radical disruption of the mainstream consumption of rock music.

A useful point of departure for the consideration of irony, amateurism, and the childlike can be found Bertolt Brecht's ideas about the radicalizing effect of amateur acting. Brecht was always suspicious of the political implications of naturalistic professional acting styles that led audiences to believe in the reality of the artificial construct of the play. This Platonic distrust of the power of the arts to deceive stemmed in Brecht from a critique of the ways in which ideologies of power concealed their constructed, class-based origins through appeals to nature and common sense. Instead, Brecht wanted to create a radical theater that encouraged its audience to question the assumed inevitability and rightness of the status quo outside the theater by challenging the supposed naturalness of the acting inside the theater.

Brecht found one such strategy in the practice of amateur theater companies. Through their awkward attempts at naturalistic acting, such unintentional bad actors created a crisis of representation that ultimately deconstructed representation itself: by revealing the constructedness of theatrical representation, amateur acting could be used to expose by extension the constructedness of the everyday actions they struggled to imitate. Brecht tried to turn this mistake into a deliberate acting style, a professional amateurism that worked to foreground the means of theatrical production and by extension the contingency and changeability of all social relationships. Brecht describes this effect of amateur acting through an analogy with the education of children:

One easily forgets that human education proceeds along highly theatrical lines. In a quite theatrical manner the child is taught how to behave; logical arguments only come later. When such-and-such occurs, it is told (or sees), one must laugh. It joins in when there is laughter, without knowing why; if asked why it is laughing it is wholly confused. In the same way it joins in shedding tears, not only weeping because the grown-ups do so but also feeling genuine sorrow. This can be seen at funerals, whose meaning escapes children entirely. These are theatrical events which form the character. The human being copies gestures, miming, tones of voice. And weeping arises from sorrow, but sorrow also arises from weeping.[3]

In "Brecht and Rhetoric," Terry Eagleton extends this analogy between Brecht's theories about the destabilizing effects of bad acting and the uneasy relationship between rhetoric and logic, assertion and justification, in the ideological enculturation of young children.[4] Eagleton uses Brecht's suggestion that children are in many ways amateur actors, trying to imitate, through their play, the "play" of adult social life, to draw a distinction between rhetoric and logic. Children imitate the actions and language of adults before they learn the supposed justification for these behaviors and beliefs. In effect, they begin by imitating the rhetoric of cultural gestures, mimicking the lines they hear adults speak. It is only later, often as part of the process of institutional education, that they learn to see these gestures as validated by, to use Eagleton's coinage, "(ideo)logic." According to Eagleton, children thus unwittingly expose the constructedness and thus contingency of particular ideological structures and practices in two ways: first, by the impertinence of their naive questions (Why is that man hungry? Are we rich or poor?); and, second, by the disconnection between their efforts to act like adults and their in a sense preideological understanding of these actions. As a cultural theorist who prides himself on the impertinency of his own questions, Eagleton claims common cause with children, whom he labels "incorrigible theoreticians," and argues that one goal of Brechtian or any radical performance theory is to "breed bad actors" through the strategic—hence rhetorical—use of the "faux-naïf" (171).

This practice of ideological demystification through a self-conscious foregrounding of the constructedness of cultural texts and performances is, of course, neither original nor unique to Brecht; it is a version of left-wing modernism and has been a staple of radical avant-garde cultural movements in the twentieth century. In Lipstick Traces, Greil Marcus constructs his own genealogy of the cultural politics of ideological demystification centered on the links connecting the dada movement to situationism and situationism to the Sex Pistols. Marcus's description of the denaturalizing effects of punk rock includes echoes of Brecht: "The music made it possible to experience all those things [God and the state, work and leisure, home and family, sex and play, the audience and itself] as if they were not natural facts but ideological constructs: things that had been made and therefore could be altered, or done away with altogether. It became possible to see these things as bad jokes."[5]

Just as Brecht's radical cultural politics focused on the theater (including musical theater and burlesque) that was the dominant leisure industry of the early twentieth century, punk recognized the centrality of pop music to consumer capitalism in the late twentieth century. There was an irony already implicit in the radical deconstruction of rock 'n' roll, however, because an element of rebellion had always been a part of the cultural practice of the form and had in fact become a part of rock's consumer appeal. Therefore, according to Marcus, "If one could show that rock 'n' roll, by the mid-1970's ideologically empowered as the ruling exception to the humdrum conduct of social life, had become simply the shiniest cog in the established order, then a demystification of rock 'n' roll might lead to a demystification of social life."[6] This demystification of rock has been a component of alternative rock ever since. The problem has been that every new attempt at demystification through a greater exaggeration of the most identifiable signifiers of rock music (volume, aggression, hedonism) has all too easily become an even shinier, noisier cog.

The analogy Eagleton draws between Brecht's dramatic theory and the ideological enculturation of children, though, can help us understand the potential of Jonathan Richman's strategic difference. While a strategy of amateurism is at face value oppositional within the conventions of professional theater (redrawing radical connections between a thoroughly canonized and institutionalized adult cultural activity and the childhood game of "let's pretend"), the use of faux naïf has had a double-edged meaning for the practice of rock, as rock performers and critics have self-consciously struggled with the identity of rock 'n' roll as youth music and at the same time so-called serious art. Such a struggle has led to rock 'n' roll performers themselves imitating the rhetoric of high culture in the form of rock opera, concept albums, and the self-important use of the term "concert" to refer to rock performances, but often with a shaky grasp of the ideological implications of such imitation. Part of the rebellion of punk was precisely against this effort to turn rock into concert—and by extension "adult"—music. Bands from the Ramones to Green Day have used cartoon graphics along with deliberately childish lyrics and even album titles as a form of resistance to what were seen as efforts to intellectualize (and thus stultify) rock music.

While these faux-naïf gestures have been grounded in an understandable reaction against the increasing dullness of mainstream rock, they have also seemed excessively nervous and self-conscious in very unchildlike ways. For all their rejection of cultural status seeking, they seemed at the same time calculated to maintain a certain ironic space between, say, the Ramones chanting "Gabba gabba hey" or the mannered naïveté of the early Talking Heads and the supposed "real" attitudes of the artists. In the end, the implication remains that these rebels against pretension are in fact trying to prove themselves in the long run to be more intellectually profound than openly pompous and portentous bands like Pink Floyd or their even more ludicrous descendants such as Kansas or Emerson, Lake, and Palmer. Thus, while seeming to distance themselves from growing trends toward securing rock a cultural position as "adult" music, punk and/or alternative rock have also tried to resist the effort to trivialize rock 'n' roll as "kids' " music. Such a project exposes and expresses important contradictions and ambivalences toward the dominant cultural practices to which alternative rock claims to represent an alternative.

Before turning to Richman's particular use of the faux naïf as it relates to this particular double bind, it would be helpful to explore this larger cultural context further in terms of the ideology of rock, particularly in relation to the concomitant desires for acceptance and rebellion vis-à-vis bourgeois standards of cultural acceptability. Neil Nehring, for example, has argued that much contemporary rock criticism from the sixties to the present has modeled itself on the decontextualizing and fetishizing practices of literary New Criticism as a means of subjecting rock lyrics to the same kinds of close literary analysis as a Keats ode, thereby claiming equal literary and cultural status for this rock "poetry." Nehring points out that such an approach fails to account for "popular music in ways relevant to its actual performance, production, and consumption" and that it buys into (and the economic metaphor is relevant here) a certain conservative, even reactionary, modernist construction of the artistic authenticity of the rock artist as isolated romantic genius transcending the limitations of history and politics.[7] Wicke has described this ideological formation of rock as art in terms of the contradictions that exist between rock music as a highly intense means of personal self-expression and its material reality as a mass media consumer product:

> The value criteria and measures which musicians had developed for judging music—communication, creativity and a common experience through music—were born of an extreme individualism, with which

they hoped in ideological terms to avoid the constraints of the capitalist music business. As long as musicians succeeded in asserting themselves against the commercial pressures of the industry and being successful in spite of this, they felt they had achieved an element of self-realization, which, as they saw it, undermined the logic of capitalism and countered the cultural production line steered by capitalist interests with something of a more personal nature.[8]

Wicke correctly calls this a "beautiful, but enormous illusion," in that it depends on a simplistic, romantic opposition between personal expression and market forces, between "sincerity" and marketability (112). In fact, the marketing of rock 'n' roll depends on the mass reproducibility of a supposedly unreproducible artistic act and, by extension, the continuous production of new and improved uniqueness. The desire to carve out a space of intellectual distance and superiority on the part of much alternative rock—and of the rock criticism that provides the ideological justification for this superiority—contributes to the cultural logic informing these marketing needs by working to invest the cultural capital of romantic genius into mass-market products. Presumed profundity or the purity of one's cultural rebellion thus becomes a powerful marketing tool.

Given this seemingly vicious circle of cultural rebellion and co-optation by market forces, Richman's continuing economic marginality—never achieving widespread commercial success yet maintaining, sometimes barely, a recording contract—along with his uncertain canonical position, make his use of the faux naïf especially intriguing. Consider Richman's own third-person description of his move away from the protopunk sound he had helped pioneer:

> He needed some songs which would make pre-teens laugh. See, he'd already started playing a lot for kids and the regular "children's songs" just weren't funny enough. Richman's idea was not to make songs aimed specifically at children but ones they could enjoy along with the rest of the audience. Sometimes this works and sometimes it doesn't and Mr. Richman sure doesn't consider all his efforts in this to be successful— those songs which had this subject matter.[9]

There are two significant points here for our purposes. The first is Richman's habitual use of the third person in talking about himself, not only here but in performance and in his songs. Like other alternative rock performers, Richman has consistently foregrounded the constructedness of his musical identity.[10] Unlike the uses of faux naïf referred to above, however, Richman doesn't refer to the childlike as simply a pose; instead, he claims to be interested in children as an audience for his music. This represents a crucial elaboration on the Brechtian formulation that Eagleton describes, in that Richman in effect trades on the tradition of rock 'n' roll as youth music to supplement the idea of regressing to a childlike condition with the notion of creating solidarity between children and more mature—but also therefore more ideologically enculturated—consumer/listeners.

Richman's desire that children enjoy his songs "along with the rest of the audience" creates the opportunity for the possible disruption of marketing categories for music by unhinging the neat distinction between the "staged" childishness, or naïveté, and the "real" intellectual sophistication informing the faux naïf of much alternative rock. Perhaps his most famous "children's" song, "Ice Cream Man," can serve as a case in point. The centerpiece of *Rock 'n' Roll With the Modern Lovers*, his most fully realized album of faux naïveté, "Ice Cream Man" features a combination of the sophisticated and childlike, perhaps best personified by D. Sharpe's percussion, a spare but ingenious backbeat played on what sounds like a drum kit made of cardboard boxes. Richman's repetitious lyrics, warbled only variably in key in the energetic sing-song style associated with children at play, offer a tribute to the sensory experience of listening to an ice cream truck coming down the street: "Ice cream man, ring your bell / Play that music I love so well." It is less about the taste of ice cream than the feelings of joy in children occasioned by the sound of the truck's approach. The tone would be unabashedly nostalgic and sentimental save for the fact that Richman sings it in the present tense, insisting on the experience not simply as a childhood memory but as a contemporary experience available to his audience right now. Even while it evokes a sense of longing in the adult audience with its invocation of the ice cream truck, the song's rhyming of "ice cream man, on my street" with "your little truck outside, it sounds . . . a-neat, a-neat, a-neat" makes it an easy sing-along for children.

Even this exegesis of the song, however, points to the ways "Ice Cream Man" disrupts the cultural logic of the conventional faux naïf in that this reading suggests a semiotic stability to the song belied by its actual performance history. The interpretation I have offered tries to tease out, identify, and categorize the various "adult" and "childlike" components of the song, the end result being the creation of a safe interpretive position for the self-described sophisticated consumer within the song, recognizing the childlike and identifying with the adult nostalgia. But in practice, the effect of the song has been to create anxiety in listeners intent on maintaining a practice of cultural consumption that, however nominally rebellious, can still be recognized as legitimate according to conventional bourgeois cultural standards. In simpler terms, most first-time listeners want to know if Richman is serious or not, when it is just this distinction, between the serious and the childish, between the sophisticated and the immature, that is troubled by the song. In this sense, the song becomes "incorrigible" in the way that Eagleton used the adjective when he described children as "incorrigible theorists."[11]

This disruption of interpretive categories also involves, of course, a disruption of marketing categories. Unlike, for example, other examples of rock artists performing children's music—the Spin Doctors on *Sesame Street*, for example, or Little Richard singing the theme song to *The Magic School Bus*, or even the resurgence of teeny bop music in the persons of the Spice Girls and Hanson, the latter literally a band of children—performances aimed primarily at the reified musical tastes of adult consumers, Richman's album sends contradictory signals. Where more conventionalized performances for children by other artists work in part as a means of shaping the tastes of junior consumers to fit preexisting marketing niches, "Ice Cream Man" tends to destabilize the tastes of its adult consumers by simultaneously suggesting the most deliberate artistic calculation and affirming an almost reckless amateurism. In short, "Ice Cream Man" is finally not about logic, in Eagleton's terms; it is about rhetoric: that is, the playful mimicking of performative styles in order to undermine just such attempts at constructing "(ideo)logic" as my initial interpretation of play between childhood innocence and adult nostalgia in the song.

The argument, in other words, is not that "Ice Cream Man" is real or authentic children's music, in contrast to the arch faux naïf of alternative rock or the tasteful children's rock designed for the yuppie market. In all these cases, including the Brechtian case, at issue is the faux naïf, a deliberate construction of the childlike. My interest here is instead in the ways this particular construction works to open up a preideological space, Eagleton's space of the incorrigible child theorist. I am not arguing, however, for the actual existence of a preideological cultural space as a utopia of innocence but the strategic use of the idea of the preideological as a part of radical, antihegemonic practice within rock 'n' roll. Children, after all, do not exist in a preideological world: playing house or cops and robbers is nothing if not ideological. But because these games are played more in terms of imitation than understanding, they contain within them potentially subversive cultural actions. At the very least, through the questions they raise in children they force a few parents to confront their own roles as transmitters of ideological values. Similarly, "Ice Cream Man" contains a potentially subversive potential for the investigation of the relation between our musical tastes and the shaping forces of both the consumer market and the hierarchy of consumer capital.

It is important as well to underline the word "potentially" in potentially subversive, though. The opening up of a constructed space of preideological understanding does not in itself imply a specifically radical politics, nor does it preclude the necessity for adult theorizing in the construction of any such politics. Indeed, one of the assumptions often left unexplored within the cultural politics of alternative rock is whether and to what extent the alternative is necessarily synonymous with the progressive.

Richman himself would probably reject all such political formulations of his art and instead describe the purpose of his music not as the creation of the preideological but of the preartificial, part of his desire to restore "communication and intimacy" to music, which, of course, sounds just like the kind of naive romanticism to which I am arguing Richman's music stands in some kind of opposition.[12] In fact, my praise of Richman's music could be taken as just the kind of invocation of individual genius and creativity that still defines bourgeois standards of artistic excellence even in postmodern late capitalism. An important qualification is therefore necessary. There are no reasons to doubt Richman's claims of sincerity (one of his most recent CDs, after all, is entitled *You Must Ask the Heart* [Rounder 9047, 1995]). The point of this essay is not to argue that, in true New Critical fashion, Richman's music resolves the cultural contradictions under discussion here as a result of his unique personal genius (unique personal genius though he undoubtedly is) but to examine how a particular cultural practice situated strategically within the development of alternative rock helps us understand the potential of and problems with "irony rock" as antihegemonic practice. It is this strategic placement that brings me back to Richman's unstable canonization as punk precursor, with which this essay began.

As I have mentioned, Richman is not alone within alternative rock in his use of the faux naïf, nor does the use of the faux naïf in itself represent some kind of ultimate strategy of ideological destabilization. Rap music, for example, also creates and exploits a crisis in the marketing of authority and originality as cultural capital through the use of pastiche and technological appropriation as well as the faux naïf. Richman's particular career, however, span-ning as it does the evolutionary history of alternative rock, from his virtual internship with the Velvet Underground in the late sixties, through his decisive turn to children's music at the height of the punk explosion, and finally to his latest work, which often involves a metacommentary on his own career, offers convenient sites to chart the development of irony as an anti-hegemonic device in alternative rock.

"Pablo Picasso," for example, from early in Richman's career, stands almost as a textbook example of the invocation of high-culture references within alternative rock, a tactic Richman has turned to throughout his career, particularly in relation to painters.[13] An almost slavish imitation of the droning, midtempo sound of the Velvets (particularly on the recorded version produced by ex-Velvet John Cale), "Pablo Picasso" maintains a carefully modulated level of educated snottiness and irreverence, as exemplified by the unforgettable but too clever rhyme of "Picasso" and "asshole," along with a punk hostility toward the audience, as Richman contrasts Picasso's sophisticated sex appeal with the crudeness of the (presumed male) listeners to the song: "As he walked down the street girls could not resist his stare / Pablo Picasso never got called an asshole, not like YOU!" This strategy, of citing a high-culture reference supposedly in order to distance the artist and audience from that culture while all the while invoking the cultural capital that comes with such a reference, has become almost a reflex in alternative rock, ranging from the witty (Elvis Costello's sly suggestion in "This Is Hell" that in the contemporary consumer dystopia " 'My Favorite Things' are playing again and again / But it's by Julie Andrews and not by John Coltrane") to the ham-fisted (Sting, for example, seems almost compelled to include in his work labored signifiers of his cultural bona fides—and by extension those of his fans—the nadir of which may be his pedantic middle-brow reference to Nabokov in "Don't Stand So Close to Me"; the relentless self-importance of his cultural appropriations has eased the way for his shift from alternative status to adult contemporary superstardom).[14] One technique, a gesture Richman himself often makes, reinscribes the supposed separation between art and commerce by supposedly saving the true meaning of the referent's work from the contamination of money and status seeking ("Vincent Van Gogh" is exemplary in this regard, as would be the Jam's quotation of Shelley on the back cover of their *Sound Affects* record [Polydor 823284-2, 1980]).[15] Another technique, closer in strategy to "Pablo Picasso," tries to act as an anarchistic desecration of the referent, a pop music equivalent of taking a razor to the Mona Lisa. In fact, in many ways this latter stance, with a long history of pre-rock pop culture antecedents ranging from the Marx Brothers to Spike Jones and his City Slickers, defines a classic rock 'n' roll gesture, from Chuck Berry's "Roll Over, Beethoven" to John Lennon's dadaesque "I Am the Walrus" ("Man, you shoulda seen 'em kickin' Edgar Allan Poe"), and ultimately to the Sex Pistols' "God Save the Queen."

My descriptions of these two forms are meant to express the ultimate limitations of each strategy, although both may be locally effective, particularly in terms of disrupting the habitual consumption practices of individual listeners. Like many radical gestures, however, they run the danger of becoming themselves icons, subject to market classification under the nostalgia of rebellion. Indeed, "Pablo Picasso" is still frequently requested at Richman performances, even though he has made it clear that the song is no longer part of his regular repertoire. Clearly, many of those who make up Richman's cult following are themselves heavily invested in the cultural logic described above.

Interestingly, while Richman has largely removed songs like "Pablo Picasso" from his performing repertoire, he has not exactly disowned them nor the influence of the Velvet Underground from which it derived. Instead, in true postmodern style, Richman has involved his protopunk activity as part of his ongoing project of reinvention. The most explicit example of this may be his live performance of "Bermuda" on *Having a Party*, in which he interrupts the song to explain how his exposure to the simple, folk-based music of the Nassau street musicians caused him to turn away from his too-serious and, in his term, stiff performing style.[16] This anecdote, while amusing enough, invests heavily in a primitivist myth about the emotional purity of black folk music and thus renders any association with the childlike problematic indeed, as it skirts too closely traditions of racist condescension.

More to the purpose of the faux naïf and Richman's relation to the construction of alternative rock is his recent homage to the Velvets—simply titled "Velvet Underground"—that deliberately constructs a contrarian appreciation of the Velvets as themselves a childlike band.[17] Such a strategy potentially turns alternative music's dominant use of the faux naïf—as a means of ironically claiming postmodernist cultural authority within the logic of the dominant cultural system—on its head by playfully deconstructing the distinction between parody and homage. In fact, the song celebrates the Velvets as playful and joyous, hardly the critical consensus on the band and an estimation definitely at variance both with the emerging canonical representation of the band's work and with what most alternative musicians would cite as subversively inspirational in the band's music. In effect, this song works to point out that the Velvets' realistic, or at least neorealist, representations of urban alienation, drug addiction, and sexual perversion were part of carefully calculated musical performances that worked to suggest both high romantic despair and an artfully amateur musicianship signified by the conjunction of Lou Reed's dorm-room guitar style with John Cale's avant-garde virtuosity. The trick in Richman's performance is both to reveal the deliberateness of this strategy and still to proclaim the importance of the Velvets, not so much on their own terms or the terms of their canonical status but as of all things performers of a kind of children's music.

Richman's recording is a model of the faux-naïf strategy turned against itself. Throughout the song, Richman points to the contradictory cultural positions the Velvets tried to embrace, summed up in phrases such as "the biker crowd meets the college kind," claims of patriotism ("they were wild like the U.S.A. / a mystery band in the New York way"), and even how much the Velvets trade in stock clichés about urban despair ("like your heat's turned off and you can't pay the bill"). Yet the song finally focuses not on the specific lyrical content of the Velvets' material, but on the crucial question of sound, as the chorus repeatedly asks, "How in the world are they makin' that sound? / Velvet Underground." The sound of Richman's own performance in the song could not be more out of keeping with the Velvets: playing at a kind of modified rockabilly tempo, like a preteen Chuck Berry, Richman vocally mugs and jokes around though most of the song while singing the praises of "rock and roll, but not like the rest / And to me, America at its best." Suddenly, however, in the middle of the song Richman answers the question posed by the refrain by launching into an uncanny imitation of an all-purpose Velvets' song, slowing way down and imitating Lou Reed's own Bob Dylan-affected singing style. In effect, the rhetorical question of the chorus moves from a suggestion of the Velvets' sound as ineffable and irreproducible to a more radical conception of rhetoric more in line with Eagleton's use of the term: in essence, that the Velvet's sound is rhetorical, capable of being mimicked and playfully transformed. Simultaneously praising the inimitability of the Velvets's sound and demonstrating just such an imitation, "Velvet Underground" not only makes meaningless the distinction between parody and homage but raises the question of just why such a distinction, with its implications of establishing a fixed cultural hierarchy, would be important in an alternative cultural practice in the first place. The song thus takes dead aim at the larger ideological structures of individual genius and absolute authenticity that mark the site of the strategic oppositional weakness of alternative rock.

Now all of this is a lot to hang on one song, and it is worth reemphasizing the point that I am talking more about the subversive potential of a particular cultural practice involving the faux naïf than a reified real meaning for the song. It is not the case that "Velvet Underground" has an automatic antihegemonic function every time it is played on a CD player or performed onstage or even that a phrase like "antihegemonic function" has a single, stable meaning or value. Nonetheless, Richman's performance, particularly now in the light of his own growing canonical status, itself embodies alternative oppositional strategies for alternative rock. By suggesting that the Velvets' music is fun, he confronts the critical stumbling block within the alternative rock tradition of how to negotiate the desire for cultural seriousness with the fear of a solemnity that undermines the potential fun, irreverence, and anarchism latent in the sound of rock 'n' roll. This negotiation also takes place within constructions of style and attitude crucial to the marketing of rock 'n' roll as part of the larger economic regulation and exploitation of dissent within pop culture, particularly the style of alienated hipness and cynicism that harnesses social discontent in the endless maintenance of a pose balanced exquisitely between the embrace of the latest cultural attitude and a supposed rejection of trendiness.

The pose implied by Richman's performance—that singing about poverty and drug addiction can be fun—comes across not so much as a trivialization of human suffering but instead as a gesture toward the idea of the Velvets' music as children's music and of solemnity and seriousness as not incompatible with playfulness. For part of the point made by Eagleton in referring to children as "incorrigible theoreticians" is not that children don't take their questions—or their play—seriously. Their uncertain orientation between rhetorical imitation and the assimilation of cultural (ideo)logic demonstrates the radical instability of all ideological structures and that in fact the most critical points of ideological intervention may not necessarily come in the university classroom or academic essay, where ideological debate is authorized and thus to a certain extent contained. If we follow the logic of Richman's performance, however, we can argue that it is not so much the artistic self-consciousness of the Velvets that poses the most significant antihegemonic challenge (although artistic pretension can also be a source of play and imitation) but the degree to which they are playing at artistic self-consciousness and thus provide a model for playful imitation that, given the

variabilities of cultural context, is radically unpredictable and therefore destabilizing of settled constructions of cultural status and the marketing categories attached to them.

Such a potential marks both the promise and danger of the faux naïf as a
disruptive strategy within rock 'n' roll, which is to some degree embodied in
the fragility of Richman's own career. Without a recording contract for several years in the late seventies and early eighties, Richman then spent several
years with Rounder records, a label specializing in folk-based music and with
a reputation for providing an outlet for worthwhile artists of marginal sales
appeal, before recently signing with Vapor, Neil Young's designer label. Even
at a friendly label like Rounder, Richman had difficulty releasing his album of
songs in Spanish, *¡Jonathan, Te Vas A Emocionar!*[18] Given the market demand
for so-called world music, such a recording might seem economically shrewd.
Linda Ronstadt's recordings of Mexican *rancheras*, for example, fit precisely
into the logic of crossover marketing by introducing a music with its own
preestablished, Latino consumer base to her English-speaking fans through
the homogenizing (or hybridizing, depending on your point of view) effects
of mainstream pop music production. Richman, on the other hand, seemed
intent on subverting this crossover strategy by baffling his almost exclusively
white English-speaking audience with a mixture of obscure (to this audience)
Spanish-language songs and now-unintelligible Spanish-language covers of
his own previously recorded material, all sung in his amateurish Boston-
inflected Spanish, while at the same time potentially alienating Spanish-
speaking listeners with the idiosyncrasy of his songs, laden as they are with
references to his very middle-class New England suburban upbringing. As a
result, Rounder decided that the project might be too economically marginal
even for them. Thus Richman has managed to disrupt expectations even
within the supposedly predictable marketing category of the cult artist.
Unlike punk and most alternative rock, which has repeatedly run up against
the problem of co-optation and the creation of ever new categories of protest
music and the use of revolution as a marketing tool, the faux naïf as Richman
has practiced it has proven adept at resisting containment. The cost, however,
has been the loss of mass media access and career stability.

The operation of the faux naïf in Richman's work, however, does open a
new line of analysis for the consideration of alternative rock as antihegemonic practice, particularly in creating a strategic potential out of the intersection of two seemingly contradictory structures of feeling within rock 'n'
roll: cynicism and naïveté. By celebrating the joy of imitation within a system

of cultural commodification dependent on the reproduction of the supposedly irreproducible, the Brechtian faux naïf as utilized by Richman challenges the separation between performer and audience, producer and consumer, by extending indefinitely the punk proclamation that anyone can be in a band. Brecht's strategic imitation of bad acting does not in itself answer the question of how to counter the challenge posed by the subsequent conventionalization and stylization of this very strategy, just as the studied amateurism of much punk and alternative rock found itself turning into just another marketable style. By returning to the idea of children's music, however, the faux naïf also returns to the site of all first attempts at the ideological colonization of human imagination and desire. Through the subversive effects of the preideological space created by the gap between the rhetorical and the (ideo)logical, the faux naïf contains the potential to destabilize any reified performance style or marketing niche through the endless play of imitations of imitations of imitations.[19] In the final analysis, this focus on imitation functions as the basic strategy central to all antihegemonic cultural practice: exposing and thus making available for possible intervention the means of production, thus potentially transforming consumers into producers. For listeners to Jonathan Richman, this is one possible outcome of simply asking with him, as a child would, "How in the world are they makin' that sound?"

NOTES

1. The song can be found on Jonathan Richman and the Modern Lovers, *Rock 'n' Roll with the Modern Lovers* (Beserkley, LP JBZ-0053, 1977).
2. Peter Wicke, *Rock Music: Culture, Aesthetics, and Sociology* (Cambridge: Cambridge University Press, 1990), pp. 136–37.
3. Bertolt Brecht, "Two Essays on Unprofessional Acting," *Brecht on Theatre*, trans. John Willett (New York: Hill and Wang, 1964) p. 152.
4. Terry Eagleton, "Brecht and Rhetoric," in *Against the Grain: Essays, 1975–1985* (London: Verso, 1986), pp. 167–72.
5. Greil Marcus, *Lipstick Traces: A Secret History of the Twentieth Century* (Cambridge: Harvard University Press, 1989), p. 6. See also Neil Nehring, *Flowers in the Dustbin* (Ann Arbor: University of Michigan Press, 1993), on the connections among the idea of an avant garde, cultural subversion, and pop music.
6. Marcus, *Lipstick Traces*, p. 56.
7. Neil Nehring, "Rock Around the Academy," *American Literary History* 5 (winter 1993): 766.
8. Wicke, *Rock Music*, p. 111.

9. Jonathan Richman, "Jonathan Richman's First Twenty Years in Show Business," Rounder Records Web page, http//harp.rounder.com/rounder/artists/richmanjonathan/richman.html (1996).

10. See David R. Shumway, "Rock and Roll as a Cultural Practice," *Present Tense: Rock & Roll and Culture*, ed. Anthony DeCurtis (Durham, NC: Duke University Press, 1992), pp. 117–133.

11. Ken Tucker similarly notes the disarming quality of Richman in relation to his influence on alternative rock:

    > Unlike nearly all other rock artists, Richman gets less self-conscious as he proceeds—he works at it, and, remarkably, he achieves it: a serious naiveté that allows him to deal with whimsical or trivial occasions with enormous gravity and spirit.
    >
    > Although his music grows richer in mooncalf lyricism all the time, the influence of Richman's recent work seems negligible; if anything, his guileless originality seems to unsettle many of the post-infants in the audience.

    ("New Wave: America," in *The Rolling Stone Illustrated History of Rock & Roll*, ed. Jim Miller [New York: Random House/Rolling Stone Press, 1980], p. 441)

12. Richman, "Jonathan Richman's First Twenty Years in Show Business."

13. Jonathan Richman and the Modern Lovers, *The Modern Lovers*.

14. Elvis Costello, "This Is Hell," *Brutal Youth* (Warner 45535, 1994); The Police, "Don't Stand So Close to Me," *Zenyatta Mondatta* (A&M SP-3720, 1980).

15. Jonathan Richman and the Modern Lovers, "Vincent Van Gogh," *Rockin' and Romance* (Twin/Tone TTR-8558C, 1985).

16. Jonathan Richman, *Having a Party with Jonathan Richman* (Rounder 9026, 1991).

17. Jonathan Richman, *I, Jonathan* (Rounder 9036, 1992).

18. Jonathan Richman, *!Jonathan, Te Vas A Emocionar!* (Rounder 904, 1994).

19. Eagleton similarly describes Brecht's focus as "at once representational and anti-representational, mimetic and performative together. The child grows towards representational meaning by redoubling rhetoric, miming a miming, performing a performative; indeed, when Brecht writes (perhaps by a slide of the signifier) of the child *copying miming*, he suggests the possibility of performing the performing of a performance" ("Brecht and Rhetoric," pp. 169–70; emphasis Eagleton's).

8

THIS IS FASCISM?

(RAVES AND THE POLITICS OF DANCING)

SEAN PORTNOY

Over sixty years ago, Theodor Adorno, in his essay "On Jazz," wrote about the popular dance music of his era that it "can be easily adapted for use by fascism." The agit-rap band Consolidated recently came to a similar conclusion about contemporary dance music: in 1991 they put out a song called "This is Fascism," set to a driving beat and with a soulful diva exhorting/critiquing: "Keep dancing, dancing to the beat / Keep marching, marching in unison. / . . . / Keep moving, no questions / This is fascism."

What is it about popular dance music that its critics could possibly find adaptable to fascistic tendencies? What does it mean to call music "fascist"? Even to ask these questions raises the difficult issue of defining fascism, an ideology so wrought with contradictions that it defies almost any attempt at definition. Fascism is at once materially stable (i.e., no talk about the redistribution of income) yet ideologically revolutionary, fascinated with the potential of the machine while clutching to mythic constructs. Alice Yaegar Kaplan provides a starting point when she writes, "Fascist aesthetes intentionally borrow the vocabulary of literary romanticism, but it is nascent technology that inspires them to put their vocabulary to political use."[1] Two comments must be made about Kaplan's statement. If it is to be claimed, as Andrew Hewitt recently has in his *Fascist Modernism*, that fascism stridently foregrounds the inherent aestheticization of politics (rather than destroying the gap between the supposedly separated spheres of art and politics), then there is no such thing as a "fascist aesthete," instead merely a fascist, and this fascist does not "borrow" from the aesthetic realm but sees the intrinsicness of that vocabulary in politics.[2] Further, the "nascent" state of technology must be explicated; as Walter Benjamin writes in "Theories of German Fascism," "Instead of using and illuminating the secrets of nature via a technology mediated by the human scheme of things, the new nationalists' metaphysical abstraction of war signifies nothing other than a *mystical* and *unmediated* application of technology to solve the mystery of an idealistically perceived nature."[3]

Thus to rewrite Kaplan's statement is to say that to begin examining the fascistic potential of a cultural practice demands an examination of that practice's potential for revolutionary violence that serves the ritualistic aims of a totalized state. This is not to say that popular music can be found to be inherently fascistic but to examine any potential for it to be appropriated for authoritarian purposes. As Kaplan notes about the role of radio in fascism, "Like any new technology, radio created a need for what it could satisfy—in this case, amplified, telephonic invective."[4] Fascist discourse filled this need for invective and adapted itself to radio as well as adapting radio to itself. The technology of popular music making therefore needs to be analyzed for this potential to demand and serve the interest of totalizing elements of society.

I

Walter Benjamin, in "The Work of Art in the Age of Mechanical Reproduction," argues that by the turn of the twentieth century the aesthetic of sound had been revolutionized through the process of technical reproduction, that is, the invention of the sound recording.[5] This invention, coupled with the development of electronic microphones, amplification, and the medium of the radio, not only altered how sound was heard in the everyday but, as John Cage's avant-gardiste compositional experiments revealed, reproduced the sound *of* the everyday. Cage and, later, experimental pop acts like Can and Cabaret Voltaire, among others, also worked at cutting and splicing recorded magnetic tape to create musical montages, much the way editors cut and splice film to produce motion pictures. The handicraft of this cutting and splicing, however, was more laborious than film editing until the introduction of computers helped to create the digital sampler.

The sampler automates the process of juxtaposing disparate sounds just as film-editing machinery sequences images. The aesthetics of the sampler as montage machine still need extensive exploration in musical discourse,[6] and it may be fruitful to compare the sampler to its visual counterpart in order to grasp its revolutionary potential in sound manipulation. The montage machine technically reproduces the process created by early-twentieth-century artists to develop film montage as a radical aesthetic form, a process Peter Bürger details in *Theory of the Avant-Garde*. As Burger describes montage, it is a process that violently disrupts the autonomy of institutional art by introducing pieces of so-called reality into the work.[7] The process of montage also coincides with the avant-gardists' consciousness of traditions, and traditional artistic materials, as materials: "Their activity initially consists in nothing other than in killing the 'life' of the material, that is, in tearing it out of its functional context that gives it meaning" (70). The sampler, like the movie camera, transplants this process into the realm of technical reproducibility, electronically cannibalizing past recordings as well as current found sounds in order to create new work, thus "killing" the original materials. Bürger notes that the avant-gardists "liquidated the possibility of a period style when they raised to a principle the availability of the artistic means of past periods" (18). In the same way, the institutions of popular music making worry that the sampler will halt the progress of new music through its raids on past recordings (not surprisingly, a British sampling band named itself Pop Will Eat Itself, and a recent book on the subject is titled *Will Pop Eat Itself?*).

The revolutionary aspects of montage, then, are its violence to traditional aesthetic materials and the subsequent violence done to traditional aesthetic practices. A recent example of this process is the work of the electronic act μ-ziq, which sampled approximately one minute of material by the rock band the Auteurs and embedded it within forty-five minutes of new electronic music. As one reviewer comments on the result, "[μ-ziq's Michael Paradinas] hasn't remixed these songs—he's hijacked them and held them hostage in an underground laboratory, giving them electroshock until they scream for mercy."[8] Benjamin argues that through the technical introduction of montage, via the motion picture, to a mass audience, the destruction of tradition extends itself to a political dimension: "[The film's] social significance, particularly in its most positive form, is inconceivable without its destructive, cathartic aspect, that is, the liquidation of the traditional value of the cultural heritage."[9] The process of montage is thus theoretically dialectical—it uses the material of tradition to destroy tradition itself—as well as inherently violent. The sampler's violent potential is even greater because it threatens traditional notions of artistic property. Unlike analog methods of montage, the sampler digitizes sound into computer code of zeros and ones, a process that allows sampled sound to be altered beyond recognition and distributed anonymously over vast computer networks. As Andrew Goodwin notes, "There are those DJs, musicians, and engineers . . . who have made an aesthetic out of sampling . . . and in some cases, a *politics* out of stealing."[10]

The technical media that are constituted in montage turn on reality in a similarly dialectical, violent fashion. As Ernst Junger, the German protofascist intellectual, noted about the camera in the 1920s, it liquidates both what is filmed—"the event itself is completely subordinated to its 'transmission' "—and the person using the lens (both the camera person and the viewer), who yields to the sight of "an insensitive and invulnerable eye."[11] Correspondingly, the sounds a sampler records are liquidated out of reality, as the person sampling, as well as the listener, are liquidated through their subordination to the technical ear. What Frances Dyson writes about Cage's electronic experiments becomes a mass phenomenon of listening in the digital age: "The perceiver is also rendered invisible, becoming a subject who, lacking intentionality, is bound to act only via the prostheses and spaces that technology supplies: the loudspeaker, the computer, and the audiophonic and informational interface."[12]

The listener, however, is not only liquidated through yielding to the technical ear. He or she must also face the assault of the music's beat. Though not all sampled music has a beat, the link is there: most popular music created through sampling—house, rap, techno, industrial, etc.—is set to a dance rhythm, and it is a correspondence that should not go unexamined. As Goodwin notes, "Pop musicians and audiences have grown increasingly accustomed to making an association between synthetic/automated music and the communal (dance floor) connection to nature (via the body)."[13] This link between rhythm and technology has one of its historical bases in modern music's attempt to replace traditional notions of harmony as the ordering structure of music. Cage argues, in his deconstruction of the relationship between sound and silence, that duration should replace pitch as the ordering process for music: "A structure based on durations (rhythmic: phrase, time lengths) is correct (corresponds with the nature of the material), whereas harmonic structure is incorrect (derived from pitch, which has no being in silence)."[14] Cage does not specify that "the nature of the material" can include electronic and computer music, but his statement can be appropriated for this purpose. The sampling process—that is, making timed recordings of sound that is converted into computer code—thus replicates Cage's reversal of the traditional musical hierarchy, turning time lengths of sound into digital phrases. The process of sampling is thus constituted in technically reproducing musical duration. The effects of this process are complemented through the use of the drum machine, a computerized device that reproduces digitally created rhythms. As a consequence, rhythm in digital music has been further quantified into a measurement of beats per minute (bpm).

The bpm of a modern dance track has become fetishized in the dance subculture looking for ever-faster music. Dance acts often label their compact discs (the commodity end of the digital music process) with individual tracks's bpm measure, and some genres of dance music are defined by bpms. Techno, for example, hovers around 140 bpm, while drum 'n' bass can track in at around 170 bpm or higher. What is the effect of this fetishization of the beat in popular music? Adorno warns that the rhythm of jazz (and by extension of any commodified dance music) is inherently linked to the march: "Insofar as dancing is synchronous movement, the tendency to march has been present in dance from the very beginning; thus jazz is connected in its origins with the march and its history lays bare this relationship."[15] Adorno also argues that the rhythm of modern music is linked to a violence that derives from primitive urges. "Is the drum the successor of human sacrifice or does it still sound the command to kill? In our music it resounds as an archaic survival."[16] It can be argued that the continuum between the dance and the march, both assumed to be violent by Adorno, depends on the social functioning of the music; that is, the bourgeois capitalist state propagates the rhythm of dance as a self-liquidizer of individuals, while the fascist state (toward which, according to Adorno, the capitalist system inevitably heads) appropriates rhythm for the march of self-liquidized individuals into war (violence toward others).[17]

This sense of losing oneself to the beat, of self-liquidation, is analogous to the loss of critical distance that Benjamin cites in the film spectator: "The film makes the cult value recede into the background not only by putting the public in the position of the critic, but also by the fact that at the movies this position requires no attention. The public is an examiner, but an absent-minded one."[18] The listener as dancer is similarly "absent-minded," in the sense that he or she empties the mind in order to enter into a trance with the beat (not coincidentally, one of the various subspecies of computer dance music is called "trance"). The raver (as the most prominent consumer of computer dance music in known) enters into a state of distraction that precludes the cognizance not only of his or her material existence but of the dialectical process that constructs the music he or she consumes. Marcus Paul Bullock, in the introduction to his text on Junger, offers a similar description of the type of music Junger's aesthetic portends: "Music that hammers a way to the ear, and for which the ear does not have to come searching, or which repeats an idea without development so that nothing is lost by giving it only intermittent attention."[19]

Both Cage and Adorno argue that this collapse of critical distance is inherent in electronic music. For Adorno, "there is electronic music whose material laws seem to preclude the subjective intervention of the composer, just as they preclude that of the interpreter";[20] for Cage, electronics replaces discourse.[21] Of course, it can be stated that through the writing of their theories of electronic music, Adorno and Cage have created a space of interpretation and discourse within this supposedly hermetic musical form, which allows for further discourse to stem from their initial discourse and so forth. But the point remains that the state of computer music seemingly resists the unveiling of its dialectical construction through the seduction of the beat. The construction of computer dance music therefore resembles the system of commodities in its immediacy and absence of meaning outside its self-constructed system of exchange. Jacques Attali also argues that the role of repetition in contemporary popular music further expresses its ties to the dominant economic system: "Musical repetition confirms the presence of repetitive consumption, of the flow of noises as ersatz sociality."[22]

This analogy of electronic music and postmodern economics is further complicated if the politics of the body are introduced into the equation. "Nothing is ever resolved: house is the beat that can never satisfy or be satisfied. . . . Every bar of the music becomes an orgasm, making the idea of climax meaningless."[23] According to Hewitt, the Italian futurist F. T. Marinetti believed that the machine displaced eroticism from the genitals to the body as a whole. He did not, however, see this as resulting in libidinal excess but in the machine's totalitarian control over the body. This is the sense in which Adorno decries the false liberation from the jazz beat, in which he sees a "coming-too-early" that is unproductive: "It is purposeless; it leads nowhere and is arbitrarily withdrawn by an undialectical, mathematical incorporation into the beat."[24] It is in this notion of an economy of the body that is circular, dispersive, and undialectical in its desires that popular dance resembles the commodity system. "Within its economy, the body becomes a medium, a process, and enters into a system of energetic exchange that will necessarily destroy it as an autonomous entity."[25]

II

The introduction of computers into popular music thus produces a contradictory, though doubly violent, process of creating dance music. The use of the digital sampler can be viewed as a dialectic technique that negates tradition by using tradition against itself, a technique that resembles the liberatory principle of film that Benjamin observed. Coupled with this technique, however, is the beat that allows the individual to liquidate himself or herself, along with his or her critical distance. This construction of modern dance music resultingly resembles an economic system of exchange, which (according to Marxism) is inherently dialectical but attempts to liquidate the critical potential to see its construction as such. And yet, despite its theoretical links to violence and the commodity system, the culture of computer dance music, particularly the cultural manifestation known as rave, holds itself to be generally nonviolent and anticommercial. How then can such a discrepancy be explained?

It can be argued that rave culture attempts this alternative consciousness through the reritualization of art. Benjamin links the notion of ritual to an earlier perception of art, before technology liberated aesthetics from ritualistic tendencies: "For the first time in world history, mechanical reproduction emancipates the work of art from its parasitical dependence on ritual."[26] But the political potential Benjamin sees in technology's liberation of art from ritual is as often replaced by a sense of alienation through the mechanical influence on the aesthetic realm. In terms of computerized dance music, this sense of alienation is most often reflected in what is known as industrial music, which mixes equal parts individualistic angst with political commentary. Named for its distinctive sound, usually an aggressively noisy mix of drum machine beats, distorted vocals, sampled sound bites, and scratchy, metallic guitar licks (thus sounding like an industry at work), industrial music stretches the limits of violent electronic music while often railing against the excesses the misuse of technology makes possible. The band KMFDM, for example, calls itself and one of its songs "A Drug Against War" while sounding like the soundtrack to the war it purports to prevent. In its aesthetic and its ideology, much of industrial music begins to reflect what Adorno sees as necessary to come to grips with the alienating effect of mechanization on modern consciousness:

The positive values [of humanity] have degenerated into a mere device to prevent anyone from reflecting on the fact that none of them has been made real in practice. Anyone who is truly concerned about them feels unable to express them in words and feels compelled to deconstruct them when others venture to do so. He thereby puts himself in the wrong and gains a reputation as the foe of all that is noble, good, true and beautiful, thus strengthening the hegemony of evil. *Anyone who wishes to speak of electronic music must draw attention to this vicious circle. Otherwise the whole ethical machinery will be set in motion and he will be sucked into it.*[27]

It is necessary to quote Adorno at such length (and to raise the subject of industrial music) because this perception of electronic music seems diametrically opposed to the general mentality of rave culture. In its belief in the power of technology to create peaceful states of mind (either through the trance of the beat or the chill-out room to which one goes to escape the beat and listen to soothing ambient music), rave culture replicates the Cagean notion of the spiritual release of the machine: "In the imaginary of Imaginary Landscapes, sound occupies the non-space of electronics, possesses the nonbeing of the invisible and intangible, and releases the spirit, not of objects, but of the quasi-objects that constitute technology and are themselves permeated by the animating force, or spirit, of electricity."[28] At raves, this vague notion of technological spirituality is transferred from the music to the body, with both serving as mediums. For example, in a discussion on the Internet of the rave philosophy, one raver wrote, "If there is spirituality in a rave, it is a straightforward ecstatic experience that transports you. . . . Certainly the DJ and the visual FX people are serving as 'shamans' to some degree, transporting you through the environment they create."

In its attempt to produce ecstasy-inducing states in a large group of people (sometimes numbering in the thousands), the rave resembles the notion of festival developed by Roger Caillois, one of the principal of the Collège de Sociologie, a French intellectual group writing in the 1930s: "These huge gatherings are eminently favorable to the birth and contagion of an intense excitement spent in cries and gestures, inciting an unchecked abandonment to the most reckless impulses."[29] Further, the reference to the shamanistic quality of the DJ playing music at raves seems hardly coincidental when placed next to what Anatole Lewitzsky, another Collège de Sociologie writer, details in an anthropological view of the shaman: "Note the presence of the *drum*, widespread from the Lapps to the Eskimo of Greenland, ecstatic *dances*, the clearly pathological nature of the shaman's personality, and finally the idea of a profoundly intimate contact with the representatives of the spirit world, the notion of levitation and, more generally, of penetration into other worlds."[30] The primitivist relationship between the rave and the ritual is more than purely discursive; some elements of rave culture clearly link themselves to the idea of the primitive. One pop techno band is known as the Shamen, for example, while there is a techno offshoot known as "tribal." In addition, some electronic music mixes samples of ethnic music into its computerized dance concoctions to create "ethnotechno," as one compilation album calls the music it features (a popular version of this phenomenon, and one not linked to the tribal scene, is the French act Deep Forest, which has combined drum machine beats and synthesized music with sampled recordings of Pygmy singing). Cage's notion of releasing the technological spirit is revealed in the sampler's ability to tap primitive musical sources for use in new ritualistic experiences (though experiences, as I note more extensively below, that are already heavily mediated).

Thus, while the rave is not nearly as orgiastic (or as violent) as Caillois's festival, it is clearly a celebration of excess and an attempt to reach a state of consciousness beyond materiality, aided for some ravers by the use of drugs, including the designer drug known as Ecstasy. This is the sense in which the rave aesthetic—like other popular music forms such as jazz and rock before it—can be viewed as an attempt to reritualize art. Benjamin writes, "We know that the earliest art works originated in the service of a ritual—first the magical, then the religious kind."[31] But with the change of the material base brought on by technology, art can no longer be expected to serve that function (as it is produced in the realm of the technology of the everyday). The rave then is something of a reversion, or regression, from the modern function of art, one that attempts to justify itself as a liberating force against daily alienation. This sense of an alternative site beyond material alienation links both Caillois and the testimony of another Internet raver, who observes, "One can understand how festival, representing such a paroxysm of life and contrasting so violently with the petty concerns of daily existence, seems to the individual like another world, where he feels himself sustained and transformed by powers that are beyond him."[32] The experience of the rave grew out of dissatisfaction with the outside world, so an enclosed space was created, a space where people could be nice to each other without incurring suspicion or violent reactions. In many ways, this alternative realm of ritual attempts to counter notions of commodified leisure time that isolates the individual. Caillois critiques the modern notion of vacation as killing off the possibility of festival in its atomizing quality: "Vacation (its name alone is indicative) seems to be an empty space, at least a slowing down of social activity. At the same time vacation is incapable of *overjoying* an individual. It has been deprived of any positive character" (302). Rave culture attempts an opposition by recreating the vacation *as* festival.

But how much of an opposition can be created by making a ritual out of sanctioned leisure time? In attempting to create an alternative sphere that the work schedule sanctions, rave culture in some ways unwittingly replicates the role art has traditionally held under capitalism. As Bürger notes, "In bourgeois society, art has a contradictory role: it produces the image of a better order and to that extent protests against the bad order that prevails. But by realizing the image of a better order in fiction . . . it relieves the existing society of the pressure of those forces that make for change."[33] Rave culture, while hardly fictional, reveals that the limits of its critique (limited to the realm outside daily conditions of existence) threaten its viability as a cultural alternative. As Bürger concludes, "Art thus stabilizes the very social conditions against which it protests" (11). In the futility of its critique, rave culture resembles those jazz and rock subcultures that hoped to change the world and yet never did. In fact, the failure of 1960s' hippies to revolutionize the world through rock music already affects the raver's mentality. He or she now fears making bold claims for the music like those of the hippies and knows the history of commodifying formerly alternative music. A musical example of this cynicism occurs in the ambient techno band the Orb's song "Little Fluffy Clouds," which includes a sampled snippet of comments from folkrock singer Ricki Lee Jones (representing hippiedom) rambling on about cloud watching for a children's show; the almost parodic editing of Jones's comments suggests an older generation out of touch with the real world.

Far from radicalizing rave culture further, this pessimism usually prevents attempts at radical thought at all: if it's all going to be appropriated anyway, why make it any more difficult to do so? This willingness to submit one's self to the system leads to what Susan Sontag sees as a willingness to seek out authoritarianism in different guises. Writing about the renewed interest in the Nazi-sponsored films of Leni Riefenstahl, Sontag argues: "Their longings are still felt, because their content is a romantic ideal to which many continue to be attached and which is expressed in such diverse modes of cultural dissidence and propaganda for new forms of community as the youth/rock culture, primal therapy, anti-psychiatry, Third World camp-following, and belief in the occult. The exaltation of community does not preclude the search for absolute leadership; on the contrary, it may inevitably lead to it."[34] This desire for community becomes further susceptible to fascistic tendencies without a more cogent social critique that resists appropriation from the commodity system. The rave philosophy thus takes on an eerie aspect when placed beside Benjamin's assertion that "fascism attempts to organize the newly created proletarian masses without affecting the property structure which the masses strive to eliminate. Fascism sees its salvation in giving these masses not their right, but instead a chance to express themselves."[35] The tendency of rave culture to express notions about a classless ritual that temporarily overcomes the alienation of the everyday not only suggests that its correspondence to fascist spectacle is unwitting but that fascism itself but is an ideology antithetical to its own regular violation of property laws. Raves were once held anywhere possible, spaces that included open fields, warehouses, and other properties that often were not officially sanctioned for such events. The most notorious attempt to question traditional notions of property occurred in the Castlemorton case, in which a six-day rave was held on British Common Land (named so because of the supposed free access of all citizens to the space) and finally busted by authorities on the basis of criminal trespassing. At the end of 1994 the British government passed the Criminal Justice Act, which gives the state wide power over public gatherings, including those that use loudspeakers to transmit music with repetitive beats (i.e., raves, among other forms of popular music shows).

As a result of crackdowns by authorities, who seemed to decide to regulate such excessive rituals of drugs and music only when the specter of breaching property laws through trespassing was raised, some raves are now held at secret locations that are unknown until a few hours before the event. This secrecy gives rave culture a slightly dangerous allure, but this is usually framed in terms of youthful rebellion rather than a critique of property rights. In fact, promoters' difficulties in cutting through the red tape to present legally authorized raves have generally led not to resistance but to laments that the growth of the culture has been stunted by its quasi-legality. This ambivalence over the potential growth in rave culture is most problematic in terms of the record industry's attempts to sign and market computerized dance acts. That major companies would be interested in a successful subculture (granted one that is already commodified in its production and distribution) seems inevitable, but the response of one of the culture's biggest stars, Moby, reveals the contradictory nature of what is called social critique today. Moby, unlike many other rave acts, is interested in politics and in making rave culture into something other than sheer hedonism. His answer to continuing the development of his musical subculture is to reinject personalities into what is often viewed as a faceless form (a form that is still mostly deemed positive in rave circles and is exemplified by an album title of the ambient techno band Ultramarine: *Every Man and Woman Is a Star*), an answer that is both paradoxical and somewhat naive: "The industrial revolution effectively separated human beings from those institutions that made humans satisfied: a sense of community, a strong sense of family, a connection with your work and creativity, and a good relationship with God and the land. One of the reasons people need personalities nowadays is that it's a way of achieving intimate communication."[36] That Moby's critique parallels the rationale usually given to explain the rise of Hitler (as the personality most adept at "achieving intimate communication" with those industrialism had alienated) is left unmentioned. Moreover, the desire for personality is one that the same forces of industrialism create to compensate for people's lack of satisfaction, a desire that liquidates the possibility of a cultural form's broader critique of society: "The cult of the movie star, fostered by the money of the film industry, preserves not the aura of the person but the 'spell of the personality,' the phony spell of a commodity. So long as the moviemakers' capital sets the fashion, as a rule no other revolutionary merit can be accredited to today's film than the promotion of a revolutionary criticism of traditional concepts of art."[37] Moby's anticapitalist leanings are therefore expressed in an ideology that not only taps into the means the entertainment industry uses to dispel critique but also evokes the forces that previously gave way to Hitler's fascism. Moby's desire for "personalities" to overcome alienation follows exactly the dangerous pattern Sontag sees of romantic mass phenomena's unwitting search for authority.

III

Ironically, the naive ideology of rave culture sees itself instead as a sophisticated response to the inevitability of commodification. It knows pop and politics don't mix, that, as Simon Reynolds notes, "This is the most deluded fantasy of all—the idea that, by buying certain pieces of vinyl and by going to certain gigs, instead of consuming a commodity, you are participating and making a contribution to 'the struggle.' "[38] But some aspects of rave culture insist on an equally delusional belief that temporary escape from the commodity system altogether will bring about the positive consciousness needed to change the world. But the most effective tools of rave's critique reside not in this antimaterialist pseudospirituality; rather, it is in its attempt to challenge traditional notions of aesthetic and physical property. This fact is never fully articulated in rave culture because it is subsumed under the notions of ecstasy and harmony that substitute for any sense of radical conflict. By serving as an escape valve for everyday alienation, rave culture participates in capitalism's ability first to bracket off critical energy and then to commodify it. In this manner, it seems that the rave's idea of an alternative sphere to capitalism will wither much as the hippies's flower power did or any other aesthetic movement that attempts to circumvent its material possibilities. As Bürger comments, "Because art is detached from daily life, this experience remains without tangible effect, i.e., it cannot be integrated into that life. The lack of tangible effects is not the same as functionlessness . . . but characterizes a specific function of art in bourgeois society: the neutralization of critique. This neutralization of impulses to change society is thus closely related to the role art plays in the development of bourgeois subjectivity."[39]

Burger is equally right, however, in stating that the alternative—the reintegration of art into life, the project of the avant-garde—has a grim future as well. The avant-garde's threat of destroying the institution of bourgeois art was recouped by that institution, and Burger further argues that popular culture can be understood as "a false sublation of art as institution" (54). Reynolds thus downplays the potential the digital sampler has for music: "Sampling may well produce a groundswell of bands making their own music (as with punk) but those individuals will still be buying music-making technology from companies that are vertically linked to the major record companies (as with punk)."[40] But this connection of technology to capitalist development is precisely where Benjamin begins his dialectic critique of technology as the material means of destroying materialist society. Thus his thesis on technology—"bourgeois society cannot help but insulate everything technological as much as possible from the so-called spiritual, and it cannot help but resolutely exclude technology's right of co-determination of the social order"[41]—cannot be read through the typical raver's eyes, because the raver fails to possess the dialectic sense to understand that the "spiritual" here refers not to some sort of New Age humbug but to socialism.

The raver throws up his or her hands (and rightly so) because commodification is resilient enough to withstand and then incorporate almost any aesthetic protest against it. It seems almost ludicrous then to attempt a musical critique based on the principles of montage, when its once-liberating effects in the visual realm have been relegated to a Hollywood editing style and especially when, as Reynolds points out, sampling has already begun being fetishized (as well as circumscribed by legal decisions that place severe penalties on unauthorized sampling). But the development of musical technology has not been concurrent with its visual counterpart, and the recent development of mechanized musical montage at least can profit from the historical legacy of past aesthetic failings. Sampling occurs in an age where it is known that Goebbels used jazz to boost morale amongst Germans during World War II and that even the leftist punk group the Clash had its song "Should I Stay or Should I Go?"—one of its more commercial and less overtly political songs—used in a United States military mission to flush Panamanian General Manuel Noriega out of hiding with rock music. This is the sense in which Adorno and Consolidated can view popular music as potentially fascistic: because its denial of its dialectical construction makes it susceptible to appropriation for propagandistic or violent activities. An example of this threat is the industrial band Front 242, which is reminiscent of Junger in its attempt to overcome modern alienation through the violence of technology: "Packed with ideas as they are, Front 242 aren't thoughtful; the ideas aren't 'communicated' so much as embodied (in the sheer visceral putsch of their rhythms) and emblazoned (in the sheer spectacle of their show). . . . They turn the dancefloor into a gulag, in which the crowd work with a will, happily turn themselves into appendages of flesh attached to the machine beat."[42] To understand the vulnerability of music technology to what Front 242 calls "micro-fascism" is to recognize that this aesthetic is not yet equipped for self-reflection, "a subjectivity which revolts against a collective power which it itself is; for this reason its revolts seems ridiculous and is beaten down by the drum just as syncopation is by the beat."[43]

Based on statements like these, Adorno has been cast as the cultural pessimist in his relationship with Benjamin (a well-documented relationship, most notably in the *Aesthetics and Politics* collection, which collects some of the correspondence between the two men during the period of "On Jazz" and "The Work of Art").[44] But few mention Adorno's interest in the potential of the gramophone or, later, of cinematic montage.[45] He concludes about the liberatory potential of film procedure (which clearly has historical ramifications for current sampling procedure) that "the obvious answer today, as forty years ago, is that of montage which does not interfere with things but rather arranges them in a constellation akin to that of writing."[46] Even earlier, Adorno acknowledged the possibility of audience critique in modern, commodified music: "The present mass reactions, for which musical reactions stand as the model, are only separated from consciousness by a thin veil. This veil should be broken through, but this is the very thing which is almost impossible to achieve."[47]

At the moment, the digital sampler provides one tool to break through that veil, a tool that can greatly expand the ability to manipulate sonic materials: "The real 'crisis,' or challenge to rock and pop posed by sampling concerns aesthetic possibilities and the fearsome prospect of the future and infinity of sounds imagined by precursors such as Varese and Schaeffer."[48] To view the possibility of computerized dance music as dialectical, as breaking through the veil, does not demand a didactic and joyless process of music making (as much of political pop, including a good portion of Consolidated's work, is); it questions the beat but doesn't eradicate it. "This is Fascism," after all, is intentionally set to a driving beat, in order to call into question the beat as a yet-unconsidered phenomenon. By calling into question the undialectical consumption of a dialectically produced music, Consolidated has created a song more politically astute than much of what can only be called the nascent philosophy of rave culture.

NOTES

1. Alice Yaegar Kaplan, *Reproductions of Banality* (Minneapolis: University of Minnesota Press, 1986), p. 138.
2. Andrew Hewitt, *Fascist Modernism* (Stanford, CA: Stanford University Press, 1993).
3. Walter Benjamin, "Theories of German Fascism," trans. Jerolf Wikoff, *New German Critique* 17 (spring 1979): 126–27; emphasis added.
4. Kaplan, *Reproductions of Banality*, p. 133.
5. Walter Benjamin, "The Work of Art in the Age of Mechanical Reproduction," in *Illuminations* (New York: Schocken, 1968), p. 219.
6. Starting points include Andrew Goodwin, "Sample and Hold," in *On Record: Rock, Pop, and the Written Word*, ed. Simon Frith and Andrew Goodwin (New York: Pantheon, 1990); Ross Harley, "Beat in the System," in *Rock and Popular Music*, ed. Tony Bennett, Simon Frith, Lawrence Grossberg, John Shepherd, and Graeme Turner (New York: Routledge, 1993); and John Mowitt, "The Sound of Music in the Era of Its Electronic Reproducibility," in *Music and Society*, ed. Susan McClary and Richard Leppert (New York: Cambridge University Press, 1987).

7. Peter Bürger, *Theory of the Avant-Garde* (Minneapolis: University of Minnesota Press, 1984), p. 77.

8. Rob Sheffield, "Listen Up," *Details* (April 1995): 198.

9. Benjamin, "Work of Art," p. 221.

10. Goodwin, "Sample and Hold," p. 271.

11. Ernst Junger, "Photography and the 'Second Consciousness,'" in *Photography in the Modern Era*, ed. Christopher Phillips (New York: Metropolitan Museum of Art, 1989), pp. 208–9.

12. Frances Dyson, "The Ear That Would Hear Sounds in Themselves," in *Wireless Imagination*, ed. Douglas Kahn and Gregory Whitehead (Cambridge, MA: MIT Press, 1992), p. 401.

13. Goodwin, "Sample and Hold," p. 263.

14. John Cage, "Forerunners of Modern Music," in *Silence* (Middletown, CT: Wesleyan University Press, 1961), p. 63n, quoted in Dyson, "The Ear," p. 375.

15. Theodor Adorno, "On Jazz," trans. Jamie Owen Daniel, *Discourse* 12 (fall–winter 1989–90): 61.

16. Theodor Adorno, "Motifs," in *Quasi Una Fantasia* (New York: Verso, 1992), p. 34.

17. Of course, many popular music scholars regard Adorno as a sort of bogeyman for making such seemingly reactionary statements about pop that fail to acknowledge the liberatory potential of mass-produced music, particularly in relation to its roots as resistive African-American music. Some have even branded Adorno racist, claiming that his essays on jazz display essentialistic tendencies towards black music and musicians. But as Jamie Owen Daniel argues in his introduction to the translation of "On Jazz," Adorno's position is a critique of the consumption of blackness in some essentialized way: "Clearly, Adorno is condemning . . . the fetishization of the black American and his/her supposedly more 'natural' or 'unmediated' sexuality, a fetishization that was very much in vogue at the time" (41). What also gets overlooked in analyzing the more outlandish (and hence read as naive) statements Adorno offers is the formal elements of their construction. Thus famous aphorisms, such as the one linking Mickey Mouse to fascism in *Dialectic of Enlightenment*, are too quickly dismissed without considering the role juxtaposition plays in the sentence's construction (see Fredric Jameson's chapter on Adorno in *Marxism and Form*, ed. Fredric Jameson [Princeton, NJ: Princeton University Press, 1971], especially pp. 53–55, concerning the "dialectical sentence"). The sentence-level "constellation"—to use one of Adorno's favorite terms—of Disney and fascism, or raves and fascism, works precisely through its unlikely associations. In other words, the naive reading actually refuses to take seriously the question of what links exist between fascist spectacle and the popular-culture phenomena of so-called democratic societies.

18. Benjamin, "Work of Art," pp. 240–41.

19. Marcus Paul Bullock, *The Violent Eye* (Detroit: Wayne State University Press, 1992), p. 27.

20. Theodor Adorno, "Music and New Music," in *Quasi una Fantasia* (New York: Verso, 1992), p. 268.
21. Dyson, "The Ear," p. 400.
22. Jacques Attali, *Noise* (Minneapolis: University of Minnesota Press, 1984), p. III.
23. Simon Reynolds, *Blissed Out* (London: Serpent's Tail, 1990), p. 178.
24. Adorno, "On Jazz," p. 66.
25. Hewitt, *Fascist Modernism*, p. 155.
26. Benjamin, "Work of Art," p. 224.
27. Adorno, "Music and New Music," pp. 265–66; emphasis added.
28. Dyson, "The Ear," p. 381.
29. Roger Caillois, "Festival," in *The College of Sociology*, ed. Denis Hollier, trans. Betsy Wing (Minneapolis: University of Minnesota Press, 1988), p. 281.
30. Anatole Lewitzsky, "Shamanism," in *The College of Sociology*, ed. Denis Hollier, trans. Betsy Wing (Minneapolis: University of Minnesota Press, 1988), p. 251; emphasis in original.
31. Benjamin, "Work of Art," p. 223.
32. Cited in Caillois, "Festival," p. 282.
33. Bürger, *Theory of the Avant-Garde*, p. 50.
34. Susan Sontag, "Fascinating Fascism," in *Under the Sign of Saturn* (New York: Random House, 1980), p. 96.
35. Benjamin, "Work of Art," p. 241.
36. Cited in Erik Davis, "Monsters of Techno," *Spin* II (April 1995): 84.
37. Benjamin, "Work of Art," p. 231.
38. Reynolds, *Blissed Out*, p. 87.
39. Bürger, *Theory of the Avant-Garde*, p. 13.
40. Reynolds, *Blissed Out*, p. 168.
41. Benjamin, "Theories of German Fascism," p. 120.
42. Reynolds, *Blissed Out*, p. 163.
43. Adorno, "On Jazz," p. 68.
44. Ernst Bloch, et al., eds., *Aesthetics and Politics*, trans. Ronald Taylor (New York: Verso, 1977).
45. See *October* 55 (winter 1990) for recently translated writings by Adorno on the phonograph.
46. Theodor Adorno, "Transparencies on Film," trans. Thomas Y. Levin, *New German Critique* 24–25 (fall/winter 1981–82): 203.
47. Adorno, "Commodity Music Analyzed," in *Quasi Una Fantasia* (New York: Verso, 1992), p. 51.
48. Reynolds, *Blissed Out*, p. 171.

9

THE RIOT GRRRLS AND "CARNIVAL"

NEIL NEHRING

Young women in the United States have understandably seized on punk rock in the 1990s. I know I have to wear a drool cup for my bile: we live in a plutocracy so brazen that decent people avert their eyes. It's so transparent, but it's also so muddy; it seems as if there's nothing you can say that they can't pervert, can't turn into their own to silence you: "Just say no" ought to be an anarchist slogan, not a Nancy Reagan/Bob Dole bromide. It even makes you feel schizophrenic, as postmodern theorists claim, but George Orwell pointed out well before postmoderns that political language doesn't seem to have much connection to material reality anymore. The worst is channeling all the wealth to a few greedheads on top and calling it a revolution.

The moral bankruptcy and social breakdown that result from living in a plutocratic military state, worse still, are explained away by politicians and pundits as being the fault of unwed mothers. That's nothing, of course, compared to the real violence done to women every day. I'm not going to recite statistics on rape and domestic abuse, though, and all the other forms of violence everyone knows about but seems to consider just part of the scenery. Stalking women is the national sport; in the city I live in (Austin, Texas), some husband, ex-husband, or boyfriend kills his wife, ex-wife, or girlfriend just about every week. The routine is so dull it's middle-of-section-B stuff (at least when the victim is poor and not white).

Setting aside actual physical violence, any sensate, honest male knows full well that supposedly wild-eyed radical feminists are absolutely right about our culture's representation of women, who are on constant display, everywhere, as semen receptacles. The gaze, when it comes to women, is real; riot grrrls write BITCH, RAPE, SLUT, and WHORE on their bodies because that's what a lot of men already see there. Beyond pornography and the whole sex industry, the problem is how so-called normal guys have learned to look at women, as well as how *not* to hear them, a problem women in punk rock are obviously working on. (They're not preaching to the converted; even at shows by female-led punk bands, I've heard men in the presumably progressive audience enthuse about the performers' breasts.) In referring to ordinary guys I'm not talking in the usual academic mode about some imaginary uneducated goons; I'm talking about myself. And let me assure you, the only difference between Hugh Grant's hooker and his tony actress-model girlfriend with her cleavage falling out of the newspaper is how much they get paid and their distance from the men they're servicing. A privileged woman in our culture is one who can stick to inspiring masturbation. In this respect, one of the finest moments in riot grrrl history occurred on the British talk show *The Word*, when the group Huggy Bear returned unexpectedly after its own performance to heckle host Terry Christian with cries of "Shame!" when he showed a film report on two topless models.

Because any words you could use to condemn the ugliness at present have already been taken and twisted, the only thing left for any sensible person to do is scream, which is exactly what a lot of young people are doing. They're not worrying about a message, which Newt Gingrich and Rush Limbaugh, given the absence of anyone in the government or news media to contradict them, would just spin into a sound bite. Pure screaming is what grunge, metal, punk, rap, and riot grrrls have in common, not scream therapy, either: the point isn't letting it out and feeling better (or a catharsis) but enlisting other screamers, and they're doing it in the public eye while the authorities hate it. "Screaming," says Kim Gordon of Sonic Youth, "is a kind of vehicle for expressing yourself in ways society doesn't let you."[1]

Writing on the riot grrrl subculture, Joanne Gottlieb and Gayle Wald toy with reducing the scream to dead-end postmodern terms of a purely bodily "jouissance" and "a radically polysemous nonverbal articulation," but they resist discounting the emotion involved: "Far from being a fluid signifier, screams are also emotional ejaculations bearing specific associations with highly charged events—like rape, orgasm, or childbirth." Since those events are "associated with femininity at its most vulnerable, the scream in its punk context can effect a shocking juxtaposition of sex and rage," going well beyond the evident assertion of a "form of expression both denied to women in public (screaming is unladylike) and devalued in private (women are so emotional)." (Gottlieb and Wald contrast quite starkly with Joy Press and Simon Reynolds's postmodern celebration of the bliss of the mother's womb, which leads them to a quick dismissal of the riot grrrls in *The Sex Revolts*). The expression of "collective outrage at abuse," I would add, is attributed by Donna Gaines to the whole "fucked generation"—male and female alike—in an obituary for Kurt Cobain that she wrote for *Rolling Stone*.[2]

Most young people wouldn't provide such a full account of why they're screaming, but that doesn't mean they couldn't, that they haven't absorbed, at some level, plenty of good reasons for screaming. And many of them are trying like mad to dredge those reasons out of the swamp of incoherence the culture's inundated them with. Cacophony in music, by their own account, is an attempt to get a grip on the way the whole culture sounds, and there's nothing (like po-mo's beloved "power") that guarantees they won't do so. Of course much of the music is merchandised by multinational corporations, but even if angry music were only a caricature of truly deviant, subversive impulses—which it's not—the response to it is never predictable. There could be a backlash or even an upheaval of the genuine feelings supposedly being prostituted: "There is always the chance that the promise of revolution on a billboard will be taken literally in the streets."[3]

I don't think we have to fall back on last-gasp ironies like this, however, though I'm compelled to make the point because so many complacent post-modernists will insist despite all the evidence to the contrary that commercial incorporation is universally damaging. Just because "a particular form [is] marketed for profit," says Rita Felski, in arguing specifically for feminist forms in mass culture, "we may not automatically conclude that it is irredeemably compromised and cannot constitute a legitimate medium of oppositional cultural activity." Feminist theorists need to pay "serious attention . . . to the political potential of more popular forms such as . . . rock music."[4]

The new wave of young women making rock music in the 1990s, whether on independent or corporate labels, has similarly had no truck with postmodern notions that popular music, given its commerciality, can only be subversive by being "deadpan, indifferent, depersonalized, effaced, . . . effectively cancel[ing] the possibility of traditional audience identification."[5] The new female rockers have tried like hell, instead, to open up a new way of living for hordes of young women, basically involving the refusal to be victims of gendering that feminists have long sought but breaking with the elders' intellectual-literary bent by making self-creation a more exciting and attractive matter than studiously absorbing feminist tracts and/or spinning out *écriture féminine* for literary theorists. Groups such as Bikini Kill, says Sandy Carter, defy "traditional roles and images open to women while simultane-

ously slashing through doctrinaire notions of feminism." The members of
the British group Huggy Bear "see Riot Grrrl as connecting theory with
action, connecting feminism with nothing less than the urge to live. . . . The
music, the literature, the hanging out—all reveal this relentless urge, the
speed and seriousness of this impulsion. A call to any girl open to it."[6]

At first, though, the riot grrrl movement existed primarily "in the minds
of a handful of boho progeny with access to copy machines and feminist
reading lists," such as Kathleen Hanna writing in *Jigsaw* (which was founded
by BK drummer Tobi Vail) and Allison Wolfe and Molly Neuman of Bratmobile, publishers of *Girl Germs*[7] (organized groups such as riot grrrl NYC
emerged about two years after the public attention the first wave received in
1991). Riot grrrl feminism is hardly a single platform but "a crazy salad that
mixes rhetoric from 1960's-style women's liberation, green politics, vegetari-
anism, Susan Faludi's *Backlash*, Naomi Wolf's *Beauty Myth* and other disparate sources."[8] The result is exemplified by Bikini Kill's "florid, pen-pal
rhetoric . . . an essential emotional and intellectual process primarily because
it's so much *fun*: Revolution as everyday play; girls getting off on rock gestures and nonsense without ever *considering* boy consent."[9]

Musicians and audience have together overcome a problem the editors of
Emotion and Gender recollect in their girlhoods: "There are very few examples
where we as girls played to an audience of peers. . . . There was a collectivity
of action in many of the young men's [activities] that was almost completely
absent from the women's." We can see the significance, then, of women in
rock music creating a "feminist public sphere" much like that advocated by
Felski in her defense of feminists working through both the mass media and
independent popular forms (such as the fanzine): "*internally*, it generates a
gender-specific identity grounded in a consciousness of community and solidarity among women; *externally*, it seeks to convince society as a whole of
the validity of feminist claims, challenging existing structures of authority."[10]

Kathleen Hanna describes just such a public sphere in the riot grrrl movement, which at a time "when *Time* or *Newsweek* said feminism was dead,
around '89, [told] girls who are not involved in tight feminist communities"
that the possibility "*does* exist" and needs to keep being created. She feels that
she achieved her original goal because "feminism really *is* cool now," and
Andrea Juno likewise finds that the recent changes women have brought
about in rock and roll "reflect the thriving and flowering of feminism, despite
the perpetual media-pronounced deaths and backlashes" (and the death of
rock has been refuted, too, in the process). But as Candice Pedersen of K

Records points out, riot grrrl continues to be important for its original function, which was simply to provide young women "with a network that prevents them from thinking they're insane." The level of organization in the riot grrrl subculture is unusual in youth culture, in fact, belying the doomsaying of all the serious politicos who castigate the whole idea of popular cultural pastimes having political results. The subculture extends beyond the making of music and the creation of expressive subcultural styles, Gottlieb and Wald emphasize, "into the realms of political strategizing and continually re-rehearsed self-definition through fanzine publication." Ann Powers, a member of Strong Women in Music (or SWIM), notes that the new wave of women in rock has also affected the production end of the music business in the United States, with "women getting more involved at all levels," an essential development if the new prominence of women is to have a lasting impact.[11]

The music that young women have recently found most useful in forming an audience of other young women is punk rock, of course: the riot grrrl "movement is above all a triumph of punk." The riot grrrls and virtually every other new rock band featuring women "say they owe their existence to punk's do-it-yourself ethic: if you have something to say, pick up a guitar, write a song and say it. 'There's no way any of this could have happened if it wasn't for punk rock,' says Molly Neuman, Bratmobile's 21-year-old drummer."[12] Perhaps the best-known of female rock critics (if one excludes Patti Smith for being better known as a performer), Ellen Willis, had written in 1977 "that she preferred the Sex Pistols to the women's music genre because 'music that boldly and aggressively laid out what the singer wanted, loved, hated . . . challenged me to do the same. Even when the content was antiwoman . . . the form encouraged my struggle for liberation.' "[13]

As Simon Frith and Angela McRobbie also noted at the time, in the 1978 essay "Rock and Sexuality," women in popular music before punk tended to take the role of the "singer/songwriter/folkie lady—long-haired, pure-voiced, self-accompanied on acoustic guitar"—and thus "reinforced in rock the qualities traditionally linked with female singers, sensitivity, passivity, and sweetness." Exceptions such as Janis Joplin and Grace Slick found it necessary to "become 'one of the boys' " (Whether tomboyism is actually a bad thing, as I will discuss later, is a hotly debated issue among present-day female rockers). Punk, given its do-it-yourself amateurism that rejects musical virtuosity and especially its antiromance stance, allowed "female voices to be heard that are not often allowed expression on record, stage, or radio—shrill, assertive,

impure" voices of "strident insistency" such as those of the Pretenders'
Chrissie Hynde (who worked in Malcolm McLaren's Sex Shop, after which
the Sex Pistols were named), Pauline Murray of Penetration, Siouxsee Sue of
the Banshees, Poly Styrene of X-Ray Spex, and groups like the Raincoats and
the Slits.[14] The riot grrrls are not simply a second coming of female punk,
though, but "a new moment in this history," Gottlieb and Wald believe, moving well beyond the first wave of iconoclasts playing back images of women
by adding "a deep sense of abuse and a stronger critique of patriarchy."[15]

The hiatus between the trailblazers of the 1970s and the emergence of the
female punk bands in 1991 accords with the submergence of punk, in popular
attention, in the decade before Nirvana. But Gottlieb and Wald note that the
successor to punk in the United States, the hardcore music of the 1980s, was
"aggressively masculinist" (252) and often "resorted to blatant misogyny"
(253), to some extent disenfranchising women interested in punk music (I
would object that Exene Cervenka of X, who came out of the hardcore scene
in Los Angeles, goes unmentioned in the article). Gottlieb and Wald conclude
nonetheless that the "potent combination" (253) of anger and "frank expressions of sexuality" (252) in punk has served to open "a fertile space both for
women's feminist interventions and the politicization of sexuality and female
identity" (253). They also note an "incremental, progressive change" (255) in
the eighties in the increasing number of female instrumentalists participating
relatively equitably with males, such as Georgia Hubley of Yo La Tengo, as
well as the godmother of riot grrrls, Kim Gordon. (All the biggest bands in
Austin in the mid-eighties, such as Glass Eye, Grains of Faith, and the Reivers,
seemed to be made up of two men and two women.)

By the 1990s, says Carola Dibbell, "What had changed was not so much
the issues, but who cared about them. In the '70s a critical fringe had con-
templated gender in punk, in the '80s an academically hip media had debated
Madonna's sexuality, but by the '90s riot grrrls had helped make feminist
issues, if not cool, at least impossible to ignore."[16] I think it's safe to say as well
that the fact that it took over a decade for female punk performers to coalesce
into a broad-based phenomenon also indicates the continuing difficulty
young women face in breaking with conventional expectations of femininity,
which makes the breakthrough of female punks in the nineties all the more
exciting.

The results of woman making punk rock are hardly appealing only to
other women, either. Greil Marcus, for example, agrees with female critics
that the general effect has been a resuscitation of rock and roll by "the most

vital and the most open punk music . . . heard in years." Few rockers "play music that genuinely challenges the dominant mind set of the pop audience," says Sandy Carter, and the "clearest and freshest exceptions to the rule are coming from rock women." Thus their "arrival signals serious change in the landscape," according to Ann Powers, offering "a different vision to fans: that of a woman setting a spark to herself." The enormous possibilities opened up by over half of humanity finally making space for itself in rock music—hardly a small minority creating a fad—makes the "subtext . . . almost always the joy and liberation found in a woman's own act of expression." Andrea Juno like- wise asserts that no one could be better suited to take over the image of rock- and-roll outlaw from exhausted "geriatric 'Rock Gods' " than women being "bold, brash, and loud, all the things they were taught not to be." The sheer exhilaration created by punk women leads Elizabeth Wurtzel (author of *Prozac Nation*) to say simply that "women playing hard-and-fast rock music do bring something to the style that is different from—and often, I think, better than—what the men, who have been doing it forever, bring," without feeling compelled to specify what that "something" is.[17]

Revolution, girl style, is quite thrilling not just for critics but for many males in the audience, too; I, for example, have become a compulsive buyer of punk (or quasi-punk) music by women. The rock audience in general, says Carter, "seems increasingly willing to accept the fact that women can create hard, exciting guitar [and vocal] sounds on par with their male peers."[18] Female performers are just more interesting, their discoveries more relevant, in my own case, to my desire to discover similarly pissed-off people with new ways of speaking and singing—and, in the best cases, with a sense of humor about themselves. Men and women are not all that dissimilar in their anger (just in what they get angry at), and this is especially true for younger people: one of the few instances in postmodernism of any belief in new progressive social forces derives from feminist psychoanalytic work on incomplete oedi- palization—or an incomplete entry into patriarchy and masculinity—which finds that "the contemporary boy [is] in [a] developmental position that looks much like that traditionally characteristic of little girls."[19]

In light of the broad appeal of the new wave of women in rock, it's understandable that the riot grrrl label is actually seen by many female musi- cians as a way of pigeonholing them as a novelty or a specialty item or, when they succeed on a larger level, of incorporating them as a fad (thus I've mostly been using terms like "women making punk rock"; Andrea Juno's title *Angry Women in Rock* is another suitably broad rubric). With increasing attention from establishment media and the music press, in fact, adherents of the riot grrrl movement launched a nationwide media blackout in late 1992. Bikini Kill even felt compelled to disavow the riot grrrl label: in the liner notes to *The C.D. Version of the First Two Records*, BK insists that it is not "the definitive 'riot girl band,' [nor] in any way 'leaders of' or authorities on the 'Riot Grrrl' movement. . . . Tho we totally respect those who still feel that label is important and meaningful to them, we have never used that term to describe ourselves *as a band*." BK does add, however, that its members "subscribe to a variety of different aesthetics, strategies, and beliefs, both political and punkwise, some of which are probably considered 'riot girl.' "[20]

As the term "riot grrrl" doesn't give total offense, I've used it in my essay's title. But in doing so I risk appearing to incorporate the subject into "the male-defined spaces of academia and academic discourse," another form of "recuperation" that has met with resistance by riot grrrls (I trust that my account of the riot grrrls, set in the larger context of validating anger and given my excitement at their music, doesn't seem like exploitation, trivialization, and tourism). From their point of view, report Gottlieb and Wald, even "left or feminist" intellectual work has a "cultural centrality" that threatens to appropriate the ability of the riot grrrls to speak for themselves "as a marginal group."[21]

But in resisting an "undifferentiated 'mainstream,' " Gottlieb and Wald argue, "Riot Grrrl risks setting itself up in opposition to the status quo" with the same "elitism [as] independent music generally." As in the aesthetic tradition running from romanticism to postmodernism, rejecting the popular may simply serve to "preclude the possibility of having a broad cultural or political impact." Resisting popularity also seems belated in this case, given that the mass-circulation magazine *Sassy* has already been instrumental in popularizing the riot grrrl movement. *Sassy*, moreover, treated it with "respect and even commitment," hardly diluting riot grrrl ideology, another good reason to question postmodern notions about the complete ideological incorporation of deviant subcultures by commercial popularity: "The media, beyond its function to control and contain this phenomenon, may also have helped to perpetuate" and encourage it in a relatively positive fashion" (270–71). This is not unprecedented, either; in *Reconstructing Pop/Subculture*, Van Cagle documents how Andy Warhol and camp sensibility were transmitted by the mass media (unwittingly in this case) to gender-bending rockers such as David Bowie and their followers in the glam subculture, an important precursor to riot grrrl work on gender, argue Gottlieb and Wald. Kathleen Hanna confirms this view in her account of how her lie in an early interview about riot grrrl chapters had cropped up in several cities, with the result that a year later she found that young women in those cities had gone looking for the groups, hadn't been able to find them, and had decided to create their own.[22]

The 1992 media blackout also risks endorsing the perception that feminine agency in popular music can never overcome co-optation, which in the hands of male critics becomes a source of ridicule. Women are assumed, not without reason, to have little choice in the matter of selling out because they have long been commodities or been linked to commodities in advertising and thus have little or no distance from commercial culture to relinquish. The problem with acceding too easily to the view that women are deeply embedded in the production of mass culture can be seen in its most extreme form: the misogyny with which elitist critics, such as Theodor Adorno bewailing castration by jazz, have traditionally cast the supposedly pacifying effect of mass culture as the threat of feminization.

Even from a less extreme perspective, the best that can presumably be said of a commercial success such as Madonna is simply that she has been in charge of her own selling-out process. These terms have been used to describe male performers, too, especially the early Rolling Stones and the Sex Pistols. But there has always been a sense that these male exemplars combined an exposé of selling out with an undiminished, blisteringly caustic outrage. Madonna, in contrast, can only manipulate conventional expectations of feminine sexuality to little or no subversive end, leaving a large part of the audience completely oblivious to any feminist component in her work.

Many female performers understandably resist consignment to this fate by disavowing Madonna. Chrissie Hynde wonders "why people pay such tribute" to Madonna for having "kicked open doors" when at best "she was a great disco queen." Though Courtney Love is often described as building on Madonna's legacy of overt sexuality (a legacy Gottlieb and Wald read into the riot grrrl movement as well), Love pointedly distances herself in observing that Madonna's dance music "has always sucked." Liz Phair, on the other hand—whom Hynde does consider important—cites Madonna as a precursor, and I know from personal experience that many riot grrrl followers despise Phair for capitalizing, however ironically, on physical attractiveness. Phair wonders, as a result, how "you get away with this kind of thing" if "you vote *for* sex and yet *against* sexism." The thought has undoubtedly crossed Madonna's mind, too, but I find Phair's parody of the Rolling Stones on *Exile in Guyville* more compelling than Madonna's incessant mining of whatever is cutting edge in black culture, which bell hooks execrates in *Black Looks*.[23]

As the example of Liz Phair indicates, there might be some middle ground between Madonna's overexposure (in more than one sense) and a media blackout. Rather than resisting commercial incorporation so strenuously, could women not highlight it, just as men have done, while remaining rebel rockers, the classic punk formula? Kathleen Hanna endorses the original press blockade as necessary to getting the riot grrrl movement off the ground with some authentic roots, but she also resists a permanent adherence to the romantic rejection of commerce: "Getting trapped in little circles of shame and blame isn't going . . . to make corporations or co-optation go away." (Valerie Agnew of 7 Year Bitch criticizes another self-defeating exclusionary practice, the refusal of some women at riot grrrl shows to give fanzines to men, which just "takes you back ten steps.")[24]

The primary problem in discussing the riot grrrl movement, finally, is simply that it doesn't encompass the music of the wide range of groups and individuals that can be roughly lumped together as women playing punk rock, angry women in rock, or whatever. "When it comes to women in music," says Wurtzel, "one size certainly does not fit all." The diversity of the musicians whom I've actually heard and could have examined indicates that "generalizations about them [are] difficult if not ridiculous," as Ann Powers puts it:[25]

Babes in Toyland
Belly
Bikini Kill
Bratmobile
Breeders
Concrete Blonde
Elastica
Fluffy
Kim Gordon
P. J. Harvey
Juliana Hatfield
Heavenly
Heavens to Betsy
Hole
Huggy Bear

Joan Jett
L7
Lunachicks
Mecca Normal
Liz Phair
Pork
Red Aunts
Scrawl
7 Year Bitch
Siren
Slant 6
Sleater-Kinney
Team Dresch
Throwing Muses
Veruca Salt

I spent a lot of time listening continuously to everything by all of them, which was a bad idea, in part because I wound up preferring the poppier ones for being easier to take in large doses than the straightforwardly angry, screaming ones.

I think that the single best song *about* anger may nonetheless really be Veruca Salt's MTV hit "Seether," sung by Nina Gordon and Louise Post (also the guitarists), who have nice high-pitched "feminine" voices that set up a jarring chasm of contradiction with their account of the monster "at the center of it all," their seething anger, which they just can't seem to "cram back" in their mouths. The "lovely daughters" in Veruca Salt (which has since broken up, unfortunately) are the most subversive and the most enjoyable of the whole lot, by my standards. I agree with music critics, though, that the most significant performer in the long run is likely to be P. J. Harvey, whose invocation of the whole of popular music's history on *To Bring You My Love* does suggest a genius at work. Harvey's voice bends gender (as well as race), though—a British woman in her early twenties singing, at times, like Howlin' Wolf—and thus Courtney Love of Hole "may be the first [female rock performer] to demand the audience's total immersion in a woman's world."[26]

Love's virtual abandonment of music after her success as an actress is unfortunate because she was often a shrewd commentator on women in rock. Her devotion to the "total" world of women led her to attack "fascistic" musicians and critics who draw lines between female performers (though

Love later mocked riot grrrls as "estrogen lemmings"). She is particularly incensed by accusations of "assimilationism," a term used by Kathleen Hanna to criticize tomboy groups like L7 who are "trying to just fit in" with male musicians.[27] (I think L7 deserves more credit than this, too; its best-known song, "Pretend We're Dead," rewrites *Society of the Spectacle* as a catchy pop song, no mean feat.) Love may be sensitive on this account because she, too, invites the assimilationist charge, if for a different reason: her professed desire to demonstrate to young women that expressing virulent anger does not preclude being conventionally attractive, even sexy (if not oversexed), that being a feminist doesn't mean one can't make it as a woman. Hanna is no absolutist, though, having worked with Joan Jett, who is often mentioned in the same breath with L7. I should note that I'm reading political differences out of more publicized personal ones: Hanna and Love came to blows at a Lollapalooza show in 1995 after Hanna reportedly antagonized Love with cracks about her fitness to raise her daughter by the late Kurt Cobain. Hanna knew Cobain before Nirvana became famous—her graffiti, in most accounts, having supplied him with the title of his breakthrough single "Smells Like Teen Spirit"—and the hostility between her and Love apparently stems from that earlier relationship.

With respect to the politics of music, Love's argument for inclusiveness has been strongly seconded by Evelyn McDonnell: to dismiss "L7 for simply doing what boys do [is] an underestimation of tomboyism woefully au courant among cultural feminists. The point of . . . 'female machisma' is not simply to emulate and assimilate, but to invade men's exclusive realms of privilege and freedom." Besides, as Rita Felski points out, there has never really been any form of expression, including musical genres, that can be said to be distinctly gendered or inherently masculine or feminine. Rather than worrying about such classification, we should recognize an important achievement on the part of all the female performers listed above: for women to play and sing through the same forms as men is inherently a form of resistance, refusing to accept the definition of woman as the male's subordinate Other. This is true in terms not only of the voice, Gottlieb and Wald note, but also of the guitar: "Something potentially radical happens when women appropriate [an] instrument . . . tirelessly resurrected [as] signifying male power and virtuosity, the legitimate expression of phallic sexuality, perversity (Jimi Hendrix [*sic*]), and violence (Pete Townshend)."[28]

I'm going to deal now with just a single song by Bikini Kill, "Carnival" (*The C.D. Version of the First Two Records*). The appeal of "Carnival" is obvious enough: it blasts along at a speed dance-music fans (who live for bpms, or beats per minute) would be hard-pressed to keep up with, as drummer Tobi Vail repeatedly forces the tempo with double time and rolls. Like all great punk songs, "Carnival" attacks the viscera through a roller coaster ride, up and down, between two chords (if a different pair in the chorus than in the verses). In keeping with the two-chord minimalism, guitarist Billy Karren, the token boy, plays a hilarious two-note guitar solo. The song only lasts less than a minute and a half before collapsing in an exhausted heap; no one could possibly sustain the energy, musician or audience. Hanna's vocal is simultaneously blasé and celebratory (as ambiguous as the song's content, as I'll show) and supplies a rhythmic counterpoint—a melody, even—over the band's unvaried thrashing.

Most angry girl bands are in fact pop rock, or melodic; Bikini Kill "rarely *just* 'rock.' "[29] The sound may be harsh, but female punks are not averse to caring about songwriting and finding hooks. This is not to suggest this comprimises them in any way; the frequent combination of pop vocal stylings from girl groups of the sixties with punk arrangements, for example, is intended to set up the same contradictions between prettiness and hardness found in "Seether." It doesn't hurt the simultaneously catchy and abrasive effect of "Carnival," either, that Kathleen Hanna accidentally has a perfect nonvirtuoso voice of yowling authenticity, which has made her stand out in the same unpredictable, unlikely way Poly Styrene did in 1977. When Hanna sings "When you get right down to the heart of the matter" in "This Is Not a Test" (*The C.D. Version of the First Two Records*), I believe that's what's happening. Marcus says of BK, in fact, that for all its pop sensibility, "this stuff is so primitive and so raw and so direct that you could almost imagine that this is where punk began, and the Sex Pistols heard this stuff and made something a little more shapely out of it."[30] But judging from the attention to melody and hooks on *Reject All American* (1996)—pop qualities embraced by Sleater-Kinney, as well, on *Call the Doctor* (1996)—Bikini Kill has apparently undertaken just such a remodeling in an effort to enlarge its audience.

As to what "Carnival" is about, after the long history of inane academic work focused on lyrics as poetry, I'm loath to dwell on lyrical content. So it should be understood throughout what follows that the meaning—or different meanings—that make the song great art lie in the intersection of the lyrics with the emotional and musical performance (that harmony of form and content is something of a classical ideal but includes an avant-garde emphasis that the expressive discoveries in the form or technique matter most if one is going to make people sit up and take notice of what one has to say). Rather than immediately peeling away the lyrics, moreover, I'd rather have a go at explaining the song by telling a story about what happened when I played "Carnival" at an academic colloquium.

Like all great rock songs, "Carnival" provides only a few intelligible lyrics, just enough to give the listener a vague start on figuring out what's going on. Hanna makes a point of doing this, in fact, in a spoken introduction over just a drumbeat, in which she describes the "seedy underbelly" of the carnival, "the part that only the kids know about," where sixteen-year-old girls give "head to carnies for free rides and hits of pot." As the song revs up, the last intelligible bit after this fairly horrific picture of vulgarity and abuse immediately complicates matters: Hanna doesn't decry the scenario, as one might expect, but instead declares "I wanna go to the carnival," too, as if she wants in on the action.

The move, at first listen, invites the response it got as soon as the panel I was on had finished. A female graduate student from the English department simply said, "I find that song very disturbing." The words are engraved on my brain because they put me seriously on the spot, though they shouldn't have: "Carnival" was disturbing to her, I am quite certain, because she assumed Hanna eagerly wanted to be defiled by carnies. The assumption, in other words, is that performers of popular music, unlike those involved in literature, are to be taken absolutely literally because they are incapable of complexity, ambiguity, parody, and other traditional shibboleths of literary criticism.

I couldn't say any of this, in part, admittedly, because it didn't all occur to me right away but also because I was stunned and embarrassed by the clear implication that I was insensitively and uncritically, even vicariously, exulting in a song that glorifies the sexual abuse and self-degradation of adolescent females. I suspect the motive behind the student's comment was a reflexive faultfinding with men not uncommon among academic feminists, not that I blame them, but if the further inference was that I had no business discussing riot grrrls in the first place, I would have to object that identity politics don't work with regard to tastes in popular music. What I wish I'd said about "Carnival" itself is that it is, in fact, about as ambiguous a work of art as William Empson (author of the classic *Seven Types of Ambiguity*) could hope for: it has an aura of authentic conviction in its performance but is also highly self-reflexive in setting up different ways of understanding it.

I want to dwell on that ambiguity, on the possible explanations for why a tale of degradation leads to celebration, desire, and a little ennui as well, because such an examination yields an appreciation of the significance not just of angry girl bands but of the best popular music in any genre. In dwelling on the possibilities in understanding "Carnival," mind you, I am not arguing for the complexity of the song itself or that it rewards intense inspection and interpretation just as a literary text does. The reasons for the meanings I make of it are not hard to detect, for one thing. If I elaborate them at some length here, the point is to demonstrate that the real complexity of simple popular songs lies in the meanings and uses people can make of them, with myself as illustration. As Georgia Christgau would have it, I'm going to stick to my own impression of what the artists are trying to get me to see and feel and think; I'm sure it's not completely idiosyncratic and with luck it will add at least a little to the experience of other listeners, as useful criticism has always done.

I don't want to seem oblivious to the sociological question of how BK is understood by a variety of members of its audience, however, because some interpretations may indeed offer reason to be disturbed. As I was writing this, a female undergraduate complained about young women she knows who sleep around indiscriminately while professing to be followers of BK and Hole and thus to be exercising a new, radical self-assertion. I don't mean to deny this possibility; sexual freedom as advocated by sixties-style women's lib is certainly expressed by some angry young female performers such as Courtney Love, though more in her self-presentation than in her songs, like "Asking For It," which hardly suggest that sex is always good. But if the riot grrrls are understood by some young women, apparently, to offer a glamorous rationale for being used quite traditionally by young men, we have a situation that does resemble the repressive hypothesis described by postmodernist icon Michel Foucault in his *History of Sexuality*: the mistake of equating the unleashing of sexuality with social liberation, when one may only wind up subjected all the more. This is the age of AIDS, moreover, and one may wind up dead as well.

For me, at any rate, there are at least three ways to take "Carnival," if one pays any attention at all to the song itself and knows something about Bikini Kill's general approach. The most direct understanding would likely be that "Carnival" in sum total serves to confront us with sexual abuse. Making listeners face unpleasant realities about sex and violence is a staple of riot grrrl subject matter, part of the whole confrontational approach including Hanna's scrawling of SLUT on her belly (which was more specifically a parody of Madonna's "Boy Toy" phase). Considering that Hanna has worked in domestic violence shelters, has suffered rape (by her own account in an interview with Andrea Juno), may have been a victim of parental abuse (but "that's for *me* to know," she tells Juno), and objects to songs based on those experiences being "framed as part of a victim or a freak show,"[31] she would hardly mindlessly glory in the wantonness my nemesis at the colloquium was disturbed to discern.

"Carnival" certainly seems to establish some linkage between its spoken introduction and the song, if one cheats and consults the lyric sheet: Hanna sings repeatedly about the carnival costing sixteen dollars, through a sort of numerology, apparently, echoing the opening invocation of sixteen-year-old girls who can't afford rides. If she does take the role of willing participant, though, at first glance a puzzling and even shocking move, Hanna accomplishes more than just putting the subject matter all the more directly in our faces; above all, she refuses to condemn other women, eschewing the lofty, judgmental view of a detached observer. In the fanzine *Jigsaw*, Hanna expresses admiration even for the "big haired makeup girl," more than likely the kind in "Carnival" who wears plastic boots "that go way up to there," especially when she performs an act of solidarity such as alerting others as to which men are date rapists.[32]

Hanna may even be playing an edgy game championing "sluts" for doing what they want: the gusto of the performance has something to do with being bad, though definitely not everything. (Having worked as a stripper, Hanna particularly wants "other women who work in the sex industry to remember that we can be . . . writers, musicians, [or] artists" as well.)[33] I say "edgy" particularly because such celebration invites opportunistic listeners to find justification for careless sex. (For all their personal and political differences, Hanna and Courtney Love resemble each other in this respect—as their pairing by some promiscuous teenage girls seems to indicate—though Hanna certainly doesn't make sexual voraciousness such a central part of her persona.) The BK anthem "Rebel Girl" (*The C.D. Version of the First Two Records*), for example (rerecorded with Joan Jett for added punch), concerns a woman whom everyone says is a slut, but when she talks, Hanna hears the revolution, and even in the sluttish way she walks, "there's revolution" in her hips, which Hanna can taste in her kiss as well, tossing bisexuality into the whole confrontational stew. "Carnival," though, in its lyrics, expresses little if any sense of rebelliousness; the sometimes jaded tone of the vocal, accordingly, may indicate a certain abjectness to the whole business.

Either in addition to or instead of a celebration of wanton women, "Carnival" might also be taken at a second, larger level as a parody. The target of the parody is not only conventional notions about sluts but also the whole process of gender or of constructing femininity. This "parodic use and abuse of mass-culture representations of women subvert[s] them by excess, irony, and fragmented recontextualization," says Linda Hutcheon (whose work on parody predates Judith Butler's well-known *Gender Trouble*, which is less interested in political coherence). But if a song like "Carnival" may be ironic about its fragmentary subject matter, that doesn't mean it's endorsing postmodern theory, which takes irony as a simple destablizing of meaning through the tactic of being in two places at once. Irony in this sense lies not just in the difference between what one says and what one means but also in the difference between the external world from which one draws one's subjects and the internal world of art in which they're recontextualized—and typically demoted, as in romanticism and modernism, beneath free play with form. That is not the only possibility for irony, however: "It is interesting," Hutcheon finds, "that few commentators on postmodernism actually use the word 'parody' " as well, which suggests that they can't acknowledge that irony sometimes has definite political results.[34]

Parody may work through irony, but in reproducing (or imitating) common sense about a group such as women, it proposes an alternative view that one is supposed to prefer to what's being parodied rather than just remaining suspended between the two. That distinct alternative is an exposé of "the *politics* of representation [and] the entire representational process" (94). When a student of mine says the cacophony of angry music captures the way the whole culture sounds, he has essentially this sweeping sort of parody in mind. Even gangsta rap does something very similar to the riot grrrls: the face it presents to white audiences, at least, seems to parody the hysterical mainstream images of urban black youth that substitute for any concern for their deprivation: they're presumably only depraved, instead. That gangsta-rap performers sometimes feel compelled to live out their subject matter suggests that even artists, let alone the uninitiated, don't always get the point.

Such misunderstandings occur because parody, by imitating conventional representations, is partially complicit with them and is only going to reinforce such images for many people. But Hutcheon makes an exception for feminist art that parodies conventions of femininity because it is "not content with exposition" (152) but has the ultimate purpose of "real social change" always in sight (168). This political intent distinguishes feminist parody from postmodernism, which "has not theorized agency" (but only what prevents it: power) and thus must be resisted (168). "While feminists may use postmodern parodic strategies, . . . they never suffer from [a] confusion of political agenda" (153) in which the complicity obscures the critique, as detractors claim about postmodernism's poster girl, Madonna, whom Andrea Juno calls "mainstream and synthesized."[35] The best feminist artists are fully aware at all times that they are parodying conventions of female representation and the processes by which various media propagate them (whether the audience gets the joke, of course, is always a sticking point).

Hutcheon's distinction of feminist work from other forms of postmodern parody may seem somewhat arbitrary, but her claim that feminists are more lucid in their politics holds up in the case of the riot grrrls. Simply "reclaiming the word 'girl' " in the first place, Gottlieb and Wald point out, "and reinvesting it with new meaning within their own feminist punk vernacular has proved one of the most salient aspects of the riot grrrl revolution." They describe that "recuperation of patriarchal language"—of the diminution of women in the word *girl*—as parody with serious connotations, including "a nostalgia for . . . close relationships between girls prior to the intrusion of heterosexual romance." Above all, though, "the riot grrrls, in rewriting 'girl' as 'grrrl,' also incorporate anger, defiance, and rebellion into their self-definition."[36]

Writing in *Jigsaw* in the spring of 1991, when "Carnival" was being recorded, Hanna expressed a consciousness of working against precisely the stereotyping or "cardboard cut outs" generated by the entire representational process. At first she sounds postmodern, contrasting the real "world of constant flux" with the artificiality of "some forever identity." But what she actually means is that "Jigsaw Youth" first have to break with learned identities such as gender, the "boxes and labels" targeted by feminist parody, and then they can assemble the puzzle pieces of a more authentic though never static identity from the "fucked up culture" of parents and "TV people," the real chaos. "It seems like it will never come together," she says, "but it can and it does and it will," a distinctly *anti*-postmodern sentiment.[37]

One commentator on Bikini Kill, Charles Aaron, finds that "they sneer, you know, *compassionately*, and spit in the pale, male face of the Generation X cliché, possessed by a radical desire to 'do' something."[38] Placing the word *do* in quotation marks may be intended as a form of condescension akin to Nietzsche's theory of *ressentiment*, an insinuation that Bikini Kill is confined to passion, unable to act on its anger. Whatever Aaron's intent, he captures precisely the point of BK: that anger and the passion for change are powerful forces in themselves. Hanna, for example, sums up her whole project in simple terms of feelings: "I am not afraid to say things matter to me." She chides cliques driven instead by a hipness, mythologized by Douglas Coupland in *Generation X*, that tries "to dictate . . . what is and what isn't cool or revolutionary or resistance. Just because someone is not resisting in the same way you are"—because he or she values feelings over your ideology, for instance—"does not mean they are not resisting," a point lost on intellectuals. "Resistance is everywhere," Hanna believes; "it always has been and always will be [among] Jigsaw Youth, listening, strategizing, tolerating, screaming, confronting, fearless."[39]

This impassioned advocacy, including but going well beyond the element of parody, is the last and most profound sense in which I understand "Carnival." The song's greatest resonance for me has everything to do with the music and virtually nothing to do with the words except for the title, a sort of keyword. I take "Carnival" most fundamentally to be a complete reversal of the dire, depressive effect of the opening subject matter, in a celebration of young women liberating themselves not only from abuse but in a much larger respect summed up in the use of "carnival" as a metaphor for the whole breakthrough of the riot grrrls and angry girl bands.

Most of the original riot grrrls were college students, and I have a sneaking suspicion someone in BK knows about Mikhail Bakhtin. A number of academics, such as Natalie Davis, Teresa Ebert, Nancy Fraser, Mary Russo, and Robert Stam, find his concept of carnival promising for feminism, like his general materialism or his argument (similar to Hanna's) that a social contest is always occurring in the emotional inflection of language. Bakhtin refers to a "material *bodily* principle" in his description of carnival as "grotesque realism," but he has in mind a dialectic between feelings and reason (of the sort described in recent cognitive philosophy and social psychology), specifically an antiauthoritarian attitude, rather than the body alone.[40] As in feminist cognitive philosophy, in particular, his bodies are the meeting point of affect and intellect: expressive, intelligent bodies capable of challenging authority, unlike the mute, dominated bodies described in postmodern footnotes to Foucault.

As Stam sums it up, carnival "is more than a party or a festival; it is the oppositional culture of the oppressed, a countermodel of cultural production and desire" like the feminist public sphere created by the riot grrrls, in which "all that is marginalized and excluded . . . takes over the center." Especially by advancing the unruly or disorderly woman, says Davis, the function of carnival in early modern Europe was "first, to widen behavioral options for women . . . and second, to sanction riot and political disobedience for both men and women in a society that allowed the lower orders few formal means of protest," a description obviously meant to pertain to the present.[41]

Bakhtin most extensively develops his concept of carnival in *Rabelais and His World*, which was written in the 1930s but unpublished until 1965 (and fairly quickly translated into English, in 1968). Taken at face value, the book concerns the High Middle Ages; it couldn't be published for three decades, however, because the book is an allegory repudiating not only the insipid version of folk culture, reduced to the decorative arts, that Stalin's minions encouraged but also the authoritarianism of Stalinism in general.

Bakhtin's description of carnivals in medieval marketplaces clearly has something larger in mind: "During carnival there is a temporary suspension of all hierarchic distinctions and barriers among men"—and women, we obviously need to add—and of the "prohibitions of usual life."[42] The result of this "world inside out" (11) is a "new type of communication [that] creates new forms of speech or a new meaning given to the old forms"—like rock and roll—"impossible in ordinary life" (16). The context of the marketplace clearly suggests work in contemporary mass culture; an opponent of modernist literary elitism (as evidenced by his attack on Russian formalism), Bakhtin is well aware that references by aesthetes to their loathing of the market, commerce, and the like, always connoted mass culture. In the process of assaulting decorum, carnival is very specifically an assertion of the powers of mass culture against the contempt of official culture, not only high culture but the mass media, which constantly insist on their own banality. The poet's pose of superiority is attacked by mixing up the sacred and the profane— making a montage out of them, in other words, along lines similar to those laid out by Walter Benjamin—as in the riot grrrls' combination of feminist intellectual work and rock and roll. Carnival works with mass culture, instead, to challenge its admittedly largely oppressive contents with "dynamic expression . . . opposed to all that was ready-made and completed"—such as identity, as Hanna describes it—and "to all pretense at immutability" (11), or the usual instruction in the mass media, emotional as well as ideological, that the status quo is forever, whether Stalinism or capitalism.

As one might expect, academic postmodernists have a simplistic, knee-jerk response to any optimistic reference to carnival: it's all authorized transgression, part of the closed circuit organized by power, whether in the medieval period or the present. Bakhtin himself, supposedly, inadvertently demonstrates this in depicting the medieval carnival as a permitted release of energy. In fact, he takes pains to resist such a view, contrasting carnival with officially sanctioned feasts that "did not lead people out of the existing world order" but "asserted all that was stable, unchanging, perennial" (9), precisely what carnival opposes. The unleashing of energy in carnival, moreover, had a long preexistence that the diminished official festivals of the Middle Ages could never suppress. If carnival has at times been a tool of the powerful, used only to "channel energies that might otherwise fuel popular revolt, it has just as often been the case that carnival has been the object of official repression" out of fear of the danger it poses.[43]

In contrasting carnival and official feasts, to read this matter into the present, Bakhtin in essence distinguishes good and bad outcomes in mass culture, as did his contemporaries in the thirties, Walter Benjamin and Bertolt Brecht. The mass media, Stam points out, do offer ersatz, "weak or truncated forms of carnival" that trivialize its "utopian promise," such as patriotic celebrations, icon-worshiping rock shows, and "festive soft-drink commercials."[44] But that is hardly the whole story, and it takes a willfully ignorant postmodern theorist to insist that only a negative outcome is possible. Umberto Eco, for example, echoes Derrida, Foucault, Lyotard, et al., in declaring that "the law" is always "overwhelmingly present at the moment of its violation" in carnival.[45] Carnivalesque attacks on authority, through mass-culture forms such as rock music, presumably only serve to drain away rebellious energies. This postmodern view, as always, is nothing more than the hoary elitism of Nietzsche, belittling the disenchanted for not immediately having a revolution but instead settling for being angry (the syndrome known as *ressentiment*). Bakhtin's theory of carnival, though, actually owes a good deal to Nietzsche's description of Dionysian festivity in *The Birth of Tragedy*. As Stam points out, both contrast "a stifling official culture with a vital unofficial one" based in collective folk rites of physical exuberance. The crucial difference is that Bakhtin is a populist, preferring the masses to the "finer sensibilities" of the "higher souls" that Nietzsche opposes to the "herd."[46]

Bakhtin proposes this populism to the avant-garde or other movements trying to integrate art and everyday life: carnival is defined as "the borderline between art and life" or as "life itself, but shaped according to a certain pattern of play," namely, that found in the best of mass culture and its popular audience.[47] Bakhtin opposes the "aesthetics of the beautiful" (10) of romanticism and modernism (again much like Benjamin) for leading to "a private 'chamber' character" (37), or veneration of the isolated artist in the garret. Romanticism "cut down" grotesque realism and its parody of official culture to "cold irony" (38)—and here we find the roots of postmodernism (as Franco Moretti has argued). Bakhtin actually draws a contrast between the "Romantic tradition" (46), including modernism, and the "realist grotesque" (46) art of none other than Bertolt Brecht, who was busy at the time incorporating popular music and other "bad" new forms into the theater, an approach Bakhtin commends as reflecting "the direct influence of carnival forms" (27).

The bad new forms of speech that empower "the people" in carnival, Bakhtin specifies, are comic compositions, specifically parodies, combined with "various genres of billingsgate" or "curses, oaths," (5) and other "abusive language" (16) directed at people with power. This is a matter of collective activity, of individuals celebrating unification with a regenerated social identity and purpose. Marketplace speech permits "no distance between those who come in contact with each other," liberating them "from norms of etiquette and decency"(10), a formulation clearly pertinent to women. People are thereby "reborn for new, purely [and truly] human relations" (10), for a new life, even, much as Bikini Kill once wrote in a fanzine that "this world doesn't teach us how to be truly cool to each other, and so we have to teach each other."[48]

The two essential forms of speech in carnival—parody and billingsgate—are, of course, abundantly apparent in Bikini Kill's own "Carnival." The song's parody of conventional representations of women, in particular, is exactly what Stam's contemporary rewriting of Bakhtin advocates: "By appropriating an existing discourse for its own ends, parody . . . assumes the force of the dominant discourse only to deploy that force, through a kind of artistic jujitsu, *against* domination."[49] Complicity, in other words, turns into critique, into the negation of conformist common sense.

Bakhtin's work on parody is most extensive in essays written at the same time as *Rabelais and His World* and collected in *The Dialogic Imagination*. In carnival, the clown and the fool, "struggle against conventions, and against the inadequacy of all available life-slots to fit an authentic human being," against the cardboard cutouts of static identity attacked by Kathleen Hanna. When an artist like Hanna dons the "mask" of the clown—and she's certainly clownish in "Carnival" in tempting us to think that she exults in abuse and vulgarity—she acquires the ability "to rip off [other] masks . . . to rage at others," and "to betray to the public a personal life." Bakhtin, in other words, contains very nearly the whole riot grrrl catalog: the exposé (or *parody*) of the whole process of feminine representation, the cultivation of the energy of anger (or *billingsgate*), and the revelation of personal experience according to the feminist commonplace that the personal is the political.[50]

In ensuring that "no language could claim to be an authentic, incontestable face," the clown's parody is "aimed sharply and polemically against the official languages of its given time" (273). This antiauthoritarian emphasis in parody, in *Rabelais and His World*, leads directly on to the outright terms of billingsgate, or curses and oaths against authority. The combination of comic parody and angry billingsgate, moreover, is explicitly linked to negation. In a description of carnival laughter, stressing that billingsgate speech must have the clown's sense of humor about itself, we find a fundamental anarchism, which I want to take up in part because literary scholars argue endlessly and unhelpfully about whether Bakhtin's a Marxist, a good Orthodox Christian, or whatever.

Bakhtin's anarchism is apparent in his description of the "ambivalence" that results from the mixture of billingsgate speech, not in itself obscene, with "profanities and oaths." In the marketplace and its carnival atmosphere, obscenity "acquired the nature of laughter and became ambivalent."[51] What Bakhtin actually means is that it became dialectical, and the dialectic he has in mind is Michael Bakunin's famous line that the destructive passion is the creative passion, which he derived from Hegel's theory of negation and extended to include common sense about feelings as well as ideology. In the combination of anger and laughter, in Bakhtin's further derivation from Bakunin, "the element of negation" (23) has a positive, regenerative outcome; the "degradation" of profane billingsgate, in "contact with earth," simultaneously brings "forth something more and better. . . . It has not only a *destructive negative* aspect, but also a regenerating one" (21; emphasis added). Something better—terms ridiculed by postmodernism, in fact, since at least Donald Barthelme's novel *Snow White* (1967)—appears when "primitive verbal functions" infused by "a general tone of laughter" (also scoffed at by postmodernism, as affect without meaning) become "sparks of the carnival bonfire which renews the world," or the social community (17). The dialectic between anger and laughter, and its positive, regenerative outcome, is precisely what critics infected by cynical postmodernism are unable to comprehend. An article about the "bratty" punk group Green Day, for example, observes that music critics "still puzzle over the band's importance, citing joie de vivre as its only tenuous hold on the popular imagination."[52] Bakhtin's account of carnival laughter ought to make us skeptical of a perspective that appends the reductive terms "only" and "tenuous" to joie de vivre.

"Modern indecent abuse and cursing," unfortunately—and this remains true—"have retained dead and purely negative remnants of the grotesque concept of the body," Bakhtin notes.[53] What we lack in particular is an "important trait of the people's festive laughter: that it is also directed at those who laugh." Bakhtin's description of the "satirist whose laughter is [only] negative, plac[ing] himself above the object of his mockery" seems to anticipate Rush Limbaugh, whose humor consists entirely of ridiculing people he believes inferior to himself and enlisting only white males in his mean-spirited divisiveness. A properly "ambivalent" or dialectical laughter, aimed at those with power and trying to heal divisions between those without it, "expresses the point of view of the whole world," offering a source of social renewal and counteracting "cosmic fear" (like that many consider characteristic of postmodernism) (12).

As a renewal simply of belief, carnival, finally, is "not actually directed against institutions," Renate Lachemann points out, "but rather against the loss of utopian potential brought about by dogma and authority." The dogma, the counseling of resignation by authority, is assailed and "dispersed through ridicule and laughter," the dialectic of negation and regeneration. The postmodern accusation that carnival is only authorized transgression, in other words, is moot; the point isn't to escape from or overthrow the organization of power immediately. Even the best of contemporary carnival "ultimately leaves everything as it was before" as far as social institutions go. The music of Green Day and others such as the riot grrrls may indeed have only a tenuous (or transient) impact, but that expression of carnival energy nonetheless "offers a permanent alternative to official culture," a lasting, "irrepressible, unsilenceable" example of the possibility of refusing to express oneself in permitted ways.[54]

This is negation in the tradition of the best of anarchism and the avant-garde, a quest simply to hold open the possibility of refusing to go along with the status quo. Just as Bakhtin describes it, negation actually has a positive, regenerating result in creating a sense of solidarity and sustenance for everyone angry at the authoritarian conformity that allows the misery of so many to go unchallenged. That anger should include laughter at its own excess not simply because it's the authoritarian who takes himself entirely seriously but also because the prospect of changing the world, however dim it may be, ought to promise pleasure. As Lachemann emphasizes, though, a revolution doesn't have to occur for carnival to be successful. People just have to come together—including at a distance that may even be mass-mediated—and rediscover the possibility of refusal, precisely the effect of movements related to popular music like the riot grrrls. Much of the angry music at present belongs to the anarchist avant-garde tradition, but the angry girl bands are the most exciting because women have hardly even begun to expand that tradition.

Taken as a metaphor—in terms of the energy of its performance as much as the title's connotations—Bikini Kill's "Carnival" celebrates that beginning. As Kurt Cobain once said, the future of rock belongs to women. And with "women entering as a steady and unstoppable force" into popular music, says Andrea Juno, "they can't help but change the [whole] status quo in as yet unknown ways."[55]

NOTES

1. Quoted in Kim France, "Angry Young Women," *Utne Reader*, no. 53 (September/October 1992): 24.
2. Joanne Gottlieb and Gayle Wald, "Smells Like Teen Spirit: Riot Grrrls, Revolution, and Women in Independent Rock," in *Microphone Fiends: Youth Music and Youth Culture*, ed. Andrew Ross and Tricia Rose (New York: Routledge, 1994), pp. 261–62; Joy Press and Simon Reynolds, *The Sex Revolts: Gender, Rebellion, and Rock-'n'Roll* (Cambridge: Harvard University Press, 1996); Donna Gaines, "Suicidal Tendencies: Kurt Did Not Die for You," *Rolling Stone*, 2 June 1994, pp. 60–61.
3. Sadie Plant, *The Most Radical Gesture: The Situationist International in a Postmodern Age* (New York: Routledge, 1992), p. 85.
4. Rita Felski, *Beyond Feminist Aesthetics: Feminist Literature and Social Change* (Cambridge: Harvard University Press, 1989), pp. 174, 181.
5. Fred Pfeil, "Postmodernism as 'Structure of Feeling,' " in *Marxism and the Interpretation of Culture*, ed. Lawrence Grossberg and Cary Nelson (Urbana: University of Illinois Press, 1988), p. 384.
6. Sandy Carter, "Courtney Love and Liz Phair," *Z Magazine* 7 (November 1994): 68; Huggy Bear, quoted in Amy Raphael, *Grrrls: Viva Rock Divas* (New York: St. Martin's, 1995), p. 150.
7. Charles Aaron, "A Riot of the Mind," *Village Voice*, 2 February 1993, 63.
8. Dana Nasrallah, "Teenage Riot," *Spin* 9 (November 1992): 81.
9. Aaron, "A Riot of the Mind," p. 63.
10. June Crawford, Susan Kippax, Jenny Onyx, Una Gault, and Pam Benton, *Emotion and Gender: Constructing Meaning From Memory* (Newbury Park, CA: Sage, 1992), p. 189; Felski, *Beyond Feminist Aesthetics*, p. 168.

11. Kathleen Hanna, quoted in Andrea Juno, *Angry Women in Rock: Volume One* (New York: Juno, 1996), pp. 89, 101; Juno, *Angry Women in Rock*, p. 5; Candice Pedersen, quoted in Juno, *Angry Women in Rock*, p. 177; Gottlieb and Wald, "Smells Like Teen Spirit," p. 253; Ann Powers, quoted in Raphael, *Grrrls*, p. xxxiii.

12. Ann Japenga, "Punk's Girl Groups Are Putting the Self Back in Self-Esteem," *New York Times*, 15 November 1992, sec. H, p. 30.

13. Ellen Willis, in Evelyn McDonnell, "The Feminine Critique: The Secret History of Women and Rock Journalism," *Village Voice Rock & Roll Quarterly*, fall 1992, p. 8.

14. Simon Frith and Angela McRobbie, "Rock and Sexuality," in *On Record: Rock, Pop, and the Written Word*, ed. Simon Frith and Andrew Goodwin (New York: Pantheon, 1990), pp. 377, 384

15. Gottlieb and Wald, "Smells Like Teen Spirit," p. 256, 268.

16. Carola Dibbell, "Better with Age," review of the Raincoats, *Looking in the Shadows*, *Village Voice*, 21 May 1996, 52.

17. Greil Marcus, in Mark Kendall Anderson, "More Than a Trace of Lipstick," *Houston Press*, 19 August 1993, p. 73; Carter, "Courtney Love and Liz Phair," p. 68; Ann Powers, "When Women Venture Forth," *New York Times*, 9 October 1994, sec. H, p. 32; Juno, *Angry Women in Rock*, p. 4; Elizabeth Wurtzel, "Girl Trouble," *New Yorker*, 29 June 1992, p. 70.

18. Sandy Carter, "Women, Guitars, and Rebellion," *Z Magazine*, May 1993, p. 52.

19. Stephanie Engels, quoted in Pfeil, "Postmodernism," p. 396.

20. Bikini Kill, liner notes to *The C.D. Version of the First Two Records* (Kill Rock Stars KRS/204, 1994).

21. Gottlieb and Wald, "Smells Like Teen Spirit," p. 265.

22. Van Cagle, *Reconstructing Pop/Subculture: Art, Rock, and Andy Warhol* (Thousand Oaks, CA: Sage, 1995); Hanna, quoted in Juno, *Angry Women in Rock*, pp. 99–100.

23. Chrissie Hynde, *quoted in Juno, Angry Women in Rock*, p. 199; Courtney Love, quoted in Raphael, *Grrrls*, p. 14; Liz Phair, quoted in ibid., p. 225; bell hooks, *Black Looks: Race and Representation* (Boston: South End, 1992). For an in-depth analysis of the feud between Courtney Love and Madonna—and what that ongoing dispute tells us about the gender politics of contemporary rock—see chapter 3 in this volume.

24. Hanna, quoted in Juno, *Angry Women in Rock*, pp. 86, 99; Valerie Agnew, quoted in ibid., p. 108.

25. Wurtzel, "Girl Trouble," p. 63; Powers, "When Women Venture Forth," sec. H, p. 32.

26. Powers, "When Women Venture Forth," sec. H, p. 39.

27. Courtney Love, quoted in Kim France, "Grrrls at War," *Rolling Stone*, June 8/22, 1993, p. 23–24; Love, quoted in Raphael, *Grrrls*, p. 12; Kathleen Hanna, quoted in Wurtzel, "Girl Trouble," p. 70.

28. Evelyn McDonnell, "Rebel Music," review of *The Sex Revolts: Gender, Rebellion,*

and Rock'n'Roll, by Joy Press and Simon Reynolds, *Village Voice,* 18 July 1995, 68; Felski, *Beyond Feminist Aesthetics;* Gottlieb and Wald, "Smells Like Teen Spirit," pp. 257–58.

29. Aaron, "A Riot of the Mind," p. 66.
30. Marcus, quoted in Anderson, "More Than a Trace of Lipstick," p. 73.
31. Quoted in Juno, *Angry Women in Rock,* pp. 85, 89–90.
32. Kathleen Hanna, "Jigsaw Youth," *Jigsaw* (spring 1991), reprinted in the liner notes to *The C.D. Version of the First Two Records.*
33. Hanna, quoted in Juno, *Angry Women in Rock,* p. 96.
34. Linda Hutcheon, *The Politics of Postmodernism* (New York: Routledge, 1989), p. 94.
35. Juno, *Angry Women in Rock,* p. 200.
36. Gottlieb and Wald, "Smells Like Teen Spirit," p. 266.
37. Hanna, "Jigsaw Youth."
38. Aaron, "A Riot of the Mind," p. 66.
39. Hanna, "Jigsaw Youth." See Douglas Coupland, *Generation X* (New York: St. Martin's, 1991).
40. Mikhail Bakhtin, *Rabelais and His World,* trans. Hélène Iswolsky (Bloomington: Indiana University Press, 1984), p. 19; emphasis added.
41. Robert Stam, *Subversive Pleasures: Bakhtin, Cultural Criticism, and Film* (Baltimore: Johns Hopkins University Press, 1989), pp. 86, 95; Natalie Davis, quoted in Mary Russo, "Female Grotesques," *Feminist Studies/Critical Studies,* ed. Teresa de Lauretis (Bloomington: Indiana University Press, 1986), p. 215.
42. Bakhtin, *Rabelais and His World,* p. 15.
43. Stam, *Subversive Pleasures,* p. 92.
44. Robert Stam, "Mikhail Bakhtin and Left Cultural Critique," in *Postmodernism and Its Discontents,* ed. E. Ann Kaplan (New York: Verso, 1988), p. 137.
45. Umberto Eco, quoted in Stam, *Subversive Pleasures,* p. 91.
46. Stam, *Subversive Pleasures,* pp. 89–90.
47. Bakhtin, *Rabelais and His World,* pp. 5, 10.
48. Bikini Kill, quoted in Japenga, "Punk's Girl Groups," sec. H, p. 30.
49. Stam, "Mikhail Bakhtin and Left Cultural Critique," p. 139.
50. Mikhail Bakhtin, *The Dialogic Imagination: Four Essays,* ed. and trans. Caryl Emerson and Michael Holquist (Austin: University of Texas Press, 1981), p. 163.
51. Bakhtin, *Rabelais and His World,* p. 17.
52. Gina Arnold, "Making Green Day," *Reverb,* 8–14 December 1995), 4.
53. Bakhtin, *Rabelais and His World,* p. 28.
54. Renate Lachemann, "Bakhtin and Carnival: Culture as Counter-Culture," *Cultural Critique* 11 (1988/89): 125, 130.
55. Juno, *Angry Women in Rock,* p. 5.

10

TIME TO HEAL, "DESIRE" TIME

THE CYBERPROPHESY OF U2'S "ZOO WORLD ORDER"

ROBYN BROTHERS

"If a society is identical with its structures—an amusing hypothesis—then yes, desire threatens its very being. It is therefore of vital importance for a society to repress desire, and even to find something more efficient than repression, so that repression, hierarchy, exploitation, and servitude are themselves desired."
—Gilles Deleuze and Félix Guattari

Cyberpunk guru William Gibson interviewed the Irish rock band U2 in 1993 amid all the chaos of their ever-expanding Zoo TV project and labeled their efforts since 1990 a "radically self-conscious evolution-via-deconstruction."[1] Gibson's label describes U2's descent into the vortex of mass-mediated irreality—where image, surface, and simulation reign—that enables them to offer up a snapshot of the "zones of transformation and instability" in which they are quite comfortable.[2] By inhabiting the ironic world of the simulacrum, U2 admits to abusing their position in the rock music world in order to craft a more subtle political agenda in an arena where entertainment and manipulation are played against each other. Insofar as they have explored the negotiation of identity in a mass-mediated world through a high-tech appropriation, repetition, and implosion of images, U2's project could certainly be classified as postmodern. However, the music's lyrics evidence an ethically charged agenda that far exceeds their more overt criticism of technologically induced "image addiction" (to use Bukatman's term).

Those willing to look beyond the glitzy marketing of their mammoth 1992–1993 Zoo TV tour uncover strains of a moral struggle that characterizes a pervasive contemporary anxiety. On the one hand, a fragmented, desiring, dispersive subjectivity—both mesmerized by an all-encompassing tele-vision and actively engaged in the challenging realm of cyberspace—represents a threat to moral accountability. On the other hand, critical and responsible acknowledgment of this process can constitute a revolutionary force. I will argue that in order to understand U2's position on politics, religion, and the new technology, it is necessary to focus on the target of their ironic discourse: the increasingly problematic intersection of the spiritual, the political, and the technological.

Issuing out of Ireland's late-seventies punk movement, with a confus-ing—even contradictory—political message of peace and Christian love com-bined with anger and rebellion, U2's music and performances intrigued some and incited others to criticism. The connection between U2 and Christianity runs deep yet continues to be widely misunderstood and often ignored. The confusion seems to stem from the fact that there is an undercurrent of a dis-tinctly Christian perspective that is radical in that it stems more from the mys-tical tradition and is therefore more in tune with deconstructive and negative theologies than with organized religion.[3] My analysis of U2's spirituality will utilize Gilles Deleuze and Félix Guattari's philosophy of desire—particularly the idea of "becoming-woman" and their discussion of "the plane of faith"—in order to illuminate U2's distinctly Christian conceptualization of desire as the force of the Holy Spirit.[4] There have been numerous speculations about the nature of U2's faith and its relation to the aim and scope of their political message. Indeed, the radical nature of that message merits a close analysis; despite the fact that these ideas are couched in the rock medium, they are quite properly "philosophy at 33 1/3 rpm."[5] The spirit of anarchy and its trans-formative properties form the center of U2's affirmative view of both an essentially deconstructive Christian theology and the new technology, which for them spell out endless possibilities for growth beyond current religious and political strictures. They seem to share the perspective that equates deconstruction with affirmation: through the encounter with alterity, desire—as an always-affirming/never-negating force—is released.

In three of U2's recent albums (*Achtung Baby* [Island 314-510 347-2, 1991]; *Zooropa* [Island 314-518 047-2, 1993]; and their Passengers release *Original Soundtracks I* [Island 314-524 166-2, 1995]), this spiritual view of desire informs their vision of cyberplay, which, like the theories of Mark C. Taylor and Esa Saarinen, Donna Haraway, and Scott Bukatman, features the dissolution of modern identity into an infinite matrix woven by the new technology.[6] Particularly applicable to this alliance of spirituality, politics, and technology in U2's perspective is Taylor and Saarinen's philosophy of media, or "imagology," which arrived on the heels of deconstruction, celebrating uncertainty through the playful manipulation of images. Imagology bypasses artificial distinctions between institutionalized, analytical philosophical abstraction and low or popular culture, descending into the "dirt and confusion of non-verbal praxes" and invading the "realm of images, simulacra, gestures and art forms."[7] Operating as amateur imagologists, U2 is attempting to inhabit strategically and thereby subvert what could otherwise be systems of oppression, namely, the overdetermined structures of religion, nationalism, and mass media. U2's music and performances not only address the metaphysics of a new virtual reality but also offer a certain strategy for navigating one's way through this ontologically different terrain.[8]

For U2, the absolute ridiculousness of rock 'n' roll—the excessive, cartoonish, raw street-level roar that is possible through this medium—allows for an embrace of the exaggerated extremes of late-twentieth-century life. The band's lyricist, lead vocalist and primary spokesperson Bono, has always felt most comfortable communicating through rock 'n' roll, for it "has its feet down in the mud and its head up in the clouds."[9] When speaking of why he became enthralled with the explosion in telecommunications technology, Bono explains, "Wherever it makes connections, then I'm interested. I feel that music is of the spirit, and the *only* thing that interests me is where it connects with human relationships, because if technology doesn't serve that, it serves nothing."[10] By walking both the high and low roads of culture, certain discourses belonging to the worlds of rock and cyberpunk can facilitate a new breed of political resistance where manipulation is subversion. U2's brand of rock 'n' roll joins cyberpunk theory's search for an imaginative and regenerative relation to forces over which humanity seems to be losing control. For example, the band's use of U.S. artist and AIDS activist David Wojnarowicz's imagery of hunted buffalo hurling themselves off a cliff—driven by forces outside their perception—addresses both the loss of control endemic in today's times as well as the herd instinct that threatens the most potent ethical weapon: empathy through imagination.

A place where images are inhabited and exploited, U2's world is a farcical, hyperbolic, technocratic staging of the tensions inherent in postmodern society. The politically and spiritually supercharged microcosm of a four-member rock 'n' roll band has evolved into the macrocosm of what *Rolling Stone* magazine has humorously proclaimed the "Zoo World Order."[11] Reveling in the slipstream of neotechnology and the wake of the image, U2 continues their attempt to implode staid, static behemoths such as morality, faith, love, and community in a unique approximation (condemnation/revelation) of rock music and culture.

"EVOLUTION IS OVER": THE TRANSPARENCY OF ROCK

In *We Gotta Get Out of This Place: Popular Conservatism and Postmodern Culture*, Lawrence Grossberg highlights the irony that today the marriage of rock music and political activism fails to have any real impact on the most ardent followers. He writes: "The popularity of such politically motivated groups as U2, REM or Midnight Oil often depends upon a radical dissociation of the music's political content and the band's political position from their emotionally and affectively powerful appeals."[12] Going on to analyze the inextricable link and interdependence between a certain segment of society's identification with youth culture and the development of rock music, Grossberg reveals how rock culture is predicated on the interstitial space between childhood and adulthood, belonging and alienation, boredom and fun, rules and rebellion, identity and difference. The conditions of postmodernity seem to embody this precarious positioning; these are the times when "terror (the uncontrollability of affect) has become boring while boredom (the absence of affect) has become terrifying" and faith in anything seems no longer feasible (210). If "ironic nihilism" responds to the stranger-than-fiction reality we now face, if "ironic inauthenticity" is the hip reaction to a meaningless world, if we have been anesthetized by the barrage of images from the media, then U2 is still challenging the assumption that hope, solidarity, and morality have been rendered obsolete. Paul Ricoeur points to the inherent goal of utopian discourse: to undermine institutional power and authority. He asks: "Is not [the] eccentricity of the utopian imagination at the same time the cure of the pathology of ideological thinking, which has its blindness and narrowness precisely in its inability to conceive of a nowhere?"[13] It is precisely the imaginative function of utopian thinking that provides alternate ways of confronting those forces that threaten our humanity.

Grossberg calls for a new politics "articulated by and for people who are inevitably implicated in the contemporary crisis of authority and whose lives have been shaped by it."[14] Any challenge to this gradual shifting toward a "new conservatism" born of apathy and inauthenticity might—despite what he views as a widening gap between rock 'n' roll's affective power and its ideology of authenticity—draw on the inherent dynamism of rock culture even as it fights that culture's complacency. If rock culture is plagued by lack of commitment, fragmentation, and cynicism, it must be reinvigorated by its potential to "deterritorialize"[15] and produce desire from within the space of affect and to reconfigure those affects into a map charting political agency.

Drawing on contemporary phenomena characterizing day-to-day life, the title of U2's enormous project, "Zoo TV," was derived from U.S. radio station's morning zoo shows featuring talk, jokes, and music as well as from the ubiquity of MTV. Operating from within the corporate world of rock music, the band has appropriated the "MTV imaginary" that, according to Ann Kaplan, offers a schizophrenic scrambling of social codes that enables the viewer to resist the discourses of domination even as it "flattens" the potentially subversive element of any counterculture message.[16] The converging worlds of rock music, computer culture, and science fiction further yield a curious site onto which may be projected various configurations of humanity's response to the "technocapitalist" world we currently inhabit.[17] Just under the surface of the work of William Gibson—in *Neuromancer*, for example—are moral ruminations concerning the effect of cyberculture on subjective agency that echo those buried a bit deeper in the music of U2.

From 1980 to 1989 U2 delivered straightforward spiritual and political messages in a decade of excess and materialism, but since 1991 they have moved toward an ironic embrace of a high-tech, postindustrial wasteland in which the subject, the artist, and even rock 'n' roll itself are being reconfigured. Grossberg's criticism of the band's agenda no longer rings true: "U2's authenticity is an obviously staged appeal to the nostalgic possibilities of the ideology of authenticity, as they construct a community that no longer exists (and in fact never did)."[18] U2's Zoo TV project is not simply an abrupt switch from a naive ideology of authenticity to a more cynical ironic inauthenticity; rather, it is a strategic use of irony. If "the domain of political struggle is now the imaginary,"[19] then it would seem that the use of irony's slippery, equivocal voice is especially well suited to a domain in which nothing is fixed. Labeled the "Band of the Eighties" by *Time* and *Rolling Stone* magazines, U2 has dared to reinvent itself, ushering in not only the nineties but also a complex offering of soaring hope and damning critique of our mass-mediated world.

"CONTRADICTION IS BALANCE": IRONY'S UNSTABLE COMMUNITY[20]

Released in 1991, *Achtung Baby* was described by U2 as the sound of a group fighting for its artistic survival.[21] In 1989 U2's much-criticized jaunt through U.S. rock history left the band with *Rattle and Hum*, an album of pure appropriation of classic rock inspiration such as Bob Dylan, Jimi Hendrix, and B. B. King. Their future as a group was also nearly crippled by the attack of the media on their supposed attempt to boost their image through this deliberate usurpation of music legends. The sudden ascent into the fame and excesses of rock stardom gave rise to a caricatured image in the public eye and deep confusion about their role as so-called serious artists. Viewed as the pop cultural icons of political awareness and affected seriousness, the band could no longer continue the trajectory that had catapulted it into the insanity of rock 'n' roll fame. Could it be that, as the eighties drew to a close, U2 sensed that explicit political and spiritual references in their music not only, as Grossberg noted, failed to engage their primary audience (those still in their teens and twenties) but in fact alienated those who did understand the band's agenda? What began as a crisis in their musical career ended in a sophisticated reevaluation of both their position as rock stars and the commensurability of their message with postmodern society.

Linda Hutcheon, in her study of the affective and political dynamism operating on the scene of irony, locates its power in the interstices between what is and is not communicated. She states that "the 'ironic' meaning is not, then, simply the unsaid meaning, and the unsaid is not always a simple inversion or opposite of the said . . . it is always different—*other than* and more than the said."[22] Both as a reaction to their bombastic image in the media and as a way to problematize and therefore enrich their original message of hope in the face of nihilism, U2 needed the distance that exists between the ironist and his target. By embracing uncertainty, conflict, and artificiality, they have uncovered a creative resource that has enriched and empowered their critique of the interdependent realms of the political and the spiritual. Bono explains: "What's happened to us is, rather than trying to resolve contradictions, we started mining them. We're getting more from having one hand on the positive terminal and one hand on the minus and just letting the energy run through us."[23]

Returning to Hutcheon's analysis of irony's cutting "edge," the ironist may choose to speak from a position exterior to the system he or she is targeting. However, and she notes that this is the "more constructive or 'appropriative' " approach, the ironist might speak alternatively from within the system.[24] And yet by operating as a player who invokes humor while upsetting the internal workings of a system, the ironist risks the label of hypocrite if the intended audience fails to receive properly the critical message (16). Such is the case of those fans who believe that the old U2—Christian, politically engaged, authentic—has sold out, exchanging their idealism for cynicism, their anti-ego stance for the excesses of megalomania. In 1989, playing the final show of their Joshua Tree tour in their hometown of Dublin, Bono closed by saying: "This is the end of something for U2. It's just that we need to go away for awhile, and dream it all up again."[25]

The band emerged two years later with the distorted roar of *Achtung Baby*. The monochromatic clothing and dangling crosses were replaced with the shiny black leather and wraparound shades of "The Fly," the silver suit and cowboy hat of "Mirrorball Man," and the gold lamé, glitter platform boots and horns of "MacPhisto." The Fly, explains Bono, personifies megalomania: "That's what it's designed for. It's a language of scale, of surface—the Fly needs to feel mega to feel normal."[26] Combining the greed and insanity of the TV evangelist, the flash of Gary Glitter, and the equivocal earnestness of the country singer or politician, the Mirrorball Man was the spokesperson during the U.S. leg of the tour: "I'm really enjoying his glass cathedral. He's into money and he's selling a religion where you can believe in anything really. It's kinda like the 90's, y' know. It's a religion without God, it's a religion where everybody can have what they want."[27]

Mr. MacPhisto replaced the Mirrorball Man for the European tour in an attempt by Bono to clarify this persona's role as the Daddy of evil, as Goethe's Mephistopheles meets Elvis, or as "the devil as the last rock star."[28] Instead of attempting to impose order and certainty—the world of black and white—U2 has inhabited the negative image of that world, where black is white and white is black. Their Zoo TV project is a creative enactment of the exhaustion of meaning and the fatal boredom conveyed in the book of Ecclesiastes, delivered in the various diabolical voices of the Fly, the Mirrorball Man, and Mr. MacPhisto. Not surprisingly, a scene in the recent *Batman Forever* video depicts a cartoon version of Bono engrossed in C. S. Lewis's *Screwtape Letters*. Since the release of *Achtung Baby*, Bono's three alter egos confused many of the fans expecting the earnest passion of their favorite militant pacifist.

Initially it seems that the message of the actual lyrics was lost; somewhere between the ironic stance of this new character and the expectations of the receiving audience, the darkness just beneath the surface was hidden by the shine of the glitz. The Zoo TV stage boasts larger-than-life video screens that dwarf the once larger-than-life rock band, emitting second-long clips of images that at first seem quite random. This visual accompaniment to the music, once unraveled, points to the seriousness behind the flash and bravado of the band's new image. During "The Fly," for instance, computer-generated, random-sequence images are rapidly fired from the screens. "Everything you know is wrong," "You are not immune," "Reject your weakness," "Guilt is not of God," "Evolution is over," "Silence = Death," "Rock 'n' roll is entertainment," "Future is fantasy," "What a marvelous human being you turned out to be." The sequence ends with "It's your world you can change it" alternating with "It's your world you can charge it" and "Watch more TV."

When asked in 1992 if U2 had given up the idea of giving any real meaning to their music, Bono responded that from now on it would be necessary to look for that meaning under a layer of trash. "It's the diamond buried in the trashcan and no longer displayed in a case."[29] And there is indeed a certain trashiness, a dark and bitter sexuality, in the music of Achtung Baby. Pointing out that most music today tends to be unidimensional, Bono asserts that U2 is trying to bring together ecstasy, drama, and irony, a combination that might finally articulate certain inescapable contradictions. Although he once firmly believed that irony was the enemy of spirituality, the lyricist now feels that it has the capacity to heighten the spiritual tenor of the band's music (61). Elsewhere he describes their approach as a way to seek out the sacred in the sensual: "We deliberately kept the record for the most erotic form of love so as to almost exhaust it as a possibility, and I think that makes it a kind of prayer, in a strange sort of way."[30]

Many fans and critics saw merely a new attempt by the band at light-heartedness: a commercialized, commodified, neon version of the former champions of peace. Bono describes the album as a "con," noting that the flippant title Achtung Baby together with the flashy surface of the videos masks the fact that the record is "a heavy mother . . . our most serious album."[31] Having always tried to reconcile spiritual and political concerns with the ever-increasing power of rock, mass media, and the image of the megalomaniacal rock ego, it is not surprising that the social, political, affective, and ethical implications of the use of irony might appeal to U2. If they are reaching beyond Grossberg's "ironic inauthenticity" to a nonproselytizing form of spiritual politics, how is that message conveyed and received? Would this brand of politics "locate people in an affective structure of hope" and respond to Grossberg's call for a politics "rooted in the organization of distance and densities through which all of us move together and apart"?[32]

For U2, the political, the spiritual, and the sexual are inextricably bound together; trying to separate them diffuses their potency and their potential for effecting social change. And to utilize the rock medium is to reach the furthest into the dense fabric of society. Bono explains it this way:

> People might think that where U2 is right now is much more throwaway, but I think the stuff we're throwing away is maybe much more interesting than what you'd at first suspect. I've never been as turned on about rock & roll as I am now because there seem to be so many possibilities. Sex and music are still for me places where you glimpse God. Sex and *art*, I suppose, but unless you're going to get slain in the spirit by a Warhol or Rothko, I think for most of us art *is* music. We're looking for diamonds in the dirt, and the music is more in the mud now.[33]

Oscar Wilde's view on the critical distance between person and persona has greatly influenced the way in which U2 has decided to manipulate their packaging of and the media's reception of their image. Bono is fond of expressing in various ways Wilde's message that "man is least himself when he talks in his own person; give him a mask and he will tell you the truth."[34] With the advent of MTV in the eighties, image became everything; in the world of the simulacrum, image is both everything and nothing at all.

In an interview about U2's attempt to demythologize their status as rock stars, Bono admits that it is impossible to escape the omnipotent effect of image: "In fact, if it is, let's play with it, and let's distort it and manipulate it and lose ourselves in the process of it. But let's write about losing ourselves in the process of it, 'cause that's what's happening to everybody else on a smaller scale anyway."[35] It is this loss—and both the positive and negative implications of that loss—that U2's two recent albums *Achtung Baby* and *Zooropa* and the ensuing Zoo TV tour address. *Zooropa* (1993), quickly recorded during their break from the Zoo TV tour, was described by *Rolling Stone* as "the sound of verities shattering, of things falling apart, that moment when exhilaration and fear are indistinguishable as the slide into the abyss begins."[36] The complex relationship between a narcissistic circularity of self and the endless circularity of the simulacra discussed by Jean Baudrillard is one whose depths U2 continues to sound.

"I FEEL NUMB / TOO MUCH IS NOT ENOUGH":
SUBJUGATED DESIRE AND VOYEURISM[37]

The effect of televisual images, virtual reality, and online global communication is as exhilarating as it is dangerous. As Michael Heim points out, the suspension of physical being—of corporeal identity—can enhance communication, liberating it from the biases of race, class, and gender. The flip side is quite ominous, however: "The spirit migrates from the body to a world of total representation. Information and images float . . . without grounding in bodily experience. You can lose your humanity at the throw of the dice."[38] The twentieth century began with a descent into the human unconscious and closes with a freefall into the "technological unconscious."[39] Bono, discussing the merits of the band's enormous investment in a high-tech concert performance, makes the following proposition: "Ask yourself, what would Dalí or Picasso have done if they had video at their disposal. If they had samplers or sequencers or drum machines or electric guitars, photography, cinematography!"[40] Salvador Dalí painted what he described as a photographic image of the human unconscious, and although neither U2 nor any cyperpunk author or theorist has yet articulated the technological unconscious, they are again pointing to a promised land: a technological utopia that can only be reached by way of the desert or, rather, Baudrillard's "desert of the real itself."

In the Gibson interview, Bono asks: "Why are we as a society so preoccupied with irrelevancies and missing the fundamentals?"[41] Still asking the same question, U2 is now radically altering their approach by substituting irony for soul as evidenced in the song "Even Better than the Real Thing" (*Achtung Baby*).: "Well my heart is where it's always been / My head is somewhere in between. . . . We'll slide down the surface of things." Taylor and Saarinen's imagology celebrates the dissolution of solid ground, of depth, and of certainty as a path leading to cultural enrichment. Operating as imagologists in that they are now asking questions instead of providing answers and proscriptions, disfiguring and imploding words, and playing on insecurities rather than certainties, U2 has relinquished any claims to authenticity.[42] The initial reaction to their Zoo TV tour has been to gather their efforts under the rubric of postmodern rock. But the lead guitarist, Dave Evans, known as "The Edge," resists this label as much as postmodernism itself defies definition: "We are certainly not attempting to put forward a particular ideology or set of ethics or artistic concepts which you could describe as postmodern."[43] He goes on, however, to state that they are addressing the "void" in which we find ourselves, a time of endings and extreme uncertainty: what we face is not nearly as important as how we face it. The daily barrage of images by the media places us in a precarious position. The inability to distinguish between the real thing and its image—even better than the real thing—is symptomatic of Baudrillard's virus of the image, which Scott Bukatman addresses in his book *Terminal Identity*. In his analysis of the cyberpunk genre, Bukatman explores the imaginative intersection between humanity and technology, dissecting the phenomenon of image addiction.

In the song "Numb" (*Zooropa*), which could serve as an anthem for technology's encroachment on humanity, a robotic, monotone voice chants survival hints for these times. Meanwhile the backing vocal, Bono's "fat lady / gospel" voice, sings: "I feel numb / Too much is not enough." Baudrillard asserts that the effect of the media upon the individual is one of "massive *devolution*, of a massive delegation of the power of desire, of choice, of responsibility."[44] He goes on to point out that it is indeed a tiresome proposition for the masses to decide what it is that they desire. This reversal of will results from a passive belief in the artificial authority of the media, through which reality is screened. Accordingly, Bono as the "Mirrorball Man" screams to his audience: "I believe in you! *I believe for you!* I HAVE A VISION! TELEVISION!"[45]

The album *Zooropa* begins with indecipherable TV or radio voices repeating endlessly over and over. As the piano leads in, the volume of senseless voices increases until it finally gives way to the guitar and drums. A voice then asks twice: "What do you want?" a question that addresses the problem of devolution. In the concert performance, this question is flashed in different languages on huge video screens and is interspersed with "It's very simple." Confusion of the medium and the message, of the active and passive, of the subject and object leads to an implosion of meaning. The overload of information, instead of enhancing communication, destroys the possibility of it. All that is presented is what the masses desire; thus when the masses watch and absorb what is presented to them, they see only a reflected image, an image of never-ending circularity that is not the distortion of reality but its own hyperreality. Thus what is even better than the real thing is no longer itself real. "Belief, faith in information attach themselves to this tautological proof that the system gives of itself by doubling the signs of an unlocatable reality."[46] During the performance of the song "Even Better than the Real Thing," the word BELIEVE is faded out to reveal the word LIE within.[47] By confusing hyperreality with reality, the image addict becomes subjugated to the power of this circular mass-mediated view of things, whose message is broadcast from nowhere. The song "Zooropa" (*Zooropa*) conveys this sense of confusion in the wake of a technology speeding ahead beyond our control: "I hear voices, ridiculous voices, I'm in the slipstream."

In his book *Media, Culture, and Morality*, Keith Tester recalls Michael Ignatieff's essay "Is Nothing Sacred? The Ethics of Television," which posits two possible reactions to this media blitz: "promiscuous voyeurism" or the "internationalization of conscience."[48] Tester draws on Ignatieff's example of the famine in Ethiopia to clarify what is at issue: the dissection, abstraction, and consequent anesthetization of images that, left outside the media's gaze, might otherwise inspire moral responsibility and action. If television has the potential to promote solidarity by communicating moral value yet in fact thwarts its possibility, it is a medium that could be as insidiously destructive as it is entertaining.

During the European leg of the Zoo TV tour, the band managed several live satellite linkups between their concerts and Sarajevo, again eliciting a torrent of controversy and stinging criticism. The British press condemned the band for their inappropriate insertion of the horrors of the war in Bosnia into the unlikely setting of a rock 'n' roll concert. The effect on the audience and the members of the band was such that the continuation of the show seemed pointless. The Edge explained: "Continuing the show was much more the point than 'here's our Sarajevo link and now we're going to slink off stage because we're so offended by reality.' The real point is why aren't we that offended by the nightly news because it's much more graphic, much more shocking than what we've portrayed but it's been editorialized into a non-offensive, non-challenging form that people can swallow and not choke on."[49]

Communication as well as the ability to digest historical events properly, whether injustices or triumphs, has been rendered impossible. War, once bloody and horrifying in the human imagination, is now neatly packaged by the media into quick, easily absorbed bytes/bites that are fed to the masses. Baudrillard warns of a social directive opposite to that of a panic reaction in which the social dissolves into a frenzied herd. The inverse is "a chain reaction of *inertia*, each microuniverse saturated, autoregulated, computerized, isolated in automatic pilot. Advertising is the prefiguration of this: the first manifestation of an uninterrupted thread of signs, like ticker tape—each isolated in its inertia. Disaffected, but saturated. Desensitized, but ready to crack."[50] Elsewhere, in *The Illusion of the End*, Baudrillard talks about the slowing of history caused by the "deceleration, indifference, and stupefaction" of those who have become numb, half-asleep in their slavery to the screen. In turn, they themselves become a type of screen, an *"écran d'absorp-tion."*[51] Medium has overtaken meaning. Image has superseded imagination. Numbness has replaced desire.

U2's use of technology in the various "Numb" videos—using the video byte against itself through a hyperbolic, rapid-fire assault of repetitive images—draws visual and aural parallels between the blind, sleeping, numb herd instinct and extreme, dehumanized violence. The Edge wrote "Numb" and sings the lead vocal for it. In one version of the video, he is so mesmerized by the flickering images from an unseen screen that he is impervious to radical attempts to distract him. Another version (the one used in concert) features alternating, repetitive video bytes that depict heavy machinery repeating the same task over and over, marching bands, a military officer's barking command, a tribesman's call, a soldier killing, and millisecond shots from various cable channels. A barely decipherable image of a corpse's face appears midway through the video.

For U2, the incessant juxtaposition of the indecipherable satellite television images with the all-too-clear images of violence and conformity conveys the threat of mass conformity and of an all-American brand of numbness. Succumbing to a passive and voyeuristic state of apathy destroys the possibility of a globalization of conscience: numbness creates the breeding ground of fascism in its many forms. It is as though U2 is blasting this powerful and insidious dynamic through larger-than-life screens in an attempt to roll back history at the close of this century. As Baudrillard puts it: "One might suppose that the acceleration of modernity, of technology, events and media, of all exchanges—economic, political and sexual—has propelled us to 'escape velocity,' with the result that we have flown free of the referential sphere of the real and of history" (1). There is no more real communication, hence the loud signal indicating that we have been disconnected at end of the *Zooropa* album. U2 echoes Baudrillard's concern that the mass media has woven an extremely tight web: the (ir)reality that is presented via seemingly endless channels and at all hours of the day and night has ensnared the viewer, who has succumbed to an easy numbness.

"THERE'S NO SLEEPING THERE": IMAGINATION AND EMPATHY[52]

German filmmaker Wim Wenders and U2 share an interest in the interplay between erotic and spiritual desire and the empathetic role of the human imagination. Their video for the AIDS benefit album *Red Hot and Blue* was filmed by Wenders, and the band has contributed songs to two of Wenders's films, *Until the End of the World* and *Faraway, So Close!* which, together with *Wings of Desire*, comprise a trilogy. Having referred elsewhere to their tour as "an image bonfire," Bono told Wenders in an interview: "We've spent a crazy time dissecting TV and adverts to make a parody of the chaos they cause. We've done a very critical satire of them in Zoo TV."[53] Referring to Richard Kearney's book *The Wake of Imagination*, Bono goes on in the interview to point out that the Zoo TV tour was built around the idea that the overmanipulation of images ultimately results in the distortion of perception.[54]

Kearney clarifies the role of the artist in a postmodern culture by showing how the artistic experience is now a wandering "about in a labyrinth of commodified light and noise, endeavoring to piece together bits of dispersed narrative." This creative bricolage seems to be the only viable way to bridge the gap between human imagination and mass-mediated irreality.[55] Kearney points to the paradox that at a time when the image dominates our reality, saturating our existence to the point where our daily lives seem at best a representation of media-induced reality, the human imagination is at its most feeble, its most vulnerable. The song "Lemon" speaks of this powerful need to project ourselves into a visual medium: "Through light projected / He can see himself up close." But when the saturation of image paradoxically results in the death of imagination, the death of empathy—ethics' most powerful weapon against prejudice—follows close behind. Bono states that this "glimpse [of] another way of being" cannot be underestimated in its potential for cultural understanding: "The inability to put ourselves in another's shoes is the core of intolerance. . . . If we want to challenge hatred, emphatic [*sic*] imagination is central."[56] In the song "Your Blue Room" (*Original Soundtracks I*), however, from the collaborative album they recently released under the name Passengers, U2 continues to express the need for a visual medium that might reintroduce the conceptual distance without which the imagination is inept: "A lens to see the world up close / Magnify what heaven knows."

Kearney joins Paul Ricoeur and Emmanuel Levinas in an effort to reinvent the human imagination in response to the ethical challenge of the other. Kearney cites Levinas's passage from *De Dieu qui vient à l'idée* regarding technology's role in image addiction and moral anesthetization, "not because everything is permitted, and by means of technology, possible, but because everything has become indifferent. . . . There is nothing new under the sun. The crisis spoken of in Ecclesiastes is not due to sin but to *ennui*. Everything becomes absorbed, engulfed and immured in the Same. . . . Vanity of vanities: the echo of our own voices . . . everywhere fallen back onto our own feet, as after the ecstasies of a drug. Except the other who, in all this *ennui*, one cannot abandon."[57] U2 conveys this same sense of exhaustion in the song "Acrobat" (*Achtung Baby*): "What are we going to do now it's all been said? / No new ideas in the house, and every book has been read." The lyrics of "Lemon" echo the same sentiment: "And these are the days when our work has come asunder / And these are the days when we look for something other." The message of the Zoo TV tour, which Bono discloses is in part that of the book of Ecclesiastes, is to inhabit and thereby control the seductive force of this endless play of signification.[58]

It seems contradictory to let go in order better to manage something, and yet this describes the challenge to reimagine both self and other: the call to embrace multiplicity without precluding moral accountability. As Jim Collins describes it: "The shift in the metaphors from overload, bombardment, glut, to highway, dance, and surfing suggests a profound reconceptualization of both 'all that information' and how individuals manipulate it."[59] Similarly, it is when we move beyond static voyeurism into dynamic dialogue with the Other that the dream of a technological utopia might give way to real change. The song "Acrobat" (*Achtung Baby*) articulates this challenge of constructive reconfiguring: "So dream out loud / And you can find your own way out." "Zooropa" continues this preoccupation with an affirmative response to uncertainty, beginning with the slogan "Vorsprung durch Technik" (a leading edge through technology) and ending with: "Uncertainty . . . can be a guiding light. . . . / Take your head out of the mud, baby. . . ." Instead of "planting flowers in the mud" by moving rhizomatically through the underground, for U2 an analogous movement through the "overground" means a revolution of a different kind.[60]

ACHTUNG, BABY! REPRESSING DESIRE, DESIRING REPRESSION, AND THE EROTICS OF FASCISM

The European leg of Zoo TV opened with brief shots from Leni Riefenstahl's Nazi propaganda films *Triumph of the Will* and *Olympia*. The audience is bombarded with a numbing barrage of second-long images, including a Hitler Youth fervently beating his drum, Joseph Stalin, Margaret Thatcher, the shroud of Turin, the hammer and sickle, and the cartoon face from *Zooropa*'s cover, which represents the Soviet astronaut stuck in orbit during the disintegration of the USSR. In the midst of all of this, the question "What do you want" is flashed in various languages, together with "It's very simple." The musical accompaniment of Beethoven's "Ode to Joy" grows louder, gradually drowning out the noise of the video clips and finally giving way to the industrial sound of the song "Zoo Station."

The implication of the video barrage in the European tour is that the same erotic dynamic at work during Hitler's reign has the potential to reappear in the age of neotechnology. During both the video and the concert performances of the dark song "The Fly," which includes the apocalyptic imagery ever-present in U2's lyrics, Bono either whispers or screams "Achtung, baby" or "Achtung, y'all." The title of U2's 1991 album *Achtung Baby* derives from a Mel Brooks movie, *The Producers*, about a tacky musical, "Springtime for Hitler," in which an S.S. officer responds to "Danke schön, baby" with "Ze führer would never say *baby*!"[61] Thus the expression "Achtung Baby!" is meant in the most trivial of ways as well as the most serious, echoing Bono's eerie approximation of the Islamic call to prayer that opened the Zoo TV concerts: "I could've lost you. I could've let you go, slippin' through the cracks, slippin' through the cracks." Baudrillard's "devolution," or the individual's voluntary relinquishing of the will to desire and to choose, recalls Wilhelm Reich's question: What makes the masses desire their own repression? Deleuze and Guattari, taking up this question in their two-volume work *Capitalism and Schizophrenia*, attempt to analyze—in a humorous style that belies their deadly serious focus—the inner mechanisms that lead one to desire that which is inherently self-destructive.

Similarly, Bono often aligns U2's work with the attempt by the adherents of surrealism and dada to "unzip the fly of Nazism."[62] At the close of this century, there still exists the need to dismantle the sex appeal of fascism, "not only historical fascism . . . but also the fascism in us all, in our heads and in our everyday behavior."[63] In light of the resurgence of fascism in Europe today, whether manifested in the war in Bosnia or the rise of neo-Nazism, the psychological dynamic behind the seductive force of power must be analyzed and rechanneled. Deleuze and Guattari attribute fascism's appeal to the subversion or, more aptly, perversion of a desire that can never be denied. Drawing on Nietzsche's "will-to-power," they present the force of desire as always present and always productive. It is in response to difference, multiplicity, and alterity that desire constitutes a revolutionary and divine energy that always exceeds, always subverts, and always affirms. Desire is necessarily a libidinal force that, once oedipalized, loses its explosive potential. Deleuze and Guattari state that the earth may develop into a "place of healing" but that this alternative earth "is not to be found in the neurotic or perverse reterritorializations that arrest the process [of desiring production] or assign it goals."[64]

In the song "Trying to Throw Your Arms Around the World" (*Achtung Baby*), Bono sings of Salvador Dalí: "He took an open-top beetle / Through the eye of a needle." Deleuze and Guattari cite Salvador Dalí as an artist who, by purposefully cultivating a critical paranoia in his perception of reality, introduced "an element of dysfunction" within the structure of society (33). Dalí, in his attempt to induce a schizophrenic interpretation of the world, had the goal of doubling images to reveal the irrational element within the rational. Not wanting to clean up the bizarre irreality of the dream landscape, Dalí preferred instead to offer a photographic image of what might never be seen. The totally unrepressed subconscious, the mingling of the sacred and the profane—even the divine and the mystical juxtaposing the scatological and the sexual—finds its way onto Dalí's canvases. The latter stage of his career revealed a preoccupation with the "eternal feminine" (adding to his obsessive admiration of his lover, Gala Eluard) and the Christian mysticism of the medieval mystic St. John of the Cross. U2 has always been intrigued by the movements of surrealism and dada as invocations of humor and irrationality in the face of the monstrosities of war. The images taken from "Tryin' to Throw Your Arms Around the World" reveal a bird's-eye view of what fuels the energy behind U2: the surreal landscape of the dream world, Dalí with the symbol par excellence of the mundane (a supermarket cart), the eternal feminine (tryin' to throw his arms around a girl), the sexual revolution and political action (the open-top beetle symbolizing the sixties), and the reconciliation of this world with the kingdom of Heaven (through the eye of a needle).

There is an inherent eroticism in these two moments in the twentieth century (World War II and the 1960s), especially in the tension between surrealism and Nazism. Deleuze and Guattari state that "Hitler got the fascists sexually aroused. Flags, nations, armies, banks get a lot of people aroused. A revolutionary machine is nothing if it does not acquire at least as much force as these coercive machines have for producing breaks and mobilizing flows" (293). Reiterating this same dynamic at work, Bono stated the following in a speech at an antifascist evening at the Thalia Theatre in Hamburg, Germany:

The machismo—and it is machismo—of the New Right has much to do with the impotence of an electorate who feel they have only one real choice anyway. It has much to do with a consumer society that equates manhood with spending power. *Maleness* is an elusive notion, distorted but made accessible and concrete by the Nazis. We shouldn't underestimate this. The fascists feed off youth culture and if we are to overcome them we must understand their sex appeal. And what is our appeal? The neo-Nazis have a perverted idealism, but do we have any idealism left?[65]

"HERE SHE COMES": THE MYSTERIOUS WAYS OF A WANDERING SPIRIT[66]

It is interesting to note that, for U2 as for Deleuze and Guattari, woman—in that the relation of woman to man remains one of subjugated to subjugator—represents a force of becoming. They do not advocate a binarism of male versus female but rather assert that the feminine represents "the key to all other becomings." "Becoming-woman" as a concept, or rather a conceptual tool as Deleuze and Guattari would have it, is best described as "atoms of womanhood capable of crossing and impregnating an entire social field, and of contaminating men, of sweeping them up in that becoming. Very soft particles—but also very hard and obstinate, irreducible, indomitable." They suggest that "becoming-woman" is only a path to "becoming-imperceptible" or the annihilation of the ego: "To reach, not the point where one no longer says I, but the point where it is no longer of any importance whether one says I."[67]

Where U2 departs from Deleuze and Guattari's concept of desire and ego loss is in the Christian mystical conceptualization of desire as the anarchical pneuma, or wind/spirit, which is the gift of the Holy Spirit. Deleuze and Guattari do in fact state that the energy sweeping through the desiring production of a degree-zero subjectivity is divine; God would constitute its "a priori principle . . . the *Omnitudo realitatis*, from which all secondary realities are derived" (13). Thus the "disjunctive syllogism" operative in desire is what is divine. U2, however, in both interviews and the lyrics and performances of *Achtung Baby* and *Zooropa*, reveal an implicit emphasis on themes that follow closely the trajectory of much postmodern and deconstructive theological discourse: the asymmetrical nature of an ethical relation with alterity, the Holy Spirit as a distinctly feminine force, and a God that exceeds the category of Being.

U2 is informed by the tradition of Christian mysticism, and whether or not they are still deeply influenced by it, their lyrics are replete with images associated with the tradition, especially that of the medieval mystics.[68] *Achtung Baby* reflects and creatively expands the following motifs operative in the band's prior works: the relationship of the soul with the Holy Spirit, the burning flame of love, a desire for union with God through humility, and finally the utter mystery of God's revelation, which exceeds the limits of being, language, and knowledge. Although U2's music has always contained a strong spiritual element, the music produced since 1991 gains as much in rich imagery as it loses in explicitness.

The mystical tradition privileges the dynamic force of love and the Holy Spirit above everything. Previous lyrics and performances include references to the flame of love ("Where the Streets Have No Name," *The Joshua Tree*, 1987) and the naked flame ("In God's Country," *The Joshua Tree*). And the title of *The Unforgettable Fire* is as much a reference to this flame of love as it is to the painting by the survivors of the bombing of Hiroshima and Nagasaki. The eroticism of the relationship between the soul and God, that is, between the Bride and Bridegroom—or, as in the case of U2's music, between the desiring soul and the feminine Holy Spirit—pervaded the writings of medieval mystics and some early Christians. U2's lyrics often echo mystical texts that describe the soul's relationship with God in a way similar to the lovers' discourse in the biblical Song of Songs.

In Bono's lyrics, the Holy Spirit surfaces alternately as "She" or "Spirit" and most often as "Love."[69] Personified by a belly dancer in the Zoo TV concert performances, Bono woos the Holy Spirit like a lover throughout the song "Mysterious Ways." She, as in many of U2's songs and especially on the *Achtung Baby* album, is invoked either as a guide or lover who "is slippy," "turns the tide," "sees the man inside the child," and is "the real thing."[70] During the performance of "Mysterious Ways," Bono is dwarfed by a huge screen showing either the belly dancer or an oscillating disc depicting a woman's face with a bar over her eyes, nose, and mouth. He beseeches her to instruct him in the ways of love: "Move my spirit teach me / To move with it." Asking love to "lift up [his] days, light up [his] nights," he hesitatingly draws nearer to the gyrating, veiled dancer and then backs away from her as she advances. At the end, all he is left with is a fragment of her veil as she spins out of sight. She is "your sister the moon" and "your sister in the rain" who "talks about the things you can't explain." Her "mysterious ways" are not to be questioned but indicate a movement of the soul toward love as an act of transformation. In the video for "Mysterious Ways," filmed in Morocco, scenes of the labyrinthine Casbah of Fez and veiled women end with increasingly distorted shots of Bono ecstatically singing about the movement of the spirit, his body visually dissolving into pure fluid, vibrating movement. Instinct over intellect, faith over reason, desire over stasis is how, according to U2, "to ride on the waves that [Love] brings," "slide down the surface of things," and "let go of the steering wheel."[71]

"ON YOUR KNEES BOY!" U2'S POLITICS OF FAITH

Perhaps unwittingly placing themselves within the debate between traditional and deconstructive Christian theologies—with the latter continuing mysticism's concern with apophatic discourse—U2's musical message continues to provoke controversy. Although they have repeatedly brushed aside attempts to pin them down with regard to their spiritual orientation, they have made it clear that spiritual issues are becoming increasingly urgent "after a century of being told by the intelligentsia that we're two-dimensional creatures, that if something can't be proven, it can't exist."[72] But the band has resisted the eighties' caricature of U2 as the warriors of radical Christianity in an age of meaninglessness and excess. Bono admits that the controversy over the "new U2" of the nineties has been liberating: "It's a nicely freeing position to be in to have nobody expecting it from us. We've found different ways of expressing it, and recognized the power of the media to manipulate such signs. Maybe we just have to sort of draw our fish in the sand. It's there for people who are interested. It shouldn't be there for people who aren't."[73]

Nevertheless, the apparent uncertainty of the band's spiritual message has confused many longtime fans who are indeed "interested" and prompted others to denounce them as having sold out to the excesses of the rock world.

Bono's satanic persona MacPhisto—like C. S. Lewis's devil, Screwtape, in his letters to his nephew, Wormwood—depicts reality in its negative form, where black and white are reversed. He gleefully says onstage: "I have a great interest in religion. Some of my best friends are religious leaders. The ayatollah, the pope, even the archbishop of Canterbury. . . . They're doing my work for me. . . . Nobody's going to church anymore."[74] The ironical stance elicited a scathing review of the album *Zooropa* in *Melody Maker* magazine, which included the following remarks about Bono: "The erstwhile Dublin urchin that stared God in the face and bawled, 'If you walk away / I will follow' is found muttering 'I have no compass / And I have no map . . . And I have no religion,' rendered virtually inaudible by Brian Eno's desolate, inhumane keyboards. The man that once had so many answers now sounds simply confused."[75] Indeed, U2 and particularly Bono have been sharply reproached for the development of what some seem to think is their own brand of Christian theology.

U2 was no doubt initially drawn to the unifying force of mysticism as an intense spirituality with no divisive, dogmatic moral agenda. The members of U2 have never identified with any particular sect of the church, favoring rather an intensely personal approach to Christianity. Thus the lyrics in "Acrobat" echo those of "Zooropa," revealing an unavoidable feeling of alienation: "Yeah I'd break bread and wine / If there was a church I could receive in." These words might surprise and confuse some who have forced U2 into a preconceived category. Looking back at some of their earlier lyrics, the presentation of their faith has certainly evolved from "Gloria," to acknowledgment and uncertainty in "I Still Haven't Found What I'm Looking For," to what Bono states is an ambiguous refusal of the keys to the heavenly kingdom in "The First Time" (*Zooropa*): "But I left by the back door / And I threw away the key." But if, as Bono sings in "Even Better than the Real Thing," "Well my heart is where it's always been / My head is somewhere in between" is true, then the message is being delivered in a much more subtle way.

Bono refers to John 3:8 in describing his own faith like the wind: "I believe that religion is the enemy of God, because it denies the spontaneity and the almost anarchistic nature of the Spirit."[76] Like the medieval mystic St. John of the Cross, U2 seems to be pointing out that those who obstruct the free-flowing force of the Holy Spirit because of human justifications based on fear or self-interest are to be avoided at all costs. Accordingly, Bono's various personae—Mirrorball Man, The Fly and MacPhisto—are all self-serving, manipulative personalities that appeal to the individual whose heart is "empty as a vacant lot / for any spirit to haunt" ("Who's Gonna Ride Your Wild Horses," *Achtung Baby*).

The sublimation of transcendence is the theme that the band's lyricist repeatedly admits interests him the most. Appalled by the dogmatism and rigidity of organized religion in the United States and particularly by the insane posturings of American TV evangelists, U2 denounces any form of proselytizing where guilt, judgment, and exclusion are all part of the bargain. Their lyrics refer to divine love as slippy and transparent. In "Zooropa" Bono

sings: "And I don't know the limit / The limit of what we got." The implication that we cannot ascribe limits, language, or presence to God surfaces
again in the song "Ultraviolet (Light My Way)" (*Achtung Baby*): "But your love
is like a secret / That's been passed around." U2 has consistently stressed the
importance of being wide awake both spiritually and politically; sleeping and
numbness can only lead to a dangerous state of passivism. By contrasting the
recorded version of the lyrics with a live variation—"Your love is like a light
bulb / It just goes over my head"—the invisibility and power of ultraviolet
light is revealed as a metaphor for a divine force both unseen to the naked eye
and ultimately unknowable to the human intellect.

The image of the fly as insignificant, attracted to filth, and bug-eyed—
crawling on the transparent and impenetrable face of love—continues the
idea of the futility of human action without guidance. It is interesting to note
that a b-side recording of "The Fly" alters the lyrics slightly to: "But it's never
to late / To take His call." In "Even Better than the Real Thing," the allusion
to the myth of Icarus expresses the desire for transcendence and union with
the divine sun: "We're free to fly the crimson sky / The sun won't melt our
wings tonight." These lyrics again point to union with God through Love or
Spirit, recalling the medieval mystic's desire to come face to face with the
divine by way of utter humility.

"DANGER THE DRUG THAT TAKES YOU HIGHER": RESIGNATION, MOVEMENT, AND THE LIMITS OF PERCEPTION

U2's lyrics consistently speak of the
need for the loss of self: blindness resulting from looking only at oneself ("I
Will Follow" [*Boy*, Island 422-842 296-2, 1980]), a landslide in the ego ("A Day
Without Me" [*Boy*]), a lack of direction when seeing only one's reflection ("I
Threw a Brick Through a Window" [*October*, Island 422-842 297-2, 1981]),
dying to oneself in order to live ("Surrender" [*War*, Island 422-811 148-2,
1983]), and the disposability of ego expressed in the lines "I can lose myself /
You I can't live without" ("Red Hill Mining Town," *The Joshua Tree* [Island
422-842 298-2, 1987]). Similarly, Deleuze and Guattari recall Kierkegaard's
"knight of faith" and equate him with their own "man of becoming," who
represents the proper avenue toward ego loss, or "becoming-imperceptible."[77] During the performance of "One" a few lyrics are added: "Hear me
knocking, Lord . . . / see me scratching, would you make me crawl?"

(*Achtung Baby*; reissue [as a single, entitled *One*], Polygram 866 533, 1992). These lyrics intensify the images of humility and resignation in the album version of "One": "Love the higher law . . . You ask me to enter / But then you make me crawl." Other lyrics suggest a heightened awareness attained only through the act of stooping: "If you want to kiss the sky / Better learn how to kneel . . . (on your knees boy!)" ("Mysterious Ways," *Achtung Baby*). Bono notes that the eye of the needle was actually a gate in Jerusalem that was so tight passing through it required stooping.[78] Ironically, a certain freedom of perception derives from a restriction of self. Kierkegaard describes the "movement" of faith as follows: "Precisely because resignation is antecedent, faith is no aesthetic motion but something far higher. . . . So I can perceive that it takes strength and energy and spiritual freedom to make the infinite movements of resignation."[79]

Deleuze and Guattari recall Kierkegaard's "leap of faith," expanding the concept into what they term the "plane of faith." They describe this plane of faith as an infinite movement between subject and object where "perception will confront its own limit." Both a video variation and the concert performance of "One" feature artist David Wojnarowicz's depiction of a herd of buffalo running in slow motion, then locking horns, and ultimately throwing themselves off a cliff. This image articulates the idea that unseen forces drive us that are beyond our comprehension as well as beyond our perception. By illuminating human perception's acknowledgment of its own limits and emphasizing the importance of letting go conceptually, Deleuze and Guattari attempt to clarify that moment when transcendence becomes immanent. The plane of faith then becomes the plane of immanence where "movement" is the "process of absolute deterritorialization." By exceeding the dualism of subject-object or conscious-unconscious, "desire directly invests the field of perception, where the imperceptible appears as the perceived object of desire itself, 'the nonfigurative of desire.' "[80] Bono demonstrates the idea of perception's infinite dance in his performance of "Mysterious Ways" when he beseeches "Love" or the "Spirit" to "teach [him] how to dance" and "teach [him] to move with it," stressing the constant tension and movement between the soul and the Spirit. And it is not surprising, then, that in "Tryin' to Throw Your Arms Around the World" the unprinted lyrics "You just gotta make your faith see" follow the chorus about Salvador Dalí, whose obsession with surpassing this dualism and with Christian mysticism lasted a lifetime.

Deleuze and Guattari go on to describe how drug users try to reach this

"plane of immanence" and often feel that they do attain this goal. But ultimately they assert that drug users have not chosen the correct vehicle.
Although they discuss drugs as a path to changing the perception in such a
way as to allow the flow of desire, Deleuze and Guattari ultimately denounce
them as a means of reaching this place of "becoming-imperceptible" (286).
They make the claim that faith operates much like a drug in that it has a radically transformative effect on one's perception. They make the distinction,
however, that faith acts as a drug "in a way very different from the sense in
which religion is an opiate" (282). The conceptualization of faith associated
with organized religion has unfortunately for many become reductive, operating as a sedative. Accordingly, at the end of the performance of "Running
to Stand Still," a song about the misplaced desire for transcendence through
the use of heroin, Bono enacts the injection of the drug and proceeds to sing
"Hallelujah" over and over, reaching upward into the stream of light beam-
ing down on him. U2 again falls in line with Deleuze and Guattari's view that
a radical widening—rather than the expected narrowing—of perception ultimately reveals the concept of faith as a desiring, affirming, and "deterritori-
alizing" force.

U2's project is ultimately driven by the idea that faith and faithlessness
form the core of the individual's relationship with the intimate Other (erotic
love), the social Other (the local community), the global Other (the international community), the technological Other (cyberspace), and the spiritual
Other (God). Faith is predicated on a willingness to let go, and this "spirit of
abandonment"[81] is essential in each of these encounters between the self and
the Other. What is important to consider here is how this reconceptualization of faith operative in the philosophy of Deleuze and Guattari and in the
music of U2 might afford a new perspective on the point where these various
relations intersect. If it is true that the new technology is effecting a revolution of sorts whereby any previously conceived ontological foundation is disintegrating, then a radical change in perception is necessary. Entering "the
kingdom of the simulacrum" requires a certain leap of faith or, rather, an
attempt to operate on the plane of faith (4). The "danger [of] the drug that
takes you higher" ("So Cruel," Achtung Baby) has yet to fully realized, and the
adrenaline from the danger has yet to be potentiated: "The transition from
the religious, to the chemical, to the electronic fix extends the process of sublimation in which matter becomes increasingly rarefied or idealized and thus
appears lighter until it is nothing other than light itself. To get high on light,
you don't need to inhale" (9).

"VORSPRUNG DURCH TECHNIK": PLASTICITY OF SELF AND TECHNOLOGY'S MATRIX

Where a radical yet centuries-old view of Christian spirituality intersects a radical yet futuristic view of a neotechnological landscape is the element of U2's "Zoo World Order" that is the least understood and the most stimulating. William Gibson, in *Mona Lisa Overdrive*, highlights the need to consider the spiritual ramifications of cyberspace as the infinite structure of this technological matrix recalls the problem of the infinite.[82] Lichtenberg-Ettinger joins Levinas in defining as feminine a future where the static ego gives way to a constant becoming that is always already invested in an infinite "matrixial alliance" with the Other. Correlating the infinite movement inherent in God's naming of Himself to Moses and Deleuze and Guattari's concept of becoming, Lichtenberg-Ettinger notes that the original Hebrew term EHIE means "I will become" and thus reflects absence over presence, becoming over being, wandering over stasis, a "movement of desire" in which "borderlines become thresholds for a nomadic 'becoming' identity that assembles together different *I-non-I* aspects."[83]

The current moment of humanity in the grip of increasingly advanced forms of technology points to an interesting irony: as individualism reaches a deafening crescendo, technology is allowing mass-mediated irreality to be superseded while simultaneously yielding a matrix in which the subject is "mediatized" and identity gives way to a never-ending web of relations. Taylor and Saarinen stress that the electronic realm of telecommunications technology reintroduces the problem of the subject: "Identity becomes infinitely plastic in a play of images that knows no end. Consistency is no longer a virtue but becomes a vice; integration is limitation. With everything always shifting, everyone is no one."[84]

The new technology represents this infinite matrix that challenges any static conceptions of identity, and yet at the same time it also constitutes a double-edged sword that must be examined for both its inherent danger and potential. U2's Zoo TV tour directly addresses these concerns, integrating *Achtung Baby*'s dark, ironic broodings on erotic love, morality, and faith with *Zooropa*'s smooth litany of the cynical voices of a postmodern wasteland. More recently, on their Passengers album, the spoken lyrics "never in company, never alone" express the concern of loss of emotion and intimacy as the soul dissolves into the "schizoid compromise" of mind and machine.[85] On the other hand, the crisis of "terminal identity" brought on by the intersection of humanity and technology has broken new ground in the struggle against totalizing discourses that presume the possibility of and look forward to an ultimate reconciliation of differences within any given social subset. By theorizing the world of science fiction and cyberpunk—where fiction and reality are often indistinguishable—Donna Haraway, Jean Baudrillard, and Scott Bukatman reveal that the interdependence of man and machine blurs ontologies and challenges epistemologies founded on disintegrating into obsolete essences of class, race, and gender. Haraway calls for a shift of focus onto the "social relations of science and technology" in order that a regenerative—indeed, manipulative—approach to the ambivalence of a high-tech culture might ultimately provide for an unceasing permeation of boundaries.[86]

Manipulation may now be thought to exist in the form of the playful wielding of the tools that once crafted the scaffolds of oppression and domination. In this celebration of crumbling dichotomies, ironic playfulness masks the serious work of destabilization. As Haraway remarks: "We are living through a movement from an organic, industrial society to a polymorphous, information system—from all work to all play, a deadly game . . . from the comfortable old hierarchical dominations to the scary new networks I have called the informatics of domination" (80). In the face of this incommensurability between technological advances and human desire for limits, U2's music admonishes even as it parallels these assertions that we must all learn to be players in this infinite game of cyberplay where "transcendence . . . is also always a surrender."[87] Thus Kierkegaard's "leap of faith" melts into Deleuze and Guattari's "plane of faith" as we begin the process of navigating our way through the ontologically different realm of neotechnology where what is at issue in this great balancing act is our susceptibility. At a time when the necessity of resistance to slicker forms of oppression is at its greatest, Haraway advocates a "cyborg politics" that both embraces and takes responsibility for the ensuing confusion. Perhaps we need a cyborg ethics as well. Cyberpunk author William Gibson and U2 share the task of calling attention to the urgency of this critical moment.

Mark Seem, in his introduction to *Anti-Oedipus*, states that Deleuze and Guattari arrive at the following conclusion: "There can be no revolutionary actions . . . where the relations between people and groups are relations of exclusion and segregation" (xxii). In this respect, it is not surprising that forms of communication such as satellite television, interactive video, and the Internet are all of great interest to U2. For an artistic group that has, for the past fifteen years, aimed at dissolving such divisive borders as religion and nationality, technology that permits the dissolution of borders is obviously to be exploited as an instrument of social change. Thus it seems that the band's trademark white flag of surrender, a peaceful challenge to the garish colors of nationalism, lives on in the motto "Uncertainty can be a guiding light" ("Zooropa"). There is an enormous amount of untapped potential in the political and economic uses of the Internet, for example, that might pave the way toward peace in areas overrun by war, terrorism, or famine. U2's music reminds us that there exists as well the need to explore the spiritual ramifications of the new technology's impact on the realm of metaphysics.

Perhaps this is yet another utopian fantasy, but when the intersection of technology and humanity takes on an altogether new form from the male-fantasy variety of science fiction where humans overtake technology and defeat it—rather than letting go and strategically riding it as Haraway advocates—one has to wonder. The idea of letting go of identity as we know it is, for U2, essential to any nonproselytizing form of morality or ethics and to any real social change. As this century draws to a close and as various discourses about endings multiply, the threat of numbness wrought by the proliferation of mediated images must be acknowledged. Creative interaction with the new technology offers the dream of eliminating borders and bringing the realm of the global into the realm of the personal, and yet we bear an enormous responsibility even as we let go and enter the slipstream.

NOTES

1. U2, "Turning Money Into Light," interview by William Gibson, *Details*, February 1994, p. 64.

2. Scott Bukatman, *Terminal Identity: The Virtual Subject in Postmodern Science Fiction* (Durham, NC: Duke University Press, 1993), p. 18.

3. These traditions address primarily the dissolution of identity, both of self and of God, in order to liberate—by way of negation—a revelation of the Divine. Negative theology privileges the process of apophasis, or an infinite series of negations that might approach an unnameable God, thereby respecting the inadequacy of language to a God beyond essence. Originating in the medieval theology of Dionysus the Areopagite, negative theological thinking stressed the absolute transcendence of God, yet the continuation of this tradition in postmodern and deconstructive theologies yields an emphasis on an immanent transcendence.

4. Deleuze and Guattari posit desire as a dynamic, fluid, and ultimately divine force

that, in and through its disjunctive operations, scrambles the restrictive social codes that prevent the healing transformation of *homo historica* into *homo natura*. The decentered subject, or "body without organs," becomes a "recording surface" for the sweeping energy of desire—or is "miraculated" by this energy— "and God, who designates none other than the energy of recording, can be . . . the greatest friend in the miraculating inscription" (Gilles Deleuze and Félix Guattari, *Anti-Oedipus: Capitalism and Schizophrenia*, trans. Robert Hurley, Mark Seem, and Helen R. Lane [Minneapolis: University of Minnesota Press, 1983], p. 78). Also see Edith Wyschogrod's discussion of desire as *agape*, "a wellspring of transfigurative power that breaks down egoistic boundaries. The energy coursing through the body without organs suggests a functional homology with the divine as a source of transforming love" (*Saints and Postmodernism* [Chicago: University of Chicago Press, 1990], p. 197).

5. See James Harris, *Philosophy at 33 1/3 RPM* (Chicago: Open Court, 1993).

6. See Mark C. Taylor and Esa Saarinen, *Imagologies: Media Philosophy* (New York: Routledge, 1994); Donna Haraway, "A Manifesto for Cyborgs: Science, Technology, and Socialist Feminism in the 1980s," *Socialist Review* 80:65–107; and Bukatman, *Terminal Identity*.

7. Taylor and Saarinen, *Imagologies*, p. 20.

8. See Michael Heim, *The Metaphysics of Virtual Reality* (New York: Oxford University Press, 1993).

9. Quoted in Steve Turner, *Hungry for Heaven: Rock 'n' Roll and the Search for Redemption* (London: Hodder and Stoughton, 1995), p. 11.

10. U2, "Turning Money Into Light," p. 67.

11. See Anthony DeCurtis, "Zoo World Order," *Rolling Stone*, 14 October 1993, pp. 48–54.

12. Lawrence Grossberg, *We Gotta Get Out of This Place: Popular Conservatism and Postmodern Culture* (New York: Routledge, 1992), p. 168.

13. Paul Ricoeur, *Lectures on Ideology and Utopia*, ed. George H. Taylor (New York: Columbia University Press, 1986), p. 17.

14. Grossberg, *We Gotta Get Out of This Place*, p. 396.

15. Deleuze and Guattari use the term "deterritorialization" to indicate the process of unscrambling social codes, a process in which there is a radical uprooting and liberation of a "desiring-production," resulting in "an intensive utilization [of language, music, writing, philosophy, etc.] that . . . take[s] flight along creative lines of escape" (Deleuze and Guattari, *Anti-Oedipus*, p. 26). Thus this free flow of "desiring-production" constitutes a revolutionary dynamic capable of imploding segregative structures.

16. Ann Kaplan, *Rocking Around the Clock: Music Television, Postmodernism, and Consumer Culture* (New York: Methuen, 1987).

17. See Douglas Kellner, *Media Culture: Cultural Studies, Identity, and Politics Between the Modern and the Postmodern* (New York: Routledge, 1995).

18. Grossberg, *We Gotta Get Out of This Place*, p. 235.

19. Taylor and Saarinen, *Imagologies*, p. 3.

20. This was one of the slogans flashed on the giant onstage screen during the Zoo TV tour (1993–94).

21. U2, "Le Guide du Zoo," *Best* (June 1992): 59.

22. Linda Hutcheon, *Irony's Edge: The Theory and Politics of Irony* (New York: Routledge, 1994), p. 13.

23. U2, "Turning Money Into Light," p. 133.

24. Hutcheon, *Irony's Edge*, p. 17.

25. U2, *Achtung Baby: The Videos, the Cameos, and a Whole Lot of Interference from Zoo TV*, prod. Neal O'Hanlon and Rocky Oldham, dir. David Mallet, 118 min., Island Visual Arts/Polygram Video, 1991, videocassette.

26. U2, "The Fly," interview with Alan Light, *Rolling Stone*, 4 March 1993, p. 45.

27. Quoted in B. P. Fallon, *U2: Faraway, So Close* (New York: Little, Brown, 1994), n.p.

28. Bill Flanagan, *U2 at the End of the World* (New York: Delacorte, 1995), p. 228.

29. U2, "Le Guide," p. 59.

30. U2, "Interview," newsgroup alt.music.u2 (August 1993).

31. U2, *Achtung Baby: The Videos*.

32. Grossberg, *We Gotta Get Out of This Place*, p. 396.

33. Quoted in Flanagan, *U2 at the End of the World*, p. 81.

34. Quoted in Flanagan, *U2 at the End of the World*, p. 6. See U2, "The Fly," p. 77.

35. Quoted in Flanagan, *U2 at the End of the World*, p. 45.

36. Quoted in Cole Moreton, "Introducing . . . Zoo TV . . . The Head of Taste," *Propaganda* 18 (1993/4): 23.

37. U2, "Lemon," *Zooropa*.

38. Heim, *Metaphysics of Virtual Reality*, p. 101.

39. Bukatman, *Terminal Identity*, p. 15.

40. Quoted in Flanagan, *U2 at the End of the World*, p. 38.

41. U2, "Turning Money Into Light," p. 133.

42. U2, "Lights, Camera, Achtung Baby," interview with Wim Wenders, *Propaganda* 19 (1994): 17.

43. U2, "The Edge of the Zoo," interview, *Propaganda* 18 (1993/4): 9.

44. Jean Baudrillard, "The Masses: The Implosion of the Social in the Media," trans. Marie Maclean, *New Literary History* 16 (1985): 585.

45. Quoted in Fallon, *U2: Faraway, So Close*, n.p.

46. Jean Baudrillard, *Simulacra and Simulation*, trans. Sheila Faria Glaser (Ann Arbor: University of Michigan Press, 1994), p. 81.

47. U2, *Achtung Baby: The Videos*.

48. Keith Tester, *Media, Culture, and Morality* (New York: Routledge, 1994), p. 95.

49. U2, "Edge of the Zoo," p. 9.

50. Baudrillard, *Simulacra and Simulation*, p. 91.

51. Jean Baudrillard, *The Illusion of the End*, trans. Chris Turner (Stanford: Stanford University Press, 1994), pp. 4, 3.

52. U2, "Lemon."

53. U2, "Lights, Camera, Achtung Baby," p. 17. See Flanagan, *U2 at the End of the World*, p. 353.

54. U2, "Lights, Camera, Achtung Baby," p. 15.

55. Richard Kearney, *The Wake of Imagination: Toward a Postmodern Culture* (Minneapolis: University of Minnesota Press, 1988), p. 13.

56. Quoted in Flanagan, *U2 at the End of the World*, p. 171.

57. Quoted in Kearney, *The Wake of Imagination*, p. 365.

58. Flanagan, *U2 at the End of the World*, p. 434.

59. Jim Collins, *Architectures of Excess: Cultural Life in the Information Age* (New York: Routledge, 1995), p. 5.

60. The use of the image of the rhizome by Deleuze and Guattari denotes a burrowing into and strangling of any arborescent system (i.e., Western thought has been dominated by the image of the tree with its branching, hierarchical structure): "There is always an outside where [plants, animals, humans] form a rhizome with something else." Following these lines of flight that trespass, transgress, deterritorialize, and extend "like so many 'transformational multiplicities' " is the way to revolutionize various social, political, and conceptual formations (Gilles Deleuze and Félix Guattari, *A Thousand Plateaus: Capitalism and Schizophrenia*, trans. Brian Massumi [Minneapolis: University of Minnesota Press], p. 11).

61. Cited in Flanagan, *U2 at the End of the World*, p. 171.

62. Moreton, "Introducing . . . Zoo TV," p. 16.

63. Mark Seem, introduction to Deleuze and Guattari, *Anti-Oedipus*, p. xiii.

64. Deleuze and Guattari, *Anti-Oedipus*, p. 382.

65. Quoted in Flanagan, *U2 at the End of the World*, p. 172.

66. U2, "Mysterious Ways," *Achtung Baby*.

67. Deleuze and Guattari, *A Thousand Plateaus*, pp. 277, 276, 279, 3.

68. U2, "Pure Bono," interview, *Mother Jones* 14 (May 1989): 35.

69. Flanagan, *U2 at the End of the World*, p. 379; U2, *In the Name of the Father* (Island 314-518 841-2, 1994).

70. The first three lyrics are quoted from "Mysterious Ways"; the last is from "Even Better than the Real Thing."

71. The first two lyrics are quoted from "Even Better than the Real Thing"; the third is from "Zoo Station" (also on *Achtung Baby*).

72. U2, "Le Guide," p. 59.

73. Quoted in Flanagan, *U2 at the End of the World*, p. 480.

74. Quoted in DeCurtis, "Zoo World Order," p. 52.

75. Cited in Turner, *Hungry for Heaven*, p. 183.

76. U2, "Interview."

77. Deleuze and Guattari, *A Thousand Plateaus*, p. 282.

78. Flanagan, *U2 at the End of the World*, p. 227.

79. Søren Kierkegaard, *Fear and Trembling*, ed. and trans. Howard V. Hong and Edna H. Hong (Princeton: Princeton University Press, 1983), p. 47.

80. Deleuze and Guattari, *A Thousand Plateaus*, pp. 282, 284.

81. Taylor and Saarinen, *Imagologies*, pp. 1, 4.

82. Collins, *Architectures of Excess*, p. 15.

83. Bracha Lichtenberg-Ettinger, "The Becoming Threshold of Matrixial Border-lines," in *Travellers' Tales: Narrative of Home and Displacement*, ed. George Robertson, Melinda Mash, Lisa Tickner, Jon Bird, Barry Curtis, and Tim Putnam (New York: Routledge, 1994), pp. 52, 51.

84. Taylor and Saarinen, *Imagologies*, p. 1.

85. Passengers, "Your Blue Room," *Original Soundtracks I*; Sherry Turkle, *The Second Self: Computers and the Human Spirit* (New York: Simon and Schuster, 1984), p. 307.

86. Haraway, "A Manifesto for Cyborgs," p. 85.

87. Bukatman, *Terminal Identity*, p. 329.

11

"EVEN BETTER THAN THE REAL THING"

U2'S (LOVE) SONGS OF THE SELF

ATARA STEIN

A man calls his lover from a phone booth to confess an infidelity; he sings in a seductive half-whisper, "They say the sun is sometimes eclipsed by a moon / Y'know I don't see you when she walks in the room."[1] He compounds the callousness of this disclosure by remarking, "They say a secret is something you tell one other person / So I'm telling you . . . child." He concludes the conversation because he's "running outa change," admitting his inability to rectify the situation: "There's a lot of things / If I could I'd rearrange." U2's "The Fly," from its 1991 album *Achtung Baby*, is not simply a straightforward tale of infidelity; the song is in some ways a centerpiece of the album, for Bono Hewson, the band's lead singer, self-consciously adopted his public persona at this period from the title of the song. "The Fly" wears black leather and wraparound dark goggles; in a conscious departure from the band's earlier idealistic and socially conscious public image, he cynically flaunts the stance of the ego-driven, self-absorbed, and self-destructive rock superstar or, as Bono himself puts it, "the rock star jerk supremo."[2] And just as the singer confesses his infidelity to his lover, he also makes a confession to the audience: "Every artist is a cannibal, every poet is a thief / All kill their inspiration and sing about the grief." In this essay I wish to explore the significance of that couplet to U2's love songs on their albums, *Achtung Baby* and *Zooropa*, as well as the Zoo TV concert tours. On both albums, the band self-consciously deconstructs the love song, revealing how the speaker's love object ultimately serves as a vehicle for his own self-love and self-aggrandizement, a screen or mirror of his own narcissistic self-projection.[3] She becomes his "inspiration," which he must then figuratively "kill" and cannibalize in order to find himself as an artist or poet. Love songs, then, serve not as a means to engage a romantic relationship or a lament for love lost but rather as a process of self-creation for the speaker; the loved one addressed is merely a disposable means to an end, not the end itself.[4] At the same time U2, in re-creating themselves as they do on these two albums and in their concert tours, undergo a similar process in relation to their audience. The lover's project of self-creation and self-glorification is a metaphor for the band's own self-conscious violation of its fans' expectations as a means to redefine itself.

Achtung Baby is a collection of love songs thematically linked in their exploration of changing attitudes at different stages in a relationship. "Even Better than the Real Thing" provides a good starting point for examining the process of idealization that takes place in many of the songs. The loved one addressed must herself be "even better than the real thing" in order to validate the singer's dilated view of himself. In this song she serves as a vehicle in the singer's search for transcendence, for a higher reality. Consciously defying his own understanding of Icarus's fate and undoubtedly deluding himself as well, he sings, "We're free to fly the crimson sky / The sun won't melt our wings tonight" and repeatedly demands of his lover, "Take me higher." Because something even better than the real thing cannot exist, the singer willfully submits himself to an illusion, thereby setting himself up for the disillusionment such songs as "One," "So Cruel," and "Love Is Blindness" reveal. Similarly in "Mysterious Ways," the singer describes his loved one in religious terms ("She moves in mysterious ways") and requests that she "lift my days . . . light up my nights." He then advises his listener, "If you want to kiss the sky / Better learn how to kneel . . . (on your knees boy!)." Paradoxically, this process of idealization simultaneously elevates the woman as an idol to be worshiped while presenting her as a potentially dangerous force the singer must control. We can see this juxtaposition in the chorus of "Who's Gonna Ride Your Wild Horses," where the singer asks, "Who's gonna fall at the foot of thee?" The explicitly worshipful note of the last line is rhymed with a line proclaiming the singer's willingness to lose himself in his lover: "Who's gonna drown in your blue sea?" At the same time, he negates this potential threat by asserting his ability to tame her at the same time. The song describes her as "dangerous" and as "an accident / Waiting to happen." Both an object of worship and a threat to be controlled, she becomes ultimately a trophy to be captured. The line "The hunter will sin . . . for your ivory skin . . ." anticipates the cannibalization the singer refers to in "The Fly." She must be "killed," tamed, controlled in order to serve the singer's purposes.

Several of the songs suggest that in the initial stages of a relationship, the woman serves the function of redeeming and rescuing her lover from some crisis of identity and loss of self-esteem. It is in exercising this ability to restore him to his sense of himself that she is initially perceived as a beneficent and healing figure, one to be worshiped because of her gift. In "Mysterious Ways," the singer advises the listener to "take a walk / With your sister the moon," because she will redeem him from "living underground." Her "pale light" will "fill up your room" with enlightenment and illumination. The singer assures his listener, "She'll be there / When you hit the ground." Similarly, in "Ultraviolet (Light My Way)," the singer sees his lover's function as being to redeem him from his own despair of himself: "Feel like trash / You make me feel clean." What marked the initial stages of a now-failing relationship in this song was the lover's ability to save him from being "all messed up" and hearing "opera in [his] head." Her love was a "light bulb" that protected him from his own demons. The singer's despair in this song results from the woman's withdrawal from him: "You bury your treasure / Where it can't be found." The song is a plea for her to turn back time and restore the early days of the relationship when the lovers were so involved with each other that they "could sleep on stones." He exhorts her repeatedly, "Baby baby baby light my way," to return to her initial role as his guide and salvation. The album concludes with the dirgelike "Love Is Blindness," which suggests that love can operate only through a willful self-deception, a voluntary surrender to what one knows is an illusion. The singer begs his lover to "wrap the night" around him because, as he proclaims, "I don't want to see." The singer knows that the image he creates of his loved one is false, but it is the only image that can satisfy him. He must perceive his beloved in idealized terms, so she can reflect back to him the image of himself that he desires to see.

While *Achtung Baby* opens with the optimistic "Zoo Station," in which the singer declares his willingness to give up control, "to let go / Of the steering wheel," subsequent songs reveal the danger of blindly submitting to a false image of one's own creation. If the woman, in her lover's eyes, has the ability to redeem him, to restore his self-esteem and provide him with a larger-than-life mirror image, she ultimately has too much power over him, and he can only maintain his self-image by taming or controlling or disposing of her. Several of the songs indicate this fear of giving up control to the woman, to being in her power. In "One," for instance, the singer rebels against the role of worshiper in the "temple" and "higher law" of love. His lover asks him to enter but makes him crawl. Ultimately, he complains that all she has given him is hurt. This song could well portray a latter stage of the relationship celebrated in the previous track, "Even Better than the Real Thing." No longer does the beloved take her lover higher; instead, she makes him grovel. Here he struggles with the paradox of two individuals trying to form a union: "We're one / But we're not the same." In "Who's Gonna Ride Your Wild Horses," the woman exerts her power over her lover by abandoning him ("Well you left my heart / Empty as a vacant lot") and teasing him by leaving him "Just out of reach." Rather than gaining himself in a relationship, he finds he is losing himself instead, as the song "So Cruel," asserts: "I disappeared in you / You disappeared from me." His need for her redemptive ability has become an addiction that she, in the speaker's perception, mercilessly exploits: "And you need her like a drug." He is forced to deceive himself, unwilling to lose a force that can sustain him, even if it is a delusion. Because of the "tender trap" of desperation, he puts his "lips to her lips / To stop the lie" he knows he can't avoid. Unable to maintain the elevated position he hopes for, the lover in "The Fly" is reduced to an ultimately vulnerable position, begging and crawling "On the sheer face of love / Like a fly on a wall." His infidelity, then, is part of a strategy to regain control; unwilling to be squashed like a fly on the wall, he must kill his inspiration instead.

The album's title, *Achtung Baby*, can thus be taken as a warning. The woman who allows herself to be placed on a pedestal, to be worshiped as a means of salvation and redemption, will ultimately have to be erased by her lover, so he can preserve his dilated image of himself. She may initially serve as his inspiration, but he has to "kill" her so as not to lose himself in her. The visual imagery of the videos and the Zoo TV tours repeatedly reinforces the impression that the singer's goal is simply to aggrandize himself, to render himself in larger-than-life terms, using his loved one simply as a medium and disposing of her when she no longer serves her function. Although the original album is, without question, a serious exploration of idealization and disillusionment in love, I believe the ironic stance Bono projects in the videos and on the tour is simply an exaggerated version of the irony hinted at in the title and in the couplet about the artist and the poet. That couplet suggests that Bono fears the whole project of *Achtung Baby* may simply be an exercise in self-indulgence as he deliberately kills his inspiration and self-consciously sings about the grief. He has to maintain an ironic distance, then, to avoid the trap of taking himself too seriously. In concert, during the Zoo TV tour, Bono would hold a video camera up to himself, as his image filled several video screens, later bringing a woman from the audience on stage and handing her the video camera with which to film him. Her role is not to interact with him but simply to provide him with a means of self-projection whereby he appears larger than life. Bono would also mime a sex act with a video camera, pulling it toward himself and pushing it away, filling the video screens with the oversized image of his leather-clad pelvis. In both cases, the cameras serve as a surrogate for the audience; like the woman addressed in the love songs, the audience must serve the project of the singer's own self-definition and self-glorification. In a similar form of visual commentary, during the video of "The Fly," the singer sings to a video monitor showing his own face, as he confesses his infidelity; instead of reflecting the face of the person he is addressing, his sunglasses reflect his own face.[5] The woman is also erased from the video version of "Even Better than the Real Thing," where she never appears. Instead, we see a repeated image of the singer as well as other band members tumbling through space, interspersed with frames of such rock icons as the Beatles, Elvis Presley, and Prince. The singer again projects an image of himself as larger than life, in effect, "even better than the real thing."

Both in concert and in the videos, Bono simultaneously mocks and glorifies the rock-superstar image he projects. He explains, "Playing the characters started as fun. People had read reports of egomania and suddenly they were seeing their worst nightmare on stage and they were agog. You have all these rock stars grabbing their crotch, and here I was screwing the entire audience via the camera."[6] He in effect proclaims his utter autonomy and self-sufficiency by screwing the audience; his stage performance, with numerous video screens continuously projecting his figure, becomes a narcissistic exercise in self-gratification, as he simultaneously taunts the audience to worship him while disdaining their worship. As he explains, "We felt we were being made a cartoon of—the good guys of rock and so forth—so we decided to make some cartoons of our own and send them out as disinformation" (72).

The *Achtung Baby* and Zoo TV tours were essentially the band's attempt to re-create itself, to redefine their relationship with their followers, as the singer strives to do with the love object he addresses. Refusing to live up to the idealized self-image of its earlier albums, U2 here deliberately violated its fans' expectations. As Bono remarks, "There are a million clichés to be exploded and we're having lot of fun exploding them. The whole zoo TV philosophy was about standing the perceived image of U2 on its head 'cos, really, it's all surface. Everything, except the actual music, is pure surface" (71).[7] Of course, that statement itself does not have to be read straight either. Does Bono truly believe that the music can be separated from its performance in videos and onstage or, for that matter, from the record company's desire for profits? While the band ironically increased their popularity and profits, U2's shift in image did in fact leave many fans feeling betrayed. One of my students, for instance, repeatedly derides the band as sellouts for apparently turning away from their earlier idealistic and sincere sound and image. Such fans seem offended that U2 is making money and enjoying their fame while taking on a glitzier, more consciously artificial and ironic stance. As one commentator notes, "They have . . . skirted the globe with a multi-media live show that redefined the term state-of-the-art and offended as many people as it enthralled with its wilfully overloaded mélange of video imagery, subliminal sloganeering, and general techno-artiness" (71).

One could read the plot of the love story in *Achtung Baby* as a metaphor for the band's relationship with its fans. The band, of course, initially needed its fans in order to attain its fame and reputation. Early in their career a band is inspired by its audience's support and fervor, but later it may feel trapped by the audience's desire for them to keep producing the same type of music over and over. Bono remarks, "People come to the shows who have seen U2 before, and you're constantly having to deal with their expectations as opposed to what you're trying to do."[8] At this point, the audience has a good deal of power, for they can withhold their money and their adulation if the band goes in a direction they disapprove. Bono's image of screwing the audience suggests a proclamation of independence from his fans: they can follow him if they wish and if they can adapt to the band's changing image and music, but he will not conform to the image of idealistic singer of rock anthems that they desire. In his interview with the *Los Angeles Times* he declared, "In being these characters, I was kind of saying, 'So what? So even if the rumors about me being out of control are true, what does that mean? Does what you wear or how you act on stage make your music any more or less interesting?' "[9] In a telling quote, which appears in the *Achtung Baby* video and perhaps reflects on the backlash against the *Rattle and Hum* film and album (which were widely perceived as exercises in self-aggrandizement), he tells an interviewer, "You people, you need heroes. The people want, the media want to create heroes. But if I agree to the job you'd kill me. So I'm backing out." Typical of the critical backlash against the band at that period are one reviewer's descriptions of it as "pompous," with a "frightening . . . lack of humor," descriptions that she used to contrast to U2's achievement in

Achtung Baby, which she lavishly praised for its "intelligent approach to love songs" and for its turn from the political to the personal and private.[10] The audience and the media have a real power to cannibalize the singer, to render him into a parody of himself if he does not proclaim his independence from them. Paradoxically, they want a hero, as long as he is a reluctant one; as soon as he agrees to the job, he becomes a sellout. At the same time, however, Bono himself has contributed a good deal to his perception as a hero, "the conscience of rock." His very overt championing of politically correct causes in his lyrics and public pronouncements provoked listeners into viewing him as a role model. In his current incarnation, however, Bono recognizes the utter ludicrousness of being perceived as a hero in the first place, remarking, "Rock and roll is ridiculous. It's funny, I mean, four jerks and a police escort."[11] In evoking images of himself as Elvis Presley, complete with black leather or gold lamé, Bono mocks the audience that originally elevated him, singing "In the garden I was playing the tart / I kissed your lips and broke your heart" before metaphorically screwing them during the instrumental section of "Until the End of the World." Performing the song "One," Bono modifies the lyrics so as to answer the question, "Have you come here to play Jesus?" with "I did."

If his audience desires a hero, he will make himself into a parody of one, ironically maintaining his own integrity through a self-conscious adoption of the rock-superstar role, insisting "I've learned to be insincere. I've learned to lie. I've never felt better."[12] Bono describes the title of the album as a "con," remarking, "It's probably our most serious record, and yet it's our least serious title" (48). Despite the seriousness of much of the album's content, the ironic and playful title is a means of keeping the audience at a distance, throwing them off guard in order to prevent them from exercising the power they wish to exercise over the band: that of forcing them to remain in a sincere and idealistic mode. At the same time, the band's musical shifts in direction also violate expectations, as U2 employs a harder, more electronic sound reminiscent of current dance music. The irony of the title actually underscores the album's serious contribution to the band's project of self-definition. I believe that underlying the self-conscious irony of the *Achtung Baby* video and the Zoo TV tours highlights a similar seriousness of intent and a similar urgency to the band's fear of being engulfed by its fans' expectations. According to Bono, "The reason we tried to kill off the perceived idea of U2 is ultimately to give the music more breathing space, to let it stand on its own without the old baggage," presumably referring to the band's sincere and idealistic image.[13] Again, however, this doesn't seem possible in the context in which rock is produced and performed. It would be more accurate to say that the band is trying to declare its independence by writing music that by its nature calls for new baggage, a set of new personae and technologies for the band to exploit. The title serves, then, as a warning to the audience that the band will define its own direction, even if it means alienating its fans. In the singer's relationship with his lover and in the band's relationship with its fans, both must ultimately cannibalize their inspiration to be true to their images of themselves. Just as the singer must control or discard his lover to maintain his autonomy, the band must violate its fans' expectations to maintain artistic integrity.

The 1993 *Zooropa* album went even further in redefining the band's sound and asserting its independence from the desires of its audience. In the last song on the album, "The Wanderer," Bono does not appear at all, instead turning over the singing role to Johnny Cash, undoubtedly confusing beleaguered fans even more (many of U2's fans must be too young to know who Johnny Cash is). Three of the love songs on the album render many of the concerns of *Achtung Baby* even more explicit. The song "Babyface" partakes of the same alternation of idealization of the loved one and assertion of control that many of the earlier songs did. At first the lover is overwhelmed by his loved one's apparent superiority to him: "How could beauty be so kind / To an ordinary guy?" (*Zooropa* [Island 518 047, 1993]). He asserts control, however, by transforming her into an aesthetic object, capturing her with technology. He comes home to "turn [her] on," noting that he has "slow motion" on his side and has "the sound and colour / Under [his] control." Behind the camera or using a remote control, with "slow motion" on his side, he can capture the precise image of what he wants his loved one to be; she turns "round and around" completely under his control. Similarly, Bono, earlier dependent on his fans' power to make or break his career, later exerts a remarkable charismatic power over his audience. If he points his microphone out toward them, they will instantly obey his gestured command and sing the lyrics they have all memorized. Mesmerized by his presence, they will surrender their individual identities to become part of a single cause, thousands of people united in the desire to please the singer and do what he asks of them. The song "Babyface" also hints that the woman may not exist at all; she may simply be an image on a television screen, as the singer notes, "You're coming to me from outerspace," over a satellite perhaps. Whether a video image he creates or receives, the woman serves as an idealized fantasy of the singer, who controls her using a particularly nineties' phallic substitute, the TV remote.

"Stay (Faraway, So Close!)" gives another twist to the singer's simultaneous idealization of and hostility toward his love object. In this song, the persona is a clerk at a 7–11, worshipfully entranced by one of his customers, a woman who is abused by her mate. He alternates between imagining himself as her protector and resenting her for her indifference to him. The chorus reveals the singer's dream of rescuing and redeeming his beloved: "If I could stay . . . then the night would give you up / Stay, and the day would keep its trust." At the same time, his descriptions of her physical condition are hostile and degrading; he describes her as stumbling "out of a hole in the ground" and as "Dressed up like a car crash." And he takes her explanation of her refusal to leave her abusive mate at face value, essentially accusing her of complicity in her own abuse: "You say when he hits you, you don't mind / Because when he hurts you, you feel alive." For all of U2's social consciousness, the song does nothing to illuminate the issue of spousal abuse. Instead, it is a type of dramatic monologue, revealing the mindset of a particular persona, one who cannot get outside of his own feelings of rejection to empathize with the woman. He cannot decide if she is a "vampire" or a "victim," a femme fatale who is luring him with her own helplessness or someone really deserving of his sympathy. He tries to resolve his dilemma in the final verse by projecting her as an unattainable ideal, able only to be worshiped from afar, an "angel" who "runs to ground." He does not have sufficient understanding of her situation to view her as a human being; the only way he can reconcile the apparent disjunction between vampire and victim is to turn her into an angel. What is particularly curious about this song is the singer's image of paradisal coexistence with his beloved, a shared immersion in the fantasy world of television: "You used to stay in to watch the adverts / You could lip synch to the talk shows." The woman he addresses is, of course, a staple of talk shows: "Women Who Don't Mind Being Abused by Their Mates." Thus the singer's conception of her or even her own self-conception may in themselves be the product of watching those talk shows. The woman's life as a battered spouse is in effect a form of lip synching to the talk shows.

"Babyface" and "Stay" both present a protagonist who seems unable to separate a *mediated* version of reality from the actualities of daily life, and the songs suggest that perhaps it can't be done. The Zoo TV tour similarly plays on the pervasiveness of media. In concert, Bono entertains the audience by operating a bank of gigantic video screens with an oversized remote control. After flipping stations for a while and commenting on the images, he tosses the remote control behind him, yelling "This is a rock and roll show. You didn't come all the way out here to watch TV, now did ya?"[14] But, of course, this is precisely what most of the audience does. In the stadium venues in which U2 performs, the only way the audience can get a real sense of what the performers are doing visually is by focusing more on the TV screens than on the live action onstage. There is a continuous interaction between the live performance and the instantaneous re-creation of it on screen. The audience can (perhaps) see Bono himself mugging for the camera; at the same time, the screens fill with the image of his mouth or crotch or whatever part he is presenting to the electronic eye, his surrogate for the audience. Both "Babyface" and "Stay," like the concert performances, express a genuine concern that the fantasy presented on television may ultimately be more satisfying, more vivid, and more understandable than anything real life has to offer. Not only does Bono interact with the camera, the metaphoric extension of the audience, but he indicates that what the audience interacts with, his image multiplied on the video screens, is but a metaphoric extension of himself. Neither partner in the relationship between singer and fans has any genuine contact with the real thing, only with a *mediated* version that seems somehow better.

It is in the song "Lemon," however, that the singer expresses most explicitly the way his love object serves as inspiration for his art and vehicle for his discovery of self. As in the two songs just discussed, the medium for this process is film or television, making a "moving picture." The song is almost a distillation of the "plot" of *Achtung Baby*. Initially, the singer concedes his lover's power over him: "She's gonna make you cry / She's gonna make you whisper and moan." This power is so overwhelming, that he loses his sense of himself: "I feel like I'm slowly, slowly, slowly slipping under / I feel like I'm holding on to nothing." At the same time she has the ability to redeem him: "But when you're dry / She draws water from a stone." And this power is a direct result of the singer's idealization of his loved one: having made her into a source of light and inspiration, he gives her a hold over him. In an analogous fashion, the singer risks "slipping under" if he succumbs to the tight hold his fans have on him; the self-destructive excesses of so many rock musicians testify to the extent to which they can inadvertently lose themselves in the process of winning their fans' adulation. In "Lemon," art becomes the means of the singer's reassertion of control as he struggles to regain a power he surrendered to the woman in the first place. The song precisely describes the woman's dual function as a source of artistic inspiration and aesthetic object. Thus contained, she is no longer a threat. The singer describes making a "moving picture" with which "He can see himself up close." A second voice evokes the woman as "your destination" and "imagination." She is the singer's "destination" only insofar as she can further his project of self-creation, but the woman is not the ultimate goal of his quest; instead, she is merely a means for self-discovery, a vehicle for the singer's desire to examine and elevate himself. "She's imagination" and thus exists only as a projection of the singer's mind, a projection he creates to give himself the illusion of a source of inspiration outside himself.

The audience serves a similar function for the band, providing them with an opportunity to indulge their desire for narcissistic self-display, a project certainly facilitated by the video technology U2 uses so self-consciously and so adeptly. Again there is an analogy between the lover's position relative to his loved one and the band's position relative to its audience. The artist cannot operate in a vacuum; despite the solipsistic nature of his enterprise, he requires a mirror in which to see himself. Bono, in concert, hands the video camera that he had previously trained on himself to a female member of the audience; playing the dual roles of love object and adoring fan, she represents the inspiration who must be evoked and used only to be discarded. Thus the ideal woman the singer creates who is "even better than the real thing" serves both as muse and as objet d'art. The artist makes a "moving picture" to capture the object of his desire, as in, for instance, the repeated images of belly dancers in the *Achtung Baby* video or the circular, clocklike woman's face that rocks back and forth in several locations on the Zoo TV set. Ultimately, she is erased, however, and the fan who has been singled out is sent back to the anonymity of the audience, both replaced by the larger-than-life video images of the singer, holding a video camera to his pelvis and seeing "himself up close."

The culmination of the Zoo TV tour, which Bono describes as "a three-act show that moved from irony to soul to cabaret,"[15] was captured in a video recording of the final performance in Sydney, Australia, that reveals just how self-consciously and explicitly the band renders this equation of love object and audience.[16] The beginning and final portions of the concert extend and expand on the singer's love affair with the camera that the earlier portions of the tour implied, but in an even more self-conscious and self-mocking way. The concert opens with the song, "Zoo Station": singing the lines, "Standing in the station / With my face pressed up against the glass," Bono leans into the bank of photographers clustered in front of the stage, pressing his own face up to their lenses. The second song, "The Fly," does several things to distance the band from the audience. Performing in wraparound dark sunglasses, Bono struts like a self-absorbed rock star, consciously denying any intimacy afforded by a live performance. One might as well watch him on a video screen. During the song, the video screens flash a series of messages, slogans, and song lyrics at great speed, beginning with the repeated message, "EVERYTHING YOU KNOW IS WRONG." Several of the slogans emphasize the cynical stance of the couplet, "Every artist is a cannibal, every poet is a thief / All kill their inspiration and sing about the grief." These slogans deliberately thwart any desire the audience may have to take the band seriously, to find some sort of transcendent meaning in the songs:

THIS IS NOT A REHEARSAL

ENJOY THE SURFACE

TASTE IS THE ENEMY OF ART

ROCK AND ROLL IS ENTERTAINMENT

SERVICE NOT INCLUDED

BELIEVE EVERYTHING

CELEBRITY IS A JOB

ART IS MANIPULATION

REBELLION IS PACKAGED

CONTRADICTION IS BALANCE

WATCH MORE TV

The word "BELIEVE" is flashed, with the beginning and ending letters dropping off so that what remains is "LIE." Thus "one man's lie" to his lover in the song becomes projected into the band's confession of lying to their believing fans. At this point, the band does not allow the audience any possibility of being uplifted or inspired, as would be the case in pre-Zoo TV performances.

But a large portion of U2's audience does not want to view their music as mere "entertainment" or art as manipulation; listening to U2 earlier in their career, one could convince oneself that one was participating in a larger social consciousness, that the music was important. Bono himself characterized the band's earlier stance as a conviction that their music was "sacred" and "almost holy," asserting "We believed we could make a difference."[17] In the band's most recent incarnation, however, the flashing slogans mock the audience's desire for politically correct messages; "IT'S YOUR WORLD YOU CAN

CHANGE IT," a message one would expect from the old U2, alternates with "IT'S YOUR WORLD YOU CAN CHARGE IT."

In his performance of three songs from *Achtung Baby*, Bono engages in a process of self-glorification alternating with self-deprecation. While filming himself with a video camera during "Even Better than the Real Thing," he brings the camera right up to his mouth, filming down into his own throat. He then begins spinning in circles, singing, holding the video camera to his own face, getting symbolically (and not terribly subtly) hobbled by the extension cord in the process. The narcissism of the rock star is apparently a trap, if an unavoidable one. The song "Mysterious Ways" is performed in such a way as to exaggerate the worshipful stance of the lyrics. During the performance of the song, a belly dancer whirls on one part of the stage, with the singer on another. For most of the song he does not interact with the belly dancer herself but allows himself to be dwarfed by her image on a huge video screen, raising his arms as if in worship. He also addresses a similar form of worship to the large clocklike images of a woman's face that rock back and forth on a raised platform, kneeling before the images as before an altar as he sings the lines "If you wanna kiss the sky / Better learn how to kneel . . . (on your knees boy!)." The belly dancer thus becomes an unattainable ideal, a woman to be worshiped from afar. Toward the end of the song, Bono approaches the actual belly dancer, reaching a finger toward her stomach, as she teases and seduces him into trying to touch her but does not allow him to. Significantly, when she approaches him, he backs off; it is her unattainability that makes her desirable. Performing "Until the End of the World," however, the singer regains control, discarding this love object who threatens his autonomy and directly romancing the camera itself. He approaches the lens, exaggeratedly runs his finger over his own lips, kisses the lens, then proceeds to "screw" the camera. Singing the line "I reached out for the one I tried to destroy," he leans into the reaching arms of the fans at the front of the stage, allowing them to grab him and pull him into the audience. On the one hand, he must "destroy" them to remain true to his own self-conception as an artist; on the other hand, he fears they may destroy him in their Dionysian worship.

The band, though, does not maintain this stance of alienating the audience. The middle section of the concert is much more straightforward, offering the traditional idealistic anthems fans expect from the band, delivered in an intimate and personal style ("Angel of Harlem," "Where the Streets Have No Name"), alternating with harder-edged songs of U2's traditional social consciousness ("Bullet the Blue Sky"). The encore section of the concert takes a marked shift in direction, however. Describing his new persona, "MacPhisto," Bono says, "It's like taking the rock jerk that the Fly is and—if you're going to play him—take him to his logical conclusion, which is when he's fat and playing Las Vegas."[18] Bono is seen to the side of the stage in a red-lined dressing room, wearing a gold lamé suit, red shirt, and red devil's horns, applying makeup before a gold-framed mirror. He begins singing "Daddy's Gonna Pay for Your Crashed Car" (a song that in its cynicism and techno sound is about as far from the traditional U2 one can get) into a microphone in front of the mirror in an affected and campy style, allowing his assistants to help him on with his jacket and then gaudily waving them off with an irritated flick of the wrist. Finishing the song onstage, he then begins a monologue directed at the audience and delivered in a quavering, affected voice: "Look what you've done to me. You've made me very famous, and I thank you. I know you like your pop stars to be exciting, so I bought these" (at this he gestures to his gold platform shoes). The monologue continues with a tone of self-mockery combined with political commentary: "People of the former Soviet Union, I've given you capitalism, so now you can all dream of being as wealthy and glamorous as me. People of Sarajevo, count your blessings. There are those all over the world who have food, heat, and security, but they're not on TV like you are." In this persona, MacPhisto then launches into a four-song set that recapitulates the plot of the love story detailed in the two albums as well as the plot of the singer's relationship with his audience. The set begins with "Lemon." After declaring "Off with the horns, on with the show," the singer approaches the ever-present camera. He preens into it as into a mirror and then swings the camera out so that it focuses on the audience. The camera is, of course, a surrogate for the audience, and both serve as a mirror to fuel the singer's own narcissistic self-absorption. He literally makes "a moving picture." The pop star requires an audience to "see himself up close." He cannot function in a vacuum, so even as he declares his independence from his audience's desires, he concedes his ultimate vulnerability to them. Thus he directs his performance of the next song, "With or Without You," a ballad of romantic confusion and vulnerability, almost entirely at the camera's lens. Singing the chorus, "And you give yourself away," the singer opens his jacket and shirt, exposing his chest to the eye of the camera and then reaches up, gently stroking the barrel. Here he seems to be conceding his audience's power over him; he will ultimately have to give them what they want, give himself away in effect, expose, even prostitute, himself, in order to retain their approval. This song is followed by the despairing and cynical "Love Is Blindness." Here the singer seems to resign himself to accommodating the desires of his audience, willing himself to be deceived that their power over him will not destroy him. Toward the end of the song, he dances with a female fan from the audience, holding her close, embracing her, and then returning her to the audience with a kiss on the cheek. On the one hand, he appears to be reaching out for an intimate communion with the audience, but, on the other hand, he chooses to engage in this dance during the performance of one of the band's most bleak and cynical songs. The final song of the concert, however, makes the reconciliation with the audience complete. Performing a cover of Elvis Presley's "Can't Help Falling in Love," in a falsetto that he describes as a "little childlike voice" that emerges "among all those fucked-up qualities" (130), Bono admits that he requires his audience, and he furthers his connection with them by encouraging them to sing along with him. He does not do so with the typical aggressive gesture of thrusting his microphone out toward the audience, as if commanding them to sing but instead walks backward along the ramp, gesturing back toward the stage with a gently summoning wave.

Popular music has long explored and continues to explore the conception of love as a means of personal redemption, whereby the love object serves as a means of repairing a void the lover perceives in himself and reflecting an idealized and dilated self-image back to him so as to bolster his ego. From the Who singing "I'm looking for that free ride to me / I'm looking for you" in 1971 to the Nine Inch Nails singing "My whole existence is flawed / You get me closer to God" in 1994, love in rock songs frequently fulfills the function of narcissistic self-gratification.[19] Similarly, the fans' worship of rock musicians elevates them from anonymity to superstardom, from relative poverty to unimaginable wealth, giving rock stars any number of opportunities to see themselves as larger than life or as "even better than the real thing." It is to U2's credit that they explore these themes in an intelligent and simultaneously serious and ironic fashion. While the members of the band have certainly profited from their fans' adulation, they are engaging in a certain amount of truth in advertising by openly and self-consciously enacting, on their albums and onstage, their complex relationship with their audience. Spelled out, the warning contained in the title *Achtung Baby* might read, "Look, we're manipulating the hell out of you—screwing you, in effect—and we're getting a whole of money and ego gratification in the process. But don't say we didn't warn you." An apparently hopeful affirmation such as

"Uncertainty will be our guiding light" in the song "Zooropa" is undermined by being rhymed with the sarcastic "You got the right shoes to get you through the night," thereby avoiding any clear-cut statement one way or the other. The audience may choose to "BELIEVE EVERYTHING," but they have to realize that "ART IS MANIPULATION" and "EVERYTHING YOU KNOW IS WRONG." Bono onstage is not simply performing; he is playing roles. His acting goes beyond costumes; he consciously modifies his voice and inflection as well as his body movements to suit the particular character he is playing, so that it seems as though three or four different lead singers have performed during the course of the same concert. While the audience may wish to believe that the apparently sincere singer of "New Year's Day" or "Pride (In the Name of Love)" is the real Bono, that persona is as much an adopted role as the Fly and MacPhisto are. The structure of the Zoo TV performance, with its pattern of submission and self-gratification, of advance and retreat with regard to the love object, is designed to convey a very complex message to the audience. The band ultimately concedes that they remain dependent on their fans and thus they devote a portion of the concert to fulfilling their expectations, but at the same time they wish to create at least the illusion of independence and artistic integrity, which they do by adopting a self-consciously ironic mode. In Bono's words, "I've found there's a great freedom when you have your feet in two so-called mutually exclusive worlds—the world of irony and world of soul, the world of flesh and the world of the spirit, the world of surface and the world of depth. That's where most people live. That's where U2 live. Then again . . . maybe it's just a phase we're going through."[20] Typically, he undercuts a serious statement of the band's self-definition with an ironic qualifier; what it amounts to is an absolute refusal at this point in U2's career to be pinned down, to make any sort of commitment to the audience. U2's fans, then, should be wary of the danger of overidentifying with their idols, despite their mutual need for each other, and the singer gives them fair warning: "We're one / But we're not the same."

In reference to *Achtung Baby*, Bono remarked, "Rock & roll has more contradictions than any art form. U2 spent the Eighties trying to resolve some of them. Now we've started the Nineties celebrating them."[21] U2's most recent release, *Pop* (Island 524 334, 1997), celebrates those contradictions even more blatantly, with songs ranging from the techno dance number "Discothèque," to the Nine Inch Nails–influenced "Mofo," to the torchy "If You Wear That Velvet Dress" to the plaintive, melodic "If God Will Send His Angels." The singer wants to save his soul and "fill that GOD shaped hole" ("Mofo") by finding himself, "looking for the father of my two little girls," presumably a reference to Bono himself, the father of two daughters. The answers are not forthcoming. Even if God does send his angels, "would everything be alright?" ("If God Will Send His Angels"). Instead of "hope," "faith," and "love," we have the quest to get through "the gates of the Playboy mansion," where there will be "no time of sorrow" or "shame." The singer says "I know I've got to believe," but it is the Playboy mansion and what it represents that is the goal of his faith ("The Playboy Mansion"). The final track declares this "a fucked up world" and pleads to Jesus, "Wake Up, Dead Man." The utter disillusionment expressed in the lyrics, the title *Pop*, and the release of "Discothèque" (a song influenced by techno artists such as the Prodigy) as the first single, all seemed to signal an even more radical shift away from U2's roots, as did the infamous news conference in the lingerie department of a K-Mart store. Some old-time U2 fans clung to the melodic "Staring at the Sun" (the second and longest-playing single), but its lyrics are as bitter as the rest of the album. The singer is staring at the sun, not for enlightenment but because he is "happy to go blind" to the problems of the world. What U2 will do in the future remains to be seen; clearly, however, they are continuing the project of *Achtung Baby*, in adopting the stance of a band that refuses to shape themselves to their fans' expectations.

NOTES

1. U2, "The Fly," *Achtung Baby* (Island 510 347, 1991).

2. Sean O'Hagan, "Bono," *Arena* (winter 1993/94): 72.

3. I discuss the narcissism of several songs on *Achtung Baby* in a different context in an article titled *"Epipsychidion, Achtung Baby*, and the Teaching of Romanticism," *Popular Culture Review* 6 (1995): 29–44.

4. In this essay, when I refer to the "singer" of the songs, I am referring to a persona created by the writer and performer, not the writer and performer himself. "The Fly" and the red-horned "MacPhisto" of the last leg of the Zoo TV tour similarly serve as characters that Bono adopts, roles he is playing. That Bono is willfully playing roles at all indicates the shift the band has taken. In a 1989 interview, for instance, he asserted "I don't have an ironic persona like David Byrne or David Bowie to stand behind" and "I sing about the way I see things. Some people write songs about the way characters see things. Some artists perform with a wink. That's just not the way with U2" (Adam Block, "Pure Bono," *Mother Jones* 14, no. 4 [May 1989]: 34).

5. U2, *Achtung Baby: The Videos, the Cameos, and a Whole Lot of Interference from Zoo TV*, 65 min., Island Visual Arts/Polygram Video, 1991, videocassette.

6. Robert Hilburn, "It's a Global Thing with U2," *Los Angeles Times*, 12 September, 1993, Calendar, p. 72.

7. O'Hagan, "Bono," p. 71.

8. Anthony DeCurtis, "Zoo World Order," *Rolling Stone*, 14 October 1993, p. 130.

9. Hilburn, "It's a Global Thing," p. 72.

10. Elizabeth Wurtzel, "Me2," *New Yorker*, 17 February 1992, pp. 76, 79.

11. U2, *Achtung Baby: The Videos*.

12. Quoted in David Fricke, "U2 Finds What It's Looking for," *Rolling Stone*, 1 October 1992, p. 48.

13. O'Hagan, "Bono," p. 74.

14. U2, *Zoo TV Live from Sydney*, prod. Neal O'Hanlon and Rocky Oldham, dir. David Mallet, 118 min., Island Video/Polygram Video, 1994, videocassette.

15. O'Hagan, "Bono," p. 73.

16. U2, *Zoo TV*.

17. Block, "Pure Bono," p. 37.

18. DeCurtis, "Zoo World Order," p. 130.

19. The Who, "Bargain," *Who's Next* (MCA 11269, 1971); Nine Inch Nails, "Closer," *The Downward Spiral* (Nothing/TVT/Interscope 92346, 1994).

20. O'Hagan, "Bono," p. 74.

21. Fricke, "U2 Finds What It's Looking For," p. 42.

12

ELVIS COSTELLO AS CULTURAL ICON AND CULTURAL CRITIC

PAMELA THURSCHWELL

For Marx, with the commodity, "a definite social relation between men . . . assumes, in their eyes, the fantastic form of a relation between things."[1] Of course, this statement rests on the assumption that things and humans are at least potentially separable. Most early Frankfurt School–inflected Marxist discussions of the commodity presume that there is a realm of human experience that is not wholly subsumed by our consumption of objects. According to much current discussion, however, this realm is steadily shrinking and/or already vanished. Recent work in cultural studies has tried to recoup commodification as a process with potentially liberatory political effects by undermining the classic Marxist assumption of differentiation between the commodity and the human. Critics argue that within postmodernism everything, including the private sphere of the family, emotions, and relations with others, is produced and/or effected by capitalist modes of production and consumption. A nostalgic desire to reclaim a utopian precommodified moment is a revenant of a Marxism whose time has passed. The cultural logic of late capitalism insists that we accept that the boundaries set by commodity culture produce the very space we consider most intimate, most exempt from the terms set by that culture. With this set of assumptions is in place, Simon Frith has argued, recent analyses of popular culture have attempted to use this apparently depressing conclusion to turn the Frankfurt School's pessimism on its head. Critics have looked to counterhegemonic acts of consumption to find a liberatory politics within the very terms of late capitalism: "The task, beginning with American liberal sociologists in the 1950s, has been to find forms of mass consumption that are not 'passive' and types of mass consumers who are not stupefied."[2] Recent cultural-studies work attempts to redeem popular culture and the disparaged commodity form by relocating agency, in terms both of human emotions and political acts of resistance, within its boundaries. Consumers consume creatively, resistantly, counterideologically. Humans take mass-produced objects and personalize them through their strategies of consumption. One might say that mass consumption only works through making objects human.

Pop records are arguably one of the most intimately experienced commodity forms. Differing from television or films, which, according to general expectations, cause the consumer to focus his or her full attention on the screen, pop music wafts through the background of people's lives, on the radio, in dance halls, in supermarkets, becoming attached in random formations to personal meanings.[3] Furthermore, while television shows and movies may be viewed repeatedly, the usual presumption is that they will only be seen only once. Fans of pop music, on the other hand, play records over and over again—Top 40 radio formats assume that people consume songs repeatedly. Like identity itself according to a deconstructive theorist such as Judith Butler, pop music is consumed and constructs lives along the lines of repetitions with differences.[4] In Butler's analysis of sex and gender identity, repetition is what creates the human. There is no realm of the human separable from the repeated fantasmatic acting out of identity, and fantasies of identity take place in and through, as well as against, commodity culture. Humans consume and are consumed by pop music.

In this essay, I want to formulate some of the contradictory ways pop songs and pop stars function as commodities by examining how Elvis Costello and two popular novels approach the problem of the split between the human and the commodity that grounds analyses of present-day consumer culture. Elvis Costello's music criticizes the culture of consumption as fully as it participates in it. More a cranky Frankfurt School theorist than a postmodern celebrator of commodification, Costello maintains the category of the human as an index of what is dangerously disappearing under late capitalism. When Bret Easton Ellis's *Less than Zero* (1985) and Nick Hornby's *High Fidelity* (1995) engage with Elvis Costello's work they also explore this strained relationship between commodification and affect. A Costello song such as "Less than Zero" lays out a terrain of paranoia, historical amnesia, and the interpenetration of intimacy and modern mass media forms. I will then look at why *Less than Zero* and *High Fidelity* take their titles from Elvis Costello songs, how they handle some of these same topics, and how the books portray pop music as both symptomatic of a diseased commodity culture and crucially life giving.

"Less than Zero" appeared on Costello's debut album *My Aim Is True* in 1977, the heyday of British punk. The song was inspired by his seeing a then-current TV interview with Oswald Mosley, the leader of the British fascist movement in the 1930s. Costello says of the song, "I've never written a political song in the sense of political theory. . . . The first song I ever released ('Less than Zero') came from my getting very angry watching this old fascist on television being buttered up and generally accepted as if the mists of time had somehow diminished his crime. I only wrote that song because I was angry."[5] "Less than Zero" springs initially from Costello's fury at a moment of historical forgetting, a moment made possible, he suggests, by the mediation of the TV set.

With its opening image of a swastika-tatooed Oswald "carving 'V' for vandal on the guilty boy's head," the song sounds a theme common in Costello's work: the combination of violence and dehumanization that he finds occurring in everyday life, both in private and public spaces, in bedrooms and in newspapers.[6] If he is finally a humanist in his critique of the loss of values in modern society (as in his rousing and, I would argue, entirely unironic cover of Nick Lowe's "What's So Funny 'Bout Peace, Love, and Understanding?"), then what it means to be human is not self-evident; rather, it is always a term in question. In his song "Lipstick Vogue," the singer tries to escape from being defined as an object by an uninterested lover ("Select the controls and then insert the token / You want to throw me away, well I'm not broken"). The song's repeated refrain, "Sometimes I almost feel / Just like a human being," suggests that humanness is something that is only rarely achieved. In Costello's early work, the loss of the human is often a result of mistreatment by a woman. He claimed famously in a 1977 interview with Nick Kent that revenge and guilt fueled everything he wrote.[7] Costello's often vitriolic misogyny aimed at unfaithful lovers (for instance, in the misleadingly titled "I'm Not Angry" (*My Aim Is True*) (in which he spits out "there's no such thing as an original sin")) shades into his analysis of the ways in which modernity encroaches on the human. When this becomes the stuff of relations between men and women the imperative seems to be objectify women before they objectify you, as in the nightmarish "Tiny Steps," where a woman is manipulated like a miniature doll—"Make her walk or make her kneel"— building to a crescendo: "You can even shop around though you won't find any cheaper / She's your baby now, you can keep her."[8]

That same song's reference to "little tombs for your baby's ashes" brings up another of Costello's edgy rhetorical techniques. One of Costello's most dubious and interesting moves is to take the imagery bequeathed by the Holocaust as the metaphorical fodder of modern existence: "But they'll never get to make a lampshade out of me"; "Just like the place where they take your spine and turn it into soap flakes"; "She's my soft touch typewriter and I'm the great dictator."[9] The Holocaust is his reference point for a process of dehumanization that occurs on every level of personal and political life. Costello consistently documents, in a deeply Foucauldian manner, the ways in which our most intimate relationships are invaded by, indeed inextricable from, institutions of power. As Greil Marcus puts it, "The idea, scattered across *My Aim Is True* and *This Year's Model*, and then set forth with both greater subtlety and violence on *Armed Forces*, was that fascism, far from being defeated in 1945, simply went underground, where it now functions as the political unconscious of the West."[10] For Costello, the legacy of Thatcher's England, as well as of Hitler's Germany, is the threat that people will literally be melted down for pills and soap.[11] This world, also recognizable in the work of authors such as Don DeLillo, is governed ominously by emotional fascism, the original title to Costello's 1979 album *Armed Forces*. Marcus describes that album:

> On this album, every moment of personal failure or unsatisfied passion is invaded by the cruelty and shamelessness of the political world. . . . The secret, unspeakable realities of political life, realities we seem to successfully deflect or ignore, rise up to force a redefinition of relationships between men and women, the essential stuff of ordinary life, on those unspeakable terms. Costello isn't after simple culpability: American responsibility for, say, the Iranian secret police. He's after the way the Iranian secret police—and those of other places, and not distant times—invisibly shape our sense of ourselves.[12]

As in many other examples of postmodern cultural production, in Costello's work, the Holocaust becomes an uneasy reference point for our modern predicament,[13] Adorno and Horkheimer's endpoint of the dialectic of enlightenment, the constitutive moment of postmodernity's loss of faith in progressive narratives, *the* modern historical event that provokes a vast disease in response to the necessity for, and the possibility of, historical memory.[14] When Costello points toward the Mosley interview as the genesis for his song and his anger, he implies that without some sort of ethics of historical memory fascism will always reemerge, but then he also doubts that it has ever really been submerged.

At several points, "Less than Zero" connects this historical amnesia to the presence of modern media technology, most obviously in the chorus, where TV emerges as a way of drowning out the noise of what appears to be a seduction: "Turn up the TV. No one listening will suspect." The potential listeners are the prohibitive oedipal parents: "Your mother won't detect it / No your father won't know." But what sort of seduction is this? One reading would suggest that when the whitewashing drone of white noise that makes news and entertainment indistinguishable invades the domestic space of the family, it breaks down any illusion that home could be a haven safe from fascism. If Oswald Mosley can appear on a TV interview, surely everything means less than zero. You might as well let the singer of the song, the punk who's "got no respect" into your home, because, in fact, he's already there. But television is not simply a method for disguising sexual transgression or a way of putting it in a larger perspective (i.e., compared to Oswald Mosley, anything we do means less than zero). The song suggests that technologies of mediation help create a perverse and dangerously eroticized public sphere: "Oswald and his sister are doing it again / They've got the finest home movies that you have ever seen." It's not so much the charge of incest but the charge of home videoing that is threatening. It's the passage between the private and an endlessly mediated and replicated public that Costello diagnoses as part of a diseased modernity. The language of television suffuses the song: Oswald and his sister engage in "a thousand variations: every service with a smile" before they break for commercials. John Brenkman identifies a process by which media technologies create a public that is simultaneously linked to each other (in the Althusserian sense, interpellated as a public at the moment it is addressed as such) and absolutely isolated from one another: "Mass communication addresses the separate subject as constituted by the exchange and consumption of commodities. It produces a relation between the subject and the collective akin to what Sartre calls seriality—the series being the grouping in which the members are connected only insofar as they are isolated from one another. Television is but the most vivid example, in that millions of people watch the same program alone."[15]

Costello similarly points to television as creating a community that is in fact a simulacrum of community, in which intimate relations to others are replaced by the spectacular relation to the commodity. On "Satellite," from his 1989 album *Spike*, Costello sings of a sexual relationship mediated obliquely and humiliatingly through a TV set. A man watches a woman in a "transparent" dress on a screen: "with his face pressed to the screen, he muttered words he'd never dare to say if she could see him." The implication, a perhaps surprisingly cranky, conservative one, is that television's mediation of desire makes it into pornography. In Costello's view, television viewers simultaneously share "the same cheap sensation."[16] Seriality now structures the no longer private sphere of sexual desire and intimacy and the no longer collective, intersubjective public sphere. This sort of analysis speaks to the periodizing and nostalgic version of postmodernism that suggests that the aura of the authentic, the intimate truth of human relations, has been lost through mechanical reproduction and the commodification of the real.

If postmodernity is in part characterized by an inability to distinguish originals from copies, then, Costello suggests, intimate human relations are in no way exempt from this effect. "Less than Zero" takes this assumption to a specific set of political events. *1984*-like, the TV set becomes an instrument of fascism when it simultaneously publicizes the private, creating a paranoid world in which a video camera is always already aimed at you, and commodifies history. The Oswald Mosley interview on TV suggests that British history is something that can be turned off: change the channel, and it will come out differently. The television that drowns out the proceedings of the song has helped create a world in which the law is indistinguishable from its opposite ("Mr. Oswald said he had an understanding with the law") and in which consumer capitalism sets all terms for value. Oswald "heard about a couple living in the USA" who "traded in their baby for a Chevrolet." The song ends with an exhortation to "talk about the future now we put the past away." The amnesiac future of the commodity is an ahistorical, amoral one in which people happily exchange babies for cars.

Through much of Costello's work, the United States is portrayed at best ambivalently, as a land without history or memory, a land that can only create a bright-eyed future full of buying power through erasure. The differences between British and U.S. cultures, and what it means to be in the position of the exile in one or the other, is a recurring theme; consider, for instance, *Get Happy*'s "New Amsterdam" ("Back in London they take you to heart after a little while / Though I look right at home I still feel like an exile") or *Trust*'s "Luxembourg" ("You look like a lover but you're only a tourist").[17] On his album *King of America*, the United States appears as part promised land, part commodified hell, a place where "they pour Coca-cola just like vintage wine." Shifting successfully between the two cultures is difficult, as the British girl who immigrates after marrying an American GI in "American Without Tears" discovers: "It seems we've been crying for years and for years / Now we don't speak any English, just American without tears."[18] The transition from British to American for Costello provokes specific problems of translation, which are related to his sense of the United States as the apotheosis of capitalism's value system.

In his 1977 tour of the USA, when Costello appeared with the Attractions on Saturday Night Live, he aborted the band's rendition of "Less than Zero" about a minute into it, saying "I'm sorry, ladies and gentlemen, there's no reason to play this song." He switched to "Radio, Radio," which was then unreleased.[19] At the time it seemed that Costello felt that the United States wouldn't understand "Less than Zero," either because of lack of knowledge about Oswald Mosley (the critique of the United States that claims it never looks beyond its own borders) or because of the mind-numbing, commodified, fascist-friendly culture of the country itself. "Radio, Radio," a vitriolic attack on the deadening effects of Top 40 radio is a full-frontal attack on some of the same tendencies that "Less than Zero" explores more subtly. The United States required blunt instruments to make an effect, at least as far as Costello was concerned.

Costello later wrote another version of "Less than Zero" specifically for his U.S. audience: "Because the song refers to 'Mister Oswald,' some people in America early on thought it was about Lee Harvey Oswald! I saw one really long article that went into every line of the song and worked up this mad theory! Even lines you couldn't imagine how they would bend into shape. They had made a really creative effort. So I wrote another version of the lyrics and we did it in Dallas."[20]

The Dallas version of "Less than Zero" deftly collapses paranoia, history, sex, and mass media constructions of, and responsibility for, all three. Costello's translation of one historical trauma (British fascist involvement) into another (the Kennedy assassination) seems implicated in the generalized historical paranoia his song points toward. What would it mean to say that fascism and Lee Harvey Oswald are part and parcel of the same cultural phenomena? Is it mass media itself that creates these connections? In the Dallas version, a woman named Jenny undresses "while her husband rides a bumper in the president's procession." Watching him on TV "as she looks up from giving head," she apparently witnesses the assassination. Her lover then "throws her on the bed / To teach her she's alive, then suddenly he is dead." This scene in which the wife of a secret service man watches her husband (or the president—the ambiguity seems intentional) die on the TV screen while she has sex with another man handily pathologizes the political through the personal. Jenny's act of sexual betrayal is set next to the country's betrayal. Conversely, watching a president's, or a husband's, assassination becomes a sexual turn-on rather than an invasion of private space by the outside world. The song seems to ask how we tell the difference between life and death when they both come flitting across the TV set, when the sexual act as a sign of life ("to teach her she's alive") is invaded by corpses on a screen. The analogy is clear: both Jenny and the USA are screwing people over as well as getting screwed. It's a question of how we enjoy as well as feel violated by that experience and of what that enjoyment has to do with the televisual media that creates new serial versions of intimacy, new ways of sharing and not sharing experiences such as presidential assassinations and sexual encounters.[21]

The Kennedy assassination was a turning point for modern U.S. culture, not only because of the loss of shared national innocence it is usually taken to indicate but because as an event it is indelibly etched on the collective national psyche through its repeated showings—the Zapruder home movie of the assassination, Jack Ruby's shooting of Lee Harvey Oswald—the first killing captured on live TV. It's the moment of history turned into mechanical reproduction par excellence. Costello's version captures this aspect of it as part of hidden bureaucratic processes of dehumanization. Because everybody was "taking home movies" there are consequently a "thousand variations." When the now secretarial-seeming Jenny "puts on some coffee" and "comes back with a smile / She says, 'I hear that South America is coming into style.' " The thousand variations suggest that you can have your Kennedy assassination filmed to order, much as the line "they're going to take a little break, and they'll be back after a while" of the original version implies that sexual encounters are structured along the same lines as television game shows. Because TV is both a documenter of news and culture and a commodity form, it creates the sense that history is for sale to the highest bidder. The reference to South America vaguely suggests revolutions and places for political exiles to hide, another signifier of a generalized paranoid world in which the differences between fascist and communist revolutionary dogma get lost. (Lee Harvey Oswald was seen simultaneously as a Communist and a dupe of the CIA, on both sides of the Cuban situation.) That Jenny is putting on coffee, secretary style, while this discussion of witnesses and South America ensues gives the scene a business-as-usual aspect. The song ends with

Jenny, with "rubies on her fingers," turning and looking away with "her mind upon a basement out of the USA." The rubies may just be a shallow pun on Jack Ruby's name, but the basement extends the sinister feel of the song. Basements are where you hide bodies, especially in the USA. Abasement is what Costello suggests we all live with, under a regime of emotional fascism.

Reading his song lyrics too closely is bound to make me look like the Costello trainspotter I undoubtedly am. Costello himself has good-naturedly disparaged people's interpretative zeal for his songs, claiming that they're not worth the trouble: "There's certain techniques of being clear or obscuring meaning or fragmenting images—just simple techniques of writing. I've got a mind for wordplay and punning. . . . It's like some people can do crosswords, some people can do anagrams. It's just a short-circuit in the brain or something."[22] But, at the risk of facing ridicule, I'd like to suggest that both versions of "Less than Zero" diagnose a complicated combination of factors present in modernity that leads to the "everything means less than zero" of the chorus. The songs' foregrounding of media technology colludes with and shapes the historical amnesia that allows the repetition of the chorus. The types of paranoia that follow from the invasive effects of teletechnology are, as Greil Marcus says, the id of the West as well as its politics. There is no love outside of the dehumanizing TV set, no sex that's not already being home videoed, no escape from a value system in which babies are traded for Chevrolets. What a disgusted Costello documents in these two songs is the commodification of the human through the loss of a sense of value-laden history.

So what happens when we move from Costello as cultural critic to Costello as cultural reference point? At first glance, other than their Costello-inspired titles, Bret Easton Ellis's *Less than Zero* (1985) and Nick Hornby's *High Fidelity* (1995) have little in common except for high sales figures, a plethora of pop music references, and reviewers' suggestions in both cases that the books were barely disguised autobiographies.[23] Ellis's book is a deadpan exposé of the bored, spoiled, thrill-seeking culture of young rich Los Angelenos amid the malaise of the Reaganite eighties. With too much money, too many drugs, and no moral convictions to speak of, the narrator, Clay, recently returned home from college in the East for the Christmas holidays, spends his time with his friends metaphorically acting out the heavy-handed truth of the novel's opening line: "People are afraid to merge on the freeways in Los Angeles" (9). Nick Hornby's recent *High Fidelity* takes a less nihilistic view of the difficulties of merging encountered by its hero, Rob Fleming, as he grapples with the dilemma of whether it is "possible to maintain a relationship and a large record collection simultaneously" (131). The novel takes its cultural context from a North London world of pop-obsessed thirty-something heterosexual music nerds trapped in extended adolescence who work in record stores and scorn fans of mainstream rock 'n' roll to make themselves feel better about not having girlfriends. The operative question in the book that signifies Rob's movement toward an adult understanding of relationships is whether it is more important what you like or what you're like. Rob's reconciliation with his girlfriend, Laura, coincides with his ability to admit that some friends of hers who possess "the sort of CD collection that is so poisonously awful that it should be put in a steel case and shipped off to some Third World waste dump" (222) are actually lovely people. The atmosphere of the two books is radically different: High Fidelity ends chirpily with everyone on the dance floor while Rob DJ's at his revived club; Less than Zero ends with Clay fleeing for the East Coast, haunted by violent images inspired by X's song "Los Angeles" of parents eating children and teenagers being blinded by the sun from the city's asphalt. The books, however, do share an overarching concern for the possibility or impossibility of relating to others and the place that pop music fills as supplement to/replacement for those relations. The exploration in "Less than Zero" of the dangerous inextricability of the personal from the political, and mass media technology from intimate relationships, is also broached in the books, which in different ways rely on pop songs as a specific type of commodity to do a specific type of emotional work. Costello functions doubly, both as the commodity that is bought and sold and as the cultural critic who critiques his own participation in a culture that commodifies affect.

Both novels received a lot of media attention when they came out. Reviews at the time suggested that the books captured certain zeitgeist phenomena: mid-eighties' Reaganite West Coast malaise in Less than Zero, masculine arrested development and obsessiveness in High Fidelity. In High Fidelity Rob and his friends who work at his record store cathect music too much. Intense relationships to pop music take place in lieu of mature emotional relationships with other people. But Hornby also suggests that it is impossible to extricate an understanding of relations to others, particularly romantic ones, from the context of the pop songs that set their terms. For Rob, emotions are formed by and filtered through 33 rpm: "Records have helped me to fall in love, no question. I hear something new, with a chord change that melts my guts, and before I know it I'm looking for someone, and before I know it I've found her" (139). As Costello puts it, "There's a second-hand emotion on a battered forty-five."[24] Emotions are secondhand because we must learn them, and the repetition of the experience of the commodity actually functions to create subjectivity. Rob maintains that music is life in a direct way: "Everyone knows *Al Green Explores Your Mind* is as serious as life gets" (138). *High Fidelity* ironizes statements such as this yet never relinquishes their truth value. At the end of the novel, although Rob has acceded to new views on human relationships, one is by no means meant to take Al Green less seriously.

By contrast, in *Less than Zero*, no one cares about the mid-eighties' pop soundtrack that suffuses the book or about each other. As Greil Marcus has pointed out, the insistent referencing of angry music such as punk in *Less than Zero* simply serves to indicate how unangry the teenagers who inhabit the book actually seem: "Clay goes to a club to see X, a founding L.A. punk band whose music contains all the loathing and fury that Clay can't touch in himself, can't talk about. He wants to hear them do 'Sex and Dying in High Society,' but it's no accident that he leaves before the number comes up; otherwise he'd have to respond to the song."[25] Music acts as a white-noise backdrop in *Less than Zero*, serving along with drugs and movies to drown out the possibility of actual interaction. If the characters' constant discussions of MTV and recent bands indicate anything besides their less-than-video-length attention spans, perhaps they point toward the inability to differentiate that marks all the lives in the novel. One song is the same as any other.

Nick Hornby's obsessives could not be further from this assumption of indifference. His characters inhabit a world in which differentiation is of utmost importance. Rob, along with Barry and Dick, his coworkers at his record store, makes endless lists: top five songs about death, top five break-ups, top five subtitled movies, top five Elvis Costello songs.[26] When Laura and Rob argue about the importance of distinguishing between a Solomon Burke record and Art Garfunkel's "Bright Eyes," Laura winds up saying, "They're only pop records, and if one's better than the other, well who cares, really apart from you and Barry and Dick? To me it's like arguing the difference between McDonalds and Burger King. I'm sure there must be one, but who can be bothered to find out what it is?" (209). Rob responds to himself, "The terrible thing is, of course, that I already know the difference, that I have complicated and informed views on the subject. But if I start going on about BK Flamers versus Quarter Pounders with Cheese, we will both feel that I have somehow proved her point" (209). In *High Fidelity* the desire to make these sorts of distinctions is coded as both a masculine pathology and as part of the appeal of a certain version of hetero masculinity. Engaging with popular culture is a serious business; making these distinctions is what it means to be passionate, to be alive, with the qualification that women seem to have different means for achieving this goal. In *Fever Pitch*, his brilliant memoir of growing up an obsessive soccer fan, Hornby suggests that the difference between boys and girls is that boys have passions while girls have personalities, that boys define themselves by their relations to their interests (football, rugby, pop music) while girls define themselves by their relations to other people.[27] If *High Fidelity* suggests that this may be both a *différence* to cry *"vive"* to and a matter for a feminist critique of the relations engendered by commodity culture, *Less than Zero* suggests that in the decathected terrain of eighties' California all relations to commodities are equivalent and indistinguishable. *High Fidelity* both celebrates and criticizes the fetishization of popular culture that makes relations to commodities— in particular that most personal of commodities, the pop record—replace relations between people. *Less than Zero* portrays stultifying relations to a popular culture unable to replace something that has been lost between people. The book enacts the other side of Marx's dialectic of commodity fetishism, suggesting that under capitalism relations between people become like relations between things. Clay and his male friends are repetitively and monotonously described as blond and tan, indistinguishable from each other; eventually they are literally commodified in the product of the male prostitute.

Occasionally in *Less than Zero* it seems that pop music is used to refer to the loss of real relations between people rather than simply being the noise that fills that gap. Clay's relationship with his old school friend Julian provides one of the few emotional trajectories of the book. Julian is the only person in the book whom Clay actively wants to see. After Julian's repeated attempts to evade him, their eventual encounter reveals Julian's heroin abuse and employment as a male prostitute. Clay's prelapsarian memories of himself and Julian together in grade school signal, somewhat heavy-handedly, the judgments of the book, the backward glance suggesting that things might have turned out some other way. In the midst of watching Julian have sex with a businessman, Clay flashes on "an image of Julian in fifth grade, kicking a soccer ball across a green field" (175). When the two first meet shortly after Clay's arrival for the holidays, Clay asks Julian what he has been doing, and Julian can't remember. He says:

"Oh, I don't know. I've been around. Went to that Tom Petty concert at the . . . Forum. He sang that song we always used to listen to. . . ." Julian closes his eyes and tries to remember the song. "Oh, shit, you know. . . ." He begins to hum and then sing the words. "*Straight into darkness, we went straight into darkness, out over that line, yeah straight into darkness, straight into night. . . .*"

. . . I look at the Perrier bottle, a little embarrassed, and say, "Yeah, I remember."

"Love that song," he says.

"Yeah, so did I," I say. (48–49)

Moments of connection, even a half-remembered connection such as this one, are rare in the book. The fact that none of the book's characters can remember song titles, lyrics, or the names of the bands who performed them signifies a loss of coherence to lives whose main access to emotion is through the pop culture artifacts that surround them. In *High Fidelity* the pathology is that lives are lived out through, and only through, these cultural artifacts. In *Less than Zero* these artifacts have become detached from the emotions they once might have signified. Songs gesture toward an affective and sometimes political terrain that is beyond the manifest scope of the novel. Shortly before the novel ends, Clay finds himself unable to get a pop song out of his head:

The week before I leave, I listen to a song by an L.A. composer about the city . . . the song . . . confused me and I would try to decipher it. For instance, I wanted to know why the bum in the song was on his knees. Someone told me that the bum was so grateful to be in the city instead of somewhere else. I told this person that I thought he missed the point and the person told me in a tone I found slightly conspiratorial, "No, dude . . . I don't think so."

I sat in my room a lot, the week before I left, watching a television show that was on in the afternoons and that played videos while a DJ from a local rock station introduced the clips. There would be about a hundred teenagers dancing in front of a huge screen on which the videos were played; the images dwarfing the teenagers—and I would recognize people whom I had seen at clubs, dancing on the show, smiling for the cameras, and then turning and looking up to the lighted monolithic screen that was flashing the images at them. Some of them would mouth the words to the song that was being played. But I'd concentrate on the teenagers who didn't mouth the words; the teenagers who had forgotten them; the teenagers who maybe never knew them.   (193–94)

Randy Newman's song "I Love L.A." is understood by the character with the conspiratorial voice as a straightforward paean to the city rather than an ambivalent damnation of it.[28] Clay, who is a product of that city and its cultural detritus, cannot satisfactorily process the information he receives from music and television. When he watches the local dance show, it is as if he were observing a simulacrum of community. The familiar faces from the clubs he frequents are available to him as spectacle but not as potential interlocutors.[29] But Clay's fascination with the teenagers who do not mouth the words to the songs seems to indicate that pop music can provide a bridge from spectacle to community. Mouthing the words to a pop song in this scenario implies a mimicking of community and affective community ties. It is saying: "I care enough about this song to know the words." Or at least: "I have heard this song repeated enough times for it to have entered my world in such a way that I can at least mime being part of a community of pop song listeners, some of whom might actually care about the song's words, meanings, emotions." The teenagers who cannot participate in this minimal act of community formation are the end of the line. It is unclear whether, like Julian, they once knew the words and have since forgotten them or whether they never knew them at all. This investment in the pop song indicates, I would suggest, that songs as commodities are never simply spectacular or reducible to their repeatability. Rather, they become so enmeshed with their specific sites of consumption that as a specific genre of commodity, the pop song actually evokes the possibility of an outside to spectacular culture. Even if that outside is only a fantasy, its function is crucial. In *Less than Zero* this is pictured as a nostalgic desire, for a time when Clay and Julian connected to the affective meanings of pop songs, when they felt something more than they do now, something that is bound up in the very possibility of knowing the words to those songs.

The words to Elvis Costello's song "Less than Zero" are never mentioned in the book. Like the Randy Newman moment that can't quite be mentioned, "Less than Zero" as a reference point suggests the impossible separation of the personal from the political that suffuses the book. There is no discernible politics in *Less than Zero*, and there are no self-conscious characters. There is no remembered history, only the traces of a nostalgia for it. Pop songs are used by the characters in the book to camouflage their lack of historical continuity not to foreground it. Yet Costello himself appears at significant moments throughout the novel, standing in for the politics and ethics the book itself initially seems to refuse.

Costello first appears in *Less than Zero* in a poster on the wall of Clay's bedroom when he comes back to his house for the first time since returning from college:

> I look up with caution at the poster encased in glass that hangs on the wall above my bed, but it hasn't changed either. It's the promotional poster for an old Elvis Costello record. Elvis looks past me, with this wry, ironic smile on his lips, staring out the window. The word "Trust" hovering over his head, and his sunglasses, one lens red, the other blue, pushed down past the ridge of his nose so that you can see his eyes, which are slightly off center. The eyes don't look at me, though. They only look at whoever's standing by the window, but I'm too tired to get up and stand by the window. (11)

Clay returns to the poster again and again in the course of the novel. Costello's eyeglassed presence seems to hover over the book in an explicit homage to the billboard of the eyes of Dr. T. J. Eckleburg that hovers over the world of F. Scott Fitzgerald's novel *The Great Gatsby* (another arguably adolescent novel about the malaise of the too rich and the tragedies to which this malaise can lead). The eyes of Dr. Eckleburg pierce through the worlds of East and West Egg in *Gatsby*, impassively surveying the tragedy of Gatsby's life and death like the eyes of an unmoved and unmoving deity. In Fitzgerald's novel, as countless high school students have written on exams, the billboard symbolizes the replacement of moral values by commercial ones; God has degenerated to an advertisement. *Less than Zero*'s replacing Dr. Eckleburg with Elvis Costello suggests yet another displacement of the role of judgment. If the iconicity of the billboard in *Gatsby* refers simply to a culture at a loss for icons other than commercial ones, then Clay's Elvis Costello poster suggests that commercial signs can be reinvested with a critical significance that the novel gestures toward. The fact that Costello's album is entitled *Trust* is no coincidence; Elvis's surveying stare momentarily seems to promise the potential for the faith denied by everything else in the novel, but Clay can't bring himself to get up and get into his line of vision: "I sit in bed and look over at the window and then glance over at the Elvis poster, and his eyes are looking out the window, beyond, into the night, and his face looks almost alarmed at what it might be seeing, the word 'Trust' above the worried face. And I think about the billboard on Sunset and the way Julian looked past me at Café Casino, and when I finally fall asleep, it's Christmas Eve" (63). The billboard on Sunset Boulevard that Clay thinks about also recalls the billboard in *Gatsby*; it says "Disappear Here" (38), another significance-soaked phrase that Clay cannot stop repeating. If all the characters in the novel are in danger of the threat of disappearing into the abyss that is the novel's Los Angeles, or of never having appeared at all, then at least, Ellis suggests, Elvis is worried about that fact.[30] In a book singularly devoid of alarm, Costello's iconic face suggests that there is in fact something to be alarmed about.

Readings of *Less than Zero* that take the book's title into consideration often suggest that the song "Less than Zero" expresses emotions similar to the nihilistic despair they find in the novel:

> Indeed the title of the novel, taken from an Elvis Costello song title, suggests that the real subject of the book is the confrontation with absolute nothingness. The refrain of the song "Less than Zero" mentions a "mother" and a "father" and states, "They think that I got no respect, but / Everything means less than zero." The claim is certainly reminiscent of Clay's situation. Although he would appear on the surface to have a disrespectful attitude and a questionable lifestyle, he is actually grappling with his deep sense of the meaninglessness of life.[31]

Phrases such as "absolute nothingness" and the "meaninglessness of life" disregard the politicized concerns of Costello's song and, indeed, his entire output as an artist. As I have indicated, Costello tackles specifically modern forms of anxiety and negation. "Everything means less than zero" is not a response to the void; it is a response to Oswald Mosley, to the Kennedy assassination, to media infiltration of the private sphere, and to a paranoid modernity that extends into the family and back out again.

In fact, a "disrespectful attitude and questionable lifestyle" are exactly what Clay does not have: his attitude and lifestyle are exactly in sync with the society that surrounds him. Greil Marcus suggests that Costello's significance is as a marker of the need for a disappearing rebellion, the punk response to intolerable social conditions. Clay's psychiatrist also has a poster of Elvis Costello on his wall, this one a *Rolling Stone* cover with a picture of Elvis and the words "Elvis Costello Repents" printed above his face. As Marcus puts it:

The use of the headline seems to be the psychiatrist's way of suggesting that even angry young punks grow up and accept the ways of the world. It's meant to stop the patient in the tracks of his or her own willfulness. But to Clay it is "Elvis Costello Repents" that signals "everything means less than zero," not the song itself, or the angry young punk who sang it. When he damned the violation of certain moral limits, Costello affirmed that moral limits were necessary, and their violation a crime. The sign on the psychiatrist's wall reduces the social dimension Costello insisted on to neurosis.[32]

If Clay's Elvis poster implies that there may still be icons out there worth trusting, then the poster belonging to Clay's shrink, who is more interested in getting Clay to cowrite a screenplay than in trying to help him with his problems, holds different connotations. In other words, saying that "everything means less than zero" is really a way of saying that this is not so, that anger is not something that needs to be exorcised from mid-eighties' Los Angeles society but rather something that needs to be expressed in spaces with productive political or community-forming potential. If on the dance floor people are at least mouthing the words to pop songs, then it might be a marginally better place than the shrink's office. The book's ambivalent relationship to the two potential meanings of its title (that everything means less than zero and that it doesn't) leaves it in something of a double bind. Is the book laying down a moralizing position with its in-your-face repeated symbols of just how bad things have got ("disappear here," "people are afraid to merge," etc.)? Or is it detachedly portraying a society without standards of any kind, refusing to judge because, as most of the original reviews suggested, the author is so clearly of that society?[33] Both possibilities, which are really just mirrors of each other, leave the book open to accusations of adolescent writing. Heavy-handed moralizing, a childlike belief in the clear-cut difference between right and wrong, or autobiographical excess are often seen as the province of the young inexperienced writer. Clay's poster of Elvis Costello seems to fulfill a sort of intermediary role in the novel, providing an adult glance that the actual adults in the book do not supply. If there are no role models to be found in the family in *Less than Zero*, then maybe there is one to be found amid the misremembered song lyrics and rock star posters that make up the mass-mediated white-noise backdrop of the book.

When Clay's friend Alana comes over to his house and tells him about an abortion she's just had, Clay feels as if his Elvis poster is somehow threatening them:

> "Well, Clay. . . ." She laughs and looks out the window and I think for a minute that she's going to start to cry. I'm standing by the door and look over at the Elvis Costello poster, at his eyes, watching her, watching us, and I try to get her away from it, so I tell her to come over here, sit down, and she thinks I want to hug her or something and she comes over to me and puts her arms around my back and says something like "I think we've all lost some sort of feeling."   (157)

In this scene the moment of apparent communal feeling and sympathy is simply Alana's mistaken assumption that Clay is trying to reach out to her rather than trying to get her away from the poster's penetrating vision. For the paranoid, drugged Clay, anything they might feel is subsumed by the poster's accusatory stare. Here, the seriality of mass media experience becomes momentarily the one space for real emotion to dwell, even if that emotion is only guilt over not having any other. In *Less than Zero* pop music signals one crucial site of lost community, and Elvis Costello is that community's ambivalent arbiter.

In *High Fidelity* Costello is just one among hundreds of pop music references; the fact that the book takes its title from a Costello song on *Get Happy* seems somewhat beside the point. It's a catchy title, a good pun that sums up the book's obsessions with music and relationships. Costello's name comes up occasionally but primarily as a signifier of intelligent, miserable music. *High Fidelity* makes Costello out to be primarily an artist of revenge and guilt, a handy reference point for the misogyny available to men as a defense against getting dumped. Like its hero, Rob, the book avoids politics or uses it only as the backdrop for personal depression. (The fact that Rob's record store is failing might be related to Margaret Thatcher, but what's much more important to the book is how its failure affects his relationship with his girlfriend.) This is not meant as a criticism of the book for not doing something it never set out to do. As Suzanne Moore points out in her review of *High Fidelity*, "Only the especially crabby could complain that Hornby is not writing about the state of the nation, the underclass, the overclass, weird sex or bad drugs or living on the edge. *High Fidelity* is about people, men and women . . . people so instantly recognisable you could hum them."[34] But *people* is, again, one of the terms at issue. For both *High Fidelity* and *Less than Zero* are about people's relationships to commodities and the ways the boundaries between what is human and what is commodified are open to negotiation. And this is necessarily a political process, even if an unacknowledged one.

In *High Fidelity* obsessiveness about music is both a male pathology and an endearing trait. Men are people who have relationships to objects but not to other people. Learning to have relationships to other people involves learning to accept that sometimes what people are like is more important than what people like and that what people like doesn't necessarily entirely determine what they are like. The lesson of the book apparently involves recognizing a realm in which emotions are not entirely bound up with commodity culture. Rob has to learn that everything isn't like the movies or Dusty Springfield singing "The Look of Love." The fantasies that popular culture portray create unfulfillable expectations, as Rob explains after listing his favorite songs about heartbreak:

> Some of these songs I have listened to around once a week, on average
> . . . since I was sixteen or nineteen or twenty-one. How can that not leave
> you bruised somewhere? How can that not turn you into the sort of person liable to break into bits when your first love goes all wrong? What came first, the music or the misery? Did I listen to music because I was miserable? Or was I miserable because I listened to music? Do all those records turn you into a melancholy person?
>
> People worry about kids playing with guns, and teenagers watching violent videos; we are scared that some sort of culture of violence will take them over. Nobody worries about kids listening to thousands—literally thousands—of songs about broken hearts and rejection and pain and misery and loss. The unhappiest people I know, romantically speaking, are the ones who like pop music the most; and I don't know whether pop music has caused this unhappiness, but I do know that they've been listening to the sad songs longer than they've been living the unhappy lives. (26–27)

Yet despite its insistence on the dangerous fantasies capitalism initiates, the book finally insists that it is only within this same consumer world that reality is constructed and happiness achieved. *High Fidelity* suggests that intersubjective relations to others must be negotiated by recognizing others' value systems within a shared consumer culture. In the last sentence of the book Rob recognizes that he could make a compilation tape for Laura that would be "full of stuff she's heard of, and full of stuff she'd play" (253), instead of imposing his own impeccable taste on her as he has done in the past. *Less than Zero* sets up pop music as a reminder of a lost world of affect. In the midst of a consumptive landscape empty of emotion, pop music at least hints at another place: singing along with songs as a way of trying to remember connections to others, or looking to the poster of Elvis Costello on the wall as a reminder of the possibility of trust in role models. In *High Fidelity* consumer culture does not work to destroy or mask affect. Rather, in a classic example of commodity fetishism, it just misdirects it toward objects instead of people. The book suggests that the solution is to love objects and people simultaneously but differently. The relentlessly upbeat ending takes place on the dance floor of the club that Rob used to DJ for, that Laura has helped him resurrect. The club reassembles a lost community of people who recognize the songs that Rob used to play as belonging to him as much as to the songs' producers, suggesting that you can consume commodities in an authentic, creative way, rather than only having them consume you. When Rob plays "The Ghetto" it "gets a cheer, as if it's my song rather than Donny Hathaway's" (251). In *High Fidelity*, unlike *Less than Zero*, the dance floor is itself a fantasy of utopian community, apart from the dangers of seriality.[35] Instead of mass media creating isolated, interpellated subjects, the dance floor becomes a public sphere that holds out the promise of intersubjectivity through and with commodity culture.

Both books, I want finally to argue, present a threatening split between commodity culture and human affect, suggesting that commodity fetishism is, pharmakonlike, both cause of and potential cure for the loss of community that accompanies modernity. That the specific commodity fetishized is the pop record or pop star is no coincidence. It's the commodity form that can hold together personal meanings and mass media saturation, repetitive beats and revolutionary messages. It's a commodity with a specifically resistant history: one of buying to rebel as well as, sometimes simultaneously with, buying to conform. It's also no coincidence that Elvis Costello holds a particular place in both books. As political commentary, his songs, steeped initially in punk outrage, take the books' problematics of the relationship between commodity culture and the human further along explicitly political lines toward a worldview that is more wide-ranging, more Frankfurt School–inflected, and ergo more paranoid, than either of the books that take their titles from his.

One of the few moments when larger political events get referenced in

High Fidelity is when Rob and Laura argue about the relative merits of Art
Garfunkel and Solomon Burke:

> "How can you like Art Garfunkel *and* Solomon Burke? It's like saying
> you support the Israelis *and* the Palestinians."
>
> "It's not like saying that at all, actually, Rob. Art Garfunkel and
> Solomon Burke make pop records, the Israelis and the Palestinians don't.
> Art Garfunkel and Solomon Burke are not engaged in a bitter territorial
> dispute, the Israelis and the Palestinians are."   (208)

Laura's and Rob's positions (that pop songs are not as important as political
events; that pop songs *are* as important as political events) function by holding in place the dichotomy between the two. In songs such as "Less Than
Zero" Costello collapses it. Sex and politics, publicity and intimacy, are inextricable, partly because of the mass media forms that invade all sections of
modern life, the very mass media forms that Costello himself uses to get his
message across. In "Radio, Radio" he shrieks, "I want to bite the hand that
feeds me, I want to bite that hand so badly."[36] Of course, Costello recognizes
his own collusion with the mass media forces that shape his Adornoesque
nightmare: the possibility that his own mass audience will be drugged by the
promises of popular culture, the great rock 'n' roll swindle, into an acquies-
cent and uncomprehending planting ground for fascism. But he also maintains that the forces of commodification invade subjectivity in ways that
make politics a necessity for the outside world as well as the inside, that if
the two can't be separated then neither can either side of the equation be
ignored. As Costello, Ellis, and Hornby show, getting happy, or getting sad,
under the auspices of late capitalism involves simultaneous recognition and
disavowal of the politics of dancing. But when conspiracy-theorist Costello
asks, "Who put these fingerprints on my imagination?" he indicates what we
should have already known: that there's always more to a solution than
pointing toward the postmodern condition and retreating to the dancefloor.[37]

NOTES

1. Karl Marx, "The Fetishism of Commodities," trans. S. Moore and E. Aveling
   (Moscow, 1954), in *Selected Writings*, ed. David McLellan (Oxford: Oxford University Press, 1977), p. 436.

2. Simon Frith, "The Good, the Bad, and the Indifferent: Defending Popular Culture from the Populists," *Diacritics* 21, no. 4 (winter 1991): 103.

3. In *Noise: The Political Economy of Music*, trans. Brian Massumi (Minneapolis: University of Minnesota Press, 1985), Jacques Attali gives the pessimistic version of this story. For him, mass-produced music as background noise "signifies the presence of a power that needs no flag or symbol: musical repetition confirms the presence of repetitive consumption, of the flow of noise as ersatz sociality" (111).

4. See Judith Butler, *Gender Trouble* (New York: Routledge, 1990).

5. Bill Flanagan, *Written In My Soul: Conversations with Rock's Great Songwriters* (Chicago: Contemporary Books, 1987), p. 237.

6. Elvis Costello, "Less than Zero," *My Aim Is True* (Stiff [Columbia] LP 35037, 1977; reissue, Rykodisk CD 20271, 1993). "Less than Zero" obviously means much more than a reproduction of its lyrics on a printed page can indicate. Contextualizing it in terms of the punk and pub rock scenes Costello came from, thinking about its chord changes, or its highest chart position, or the situations in which it was played or wasn't, all these are arguably more valid ways in which to interpret a song's meanings than simply talking about its lyrics. But, because what I am discussing is the ways in which Costello has been used by literature and because readings of Bret Easton Ellis's novel *Less than Zero* that mention Costello's song rarely go further than talking about its lyrics, I will also confine myself primarily to them.

7. Nick Kent, "Horn-Rims from Hell: Elvis Costello," *The Dark Stuff: The Best of Nick Kent* (London: Penguin, 1994), p. 190.

8. "Tiny Steps," *Taking Liberties* (Columbia LP JC 36839, 1980).

9. Song lyrics are from, respectively, "Goon Squad," *Armed Forces* (Columbia LP PC 35709, 1979); "Poor Napoleon," *Blood and Chocolate* (Columbia LP FC 40518, 1986); and "Two Little Hitlers," *Armed Forces*. The titles themselves aptly communicate Costello's obsession with authority.

10. Greil Marcus, *In the Fascist Bathroom: Writings on Punk, 1977–1992* (London: Viking, 1993), p. 136.

11. "Pills and Soap," *Punch the Clock* (Columbia LP FC 38897, 1983).

12. Marcus, *In the Fascist Bathroom*, p. 35.

13. See *Probing the Limits of Representation: Nazism and the "Final Solution,"* ed. Saul Friedlander (Cambridge: Harvard University Press, 1992), for arguments about when or if the use of the Holocaust as a metaphor can be justified. Also see Jacqueline Rose, *The Haunting of Sylvia Plath* (London: Virago., 1991), for a brilliant defense of Plath's use in her poetry of the Holocaust as a metaphor for her own private pain. Rose explores the shifting boundaries of fantasy and identification that call into question the borders between public and private. I want to suggest that, for different purposes, Costello is doing something similar. Costello's use of puns and wordplay might downplay the seriousness of the ways in which he engages with historical trauma, but because of the way he sings it,

the emotional import of a line such as "Are you ready for the final solution?" from "Chemistry Class" is undeniable. You can't necessarily tell whether he's singing about a failed relationship or the Nazis, but that's the point. It can't be dismissed as a cheap pun.

14. Three separate broad claims might be seen to define the postmodern era: (1) that ideas such as rationality, objectivity, and progress that underlie modernity have been shown to be invalid because they ignore cultural difference; (2) that the difference between "high" culture and "low" or popular culture has disintegrated; and (3) that modern information technologies have helped create a historical situation in which it is no longer possible to separate securely the real from the copy (introduction to Jean François Lyotard, "Defining the Postmodern," in *The Cultural Studies Reader*, ed. Simon During [London: Routledge, 1993], p. 170). I don't wish to enter the argument about the validity of the term *postmodernism* or what it means here. Marxist critics have tended to use it as periodizing term, implying a nostalgia for a way of being that has been lost. Lyotard distances himself from these definitions by insisting that postmodernism questions the very teleological assumptions of historical narratives, yet for him the Holocaust remains a key moment for understanding the postmodern condition. If it is not foundational, it is at least exemplary.

15. John Brenkman, "Mass Media: From Collective Experience to the Culture of Privatization," *Social Text* 1 (winter 1979): 99–100.

16. "Satellite," *Spike* (Warner Brothers CD 25848, 1989).

17. "New Amsterdam," *Get Happy* (Columbia LP PC 36347, 1980); "Luxembourg," *Trust* (Columbia LP FC 40173).

18. "Brilliant Mistake," *King of America* (Columbia LP FC 40173, 1986); "American Without Tears," *King of America*.

19. Mick St. Michael, *Elvis Costello: An Illustrated Biography* (London: Omnibus, 1986), p. 33.

20. Flanagan, *Written in My Soul*, p. 238.

21. The alternative lyrics to "Less than Zero" were found at http://east.isx.com/-schnitzi/ec/index.html.

22. Flanagan, *Written in My Soul*, p. 244.

23. Bret Easton Ellis, *Less than Zero* (London: Picador, 1986); Nick Hornby, *High Fidelity* (London: Gollancz, 1995). Subsequent references are cited in the text.

24. Elvis Costello, "Next Time Around," *Blood and Chocolate* (Columbia LP FC 40518, 1986).

25. Marcus, *In the Fascist Bathroom*, pp. 285–86.

26. If you're curious, Rob's are "Alison," "Little Triggers," "Man Out of Time," "King Horse," and a Mersey beat version of "Everyday I Write the Book" (84).

27. Nick Hornby, *Fever Pitch* (London: Gollancz, 1993), p. 103.

28. Randy Newman seems to invite this particular problem of misinterpretation. In the case of "I Love L.A." as with his smash hit "Short People," the ironic under-

side of the thoughts expressed was often ignored. "I Love L.A." was easily adapted as a slogan for tourist advertising for the city. You simply leave out the line that disturbs Clay: "Look at that bum down there on his knees."

29. See Elizabeth Young and Graham Caveney, "Vacant Possession: *Less than Zero*—A Hollywood Hell," in *Shopping in Space* (London: Serpent's Tail, 1992), pp. 21–42, for a reading of *Less than Zero* that employs Baudrillard and Guy Debord's *Society of the Spectacle*.

30. See Nicki Sahlin, " 'But This Road Doesn't Go Anywhere': The Existential Dilemma in *Less than Zero*," *Critique: Studies in Contemporary Fiction* 33 (fall 1991): 23–42, for a reading of the novel's engagement with existentialism, that adolescent philosophy par excellence. Modern adolescence is a time defined by a combination of increased powers of consumption and choice, a time before fully entering the workforce but after having loosened some of the controlling bonds of the family of origin. It can be seen as the site of perceived exhilarating freedom and its loss in vertiginous despair. Existentialism seems peculiarly suited for adolescence because of its similar characteristics, its championing of autonomy and its threats of nullity, its refusal of political or social factors that could fix and determine the subject.

31. Sahlin, " 'But This Road Doesn't Go Anywhere,' " p. 38.

32. Marcus, *In the Fascist Bathroom*, p. 288.

33. *Less than Zero* "ends up feeling more like a '60 Minutes' documentary on desperate youth than a full fledged novel" (Michiko Kakutani, "The Young and Ugly," *New York Times*, June 8, 1986, p. I-32, quoted in Sahlin, "But This Road Doesn't Go Anywhere," p. 24).

34. Suzanne Moore, "Slipped Discs," *The Guardian*, 28 March 1995, sec. 2, p. 7.

35. The type of music that is listened to in the scenes that take place in clubs in the books signifies the potential for apparently authentic community formation. Mid-eighties techno pop is easily dismissed as soulless, while soul is exactly what Rob's club is primarily about. For more on questions of how soul and folk become defined as authentic in contrast to other forms of popular music, see Simon Frith, " 'The Magic That Can Set You Free': The Ideology of Folk and the Myth of the Rock Community," *Popular Music* 1 (1981): 159–68, and idem, *Performing Rites: On the Value of Popular Music* (Cambridge: Harvard University Press, 1996).

36. "Radio, Radio," *This Year's Model* (Columbia LP JC 35331, 1978).

37. "Green Shirt," *Armed Forces*.

13

MUSICAL CHEESE

THE APPROPRIATION OF SEVENTIES MUSIC IN

NINETIES MOVIES

KEVIN J. H. DETTMAR AND WILLIAM RICHEY

Recently, WROQ, a Greenville, South Carolina, radio station with a "classic rock" format, had a seventies weekend, featuring all the music from the 1970s that the station's moguls are trying to smuggle in under the classic rock umbrella (primarily dreck like Boston, Kansas, Aerosmith, et al.). At one point late on Saturday afternoon, the DJ came on the air at the close of a song and pleaded, with a note of some real desperation in his voice, not to have to field any more requests for the Bee Gees or Barry Manilow.

In our local battle of the FM airwaves, the other new player is a station, called "The New Q," that fashions itself as a homey, corporate alternative-rock venue (playing bands such as Pearl Jam, R.E.M., Soundgarden, Collective Soul, and Nirvana). Every Friday morning, however, they have an all-request show that features extended dance-mix versions of disco songs you haven't heard or thought about in years (but remember instantly—with a groan—when they come on). Listeners sat by helplessly the other morning as the full, unedited, and unexpurgated "Disco Duck" came on, followed in short order by Donna Summer's witty and sublime "MacArthur Park." In the few months since its inception, this retro-disco show has been successful enough that a local nightclub has installed a lighted, shamrock-shaped dance floor on which eighteen and ups can shake their boo-tays all night long: they can boogie-oogie-oogie till they just can't boogie no more. As we write this, we've now learned that they've instituted a platform-shoe night on Tuesdays. Lawsuits just waiting to happen.

So what's going on here? Just when you thought it was safe to turn the radio back on, seventies' schlock is back, in spades (and in bell-bottoms). And remember, this is South Carolina we're talking about, not L.A. or New York or Chicago. We're not a remarkably avant-garde group; this state has been sending Strom Thurmond to the U.S. Senate since before we were born.

What we would argue is that this new fondness for the disco decade is simply the South Carolina manifestation (or, to use a more regionally appropriate metaphor, infestation) of the national phenomenon that some commentators have called "cheese." Like "camp"—which Susan Sontag in the 1960s saw as so uniquely characteristic of the modern sensibility—cheese is a highly rhetorical embrace of those things that many would consider to be in bad taste. But, as a postmodern version of this mentality, cheese—we believe—differs from camp in two primary ways. First, it is somewhat more exclusive than camp, in that cheese is derived solely from the detritus of consumer culture. Thus, while Sontag can list both "The Brown Derby restaurant on Sunset Boulevard in LA" and "Bellini's operas" in her "canon of Camp," cheese is almost entirely a celebration of canceled TV shows, artless pop songs, and useless cultural artifacts like the lava lamp and the Chia Pet.[1] Second, we would argue that the attitudes encoded in cheese are even more indecipherable than those of camp. Despite camp's apparent delight in things usually considered excessive or overwrought, it never really loses sight of what good taste is. With cheese, however, the distinction between good and bad taste threatens to break down altogether, to the point that it becomes nearly impossible to tell when something is being celebrated and when it is being parodied.[2]

To explore the rather twisted metaphysics of cheese, we wish to examine how this current taste for third-rate music, to which WROQ's request line and The New Q's disco-on-demand program bear witness, has begun to assert itself in recent films, specifically how, over the past few years, movie soundtracks have started recycling some of the very worst of seventies' and eighties' pop/rock.[3] Our first example is Ben Stiller's *Reality Bites* (Universal Pictures, 1994), a film that at first glance appears to exemplify the concept of cheese perfectly. For the film's central quartet, the flotsam and jetsam of seventies' and eighties' popular culture assume an almost cultic status; they adorn their apartments with posters of Shawn Cassidy and disco-era Travolta, they pass their days watching reruns of seventies' sitcoms such as *Good Times* and *One Day at a Time*, and, of course, they delight in listening to the most mindless music from this thoroughly forgettable period in rock 'n' roll history. The most glaring instance of this adoration of cheese occurs when the Knack's "My Sharona" comes on the radio as the main characters are purchasing Pringles and diet Pepsis at an AM/PM mini-mart. After persuading the clerk to pump up the volume, the two women (Lalaina and Vicki) begin a manic but clearly choreographed dance routine to the song, much to the amazement of the forty-something clerk and the apparent distaste of their friend, Troy, the group's resident grunge philosopher.

Though the film's trailer would emphasize Lalaina and Vicki's giddy gyrations, the scene in its original context indicates that Troy's disdain is the appropriate response. Once the women have abandoned themselves to their dance, the camera cuts to a long shot in which we see them boogalooing wildly through the window of the convenience store. Seemingly, then, this moment of ironized fun soon gives way to some rather dour social commentary in which Stiller equates the music of the Knack with the disposable consumerism of contemporary society. This is junk music for a junk food culture, the film none too subtly says—or, to put it in Jamesonian terms, "postmodernism is the consumption of sheer commodification as a process."[4] The Knack, of course, provides perfect fodder for such a reading as they never pretended that they were anything more than a hit-making machine. In fact, as the *Meet the Beatles*–inspired cover of their first album suggests, the Knack's primary model was the Fab Four of the early sixties, the producers of catchy, easy-to-dance-to hits, not the Beatles' later incarnation as the prophets of universal peace and love. And "My Sharona" is essentially "I Want to Hold Your Hand" repackaged to cash in on the relaxed sexual mores of the seventies ("When you gonna give it to me, give it to me / It's just a matter of time, Sharona").[5]

A similarly ironic use of seventies' music immediately follows this scene. The film cuts directly from the convenience store back to Lalaina's apartment as she is getting ready for a date with Michael, a rising executive for a new music video network (it's "like MTV, but with an edge") whom Troy instantly deems a "yuppyhead cheeseball." Though somewhat sympathetically portrayed by Stiller himself, we soon realize that Michael is bad news, and again it is the soundtrack that provides the principal clue. As Michael and Lalaina sit in his BMW convertible drinking Big Gulps, Peter Frampton's "Baby I Love Your Way" plays in the background. When Lalaina naively asks, "Who's this again?" Michael replies incredulously, "I can't believe you don't remember *Frampton Comes Alive.* That album like totally changed my life." Frampton's music—though wildly popular in the late seventies—is no less gimmicky or vapid than the Knack's (e.g., "Ooh baby I love your way / Wanna tell you I love your way"); and so the film clearly indicates that the only fitting response to a man who claims his life was changed by such music is, "Get a life."[6] When Frampton serves as the accompaniment to Michael's seduction of Lalaina, it forcefully demonstrates how morally and aesthetically tainted she is becoming in this relationship: it's as if she's sleeping with her father's record collection. But, if Lalaina has temporarily lost her ironic distance from this seventies' dreck, Troy has not. Happening along just as Lalaina and Michael begin making love, he seems as disgusted by the Frampton as by Lalaina's taste in men. Once again, music acts as a kind of diacritical marker alerting us to the presence of irony. And the filmmakers assume that we can read the clues. While otherwise there might be some ambiguity to Michael's character, the music serves as a surefire sign that Michael is as slickly shallow as an Abba single.

Despite the film's gestures toward cheese, then, its irony ultimately takes a rather stable and traditional form: it enacts, in effect, a kind of a musical morality play. As her documentary about Gen Xer's "trying to find [their] own identity without having any real role models or heroes or anything" suggests, the character of Lalaina represents her generation's potential for optimism, and so her relationship with Michael poses the danger that her idealism might become corrupted. By contrast, Troy's problem is a deep-seated, almost crippling cynicism. During a club appearance with his band, Hey That's My Bike, he performs "I'm Nuthin', " a song that neatly sums up his sense of aimlessness and resentment. Here, he not only characterizes the nineties as a time of diminishing expectations ("I'm sick of people talkin' / About American dreams"), but he explicitly blames the previous generation, the baby boomers, for causing this situation.[7] By abandoning their youthful sixties' ideals for the greedy consumerism of the seventies and eighties, the boomers have at once destroyed their own moral credibility and sold the next generation down the river ("Before I was born / It was all gone"). In short, they pawned the future in exchange for big TVs, flashy garages, and designer drugs. The song's most potent irony, however, comes from its sly appropriation of the opening riff to the Stones' "Street Fighting Man." Whereas this sixties' rock anthem exhibits a similar sense of alienation ("'Cause in sleepy London town / There's no place for a Street Fighting Man"), the speaker's outrage seems on the verge of erupting into decisive action ("the time is right for a palace revolution").[8] For the despairing speaker of "I'm Nuthin'," this kind of action—thanks to the failed example of the boomers—has ceased to be a viable option. Sixties-style rebellion has become just another discredited cliché, a cultural myth that is no more believable than the American dream; the Beatles' "Revolution" is now just a Nike commercial. Thus, unlike the "street fighting man," who can define himself through his opposition to the status quo, this speaker has lost all sense of identity. He's "nuthin', " as alienated by the left as by the right, by the counterculture as much as by the establishment.

Ultimately, though, Troy's jaded perspective is no more valorized than Lalaina's naïveté because something like sixties' idealism consistently threatens to rear its long-haired head from beneath the film's ironic surface. Lalaina—as we have seen—hopes that her documentary will have some impact on her g-g-g-generation and makes a promise to herself not to "unintentionally commercialize it." And even Troy says that he would like his band to "travel the country like Woody Guthrie," harking back to a time before music had become a multimillion dollar industry. As a result, much of the soundtrack has a distinctly sixties' flavor. While several selections sound like warmed-over psychedelic rock (e.g., Dinosaur Jr.'s "Turnip Farm"), others have a retro-folk (Lisa Loeb's "Stay") or sixties-revival quality (the Posies' "Going, Going, Gone") that contrasts with the slickly produced hits of contemporary Top 40. But, predictably, the film's touchstone for sincerity and commitment comes from those poster boys of socially conscious rock, U2, whose ballad "All I Want Is You" accompanies the "Dover Beach"–like efforts of Lalaina and Troy to find love and security amid the chaos of nineties' America, to blend their respective idealism and skepticism into a harmonious and productive union. Clearly, then, the film's sensibility is a long way from the irony Jameson sees as characteristic of our postmodern moment, an attitude characterized by "a new kind of flatness or depthlessness, a new kind of superficiality."[9] This is not to say that Jameson misunderstands postmodernism but rather that *Reality Bites*—for all its hipper-than-thou attitude—is just faux po-mo. Troy talks bravely about "riding his own melt," and most of the characters, for most of the film, seem happy enough with Bono's injunction to "slide down the surface of things";[10] but when the going gets really tough—when Troy's dad dies, and Troy and Lalaina's relationship seems on the verge of breaking up—the film shows its true colors. It comes through with a big, orchestrally reinforced ballad to reassure us that everything'll be all right.

By now, we hope it's clear how much the value system that *Reality Bites* promotes grows out of, or is disseminated through, its soundtrack. The Knack and Frampton, we are led to believe, are "bad" because their vacuousness is symptomatic of the commercialism of the seventies and eighties; U2 and the other usually acoustic, sixties-tinged music on the soundtrack is "good" because it symbolizes the social commitment of that decade. Still, despite the simplicity of this allegory, the film's use of music is actually more sophisticated than that of most rock soundtracks. Rather than using a sixties' song simply to evoke the decade of the sixties as *The Big Chill* or *Forrest Gump* do, *Reality Bites* uses the music and musical styles of the sixties, seventies, and eighties to frame and comment on its Generation X narrative. Moreover, unlike most soundtracks, it is not simply our response to this music that is important but that of the characters as well. Throughout *Reality Bites*, we regularly see the central characters listening to, reacting to, and talking about the songs on the soundtrack, and it is principally these reactions that enable us to assess their states of mind and values. In Bret Easton Ellis's *American Psycho*,[11] we know not to trust Patrick Bateman in part because he can narrate entire chapters about Huey Lewis and the News and (post–Peter Gabriel) Genesis; in *Reality Bites*, we know that Troy and Lalaina are OK because Bono sings at their reunion.

A purer, less processed form of cheese appears in *Wayne's World*, the 1992 Mike Myers film that we would argue began this trend toward ironically recontextualizing baby boomer music in Gen X movies. Of course, *Wayne's World* takes nothing from the previous generation seriously. The movie opens with some poor middle-aged schmuck named Ron Paxton showcasing his new invention, the Suck Kut, on Wayne and Garth's public-access cable show. Bad idea, Ron. Wayne's first comment is that Ron's brain-child "certainly does suck," and while Ron's doing a demo trim on Garth's melon, Wayne surreptitiously calls in the "Get-A-Load-Of-This-Guy Cam." Poor Paxton's sent packing as the show ends, with Wayne remarking that the Suck Kut is "a totally amazing, excellent discovery. Not!" Later in the film, of course, the hapless, terminally unhip video arcade tycoon Noah Van Der Hoff gets much the same treatment when Wayne uses his idiot cards as message boards with which to make an idiot of the founder of Noah's Arcades during his live interview on "Wayne's World," calling Van Der Hoff a "sphincter boy," suggesting that "this man has no penis," and insisting that "he blows goats. I have proof."

But like *Reality Bites*, *Wayne's World*'s most sublime irony, for our money, comes when Myers gets his hands on the boomers' music. The obvious place to start is with the film's use and abuse of Queen's "Bohemian Rhapsody." Wayne, cruising down the street in the passenger's seat of his buddy Garth's vintage AMC Pacer (a.k.a. the Mirthmobile), queries the passengers about car tunes: "I think we'll go with a little 'Bohemian Rhapsody,' gentlemen?" His pilot, Garth, answers in the affirmative ("Good call"), and Wayne pops his cassette into the tape deck (though we almost expect an 8-track player), while the whole carful—including a drunk guy in the back seat named Phil who's upright only because he's wedged between two others—sing along and begin to thrash their stringy hair (in fact, obviously cheap hairpieces, like Wayne's and Garth's) in synch with the music and one another. In the process, seventies' superstars Queen—and particularly one of their signature songs, "Bohemian Rhapsody"—get "spun" in *Wayne's World*. It seems clear to us that Myers is sending the band up; the overproduced and deadly self-important music of Queen and the torch singer role so eagerly adopted by Freddie Mercury make a great source of cheese, and Myers uses Wayne and Garth's devotion to them as a way to flesh out their characterization. But it's finally a judgment call, for there's no firm textual or contextual evidence that the boys in the Mirthmobile think the song is anything but "Excellent": Wayne maintains a steady accompaniment of air guitar and air drums throughout and has a beatific grin on his face (as does Garth) as the song fades out that looks strangely like afterglow. Indeed, the sing-along participation in the song in the tight space of Garth's Pacer represents, among other things, a socially sanctioned moment of male bonding in a youth culture that provides few such opportunities. How bad can a song be, finally, if it allows adolescent males to connect in the midst of a homophobic atmosphere that forbids absolutely any such engagement?

This is the kind of unstable, postmodern irony that Linda Hutcheon describes: suspicious of "transcendental certitudes of any kind, including the subject" (and, we might add, taste), "postmodern irony . . . denies the form of dialectic and refuses resolution of any kind in order to retain the doubleness that is its identity."[12] Try as you might, you'll find no way to establish an ironic reading of this scene. To judge it an ironic treatment of "Bohemian Rhapsody," as we are, one must assert a distance between Mike Myers as writer and Wayne Campbell as narrator. This is doubly difficult because part of the dynamic in *Wayne's World* is that Myers is himself a late boomer rather than a Generation Xer: his character, Wayne, however, is an Xer, a slacker, all dressed up in black T-shirt and blue jeans—as well as "an extensive collection of name tags and hair nets"—but no place to go. It thus seems to us that the irony of "Bohemian Rhapsody" in the Mirthmobile—Schlock Opera lip-synched in the 1970's version of the Edsel—cuts two ways. The music of

Queen is shown up as cheesy through the comic stylings of Wayne, Garth, and crew; thus Myers points a condemning finger at the excesses and narcissism of the progressive seventies' art rock with which he must have grown up that contrasts so sharply with the self-consciously disposable pop of "My Sharona." At the same time, however, Wayne and Garth are indicted, for they've pulled "Bohemian Rhapsody" from the trash heap of contemporary history, dusted it off, and popped it into the tape deck; no saturation airplay has forced them to listen to, and hum along with, Queen against their will. They've brought this on themselves.

But wait: there's more. It gets weirder. After *Wayne's World*'s theatrical release, and the MTV video of the boys popping their heads to "Bohemian Rhapsody" in their Pacer got a lot of airplay, Queen actually enjoyed something of a renaissance, akin to the brief *Reality Bites*–inspired rebirth of the Knack—including a retrospective (and, in Freddie Mercury's case, posthumous) live album and live videos released and put in heavy rotation on MTV—which leads us to suspect that the irony that we think we see was missed by much of the audience. Freddie Mercury's death from AIDS in November 1991, only months before the film's release, doubtless had something to do with the revival of Queen's fortunes, and we don't wish to downplay this aspect. But an entire generation of music consumers was introduced to Queen, and "Bohemian Rhapsody," by *Wayne's World*, and they didn't see anything wrong with it: indeed, they thought it was "Excellent."

There are any number of other examples of this unstably ironic use of boomer tunes in the film. One thematic that we'd like to note briefly is the way that this avowedly cheesy music determines the structure of romantic and sexual desire in the Dynamic Duo. Garth's pure, chaste love of the Dreamwoman who works behind the counter at Stan Mikita's donut shop is figured in the soundtrack by Tchaikovsky's "Fantasy Overture" from *Romeo and Juliet*, surely a musical cliché of romantic love if ever there was one. But tellingly, when spurred on by Cassandra actually to break his silence and speak to her, Garth soundtracks his daydream/fantasy with Jimi Hendrix's "Foxy Lady." The choreography of this number is absolutely masterful; at one point in his waltz toward the counter, it appears as though Garth is being pulled toward his Dreamwoman by an invisible fishhook in the zipper of his trousers; as he gyrates toward her, he looks down in amazement at his seemingly possessed crotch. And as for the lyrics: well, most of us who listened to Hendrix before he was retro didn't listen for the lyrics, and when Garth makes little feral ears with his fingers while calling his Lady "Foxy," we're painfully reminded of *why* we ignored the lyrics. Ouch. As for Wayne and his lady, Cassandra, his theme song is—gulp—Gary Wright's eminently forgettable "Dream Weaver."

Aerosmith is the moral/aesthetic equivalent of Queen in *Wayne's World 2*. How many folks turned out to see *Wayne's World 2* simply because it contains live footage of Aerosmith? This makes for very complicated irony, of course, because Aerosmith, we think, takes itself pretty seriously even if Mike Myers doesn't. As with all interesting, postmodern irony, the use of Queen and Aerosmith in the *Wayne's World* films poses one particularly tricky question: *you* know that Mike Myers doesn't take Steve Tyler as seriously as Tyler takes himself, and *we* know it, but *how* do we know it? This irony is unstable because one can never prove with any certainty that it is even irony. Watching Aerosmith at Waynestock, the spectator is at some loss to discover precisely how s/he's to read Aerosmith's concert performance and Steve Tyler's adolescent mike humping. It's as if Wayne and Garth put Aerosmith up on the Waynestock stage and announce, "Hey, these guys are great! Not!!" But that "not" teasingly remains unvoiced.

In fact, the closest we get to a theory of irony in the *Wayne's World* films is at the end of the first movie, after the credits have been rolling for a time. Wayne and Garth are suddenly back up on the screen, to bid us adieu, and Wayne says into the camera: "Well, that's all the time we have for our movie. We hope you found it entertaining, whimsical, and yet relevant, with an underlying revisionist conceit that belied the film's emotional attachments to the subject matter." Wow! This is Wayne Campbell talking? Suddenly Wayne's become a native philosopher of postmodernism, positing in one economical sentence a theory of postmodern irony as compelling as anything written by Jameson or Hutcheon. But Wayne and Garth are a team; Wayne's brief disquisition is only half the story without Garth's rejoinder: "I just hope you didn't think it sucked." For postmodern irony can allow nothing to stand unscathed, not even Wayne's definition of postmodern irony itself.

In the soundtracks to the films of Quentin Tarantino, we also find something approaching an aesthetics of pure cheese. The director's fondness for bad pop music is unmistakable, for rather than simply mixing in an occasional rock song for period color, he constructs entire soundtracks out of successions of not-quite-forgotten pop singles. *Reservoir Dogs*, for example, uses nothing but K-Billy's "Super Sounds of the Seventies" for the film's musical score, a strategy that, according to Tarantino himself, provides "somewhat of an ironic counterpoint to what you are seeing on the screen."[13] This is, for the most part, an accurate assessment: these unrelentingly superficial songs generally do help to distance us from the blood and often gut-wrenching violence of the film. Plus the cheesiness of the soundtrack constantly reminds us of the fact that this is a story about cheap hoods. Unlike its precursors in the heist movie genre—*The Asphalt Jungle, Riffifi, The Killing*—*Reservoir Dogs* does not ask us to empathize with the characters or to find tragic dignity in their plight, something that would be far more likely to happen if it had used a more conventional Miklos Rozsa/Jerry Goldsmith score. At the same time, though, we have to take the "somewhat" in Tarantino's statement seriously. Often, his specific musical choices have an unexpected aptness as in the most famous and memorable scene from the film: the torture sequence performed to Stealers Wheel's "Stuck in the Middle with You."[14] At first, the bouncy, hand-clap–accented beat of this "Dylanesque, pop, bubble-gum favorite" seems thoroughly out of keeping with the uncompromising violence of the scene. But without this accompaniment, we would miss the glee that the torturer, Mr. Blonde, takes in his task, especially when he breaks into an impromptu dance in between his assaults on the young cop tied to the chair. Moreover, as the scene continues, the nasal drone of Gerry Rafferty's vocal becomes increasingly irritating, thereby intensifying the agony of this already agonizing scene. And, finally, if we can bring ourselves to concentrate on the lyrics to the song, we notice that Tarantino himself seems to be taking an almost sadistic glee in the grim ironies of the scene. While the opening line, "I'm so scared I guess I'll fall off my chair," clearly contrasts with the condition of this thoroughly bound and gagged cop, the words of the song's title become cruelly literalized. The cop is stuck in the middle of this warehouse where his torturer is sticking him in the gut with a razor.

In *Pulp Fiction*, Tarantino's use of music is even more creative and unorthodox. With its eclectic mix of various music genres from the sixties, seventies, eighties, and nineties, the soundtrack exhibits the kind of "depthlessness" that Frederic Jameson decries in his jeremiads against postmodern art, and so—in sharp contrast to most rock soundtracks—it provides no reliable contextual clues to ground the narrative or situate the viewer. The opening credits sequence exemplifies how this kind of aesthetic and temporal destabilization works. First, we hear Dick Dale's sixties' surf guitar instrumental, "Misirlou," and then, in what may be an ironic nod at the soundtrack of *Reservoir Dogs*, the channel is changed to a new station on which Kool and the Gang's R&B hit "Jungle Boogie" is playing. Tarantino's rationale for these choices is instructive. "Misirlou" he describes as sounding like "the beginning of like *The Good, the Bad, and the Ugly* with those trumpets, that almost Spanish sound. Having 'Misirlou' as your opening credits, it just says, 'You're watching an epic, you're watching this big old movie, just sit back.' " The sudden switch to Kool and the Gang, however, works both to startle the viewer and to signal the film's "other personality": its appropriation of "this black exploitation thing."[15]

In this way, Tarantino provides his viewer with quite a bit of information. There is no whiter music on the planet than surf music, while "Jungle Boogie" is obviously very black and urban. The only common denominator is their mutual cheesiness. With the coming of the British Invasion, psychedelia, and the Summer of Love, surf music was—until its recent Dick Dale–led renaissance—rendered terminally uncool, its clean-cut, All-American image being totally out of step with the increasingly radicalized atmosphere of the sixties. Similarly, Kool and the Gang are never going to be confused with Stevie Wonder or Marvin Gaye, and this song in particular seems designed to create as insulting a stereotype of African-American culture as possible. Nonetheless, Tarantino claims to be genuinely fond of both songs. He says that he "always really dug surf music," and while he admits "if I had to choose between Al Green or 'Jungle Boogie' I would probably choose Al Green," he maintains that "the early Kool and the Gang records were great" (8). Here, then, the irony seems to be at least as unreadable as anything in *Wayne's World*. While in that film the distinction between Wayne and Mike Myers occasionally blurs, in *Pulp Fiction* such a distinction is impossible to find because Tarantino seemingly recognizes the ironic effect that such musical choices have but refuses to pass judgment on them or to acknowledge them as bad. This is a man who truly likes surf music and who can distinguish between the early, golden age of Kool and the Gang and their later decadence—who can distinguish for us among the good, the bad, and the ugly.

This suspension of judgment—this mixture of emotional involvement and ironic detachment—is, we believe, the principle on which Tarantino's brand of postmodernism depends. To construct his narrative, he creates a pastiche of B-movie allusions (*Kiss Me Deadly, The Killers, The Set-Up*) as well as several references to more mainstream fare (*Rocky, Deliverance*), but he puts them to unfamiliar, unexpected ends; he carefully creates atmosphere and attitude but divorces them from any clearly identifiable content or message. His use of pop music works similarly. These familiar or seemingly familiar songs set our toes tapping and heads bobbing involuntarily, even as our minds ask, "What *is* this shit?" They both draw us in and draw attention to themselves. During the episode in which the hit man, Vincent Vega, takes Mia Wallace, his boss's young wife, out on date, we see two more examples of this strategy in action. When Vincent first comes to pick her up, she is playing Dusty Springfield's "Son of a Preacher Man" on the stereo. According to Tarantino, he wrote the scene with this song in mind: "That whole sequence, I've had in my head for six or seven years. And it was always scored to 'Son of a Preacher Man.' That was the key to the sequence. I can't even imagine it without 'Son of a Preacher Man' " (9). But to most viewers—ourselves included—the immediate reaction would be simply, "Why?" What is it about this song that is so central to this scene? First of all, that Mia would be playing this song seems highly unlikely given the fact that it was released before she would have been born. Plus, when we consider the lyrics to the song, they seem to contradict the situation in the film flatly: this heroin-shooting hit man is unlikely to be taken for the son of a preacher man. And yet—as in Tarantino's earlier use of "Stuck in the Middle with You"—there is indeed something right about the way the song works in this scene. Much of the tension in the episode results from the fact that Mia, like the preacher's son, is off limits; it's not just that she's the wife of Vincent's boss but that her husband reportedly ordered another employee to be thrown out of a four-story building for giving Mia a foot massage. She's forbidden fruit—something that Mia herself underscores later in the episode when she says, "Besides it's more exciting when you don't have permission"—and it's this taboo aspect of the meeting that makes Mia and Vincent so desirable to one another.

Furthermore, this white man's—or in this case—white woman's soul music helps to establish the ersatz quality that will pervade the rest of the episode. Mia's choice of a restaurant is Jack Rabbit Slim's, a faux-fifties' diner, complete with Ed Sullivan, Marilyn Monroe, and Buddy Holly impersonators and tables inside Chrysler convertibles. Though this environment creates a superficial sense of wholesomeness (the soundtrack for much of this segment is by that most clean-cut of fifties' pop idols, Ricky Nelson), the seaminess of Tarantino's pulp fiction is never far beneath the surface. For example, when Mia excuses herself—in good fifties' fashion—to go "powder my nose," Tarantino perversely literalizes this seemingly decorous euphemism by showing her snorting coke in the bathroom. Once they return to Mia's house—euphoric over their victory in the Jack Rabbit Slim's dance contest—the sexual subtext becomes overt. Now, when Vincent goes off to "take a piss," Mia puts on some mood music—which, in one further knowing anachronism, she plays on a reel-to-reel tape recorder. This time her choice is somewhat more contemporary—Urge Overkill's cover version of Neil Diamond's "Girl, You'll Be a Woman Soon"—and here, again, Tarantino seems to be constructing a largely unreadable irony. On one level, this song serves as the flip side of "Son of Preacher Man." Just as Vincent is clearly no preacher's kid, Mia—with her Cleopatraesque hairdo, her vampish makeup, and sex-kitten manner—is clearly already a woman. Still, the irony does not work through simple inversion or kitsch. Tarantino doesn't appear to be ridiculing this silly love song, and, as we might expect by now, he claims even to like the original version: "Well, I love Neil Diamond, and I have always loved Neil Diamond's version of that song, but [Urge Overkill's] version is even better" (13). Here, however, we think Tarantino is being somewhat disingenuous as there is no way that the scene would have worked if he had used the Neil Diamond version: the irony would be overdetermined, and we would laugh out loud as we do at "My Sharona" in *Reality Bites* or "Dream Weaver" in *Wayne's World*. On the other hand, by using this bass-heavy, flamenco version, Tarantino defamiliarizes Neil Diamond's cheesy ballad so that—in spite of its pedigree—the song succeeds in heightening the intensity of the scene. In this case, rock 'n' roll really does have "the beat of sexual intercourse"[16]—and so while we may be aware that this is a Neil Diamond song, we don't let that intrude on the mounting sexual tension until the scene yields a final grim irony. Mistaking Vincent's heroin for a bag of cocaine, Mia snorts it, with the result that it seems this girl will be a corpse soon.

Perhaps, though, the best way to demonstrate what makes Tarantino's use of music so distinctive is by viewing it in direct comparison with Ben Stiller's more conventional handling of his films' soundtracks. In a key scene from Stiller's recent directorial effort, *The Cable Guy*, Jim Carey's Chip Douglas, the title character, performs a thoroughly over-the-top karaoke version of Jefferson Airplane's "Somebody to Love." Gyrating in front of a TV screen swirling with psychedelic colors and patterns, he flaps the ridiculously long fringes of his sixties' leather jacket while grotesquely exaggerating the vibrato of Grace Slick's original vocal. Clearly, the song is being ironized as we are asked to participate in this knowing send-up of Bay Area psychedelia, but, at the same time, we are also intended to recognize how revealing this character's choice of songs is. After all, the entire narrative of the film revolves around the attempts of this TV-obsessed cable guy to achieve some real human contact by befriending a customer: he truly does want someone to love. Thus Stiller's basic strategy is to make fun of the song's surface features while using its lyrical content to further the plot and provide reliable insight into his character's psyche.[17] As his use of "Son of a Preacher Man" and "Girl, You'll Be a Woman Soon" indicates, Tarantino's modus operandi is the exact opposite. Unlike Stiller, he never openly parodies the music he selects, and—rather than using the soundtrack to underscore the film's narrative line—he often creates a highly unstable, even contradictory relationship between the song lyrics of the soundtrack and the action taking place on the screen.

A second example comes from what is for us a very fortuitous coincidence. At one point, Tarantino considered using "My Sharona" for the "sodomy rape sequence" during the later "Gold Watch" episode in *Pulp Fiction* because, as he explains, " 'My Sharona' has a really good sodomy beat to it." The plan eventually fell through because the Knack objected to this appropriation of their song and decided to let Stiller use it in *Reality Bites* instead. Thinking back on his original plan, Tarantino is now pleased that he had to use "Comanche," another surf music cut: "I like using stuff for comic effect, but I don't want it to be har, har, wink, wink, nudge, nudge, you know?"[18] Once again, this kind of irony is for Tarantino too broad and easily decipherable, and so he sets up a far more complex and demanding scenario for his viewers. He expects us to recognize the songs he selects and to acknowledge their cheesiness, but, by using them in unexpected and unfamiliar contexts, he alters our experience of them. As a result, we start to hear them in something like the way Tarantino himself does, a man who boasts of liking "certain music that nobody else on the planet has an appreciation for" (8).

From this last comment, it seems to us, a whole new problematic arises because here Tarantino appears to take a perverse pride in his sense of taste, a stance that appears to conflict with his usual self-representation as an aesthetic man of the people. In a recent *New York Times* interview, for instance, he dismissed the idea that he is a "collector" of pop culture by saying, "I don't believe in elitism. I don't think the audience is this dumb person lower than me. I am the audience."[19] But, as in the above quotation, Tarantino does on occasion appear to congratulate himself for having a more highly evolved sensibility, an aesthetic sense so acute that he can find beauty in things that most people see as having no socially redeeming value. It may be something of a Bizarro standard of taste, but it's a standard of taste nonetheless. Such a statement, then, reveals how difficult it is to maintain the kind of instability and undecidability that we see as the hallmarks of cheese and how tenuous the distinction between camp and cheese really is. Cheese may be, finally, all about self-consciousness, but, paradoxically, cheese that betrays its self-consciousness, its aesthetic investments, quickly spoils and loses its ability to delight and instruct.

NOTES

1. Susan Sontag, "Notes on Camp," in *A Susan Sontag Reader* (New York: Vintage, 1983), p. 107.

2. Since cheese is of relatively recent vintage, there have been few academic or theoretical treatments of it. To our knowledge, the fullest discussion is in Michiko Kakutanti's August 7, 1992, *New York Times* article, "Having Fun by Poking Pun: A New Esthetic Called Cheese" (B1, B6). Here, Kakutani usefully compares cheese to camp, noting very accurately that cheese "willfully focuses on the vulgar, the meretricious, the bogus"; she goes on to argue that, unlike the "generous" spirit of camp, "cheese tends to be judgmental, cynical, and detached" (B6). This—as the following examples we hope will demonstrate—is a severe misrepresentation of how genuine cheese functions. No less than camp, cheese "relishes, rather than judges" (Sontag, "Notes," 119), but it takes this process one step further, effectively obliterating or at least ignoring the distinctions between good and bad art, high and popular culture that underlie most standards of aesthetic judgment.

3. For other analyses of rock music soundtracks, see Claudia Gorbham, *Unheard Music: Narrative Film Music* (London: BFI, 1987); R. Serge Denisoff, *Risky Business: Rock in Film* (New Brunswick, NJ: Transaction, 1991); Lawrence Grossberg, "The Media Economy of Rock Culture: Cinema, Post-Modernity, and Authenticity" in *Sound and Vision: The Music Video Reader*, ed. Simon Frith, Andrew Goodwin, and Lawrence Grossberg (London: Routledge, 1993), pp. 185–209.

4. Fredric Jameson, *Postmodernism; or, The Cultural Logic of Late Capitalism* (Durham, NC: Duke University Press, 1991), pp. x, 17.

5. The Knack, "My Sharona," *Reality Bites* (RCA 44364, 1994).

6. Peter Frampton, "Baby I Love Your Way," *Frampton Comes Alive* (A&M 540930, 1976; reissue, 1998).

7. Ethan Hawke, "I'm Nuthin'," *Reality Bites.*

8. The Rolling Stones, "Street Fighting Man," *Beggar's Banquet* (ABKCO 7539, 1968).

9. Jameson, *Postmodernism*, p. 9.

10. U2, "Even Better than the Real Thing," *Achtung Baby* (Island 314-510 347-2, 1991).

11. Bret Easton Ellis, *American Psycho* (New York: Vintage, 1991).

12. Linda Hutcheon, "The Power of Postmodern Irony," in *Genre, Trope, Gender: Critical Essays by Northrop Frye, Linda Hutcheon, and Shirley Neuman* (Ottawa: Carelton University Press, 1992), p. 35.

13. "Truth and Fiction," liner notes to *Pulp Fiction/Reservoir Dogs* (MCACD 11188, 1994), p. 7.

14. Stealer's Wheel's "Stuck in the Middle with You," *Reservoir Dogs* (MCA 10541, 1992).

15. "Truth and Fiction," pp. 5–7.

16. This infamous quotation is, of course, from Allan Bloom, *The Closing of the American Mind* (New York: Simon and Schuster, 1987), p. 73. Bloom continues with a comment that sheds an interesting light on the flamenco feel of Urge Overkill's cover: "That is why Ravel's *Bolero* is the one piece of classical music that is commonly known and liked by them ["young people"]."

17. As in *Reality Bites*, Stiller's use of music may not be as enigmatic as Tarantino's, but it is by no means simplistic. This scene works on an additional level as well because Carey's performance is intercut with the foreplay of Steven—the Cable Guy's would-be friend—and a young woman whom we later learn is a prostitute hired by the Cable Guy. The song thus also applies to Steven—especially when we consider that he only subscribes to cable because he has just broken up with his girlfriend. This may only be a pay-per-screw version of the Summer of Love, but Steven, too, is seeking someone to love.

18. "Truth and Fiction," p. 16.

19. Lynn Hirschberg, "The Man Who Changed Everything," *New York Times Magazine*, 16 November 1997, p. 116.

CONTRIBUTORS

JOHN ALBERTI is an associate professor of American literature at Northern Kentucky University. He is the editor of *The Canon in the Classroom: Pedagogical Implications of Canon Revision in American Literature* (Garland, 1995) and has written on the issues of race and class in multicultural pedagogy.

ROBYN BROTHERS recently completed the Ph.D. in French Studies at Brown University. Her research focuses on narrative ethics, ethical theory, and philosophy of technology (including a recent article on cyborg identities in *Metaphilosophy* 28:3).

MICHAEL COYLE is an associate professor of English at Colgate University. His first book, *Ezra Pound, Popular Genres, and the Discourse of Culture*, was published in 1995 by Penn State University Press.

ASHLEY DAWSON completed his Ph.D. work in English at Columbia University and is an assistant professor of English at the University of Iowa.

ANTHONY DeCURTIS is the author of *Rocking My Life Away: Writing About Music and Other Matters* and the editor of *Present Tense: Rock & Roll and Culture*. He is also the coeditor of *The Rolling Stone Illustrated History of Rock & Roll* and *The Rolling Stone Album Guide*. A contributing editor at *Rolling Stone*, he holds a Ph.D. in American literature and has taught at Indiana University.

KEVIN J. H. DETTMAR is professor and Chair of the Department of English at Southern Illinois University Carbondale. He is the author of *The Illicit Joyce of Postmodernism: Reading Against the Grain* (University of Wisconsin Press) and editor of *Rereading the New: A Backward Glance at Modernism* and (with Stephen Watt) *Marketing Modernisms: Self-Promotion, Canonization, and Rereading* (both University of Michigan Press).

JON DOLAN writes for *City Papers*.

MARILYN MANNERS teaches humanities, women's literature, and feminist theory in the Comparative Literature Program at the University of California, Los Angeles. She has published in the fields of cultural studies and contemporary feminist cultural production and theory, as well as on the work of Sylvia Plath and Hélène Cixous. Currently, she is writing a book on feminist sexualities and irony that examines the interrelationship between high and popular culture.

NEIL NEHRING is an associate professor of English at the University of Texas at Austin. His first book was *Flowers in the Dustbin: Culture, Anarchy, and Postwar England* (University of Michigan Press, 1993), and his newest book is entitled *Popular Music, Gender, and Postmodernism: Anger Is an Energy* (Sage, 1997). He has published essays on rock music and cultural studies in journals including *American Literary History, Australian Journal of Communication, Discourse, PMLA,* and *Puncture.*

SEAN PORTNOY is currently in the Ph.D. program in English (film and literature) at the University of Southern California, where he is writing his dissertation on digital sampling, the electronic music subculture, and critical theory.

WILLIAM RICHEY is an associate professor of English at the University of South Carolina. His book *Blake's Altering Aesthetic* was published in 1996 by the University of Missouri Press. He has also published various articles on William Blake, Mary Wollstonecraft, and William Wordsworth and is currently working on a book about parody in English romantic poetry.

PATRICIA JULIANA SMITH is a visiting assistant professor of English at the University of California, Los Angeles. She is the author of *Lesbian Panic: The Homoerotics of Narrative in Modern British Women's Fiction* (Columbia University Press, 1997), editor of *The Queer Sixties* (Routledge, 1999), and coeditor of *En Travesti: Women, Gender Subversion, Opera* (Columbia University Press, 1995). She is presently at work on a study of the end of empire and the permissive society in 1960's British literature and culture.

ATARA STEIN is an associate professor of English at California State University, Fullerton. Her work focuses on British romanticism and contemporary popular culture, especially at the point(s) of their intersection.

JOEL D. STEIN received his M.S. in zoology from the University of Wisconsin–Madison. He presently teaches in the Life Science Department at Mesa Community College.

PAMELA THURSCHWELL is a research fellow at Queens' College, Cambridge. She is currently writing a book on intimacy, technology, and interest in the occult at the turn of the century.

MARK WILLHARDT is the editor of *The Routledge Anthology of Cross-Gendered Verse* (1996) and is now editing *The Routledge Who's Who of 20th Century Poetry*. He is assistant professor of English and Professional Writing at Ohio Northern University.

R. J. WARREN ZANES spent the attractive part of his youth playing guitar for the Del Fuegos. After recording three albums for Slash/Warner Brothers, he retreated to the warmth of the academy and is currently completing doctoral work in the University of Rochester's Visual and Cultural Studies Program. He remains active as a songwriter.

INDEX